ORANGE

God Said:

This Is My S

— Synoptic

In the Beginning

— Genesis

Draw Near

— James and Philemon

Worship

— Prayers and Songs

1998-99

Companion

Published by Gospel Advocate Co.
P.O. Box 150, Nashville, TN 37202
ISBN 0-89225-468-8

Foreword

More than 75 years ago, the Gospel Advocate Company began publishing a volume of annual lessons for use in Sunday morning Bible classes. Originally, these lessons were called *Elam's Notes*, but since 1982 the annual volume has been known as *Companion.*

The 1997-98 volume featured a study of Bible characters. This current volume begins a scope and sequence designed to cover the Bible in eight years. A chart showing the first four years of that design is featured on the back cover indicating which books of the Bible will be covered in the first four years.

To begin this new structure, "God Said" was chosen for this year's theme. With that emphasis on the study of God's Word, the 1998-99 volume will devote the first quarter to the synoptic gospels, the second quarter to Genesis, the third to James and Philemon, and the fourth to a study of prayers and songs in the Bible.

Returning to the quarterly format in *Companion* rather than having a yearlong topic enables each student and each teacher to focus on a specific book or topic for 13 class meetings.

Whatever the structure of the guide or the number of lessons devoted to a single subject, the most important reality is commitment to the study of God's Word, for only there can one find the "words of eternal life." Our prayer is that you will approach this study with the hunger of a learner anxious to be filled and the soul of a disciple seeking to learn what God has said.

– *The Editors*

God Said, "This Is My Son"

Fall Quarter

God Said, "In the Beginning" — Winter Quarter

God Said, "Draw Near"

Spring Quarter

God Said, "Worship"

Summer Quarter

Lesson 1

The Birth of Jesus

Week of
Sept. 6, 1998

Lesson Text

LUKE 2:8-20

(8) Now there were in the same country shepherds living out in the fields, keeping watch over their flock by night.

(9) And behold, an angel of the Lord stood before them, and the glory of the Lord shone around them, and they were greatly afraid.

(10) Then the angel said to them, "Do not be afraid, for behold, I bring you good tidings of great joy which will be to all people.

(11) "For there is born to you this day in the city of David a Savior, who is Christ the Lord.

(12) "And this will be the sign to you: You will find a Babe wrapped in swaddling cloths, lying in a manger."

(13) And suddenly there was with the angel a multitude of the heavenly host praising God and saying:

(14) "Glory to God in the highest, And on earth peace, goodwill toward men!"

(15) So it was, when the angels had gone away from them into heaven, that the shepherds said to one another, "Let us now go to Bethlehem and see this thing that has come to pass, which the Lord has made known to us."

(16) And they came with haste and found Mary and Joseph, and the Babe lying in a manger.

(17) Now when they had seen Him, they made widely known the saying which was told them concerning this Child.

(18) And all those who heard it marveled at those things which were told them by the shepherds.

(19) But Mary kept all these things and pondered them in her heart.

(20) Then the shepherds returned, glorifying and praising God for all the things that they had heard and seen, as it was told them.

Introduction

In writing to the Christians in Galatia, Paul said, "But when the fullness of the time had come, God sent forth His son, born of woman, born under the law, to redeem those who were under the law, that we might receive the adoption as sons" (Galatians 4:4-5). The birth of Jesus at that point in history was no accident; it was the time appointed by God. The world was in desperate need of change from despair to hope, and God had promised a Deliverer (Genesis 3:15; Isaiah 7:14; 9:6-7), who was to come during the days of the Roman Empire to establish God's kingdom upon Earth (Daniel 2:44). That time had finally arrived.

It was also a time of prosperity. Augustus Caesar was the emperor, and the *pax Romana*, or Roman peace, reigned throughout the empire. Roman power kept the peace. Although the world was at peace, the hearts of men were not. Spiritually, the world was bankrupt. The old religions had failed. They were powerless to change men's lives. Spiritual hunger was apparent everywhere. The world did not need another religion; it needed a Savior. And what the world needed most, it refused to accept (John 1:11-12).

The First to Receive the Message (Luke 2:8)

That the first announcement about the Savior's birth was made to the most unlikely, unworthy people – simple shepherds tending their flocks at night in the fields of Bethlehem – is fitting. That they were outside may prove the birth of Christ did not happen in the winter because sheep were kept inside during the winter unless they were destined for the sacrificial altar.

Shepherds were not among the elite. Their names would not have been found on the social registry. Jewish rabbis had pronounced six professions forbidden and shepherding was one of them. Shepherds were not allowed to give testimony in court. They were kept from the sacred places of worship – the temple or the synagogues – for weeks at a time and with good reason. They were ceremonially unclean. They walked in sheep dung; and because they virtually lived with their sheep, they were seldom clean.

They ranged their sheep anywhere they pleased, so they were constantly trespassing. They were considered to be thieves who would steal you blind and take anything left lying around. Yet when God chose to announce the birth of His Son, He sent messengers to these men first. Why? We may not know for sure, but Luke's narrative leads us to believe that these men were different (2:10-12, 15-20). They appear to have been devout men awaiting the arrival of God's Messiah.

The Messengers and the Message (Luke 2:9-14)

The word "angel" means "messenger." Angels are special servants of God, created to do His bidding. They often took on a human appearance (Genesis 18:1-2; 19:1-2; 32:22-28; Judges 13:3; Mark 16:5; Luke 24:4; Acts 1:10-11). However, we know that their appearance was sometimes dreadful to behold (Ezekiel 1:4-25; 10:1-22; Revelation 19:6-10; 22:8-9). Imagine the amazement these shepherds experienced when a heavenly messenger suddenly appeared to them. Luke tells us they were so fearful they had to be comforted by the angel before he could convey his message to them.

The literal rendering of the beginning of the angel's message is "I announce to you good news, a great joy, which shall be to all people." The verb used here is the word that refers to preaching the gospel. It is the word "evangelize" in English (cf. Luke 1:19; 3:18; 4:18, 43; 7:22; 8:1; 9:6; 16:16; 20:1). Although this word was first used to indicate the bringing of any kind of good news, it came to be used especially for carrying the gospel. What was this good news?

"There is born to you this day in the city of David a Savior, who is Christ the Lord." From Luke 2:4, we learn that Joseph had to return to Bethlehem for the census required by Augustus. This city has a rich heritage. In addition to being David's birthplace, it was the place where Rachel died giving birth to Benjamin (Genesis 35:16-20). It was where Boaz met and married a Moabitess named Ruth, one of the few women mentioned in Christ's genealogy (Matthew 1:5). Bethlehem where the prophet Micah said the Christ would be born (Micah 5:2).

The angel used three titles to identify the Son of God. The first is "Savior." This is the only time this title is used for Jesus in the Synoptic Gospels. Joseph was told, "You shall call His name Jesus, for He will save his people from their sins" (Matthew 1:21). This is no indication that this aspect of Jesus' work is less significant than others. The word "Savior" is employed many times in other books of the New Testament (John 4:42; Ephesians 5:23; Philippians 3:20; 1 Timothy 1:1; 2:3; 4:10; 2 Timothy 1:10; Titus 1:2-3; 2:10, 13; 3:4, 6; 2 Peter 1:1, 11; 3:2, 18; 1 John 4:14).

The second title the angel used was "Christ." This meant that the infant whose birth received so much attention was the Messiah, God's anointed, the One sent to be King over His eternal kingdom. Pilate asked Jesus, "Are you the King of the Jews?" (Matthew 27:11). John records that Jesus answered, "You say rightly that I am king. For this cause I was born, and for this cause I have come into the world, that I should bear witness to the truth. Everyone who *is* of the truth hears My voice" (John 18:37). Pilate had the title over the cross read: "Jesus of Nazareth, The King of the Jews" (John 19:19).

Jesus came to be the King over God's kingdom. People who look for a future fulfillment of this promise fail to understand the kingdom has come. Jesus promised the disciples that some of them would not taste of death until they saw the kingdom come with power (Mark 9:1; cf. Acts 1:6-8). This event was fulfilled on Pentecost after the resurrection of Jesus (2:1-4). In his sermon, Peter said that Jesus had ascended to Heaven to sit on the throne of His father David (2:30-31) and that He was now "both Lord and Christ" (2:36). Jesus Christ is reigning today over His church kingdom (Colossians 1:13). He will reign until the last enemy of mankind, death, has been defeated (1 Corinthians 15:24-27).

The third title used by the angel was "Lord." The Greek word for Lord, *Kurios*, is used more than 435 times to refer to Jesus. William Barclay, in his *Daily Bible Lesson* series on *The Letter to the Romans*, says that it "describes someone who has undisputed possession of a person or a thing. It means master or owner in the most definite sense." When we say "Jesus is Lord," we are saying He is the absolute Ruler and Controller of our lives. The church is not a democracy – it is a kingdom, an absolute monarchy. Only Jesus makes the rules for God's kingdom (James 4:12).

The shepherds were told that the Christ child would be "wrapped in swaddling cloths" (v. 12). Jewish mothers wrapped their newborn babies in strips of cloth to support and protect their limbs. Many babies may have been born there during this same period, and most of them would probably have been wrapped in the the same way. However, the the baby they sought would be "lying in a manger" (v. 12). This was the unique sign by which they could identify Him. The word "Manger" most likely referred to the trough from which the animals were fed (vv. 7, 16).

Following the message, the heavens came to life with a host of angels praising God. Their song declared "peace and good will toward men." The Hebrew word for peace, *Shalom*, means "well being, health, prosperity, security, soundness and completeness." Isaiah prophesied that the Messiah would be, among other things, "the Prince of Peace" (9:6). Christ's coming brought the opportunity for men to have peace with God, peace with themselves, and peace with other people (John 16:33; Acts 10:36; Romans 5:1; Ephesians 2:14-16; Philippians 4:6-7).

The Shepherds Make Haste (Luke 2:15-20)

After the angels departed, the shepherds hastened to find the Christ child. They found Him lying in the manger with His mother and father nearby. The shepherds may have been men hardened by their life in the wilds; but as an indication of their spirituality, they did not doubt the angel's words. They accepted without question that this baby was their long-anticipated Messiah. After they saw Him with their own eyes, they quickly left and began to spread the good news about His birth.

Luke tells us that they "returned glorifying and praising God for all they had heard and seen." The implication is that they returned to their shepherding task. Christians are not relieved of their earthy responsibilities. In fact, they have even greater reasons for being good citizens, workers and people. The shepherds had to see the King. Although almost 20 centuries have passed since this greatest of all events occurred, should it not elicit the same reaction from people today who hear about it? Should not the recipients of this marvelous grace be just as eager to share this good news as these humble servants so long ago?

Lessons Learned

1. God does all things in His own time. It is always the right time with God.
2 The fact that God revealed the news about Christ's birth first to lowly shepherds shows His concern for common people.
3. Angels were created by God to be special messengers. They are not to be worshiped or adored.
4. The kingdom of God exists on Earth today in the form of the church. People who are "called out" of the world are its citizens. Jesus is reigning from heaven over His kingdom now. We must not look for some future earthly kingdom to come.
5. We should be as eager as those shepherds were to spread the good news of salvation to our world.

Questions

1. What does the "fullness of time" mean?
2. How did the Roman Empire aid in the spread of the gospel?
3. Why were shepherds generally looked down upon?
4. In what form did angels often appear?
5. What is the literal meaning of the angel's message to the shepherds?
6. What three titles did the angel use to identify Jesus, and what do they mean?
7. Who makes the rules in God's kingdom and why?
8. What sign was given to the shepherds so they could be certain they had found the Christ?
9. Why is Jesus called "the Prince of Peace"?
10. Why did the shepherds have reason to rejoice after they had left the child?

Lesson 2

The Education of Jesus

Week of
Sept. 13, 1998

Lesson Text

LUKE 2:40-52

(40) And the Child grew and became strong in spirit, filled with wisdom; and the grace of God was upon Him.

(41) His parents went to Jerusalem every year at the Feast of the Passover.

(42) And when He was twelve years old, they went up to Jerusalem according to the custom of the feast.

(43) When they had finished the days, as they returned, the Boy Jesus lingered behind in Jerusalem. And Joseph and His mother did not know it;

(44) but supposing Him to have been in the company, they went a day's journey, and sought Him among their relatives and acquaintances.

(45) So when they did not find Him, they returned to Jerusalem, seeking Him.

(46) Now so it was that after three days they found Him in the temple, sitting in the midst of the teachers, both listening to them and asking them questions.

(47) And all who heard Him were astonished at His understanding and answers.

(48) So when they saw Him, they were amazed; and His mother said to Him, "Son, why have You done this to us? Look, Your father and I have sought You anxiously."

(49) And He said to them, "Why did you seek Me? Did you not know that I must be about My Father's business?"

(50) But they did not understand the statement which He spoke to them.

(51) Then He went down with them and came to Nazareth, and was subject to them, but His mother kept all these things in her heart.

(52) And Jesus increased in wisdom and stature, and in favor with God and men.

Introduction

When God chose parents to nurture His Son, He chose two devout people. Jesus was raised by His parents to respect His Father's will. He was taken to the temple at the appropriate times according to the Law, and He was brought up attending the synagogue services on the Sabbath (Luke 4:16). Mary and Joseph saw to it that He received growth in every significant area of His life (2:52).

Jesus was raised in an atmosphere that encouraged learning. Sixty years before His birth, a decree was passed by the Jewish leaders that provided for a free compulsory education for every Jewish boy. The education was centered on the Scriptures. In the Mikra, their elementary school, the main lesson content was reading and writing Scriptures along with simple mathematics. The secondary school, or Mishnah, involved more study of the oral Law and a comprehensive study of the Pentateuch. All of these studies were done with an emphasis on morality and a practical application of God's Word to everyday life. How much of this training Jesus would have received is not known for sure. Because He was raised in this cultural setting by strict parents, it is probable that He was exposed to both of these educational environments.

At age 12, Jesus was quite knowledgeable, astounding even the learned teachers of the Law at the temple (2:47). His teaching as an adult would indicate that he had an education far beyond the normal high school level of His day. That He attended any institution of higher learning is doubtful. We know that His earthly father, Joseph, was a carpenter. If Jesus followed the normal practice, He would have begun an apprenticeship under His father's direction immediately after His secondary education, so He was also a carpenter (Mark 6:3).

Galilee was not an area that encouraged extensive educational pursuits. Most of the people from there were craftsmen, laborers and fishermen who were poor because they were not well-compensated for their work. Nathaniel was astonished that Jesus came from Nazareth of Galilee (John 1:43-51). Other people who heard Jesus speak said, "How does this man know letters, never having studied?" (John 7:14-15). This meant that He had not attended any of the prestigious rabbinical schools. He did not need their accreditation or approval. How then did He have the knowledge He demonstrated?

In His answer to this question, He said, "My doctrine is not mine; but His that sent Me" (John 7:16). We simply cannot rule out the divine element. Jesus was the Son of God who became a man (1:1, 14). This being true, He was omniscient. Thus His formal education, no matter how extensive, was supplemental. He purposefully limited Himself in certain areas, but this did not prevent Him from having access to divine knowledge whenever He or the Father believed it was necessary (Mark 13:32; Matthew 27:46).

Jesus and His Family (Luke 2:40-42)

We can see how devout Mary and Joseph were in the meticulous way in which they carried out every divine decree regarding their Son. In Luke 2:21-23, they circumcised Him on the eighth day according to the Law (Leviticus 12:3). Following the 33 days required for purification after the birth of her Son (vv. 4-8), Mary carried Him to the temple to be dedicated. When God spared the firstborn of the Israelites in Egypt, He decreed that every male child should be dedicated to Him (Exodus 13:2-15). However, the provision was made for a family to fulfill this obligation by offering a sacrifice to God instead. The two turtle doves or two young pigeons mentioned here (2:24) were given by the poorer people who could not afford a lamb (Leviticus 12:8). Even their journey to Jerusalem when Jesus was 12 illustrates their devotion to God's will.

Luke, the beloved physician, makes it clear that this trip was not a once in a lifetime event or some kind of spiritual pilgrimage. They "went to Jerusalem every year at the Feast of the Passover" (v. 41). According to the Law, every male Jew of "mature age" was required to journey to Jerusalem three times a year to attend the three great feasts: Passover, Pentecost, or Harvest, and Tabernacles (Exodus 23:14-17; 34:22-23; Deuteronomy 16:16). The distance involved made it extremely difficult, especially for many poorer people, to make all of them. For this reason, many families chose to attend only one of those feasts. As in the case of Mary and Joseph, many of them selected the Passover because it was the most significant of these feasts. Why was this year different?

The wording of the text indicates that this may have been the first time Jesus had made the journey with His parents (v. 42). Many Jewish sources, although there is certainly no unanimity, relate that a Jewish boy became a "bar mitzvah," or son of the Law, when he attained the age of maturity and responsibility for keeping the commandments of the Law. The prevailing opinion is that the age was 13. Jesus may have been near that age at the time of His journey. Even if that was not the case, His parents may have believed that it was good for Him to make the trip a year earlier to see what was involved. They were certainly preparing Him to take on the responsibilities of a mature man.

The Lost Boy (Luke 2:43-45)

Mary and Joseph have often been criticized for leaving their Son in Jerusalem. Many sermons have been preached on this text condemning them for gross parental neglect. However, when the circumstances are fully known, it may be that we can excuse their negligence. They did not lose Him because He was not loved or appreciated, nor was it because of a lack of interest or because they were bad parents. The custom was for people to make these journeys to Jerusalem in the company of other people, family, friends and neighbors for safety concerns as well as companionship. There were often large caravans of people involved. The custom was also for the women to travel in the front with their younger children and the men and older children to follow behind. Mary may have assumed that Jesus was with Joseph, and Joseph may have assumed that He was with His mother. To understand how a person, especially a child of 12, could be left behind in this situation is easy.

At the end of the first day's journey, the families regrouped to be certain that everyone was all right and accounted for. That was when Mary and Joseph first discovered that their Son was not with either one of them. There was still no panic, as they supposed He would be found among His aunts, uncles and cousins. When He was not to be found there, then we can safely assume that the terrible anxiety of any parents with a lost child set in. Imagine their heightened fear as they made their way back along the way, asking other people if they had seen their son Jesus. With each "No," the apprehension would have increased until at some point any normal parent would have erupted in a torrent of emotions, culminating in a flood of tears.

Jesus in the Temple (Luke 2:46-50)

Once back in Jerusalem, the search continued and the fear grew until after three days of worry they finally find Him in the temple (v. 46). He was not engaged in frivolity, nor was He cavorting with His friends. He was sitting with the learned teachers of the Law, both asking and answering questions. This was a favorite method of teaching among Jewish rabbis. The object of this exchange was to arrive at some definitive answer. Jesus amazed these men with His knowledge and understanding at such a young age.

Mary's first reaction when she saw her Son was not astonishment at what He was doing, but hurt, even anger, that He had put them through such misery. It was a typically human response: "Why have you done this to us?" Put yourself in her place. How would you have reacted? His reply did cause deep reflection on her part (v. 51). This statement proves that even at that age Jesus knew who He was. The phrase "My Father's business" is clear evidence that He was the Son of God with full knowledge about His unique role in this world. Because of His divinity, there was perhaps no point in His life in which He did not know.

Jesus' Life in Nazareth (Luke 2:51-52)

Many stories have been told, and even books written about the boyhood of Jesus. One book, titled *The Lost Years of Jesus,* chronicles His boyish naivete and mischievousness. All such accounts are purely fabrications of imaginative minds. We have no substantial resources to deduce anything about Jesus' youthful years. Because the sacred writer is a man of few words on this matter, we must be content with that. However, if we cannot imagine Jesus being nursed from His mother's breast, burped, diapered and disciplined when necessary, then our concept of the Incarnation is not what it ought to be. He was fully divine but also fully human. He was "coming in the likeness of men" (Philippians 2:7). When God came down, He became as we are (Hebrews 4:15).

The historian tells us that when Jesus went back to Nazareth with His parents He was "subject to them" (v. 51). This means that He willingly submitted Himself to their authority and leadership although He knew His identity and what His mission was. He remained in Nazareth, growing up under their guidance for 18 more years. He left home to begin His public ministry at the age of 30 (Luke 3:23). It must have been hard for Him to feel so deeply the needs of the world, to know the job He was sent here to do, and yet to wait until the appointed time had arrived. All the while He was respectful to His parents and was obedient to them.

During those 18 years, He "grew in wisdom and stature, and in favor with God and men." The point of this statement shows that He was one of us. He was "the Son of Man," and He developed in all of the normal ways in which other human beings do. He grew intellectually through the normal processes noted before. He increased in size and strength. His physical appearance must have been imposing for no one challenged Him when He cleansed the temple (Matthew 21:12-14; Mark 11:15-17; Luke 19:45-48). He also developed in social skills and graces so that people felt comfortable in His presence and generally approved of Him as a person. Finally, He grew in His spiritual life. In His humanness, He had to deal with every kind of emotion and temptation that men confront. His behavior and conduct in all of this pleased His Father (Matthew 3:17; 17:5). Although Jesus had miraculous power and knowledge, He never used them for His personal advantage.

Lessons Learned

1. To nurture His Son to manhood, God chose as parents people He knew would perform their task conscientiously. Every child deserves such parents.
2. Jesus was omniscient, but He subjected Himself to learning the ways of mankind in the normal fashion.
3. Mary and Joseph were careful to fulfill all of the requirements of the Law regarding their Son. Parents today should be equally concerned about raising their children in God's will (Ephesians 6:4).
4. Jesus' parents did not leave Him in Jerusalem through negligence or poor parenting. He was left because of ordinary circumstances. We must be careful not to lose the souls of our children through the deceptive normalcy of our lives.
5. Although He was divine, Jesus advanced in all of the normal ways in which men develop.

Questions

1. How can we know that Jesus did not have much education beyond the secondary level?
2. Why were people astonished by His learning?
3. How do we know Jesus limited His knowledge in certain areas?
4. What evidences do we have of Mary and Joseph's devotion to God's will?
5. What two evidences of Mary and Joseph's poverty do we find in this lesson?
6. Why should Mary and Joseph not be criticized for leaving Jesus in Jerusalem?
7. What was the meaning of Jesus' reply to His mother's question in the temple?
8. What does the phrase "My Father's business" prove?
9. What do we actually know about Jesus' early years?
10. In what ways did Jesus develop? Discuss.

Lesson 3

The Baptism of Jesus

Week of Sept. 20, 1998

Lesson Text

MATTHEW 3:1-17

(1) In those days John the Baptist came preaching in the wilderness of Judea,

(2) and saying, "Repent, for the kingdom of heaven is at hand!"

(3) For this is he who was spoken of by the prophet Isaiah, saying: "The voice of one crying in the wilderness: 'Prepare the way of the LORD; Make His paths straight.' "

(4) And John himself was clothed in camel's hair, with a leather belt around his waist; and his food was locusts and wild honey.

(5) Then Jerusalem, all Judea, and all the region around the Jordan went out to him

(6) and were baptized by him in the Jordan, confessing their sins.

(7) But when he saw many of the Pharisees and Sadducees coming to his baptism, he said to them, "Brood of vipers! Who warned you to flee from the wrath to come?

(8) "Therefore bear fruits worthy of repentance,

(9) "and do not think to say to yourselves, 'We have Abraham as our father.' For I say to you that God is able to raise up children to Abraham from these stones.

(10) "And even now the ax is laid to the root of the trees. Therefore every tree which does not bear good fruit is cut down and thrown into the fire.

(11) "I indeed baptize you with water unto repentance, but He who is coming after me is mightier than I, whose sandals I am not worthy to carry. He will baptize you with the Holy Spirit and fire.

(12) "His winnowing fan is in His hand, and He will thoroughly clean out His threshing floor, and gather His wheat into the barn; but He will burn up the chaff with unquenchable fire."

(13) Then Jesus came from Galilee to John at the Jordan to be baptized by him.

(14) And John tried to prevent Him, saying, "I need to be baptized by You, and are You coming to me?"

(15) But Jesus answered and said to him, "Permit it to be so now, for thus it is fitting for us to fulfill all righteousness." Then he allowed Him.

(16) When He had been baptized, Jesus came up immediately from the water; and behold, the heavens were opened to Him, and He saw the Spirit of God descending like a dove and alighting upon Him.

(17) And suddenly a voice came from heaven, saying, "This is My beloved Son, in whom I am well pleased."

Introduction

About six months before the angel Gabriel appeared to Mary in Nazareth, he was sent to Zachariah (Greek: Zacharias), a priest of the eighth course of Abijah, who was serving at the temple. His home was in the hill country of Judea where he lived with his wife, Elizabeth, who was the cousin of Mary (Luke 1:36, 40).

King David had divided the priests into 24 divisions or courses (1 Chronicles 24:1-6). Each of these courses of priests served at the temple twice each year for one week. Luke tells us that Zacharias was chosen by lot to offer the incense at the appointed hour. To be selected for this solemn ceremony was a profound privilege. A priest could receive this honor only once in his lifetime and forever afterward was considered "rich and holy." The task was performed twice each day by a priest, once in the morning and once in the evening. While the incense was being lit, the people stood outside praying (Luke 1:8-10).

As Zacharias was going about this sacred duty, "an angel of the Lord appeared before him, standing on the right side of the altar of incense" (v. 11). Later, this angel is identified as "Gabriel, who stands in the presence of God" (v. 19). The sudden entrance and perhaps the manner of this heavenly messenger's appearance frightened Zacharias (v. 12). After comforting him with words of encouragement, Gabriel told Zacharias that Elizabeth would bear him a son and his name would be John. He also told Zacharias that this son would be a special servant who would be "filled with the Holy Spirit, even from his mother's womb" to call the people of God, the Israelites, back to Him (vv. 15-17).

When Zacharias demonstrated unbelief in Gabriel's promise because he and his wife were well past the age of childbearing, he was struck mute. He did not speak a word from that moment until he was asked what his son was to be called. He then asked for a tablet and wrote, "His name is John," and "immediately his mouth was opened and his tongue was loosed, and he spoke, praising God (vv. 63-64). John "grew and became strong in spirit, and was in the deserts till the day of his manifestation to Israel" (v. 80).

Luke 1:15 has led some people to conclude that John was to be a Nazirite. The rules governing Nazirites are mentioned in Numbers 6:1-21. Two of these are mentioned in connection with Samson – not drinking alcoholic beverages and not cutting the hair (Judges 13:1-14; 16:13-22). However, only one of these is mentioned in connection with John, and that was the drinking of alcohol. The requirement imposed upon John was much more stringent than was the one given to Nazirites. They were forbidden to drink during the period of their vow; John was forbidden to drink during his entire lifetime (NIV; NEB). This would lead a person to the conclusion that although he was a special servant of God, he was not a Nazirite.

The Forerunner of the Christ (Matthew 3:1-4)

Malachi had prophesied that God would send "Elijah the prophet before the coming of the great and dreadful day of the Lord" (Malachi 4:5). The angel had told Zacharias that his son would come "in the spirit and power of Elijah" (Luke 1:17). When John was born, Zacharias prophesied that he would "be called the prophet of the Highest" and that he would "go before the face of the Lord to prepare His ways" (v. 76). These words and the words of Gabriel to Zacharias were taken from Malachi's prophecy. Jesus later used the same words to describe John and said that he was the "Elijah who is to come" (Matthew 11:10, 14).

In our text for this lesson, Matthew describes the beginning of John's ministry in the wilderness of Judea. He must have been a sight to behold. The inspired writer says he was "clothed in camel's hair, with a leather belt about his waist; and his food was locusts and wild honey" (Matthew 3:4). The people did not quite know what to make of him, but they knew he was a prophet (11:9). When they asked him who he was, John used the words of Isaiah the prophet to describe himself: "I am the voice of one crying in the wilderness: make straight the way of the Lord" (John 1:23). His message was clear and simple, "Repent, for the kingdom of heaven is at hand!" (Matthew 3:2).

John the Baptist (Matthew 3:5-12)

John was called "the Baptist" because he baptized people. As this text begins, John was baptizing near the mouth of the Jordan, and the common people flocked to him to be baptized. While the Jewish leaders came mostly out of curiosity, even some of them came to be baptized (Matthew 3:7). Matthew says, "Then Jerusalem, all Judea and all the regions around the Jordan went out to him and were baptized by him in the Jordan confessing their sins" (3:5-6). Certainly not every person was baptized, but many people from all of these areas were.

The baptism of John was the "baptism of repentance" (Matthew 3:11), but it was also "for the remission of sins" (Mark 1:4). While the actual forgiveness was not accomplished until the death of Christ on the cross (Hebrews 9:13-28), John's baptism was valid for the purposes stated. Scripture does not tell us any of the people who were baptized by John before Christ's death were ever rebaptized. The only mention of any persons baptized with John's baptism being rebaptized is the incident involving the 12 men Paul encountered in Ephesus (Acts 19:1-7). They were baptized because they were baptized of John's baptism after Christ had been crucified, had given the Great Commission, and had ascended to heaven.

There is only one baptism that accomplishes the forgiveness of sins today, and that is the baptism of the Great Commission (Acts 2:38; 22:16; Ephesians 4:5). This is the baptism of a person who believes Jesus to be the Son of God and has confessed this publicly, who has repented of his sins, and who is immersed in water in the name of the Father, the Son and the Holy Spirit (Romans 10:9-10; Acts 2:38; 8:35-39; Matthew 28:18-20). Only at this point does the blood of Christ cleanse us of our sins (Acts 22:16; Romans 6:3-7, 17-18; Ephesians 1:7; Colossians 1:14; Revelation 1:5).

John called upon the Pharisees and Sadducees to "bear fruits worthy of repentance" (Matthew 3:8). That is, he wanted them to demonstrate that they had truly repented before he would baptize them. A reformation of life is absolutely essential to true repentance. This is indicated in John's instructions to certain individuals, including tax collectors and soldiers (Luke 3:10-14). John urged these Jewish leaders not to rely upon their national and family origin but to realize that the time of separating the wheat from the chaff had come. They could no longer count on merely being the seed of Abraham as assurance of salvation. In fact, they never could do so (Romans 2:1-29; 4:1-25); they only thought they could. The ax of God's truth had been "laid to the root of the tree," and the unfruitful ones would be "cut down and thrown into the fire" (Matthew 3:10).

John said he was baptizing them with water, but "He who is coming after me is mightier than I, … He will baptize you with the Holy Spirit and with fire" (Matthew 3:11). From this statement, some people conclude John was saying that Christ would not baptize with water. This cannot be the true meaning of his words because Jesus commanded people to be baptized in water not long after these statements were made (John 3:26; 4:1-2). John's statement obviously means that in addition to the baptism of water, Jesus would also baptize with the Holy Spirit and with fire.

When was the baptism of the Holy Spirit accomplished? Jesus promised the apostles that when He went away, He would send the Holy Spirit (John 14:16-17, 26; 16:7-15). Before He ascended to the Father, He told them "you shall be baptized with the Holy Spirit not many days from now" and that when that happened, He said they would "receive power" to be witnesses for Him (Acts 1:5, 8). On the Day of Pentecost after His ascension, this promise was fulfilled (2:1-4). Only the apostles were baptized with the Holy Spirit on this occasion (v. 4). This is the first of two occasions when the Holy Spirit came spontaneously without the laying on of apostolic hands (8:14-19; 19:1-12). The second time was at the house of Cornelius (10:24, 44-45; 11:15-17). In these two events, God sent His Spirit upon "all flesh," both Jews and Gentiles, in keeping with Joel's prophecy (Joel 2:28; Acts 2:17).

What of the baptism of fire? Some people teach that this refers to the baptism of the apostles on the Day of Pentecost. They point out that "divided tongues, as of fire … sat upon each of them" (Acts 2:3). That this incident is the baptism of fire about which John spoke cannot be the case. First, the apostles were not immersed in fire. What Luke says is that objects that appeared to be like parted tongues of fire were above the head of each one of them. They were not immersed or completely submerged, which is the meaning of the word baptized, by these objects, and neither were these real tongues of real fire. Second, John gives his inspired interpretation of these words. He says this baptism of fire is when the wicked, the unfruitful trees and the chaff from the wheat will be cast into the unquenchable fire. This can only refer to the Judgment and the time when the unrighteous will be cast into the lake of fire (Matthew 25:31-33, 41, 46; Revelation 20:11-15). People have even foolishly prayed for this baptism of fire, but this is one baptism they will not want to receive.

Jesus Is Baptized by John (Matthew 3:13-17)

When Jesus was about 30 years old, He came from Galilee to the Jordan to be baptized of John (Luke 3:23). At first, John refused to baptize Him. In his refusal, he seems to imply his knowledge of who Jesus really was. However, in John's account of the gospel, he records John the Baptist as saying, "I did not know him; but He who sent me to baptize with water said to me, 'Upon whom you see the Spirit descending, and remaining on Him, this is He who baptizes with the Holy Spirit' " (John 1:33). For this to be understood, we must put some pieces of this puzzle together.

It is not as if John and Jesus did not know each other, because they were cousins. If they were like most families, they had surely had some contact during these 30 years, as Luke 2:44 implies. John was not saying he did not know Jesus at all. He was only saying he did not know that He was the Son of God, but when he saw the Holy Spirit come upon Him as a dove, this was the sign that God had told him would reveal the Christ to him (John 1:33-34). Not until then did John testify as to Christ's true identity (John 1:36). He no doubt already knew about the sterling character and righteousness of his cousin, and his immediate response was in view of these facts and had nothing to do with His knowledge about Christ's deity

In answer to John's question, Jesus said, "Permit it to be so now, for thus it is fitting for us to fulfill all righteousness" (Matthew 3:15). Jesus did not need to be baptized for the remission of sins, for He "knew no sin" (2 Corinthians 5:21; 1 Peter 2:21-22). He did, however, have to be completely obedient to the righteous will of God to become "the author of eternal salvation to all who obey Him" (Hebrews 5:8-9).

When Jesus was baptized by John, He "came up immediately from the water," which implies full immersion (Matthew 3:16). Then the Holy Spirit came upon Him. This was a sign to John that Jesus was God's Son, and it was also the fulfillment of a prophecy made by Isaiah (Isaiah 11:2; 42:1). It was the anointing of Jesus to be the King over God's kingdom. When the Spirit came upon Jesus, God audibly spoke from Heaven and gave His witness to His Son and said, "This is my beloved Son, in whom I am well pleased" (Matthew 3:17). This was the first of three occasions when God declared His testimony to His Son's deity (Matthew 17:5; John 12:28-32). Jesus was the God who became man (John 1:1, 14).

All three persons of the Godhead (Acts 17:29 KJV; Romans 1:20; Colossians 2:9), are represented on this occasion. Christ is in the water with John; the Holy Spirit descends upon Him in the form of a dove; and God speaks from Heaven to proclaim His pleasure with His Son. This event provides a problem for those who deny the Trinity. While the word Trinity is never used in Scripture, there is biblical teaching to confirm the fact (Matthew 28:19; John 1:1-3, 14; 17:1-26; 1 John 5:7).

Lessons Learned

1. Mary, the mother of Jesus, and Elizabeth, the mother of John the Baptist, were cousins. This means that Jesus and John were cousins and had most likely known each other since childhood.
2. Although John the Baptist was a special servant of God and a prophet, he was not a Nazirite.
3. John baptized penitent people for the remission of sins. There is no record of any people who were baptized with John's baptism being rebaptized with the exception of the 12 men Paul found in Ephesus. They were baptized with John's baptism after the Great Commission was given.
4. The baptism of fire that John spoke about will be when the wicked are cast into the lake of fire.
5. The baptism of the Holy Spirit was fulfilled on the Day of Pentecost and at the house of Cornelius in Caesarea.
6. Although John's baptism was for the remission of sins, Jesus had no sin. He was baptized to fulfill the righteousness of God.
7. The Holy Spirit descending upon Jesus was a sign to John the Baptist that He was the Messiah and the fulfillment of prophecy.

Questions

1. What was Zacharias' profession?
2. What was Zacharias doing when the angel appeared to Him?
3. What happened to Zacharias as a result of his apparent unbelief?
4. Who were Nazirites?
5. How did John answer people who asked him who he was?
6. Why do we call John "the Baptist?"
7. Which of the at least five baptisms mentioned in the New Testament accomplishes the forgiveness of sins today?
8. What does repentance mean, and what does it require?
9. What was the baptism of fire and the baptism of the Holy Spirit?
10. How do the events at Jesus' baptism confirm the doctrine of the Trinity?

Lesson 4

The Temptation of Jesus

Week of Sept. 27, 1998

Lesson Text

MATTHEW 4:1-11

(1) Then Jesus was led up by the Spirit into the wilderness to be tempted by the devil.

(2) And when He had fasted forty days and forty nights, afterward He was hungry.

(3) Now when the tempter came to Him, he said, "If You are the Son of God, command that these stones become bread."

(4) But He answered and said, "It is written, 'Man shall not live by bread alone, but by every word that proceeds from the mouth of God.' "

(5) Then the devil took Him up into the holy city, set Him on the pinnacle of the temple,

(6) and said to Him, "If You are the Son of God, throw Yourself down. For it is written: 'He shall give His angels charge over you,' and, 'In their hands they shall bear you up, Lest you dash your foot against a stone.' "

(7) Jesus said to him, "It is written again, 'You shall not tempt the LORD your God.' "

(8) Again, the devil took Him up on an exceedingly high mountain, and showed Him all the kingdoms of the world and their glory.

(9) And he said to Him, "All these things I will give You if You will fall down and worship me."

(10) Then Jesus said to him, "Away with you, Satan! For it is written, 'You shall worship the LORD your God, and Him only you shall serve.' "

(11) Then the devil left Him, and behold, angels came and ministered to Him.

Introduction

Paul writes that "No temptation has overtaken you except such as is common to man" (1Corinthians 10:13). No temptation exists that people who have gone before us have not confronted. The Bible is filled with many examples of people who encountered temptation. Some succumbed to its pressures, but others overcame it. No example of overcoming temptation is more reassuring than that of our Lord Himself.

The writer of Hebrews says of Jesus, "For in that He Himself has suffered, being tempted, He is able to aid those who are tempted" (Hebrews 2:18). He adds, "For we do not have a High Priest who cannot sympathize with our weaknesses, but was in all points tempted as we are; yet without sin" (Hebrews 4:15). To understand that Jesus knew temptation is extremely encouraging. He experienced temptation, and He was tempted in every way that we are tempted. He was not tempted with every sin, but He was tempted in all the avenues through which men are tempted. These avenues are the lust of the flesh, the lust of the eyes, and the pride of life (1 John 2:15-17). He met and overcame these temptations, as well as subsequent ones, without sinning.

Some people will say, "That is great, but He was divine." Yes, He was divine, but we must never forget that He was also human. He was fully divine, but He was also fully human. In defending His divinity, we must never deny His humanity. This is what the antichrists about whom John wrote were doing (1 John 2:18-23). If He overcame temptation only because of His divinity, then He was not tempted as we are. If He could not experience the same struggle in the temptations He encountered, then the fact that He overcame them means little. The temptation of Jesus means something because with His human nature He felt the same pressure to yield that we do, but He refused to submit to it.

Paul developed the idea of the self-humiliation of Jesus (Greek: *kenosis* – emptying) in Philippians 2:6-8. Although Jesus was God, "in the form of God", He 1. emptied Himself; 2. was born like a man, or in man's likeness; 3. was obedient even to death; and 4. willingly accepted the shame of the Cross. Certainly, there was a perfect balance between Christ's human nature and His divine nature, but this in no way lessens the impact of His victory over Satan. Jesus faced this temptation and overcame it as a man. He did not sin because He chose not to sin. Our text proves He did not use miraculous power to overcome Satan. He used only what is available to each of us – His commitment to His Father's will and the Word of God. If Jesus could successfully confront temptation and overcome it, we can too. It may be harder for us, but as Paul wrote, "No temptation has overtaken you except such as is common to man; but God is faithful, who will not allow you to be tempted beyond what you are able, but with the temptation will also make the way of escape, that you may be able to bear it" (1 Corinthians 10:13).

Jesus Prepares for His Confrontation with Satan (Matthew 4:1-2)

Matthew says, "Jesus was led up of the Spirit." Mark says, "And immediately the Spirit drove Him into the wilderness" (Mark 1:12). This means that right after Jesus submitted to the righteousness of God in being baptized by John, the Spirit anointed Him, and God personally identified Him as His Son, He had to endure the trial of human affliction. After some of our most significant moments we face life's greatest trials. Many people wrongly believe that after they are baptized that they will no longer face the lure of temptation, the pain of trails, or the effects of trouble. Nothing could be further from the truth. The battle has only just begun. We must continue to "fight the good fight of faith" that we may "lay hold on eternal life" (1 Timothy 6:12). We must "finish the race, and keep the faith" before we receive the "crown of righteousness" (2 Timothy 4:7-8).

The Spirit led Jesus to the loneliness of the wilderness so that He spiritually might prepare Himself for His meeting with the devil. The Greek renders it *diabolos*. This is one of the names by which Satan is made known to us. It means "accuser," as in Revelation 12:10 where the voice John heard describes him as "the accuser of our brethren, who accused them before our God day and night." In Job 1:6-7, we find him engaged in this very activity as he appeared before God to bring accusation against the righteous Job.

To prepare for His confrontation with the devil, Jesus "fasted forty days and forty nights" (Matthew 4:2). Whether there is any significance in the time period, we cannot be certain. Moses fasted for the same period before receiving the Law of God on Mount Sinai (Exodus 24:18; 34: 28; Deuteronomy 9:9; 10:10). Elijah fasted for the same period in his flight from the wrath of Jezebel following his defeat of the prophets of Baal (1 Kings 19:8). The most significant point is the purpose for which each of them fasted because in each case, it was a spiritual one.

Fasting is not dieting, just missing a single meal, starvation, an exercise to be observed on fixed days or at stated time, or as an ostentatious show of piety. In every case in which it was observed in the Bible, it was to bring a person closer to God and to help him find strength to endure whatever difficulty or problem he was facing. Scripture does not command Christians to fast but assumes that they will (Matthew 6:16-18; 9:14-15; Mark 2:18; Luke 5:33). Jesus did not condemn fasting, but He did condemn the wrong kind, done in the wrong manner.

Jesus Faces the Tempter (Matthew 4:3-10)

When Jesus was physically purged but spiritually powerful, the tempter came to Him. Satan is always the tempter (Job 1:9-12; 2:1-7). God allows us to be tempted to test us (James 1:2-3, 12), to discipline us (Hebrews 12:3-11) or to serve some higher purpose, as in Job's case. If there is no opportunity to do evil, there is no virtue in doing good. However, God is never the tempter, nor can He be tempted to do evil (James 1:13-15).

This was no chance meeting. It was not as if Satan was just out taking a stroll and accidentally stumbled upon the Christ in prayer and meditation. The words of the text leave no doubt this meeting was planned as well as prepared for. Satan knew he would find Jesus there, just as Jesus knew that he would come.

Satan began his assault by taunting Jesus with the very words God had used in endorsing His ministry: "If you are the Son of God" "If" – was there really any doubt? Are we to believe that Satan did not know who Jesus was? The Greek construction would indicate that Satan was really saying, "Since you are the Son of God, show me what you can do." He attacked Jesus at His vulnerable point. He always comes to us at our weakest moments. After 40 days and nights of fasting, Jesus surely would have been extremely hungry. So Satan said, "Command that these stones become bread." That would have been easy for Him who could feed a multitude with a couple of fish and a few pieces of bread. It is not that He could not, but He would not satisfy Satan's desire for Him to demonstrate a lack of confidence in God's provisions. He answered this challenge, as He did each of them, with "the sword of the Spirit, which is the word of God" (Ephesians 6:17). "Man shall not live by bread alone, but by every word that proceeds from the mouth of God" (Matthew 4:4).This is a quotation of Deuteronomy 8:3 from the Septuagint, a Greek translation of the Old Testament by 70 scholars from Alexandria, Egypt.

Where the first temptation questioned God's provisions, the second questioned His protection. The devil took Jesus to the Holy City, Jerusalem, to the pinnacle of the temple. Men debate how this was accomplished. The text does not say. Was it an actual transportation of the Son of God by Satan? Does he really have such power? Could he make Jesus do something that He did not choose to do? Why could Jesus not have voluntarily gone from the wilderness with Satan to Jerusalem? See Numbers 23:13-14 and Matthew 17:1; 20:17; 26:37; 27:27 that show the expression "took Him" does not necessarily imply a person is forced against his will.

The place where they were in Jerusalem was at some high point of the temple. Eusebius says it was the same place where James, our Lord's brother and a leader in the church at Jerusalem, was martyred (*Ecclesiastical History II*, xxiii.11). Some scholars believe it was either the southeast corner of the wall around the temple or the roof over Solomon's porch. Other scholars think it was a tower that had been constructed on the east wall that was described by Josephus (*Antiquities* XV.11.5) as being so high that to look down from its lofty heights would make a person dizzy. We cannot know for sure which of these places, if any of them, was the exact location.

The devil quoted Scripture (Psalm 91:11-12), as if to say, "If you're going to use Scripture, I can too." However, although he quoted this passage exactly as it is written in the Septuagint, he used it incorrectly. As Jesus indicated, by His response from Deuteronomy 6:16, it was intended to encourage faith, never to encourage men to put God to the test. If Jesus had submitted to Satan's request, He would have demonstrated a lack of faith in God's protection rather than proving it.

The final temptation was designed to question God's promise. He had sent Christ into the world to be the King over His spiritual kingdom. What He had promised, He was able also to fulfill. However, to receive it, Jesus would have to go by way of the Cross. Satan offered Him a shortcut around Calvary. He took "Him up on an exceedingly high mountain, and showed Him all the kingdoms of the world and their glory" (Matthew 4:8). Was this merely a vision? It may have been, but it does not have to be so. God let Moses see the Promised Land from the top of Mount Nebo. From that point, he could see a large portion of the land. The text says he saw, "All the land of Gilead unto Dan and all Nephtali, and the land of Ephraim and Manasseh, and all the land of Judah unto the utmost sea, and the south and the plain of the valley of Jericho, and the city of the palm trees unto Zoar" (Deuteronomy 34:1-3).

Did Jesus actually see "all the kingdoms of the world"? The term "world" is often used in a limited sense (Romans 4:13; Luke 2:1). It likely referred here only to Palestine. Judea was divided into three parts, and each one was ruled over by one of the sons of Herod the Great, all called kings. Even so, how was Satan able to offer Christ these kingdoms? Jesus called him the "ruler of this world" (John 16:11). Paul referred to him as the "god of this age," or "world" in the King James version (2 Corinthians 4:4). He later called him "the prince of the power of the air; the spirit who now works in the sons of disobedience" (Ephesians 2:2). Two kingdoms exist side by side – the kingdom of God and the kingdom of Satan (Colossians 1:13). Satan could not give what was not his to give, but he could offer Jesus what was under his domain. He was saying, in effect, "You came to be a king, but you'll have to wait for that to happen. I'm giving you an opportunity to be one now."

Once more Jesus responded with Scripture, quoting Deuteronomy 6:13 from the Septuagint: "Away with you, Satan! For it is written, 'You shall worship the Lord your God, and Him only you shall serve' " (Matthew 4:10). Complete commitment to God was the only pathway to the throne for Christ. He had to go by way of the Cross before He could wear the crown. The only way we can wear the "crown of life" (Revelation 2:10) is to follow His example of faithfulness.

Matthew tells us that after this last temptation that "the devil left him, and behold angels came and ministered to Him" (Matthew 4:11). Luke says that "when the devil had ended all the temptations, he departed from Him for a season" (Luke 4:13 KJV). The New King James version says "he departed from Him until an opportune time" (Luke 4:13). We must not think that this wilderness encounter was the only occasion when Satan tempted Jesus. He hounded the Son of God all the way to Calvary, and even there tempted Him through the mob: "Save yourself! If you are the Son of God, come down from the cross" (Matthew 27:40). Satan will not leave us alone, either, for when we think he has left us forever, he returns with all of his fury "like a roaring lion, seeking whom he may devour" (1 Peter 5:8).

Lessons Learned

1. Every temptation we can face in this world has been faced by people before us.
2. Because Jesus was tempted in every way that we can be, He understands how we feel when we are tempted.
3. Jesus was not just a divine being in a fleshly body but was the merger of humanity and divinity.
4. When Jesus faced the temptations in the wilderness, He did so with the same power we have at out disposal – commitment to God and His Word.
5. The only reason Satan could legitimately offer Jesus the kingdoms of the world was because he is the "ruler of this world," that is this world system.
6. As long as Jesus lived in this world, He was tempted, and we should expect to experience the same thing.

Questions

1. Why is Jesus able to sympathize with our weaknesses?
2. What are the three avenues of temptation with which Satan confronted Jesus?
3. Can you name the three temptations that Jesus experienced?
4. How did Jesus meet these temptations?
5. In the passage from Philippians 2:5-8, how did Paul demonstrate the self-humiliation of Jesus?
6. What did Jesus teach concerning fasting? Should Christians fast or not, and why?
7. What does the name "Satan" mean?
8. How did Satan misuse Deuteronomy 6:16?
9. What is the only way we can wear the crown and robe of righteousness?
10. What happened after Jesus' temptation?

Lesson 5

The Trip to Nazareth

Week of Oct. 4, 1998

Lesson Text

LUKE 4:16-30

(16) So He came to Nazareth, where He had been brought up. And as His custom was, He went into the synagogue on the Sabbath day, and stood up to read.

(17) And He was handed the book of the prophet Isaiah. And when He had opened the book, He found the place where it was written:

(18) "The Spirit of the LORD is upon Me, Because He has anointed Me To preach the gospel to the poor; He has sent Me to heal the brokenhearted, To proclaim liberty to the captives And recovery of sight to the blind, To set at liberty those who are oppressed;

(19) To proclaim the acceptable year of the LORD."

(20) Then He closed the book, and gave it back to the attendant and sat down. And the eyes of all who were in the synagogue were fixed on Him.

(21) And He began to say to them, "Today this Scripture is fulfilled in your hearing."

(22) So all bore witness to Him, and marveled at the gracious words which proceeded out of His mouth. And they said, "Is this not Joseph's son?"

(23) He said to them, "You will surely say this proverb to Me, 'Physician, heal yourself! Whatever we have heard done in Capernaum, do also here in Your country.'"

(24) Then He said, "Assuredly, I say to you, no prophet is accepted in his own country.

(25) "But I tell you truly, many widows were in Israel in the days of Elijah, when the heaven was shut up three years and six months, and there was a great famine throughout all the land;

(26) "but to none of them was Elijah sent except to Zarephath, in the region of Sidon, to a woman who was a widow.

(27) "And many lepers were in Israel in the time of Elisha the prophet, and none of them was cleansed except Naaman the Syrian."

(28) So all those in the synagogue, when they heard these things, were filled with wrath,

(29) and rose up and thrust Him out of the city; and they led Him to the brow of the hill on which their city was built, that they might throw Him down over the cliff.

(30) Then passing through the midst of them, He went His way.

Introduction

Jesus was raised in the city of Nazareth in lower Galilee, about 70 miles from Jerusalem. Apparently He had lived there all of His life with the exception of the time spent in Bethlehem and in Egypt (Luke 2:11-40, 51-52; Matthew 2:13-23). At the age of 30, He left home and journeyed to the river Jordan where He was baptized by John (Luke 3:21-23). Immediately after His baptism, He was led by the Holy

Spirit into the wilderness, where after fasting for 40 days and nights, He was tempted by Satan. Following His temptation, and after being strengthened by angels (Matthew 4:11), He began His public ministry. Luke does not give us a lot of information or specific details about His activities but simply tells us "Jesus returned in the power of the Spirit to Galilee, and the news of Him went out through all the surrounding region. And He taught in their synagogues being glorified by all" (Luke 4:14-15).

John tells us that during this time Jesus performed His first miracle in Cana of Galilee by turning water into wine at a wedding feast (John 2:1-11). John the Baptist continued preaching (John 3:22-24). Soon after that he was imprisoned (Matthew 4:12; John 4:21-23). By this time, Jesus' fame had spread far and wide. He had performed miracles in Capernaum that are not specified but are alluded to in Matthew's gospel (Matthew 11:23). However, He had not yet returned to His hometown. Our text gives us the account of His first visit to Nazareth after He began to preach. He was the local boy made good, the carpenter turned itinerant preacher. The townspeople were eager to hear Him and to witness some miracles at His hand.

Jesus' Visit to the Synagogue (Luke 4:16)

Luke tells us "as His custom was, He went into the synagogue on the Sabbath day" (4:16). This was most likely the synagogue He had attended with His parents before leaving home. He would be joining family, friends and neighbors in the place where they had worshiped together so many times before. The synagogue, meaning "congregation," which is thought to have originated during the Babylonian captivity, was the center of Hebrew life. Where there were 10 Jewish males, there could be a synagogue. At one time there were more than 400 synagogues in Jerusalem alone.

The typical synagogue services began with a prayer for God's blessing and then a recitation of the *Shema*, the traditional Hebrew confession of faith. "Hear, O Israel: the Lord our God, the Lord is one! You shall love the Lord your God with all your heart, with all your soul, And with all your strength" (Deuteronomy 6:4-9; 11:13-21). This would be followed by prayer, after which the people would say "Amen." Then a prescribed portion from the Law and the Prophets would be read in the Hebrew language. The reader, or someone else, would then translate them into Aramaic, which was the language spoken by the average Jew on the street. The person doing the reading would always stand with the congregation when the Scriptures were read, unless it was a text from the book of Esther. After the reading, a brief lesson would be delivered by the men of the congregation or by a visiting rabbi (Acts 13:14-16). If a priest was present, he would close the service with a benediction, to which the congregation would say "Amen!" If a priest was not there, one of the men would lead a closing prayer and dismiss the assembly.

Whether Jesus stood up to be recognized or whether the person presiding over that particular service asked Him to read is not certain. This may have been their way of honoring the hometown boy. We can almost imagine the hushed silence and every eye fixed upon Him as He prepared to receive the book from which to read.

The Text Jesus Read (Luke 4:17-19)

Jesus was handed the book of Isaiah. It would not have been like our books but would have been a scroll, much like those still used in Jewish synagogue services today. From Luke's words, it would appear that Jesus opened the scroll and chose

Himself to read from Isaiah 61:1-2. While some people try to apply this passage to the Year of Jubilee mentioned in Leviticus 25:8-17, its Messianic implications are clearly indicated by our Lord and applied to Himself (Luke 4:21). When John was in prison and sent disciples to inquire if Jesus was the Christ, He appealed to this same text and certain others from Isaiah to convince them and John of His identity (7:22; Matthew 11:4-5).

Verses 18 and 19 refer to the event that occurred at Jesus' baptism when the Holy Spirit came upon Him. This was not to fill Christ with the Spirit, "for God giveth not the Spirit by measure unto Him" (John 3:34 KJV). This was the sign that He was God's Anointed; the King over the kingdom of heaven. It was not until this anointing that Jesus began to "preach the gospel" and fulfill the rest of Isaiah's prophecy.

While this passage specifically relates to the ministry of Jesus, it can be said that whenever the gospel is preached it brings forth the same results. The gospel does "heal the brokenhearted" and those people "who are oppressed" by helping them see the true salvation that is found only in Jesus Christ. It helps believers to overcome pain, grief and loss; it brings "deliverance to the captives" of sin; it "sets at liberty" people who are enslaved to ignorance, fear and doubt. The statement by Isaiah about "the acceptable year of the Lord" most likely refers to that fact that this was the time when God had chosen to bring this prophecy to fulfillment.

Jesus' Application of the Text (Luke 4:20-22)

When Jesus had rolled up the scroll and given it back to the attendant, He sat down. While the person who read the Scripture text was not always the person who delivered the message, it is clear that this is what the congregation expected Jesus to do. "And the eyes of all who were in the synagogue were fixed on Him" (Luke 4:20). Jewish rabbis stood to read the Scriptures, but when they taught, they always sat. Their messages were more Bible class lessons than they were discourses. The people wanted to hear Jesus speak, but they were not prepared to hear what He had to say: "Today is this scripture fulfilled in your hearing." There could be no doubt about the meaning of this statement. Jesus was declaring for all the world to know that He was the One about whom Isaiah was speaking. He was saying that the Messianic prophecies were no longer merely a matter of public reading or private devotion – they had leapt off the page and come to life in the person of Jesus.

Could they have been hearing Him right? Was this young man they had known all of His life saying He was the long-anticipated Messiah? "They said, Is this not Joseph's son?" Matthew points out that they later said, "Is not His mother called Mary? And His brothers James, Joses, Simon, and Judas? And His sisters, are they not all with us?" (Matthew 13:55). Because of this, although they "marveled at His gracious words" (Luke 4:22), they were "offended at him" (Mark 6:3). We often fail to appreciate what is right before us until it is no longer there. What an opportunity they missed. The great announcement the world had waited for had just been made in their presence, but they rejected the message because they rejected the Messenger.

Jesus Rebuked Their Unbelief (Luke 4:23-27)

Jesus knew what they were thinking. He answered, "You will surely say this proverb to me, 'Physician heal yourself! Whatever we have heard done in Capernaum, do also here in your country.' " They wanted Him to put on a healing show to prove that He was sent from God. Like others after them, they wanted a sign. He rejected their desire for Him to show His stuff. He never performed miracles on demand just to satisfy the curious. He bluntly let them know that, even if He had, they would not have believed Him because of their puny faith.

Jesus responded to their unbelief with a statement He used often, "Assuredly I say to you, no prophet is accepted in His own country" (Matthew 13:57; Mark 6:4; Luke 4:24; John 4:44). Many people since this incident have experienced the truthfulness of Jesus' words. How many preachers have returned to their home congregations in which they grew up and heard said, "I remember when you were just a little boy. I knew your father and your mother." Some preachers have even been reminded of childhood mischief and mistakes, as if these youthful indiscretions make a man eternally unfit to preach the gospel. When such happens, the man of God can take comfort in the fact that our Lord received the same reception from His home congregation.

To make His point about their lack of faith, Jesus used two illustrations from the Old Testament with which these people were very familiar. Why did He perform miracles in Capernaum and not in His hometown? He reminded them that there were many widows in Israel during the drought and the famine that followed the days of Elijah's dealings with Ahab, Jezebel and the prophets of Baal. However, Elijah was sent to the home of a Gentile widow in Zarephath in the region of Sidon and stayed in her home. It was here that he performed the miracle of the pitcher of oil that never ran dry and the flour bin that never emptied, and he raised this woman's only son from the dead (1 Kings 17:8-24). Jesus also reminded them that although there were many lepers in Israel during Elisha's time, the prophet healed only Naaman, a Gentile, the commander of Syria's army.

The people did not need anyone to interpret this message. Jesus was telling them that those two lowly Gentile "dogs" had more faith than the exalted Jews, the people of God. He was saying that He performed miracles in Capernaum, even some among Gentiles, because they had the faith to accept them when they did not. You do not gain any popularity by telling people who consider themselves to be the people of God that their faith is weaker than people whom they consider outcasts.

The Sermon's Aftermath (Luke 4:28-30)

This hometown crowd became so angry at the obvious implications of Jesus' statements that they rose up in mass and literally drove Him out of the synagogue. They led Him up to the brow of one of the many hills surrounding Nazareth. By now their anger had turned into rage, and they intended to push Him off the hill to His death. Luke simply says, "Then passing through the midst of them, He went His way" (Luke 4:30). Some people believe Jesus performed a miracle and disappeared from their midst. In Israel, guides will tell tourists that He jumped from one hill to another to escape from them. From the wording of the text, neither of these extreme measures is the necessary conclusion. The casual nature of verse 30 lends itself to the conclusion that because of the confusion and the press of the crowd, Jesus just walked away.

Lessons Learned

1. Most of Jesus' life, with the exception of the short time spent in Bethlehem and Egypt, was lived in Nazareth of Galilee until He was 30 years old.
2. From the text, it is clear that Jesus regularly attended the Sabbath services at

the synagogue; this is an example for Christians to follow in attending in worship services today.

3. The passage from Isaiah 61:1-2 proves that Jesus is the Messiah.
4. The Holy Spirit came upon Jesus as a sign and as His anointing to be King of God's kingdom.
5. Jesus' use of two Old Testament illustrations where God blessed Gentiles through His prophets showed that the ministry of Jesus, though initially to the Jews, was much broader in scope.
6. When people are confronted with truth, they will either accept it or reject it.

Questions

1. For what reasons did Jesus leave Galilee at the age of 30?
2. What was the first miracle Jesus performed and why? Can any deductions be made from this miracle concerning Christians and alcohol? Why or why not?
3. When was the synagogue form of worship thought to have originated and why?
4. What is the *Shema*, and what does it mean? Can you recite it?
5. What is the significance of the passage Jesus read from Isaiah 61:1-2?
6. How can this passage apply to the preaching of the gospel today?
7. Why was the reaction of Jesus' hometown folks to His application of this passage so negative?
8. What was the main reason that the people of Nazareth did not believe Jesus was the Messiah?
9. Why were they so angered by His use of the two Old Testament illustrations?
10. What is the meaning of Jesus' statement, "No prophet is accepted in His own country?"

Lesson 6

The First Disciples

Week of Oct. 11, 1998

Lesson Text

LUKE 5:2-11, 27-28

(2) and saw two boats standing by the lake; but the fishermen had gone from them and were washing their nets.

(3) Then He got into one of the boats, which was Simon's, and asked him to put out a little from the land. And He sat down and taught the multitudes from the boat.

(4) When He had stopped speaking, He said to Simon, "Launch out into the deep and let down your nets for a catch."

(5) But Simon answered and said to Him, "Master, we have toiled all night and caught nothing; nevertheless at Your word I will let down the net."

(6) And when they had done this, they caught a great number of fish, and their net was breaking.

(7) So they signaled to their partners in the other boat to come and help them. And they came and filled both the boats, so that they began to sink.

(8) When Simon Peter saw it, he fell down at Jesus' knees, saying, "Depart from me, for I am a sinful man, O Lord!"

(9) For he and all who were with him were astonished at the catch of fish which they had taken;

(10) and so also were James and John, the sons of Zebedee, who were partners with Simon. And Jesus said to Simon, "Do not be afraid. From now on you will catch men."

(11) So when they had brought their boats to land, they forsook all and followed Him.

(27) After these things He went out and saw a tax collector named Levi, sitting at the tax office. And He said to him, "Follow Me."

(28) So he left all, rose up, and followed Him.

LUKE 6:12-16

(12) Now it came to pass in those days that He went out to the mountain to pray, and continued all night in prayer to God.

(13) And when it was day, He called His disciples to Himself; and from them He chose twelve whom He also named apostles:

(14) Simon, whom He also named Peter, and Andrew his brother; James and John; Philip and Bartholomew;

(15) Matthew and Thomas; James the son of Alphaeus, and Simon called the Zealot;

(16) Judas the son of James, and Judas Iscariot who also became a traitor.

Introduction

Having been baptized by John, tempted by the devil, and beginning His public ministry, Jesus selected the men who would work the closest with Him. Jesus had already encountered some of these men (Luke 4:38), and at least four of them,

Simon, Andrew, Philip and Nathanael, accompanied Him on His return to Galilee (John 1:35-51; 2:2). Andrew and another unnamed disciple, probably John, spent several hours privately with Jesus. If this unnamed disciple was John, then he may have introduced his own brother James to Jesus, just as Andrew had introduced his brother Simon to Him.

The word "disciple" means "learner" or "follower." A disciple is a student of the person he follows. Jesus had many disciples at this time. Luke tells us that He sent out 70 men at one time on what has been called the Limited Commission because they were sent only to the cities Jesus was preparing to visit (Luke 10:1). From this larger group of disciples He selected 12 men who would become His apostles (Luke 6:13). The word "apostle" means a person who is "selected, charged and sent with authority to act on behalf of the person who sent him." The word is used both in a narrow sense and in a broader one. In the broader context it is used in referring to Barnabas (Acts 14:4,14; 1 Corinthians 9:5-6), to James, the Lord's brother (1 Corinthians 15:7; Galatians 1:19), and even to Jesus Himself (Hebrews 3:1). Paul also calls some "false apostles, deceitful workers, transforming themselves into apostles of Christ" (2 Corinthians 11:13). Whether these men were sent out by churches or by mere men, Jesus chose 12 men from among His closest disciples to be His apostles (Mark 4:10; 6:7).

Luke uses the term "apostle" more than any of the other gospel writers in reference to the Twelve. A clear distinction must be made between these men and the men mentioned previously. These 12 men would become Jesus' personal ambassadors or emissaries to bear witness for Him " in Jerusalem, in all Judea and Samaria, and to the end of the earth" (Acts 1:8). Mark tells us that these men were selected to be "with Him that He might send them out to preach" (Mark 3:14).

The Drought of Fishes (Luke 5:2-11)

Multitudes followed Jesus wherever He went in the early days of His ministry. On this occasion, He was walking near Lake Gennesaret, which was also known as the Lake of Tiberias (John 6:1; 21:1) and the Sea of Galilee (Mark 1:16). It must have been in the early morning (Luke 5:2, 5). The press of the crowd became so great that Jesus felt the need to separate Himself from them so He could be in a better position to teach. Then He saw Simon and probably Andrew, his brother, although he is not mentioned by name, and James and John near their boats washing their nets (Matthew 4:18; Mark 1:16, 19; Luke 5:2). These men were partners in the fishing business (Luke 5:7, 10). Jesus entered Simon's boat and asked him to push out from the shore a short distance. Then He sat down and taught the people.

When Jesus had finished His teaching, He must have realized the discouragement of Peter because of the failure of his previous night's fishing. He urged him to "launch out into the deep and let down your nets for a catch" (Luke 5:4). This incident must not be confused with the one that happens after Jesus' resurrection (John 21:5-8). Peter was at first reluctant, and we must wonder why he was. By now, he had already witnessed the Lord's first miracle of turning water to wine in Cana of Galilee (John 2:1-2). More importantly, his own mother-in-law and many of his friends and neighbors healed from various diseases. Demons had been also cast out by Jesus (Luke 4:38-41). The answer to this question probably lies in the nature of the man himself.

Peter appears to be more like us than any of the other apostles. He was impulsive, inquisitive, brash, weak and full of pride but so very human. An early description of him says that he was "hopeful, bold, confident, courageous, frank, impulsive, energetic, vigorous, strong, loving, and faithful to his Master, notwithstanding his defection before the Crucifixion. It is true that he was liable to change and inconsistency, and because of his peculiar temperament he sometimes appeared forward and rash." With this description in mind, you can understand why he might question the Lord although he had witnessed many miracles done by Him. He was a fisherman; Jesus was not – He was a carpenter. Fishing was Peter's job, and he knew where to find fish and how to catch them. Surely if he had been fishing all night and caught nothing, Jesus could not help him catch any fish.

But despite his doubts and because of his faith in Jesus, he let down his net. The catch was so great that the net began to break, and he had to call for James and John to help him. Both boats were filled with so many fish that they almost sank (Luke 5:5-7). Peter and the men who were with him were so astonished at what was done that he fell down at Jesus' knees ("feet" KJV), and said, "Depart from me, for I am a sinful man, O Lord" (Luke 5:8-9). This was not a request for Jesus to actually leave his presence but is an indication of Peter's impetuousness when he witnessed in such a dramatic way the awesome power of the Christ.

Most of Jesus' miracles were performed for a purpose, and this one was no different. The miracle was not done so that Peter, Andrew, James and John could brag about their great haul at the local fish market or so they could bring home a large catch. The miracle served the purpose of convincing these men that Jesus could provide whatever they needed to fulfill His mission. His statement to Peter and to all of them (Matthew 4:19-22) put them on notice that the job for which He had selected them was to begin right then (Luke 5:10). Luke tells us that "they forsook all and followed him" (Luke 5:11). Matthew adds that James and John "immediately left their boat and their father, and followed Him" (Matthew 4:22). They left everything, including jobs, home and families to be Jesus' apostles (Matthew 19:27-30; Mark 10:28-31; Luke 18:28-30).

Matthew the Tax Collector (Luke 5:27-28)

Publicans were considered traitors to their people. They were tax collectors for the Roman government. Because tax assessments were not as precise then as they are today, this position provided an opportunity for an unscrupulous person to make a lot of money. Many publicans were extremely wealthy (Luke 19:2), and they were often linked with sinners (5:30; 15:1-2; 19:7). Yet when we look at New Testament illustrations, we see men who were interested in spiritual matters, such as Zacchaeus who climbed a sycamore tree just to have an opportunity to see Jesus (Luke 19:1-10). When he was confronted by Christ, he promised to restore fourfold anything he had taken unjustly. Jesus used another publican as an example of a person whose sincere prayer was heard by God in preference to that of a self-righteous Pharisee (Luke 18:9-14). Even one of the Lord's first disciples came from this despised group.

As Jesus was walking on the road that led from Syria to Egypt, He came near Capernaum (Mark 2:1). There, He encountered Levi (Mark 2:13-14), who was sitting at the seat of custom. From Matthew's gospel account, we learn this man is also called Matthew (Matthew 10:3). We do not know how he got that name. Some have suggested that Jesus may have given it to him because Matthew means "gift of God" as He gave other names to Peter, James and John.

Jesus told Matthew, "Follow Me" (Luke 5:27). Just as Peter, Andrew, James and John had done before him, "He left all, rose up, and followed Him" (v. 28). In place of treasures of Earth that perish with using, Jesus offered him treasures in heaven (Matthew 6:19-21). It was an offer he could not and did not refuse. Had Matthew ever encountered the Master before? Did he hear His sermon in the local synagogue or witness some of the miracles Jesus performed in Capernaum? We do not find the answer to these questions in the Gospels. However, Matthew left this position of power, influence and wealth, and as far as we can tell from Scripture, he never looked back. This would have been strange behavior for a man who had not seen nor heard of Jesus before.

The Twelve Are Chosen (Luke 6:12-16)

For about a year, Jesus had gathered disciples from various walks of life. This provided time for Him to observe their conduct and behavior. Now the time had come to select from the larger group men who would be entrusted with the keys of the kingdom of heaven. This was a crucial decision and one that could not be made without serious consideration and prayer.

Luke portrays Jesus as a man of prayer more than any of the other Gospels and through this demonstrates His humanity. He prayed after His baptism (Luke 3:21); He prayed on the Mount of Transfiguration (Luke 9:29); He "often withdrew into the wilderness and prayed" (Luke 5:16); His disciples were influenced by His prayer life (Luke 11:1); He prayed in the Garden of Gethsemane (Luke 22:40-45); and He prayed from the cross (Luke 23:34). The only time that we are told He prayed all night was on the night before He selected His apostles (Luke 6:12). This certainly illustrates how critical this decision was.

There are four lists of the apostles in the New Testament (Matthew 10:2-4; Mark 3:14-19; Luke 6:13-16; Acts 1:13). In all of these lists, Simon, whom Jesus named Peter, appears first, and Judas Iscariot appears last, with the exception of Acts 1:13 where His name is not mentioned in the grouping of the apostles. It is mentioned in Acts verse 25 when his successor, Matthias, was chosen. When we look at all of these lists together, there are some noticeable differences in the names given. For example, Bartholomew is thought to be the same person as Nathanael (John 1:45; Matthew 10:3; Mark 3:18). Bartholomew could be a patronymic that identifies him as the son of a man named Tholomai or Ptolemy. Judas, the son of James, is thought to be same as Lebbaeus, whose surname was Thaddaeus, and Simon the Canaanite is the same as Simon the Zealot (Matthew 10:3-4; Mark 3:18). Thomas was called Didymus, meaning twin, which has led some to believe that he may have had a twin (John 11:16; 20:24; 21:2). James, the son of Alphaeus, was called James the Less, most likely to distinguish him from his illustrious counterpart, James the son of Zebedee and the brother of John (Mark 15:40). Judas Iscariot may have been from the area of Kerioth which was in Judea. If that is the case, he would have been the only apostle who was not from Galilee.

Jesus selected this particular group of men from different backgrounds, excluding Peter, Andrew, James and John, who came from a similar environment. They also had different temperaments and dispositions. Peter was the impetuous optimist (Matthew

14:28; 26:33, 35), and Thomas was a pessimist (John 11:16; 20:24-25). Simon the Zealot, who hated tax collectors, became a fellow laborer with Matthew, who had collected taxes for the government Simon despised. James and John were nicknamed "sons of Thunder" (Boanerges, Mark 3:17). Once they asked Jesus to rain down fire from heaven and destroy a Samaritan village (Luke 9:51-56). However, James was the first apostle martyred for the faith (Acts 12:2), and John came to be called "the disciple whom Jesus loved" (John 13:23; 21:20). He has also been called "the apostle of love" by later Bible students because of the tenderness exhibited in his epistles. Judas was the betrayer and a thief (12:6). Jesus said of him on one occasion, "Did I not choose you, the twelve, and one of you is a devil?" (6:70). The greatness of Jesus is seen in the fact that He could take this ragtag bunch of misfits and mold them into an evangelistic team that turned the world upside down (Acts 17:6).

Lessons Learned

1. Although Jesus had many disciples, the Twelve were chosen from among them to be His personal emissaries or witnesses.
2. The two recorded incidents about a drought of fishes is similar, but one account comes at the beginning of Jesus' ministry and the other near the end of His time on Earth. The last one appears to have reminded the apostles of the earlier event that convinced them Jesus was more than a mere mortal.
3. Peter was reluctant to accept Jesus' true identity at first because his character was so human and in this regard much like us.
4. When the miracle of fish convinced them Jesus was Lord, they immediately left everything to follow Him.
5. Jesus never performed miracles for show or merely to attract attention, but they served some practical purpose.
6. Publicans were despised by their people, but many publicans referred to in Scripture were decent people interested in spiritual matters.
7. As He often did, Jesus prayed before the crucial decision to select the Twelve.

Questions

1. What does the term "disciple" mean, and how does it differ with "apostle"?
2. What was the Limited Commission, and why is it called that?
3. What three names are given to the large natural lake on which some of the disciples fished?
4. Why should Peter have immediately listened to Jesus when He told Him to cast out a little farther?
5. What did the drought of fishes serve to prove?
6. Why were publicans so despised by their people?
7. Why did Matthew so quickly follow Jesus?
8. What did Jesus do before selecting the Twelve?
9. How do we explain the different names for some of the Twelve?
10. Who was the "apostle of love" and the "disciple whom Jesus loved"?

Lesson 7

The Transfiguration

Week of
Oct. 18, 1998

Lesson Text

MATTHEW 17:1-13

(1) Now after six days Jesus took Peter, James, and John his brother, led them up on a high mountain by themselves;

(2) and He was transfigured before them. His face shone like the sun, and His clothes became as white as the light.

(3) And behold, Moses and Elijah appeared to them, talking with Him.

(4) Then Peter answered and said to Jesus, "Lord, it is good for us to be here; if You wish, let us make here three tabernacles: one for You, one for Moses, and one for Elijah."

(5) While he was still speaking, behold, a bright cloud overshadowed them; and suddenly a voice came out of the cloud, saying, "This is My beloved Son, in whom I am well pleased. Hear Him!"

(6) And when the disciples heard it, they fell on their faces and were greatly afraid.

(7) But Jesus came and touched them and said, "Arise, and do not be afraid."

(8) When they had lifted up their eyes, they saw no one but Jesus only.

(9) Now as they came down from the mountain, Jesus commanded them, saying, "Tell the vision to no one until the Son of Man is risen from the dead."

(10) And His disciples asked Him, saying, "Why then do the scribes say that Elijah must come first?"

(11) Jesus answered and said to them, "Indeed, Elijah is coming first and will restore all things.

(12) "But I say to you that Elijah has come already, and they did not know him but did to him whatever they wished. Likewise the Son of Man is also about to suffer at their hands."

(13) Then the disciples understood that He spoke to them of John the Baptist.

Introduction

Many mountaintop experiences are mentioned in the Bible. The first that comes to mind is that of Noah when the ark of his salvation came to rest upon Mount Ararat (Genesis 8:4). Can you imagine that scene as this great man realized, perhaps for the first time, that he and his family were the only people left alive? He could still see the water receding beneath him and witness some of the devastation left by the Flood. No wonder he built an altar and offered sacrifices to God (vv. 20-21).

The second mountaintop experience that stands out prominently would have to be that of Moses when he received the Law on Mount Sinai. On that mountain, Moses saw the glory of God and received the Ten Commandments written on two tablets of stone (Exodus 24:16-17; 33:12-23; 34:1-5). He was privileged to see what few other people had ever witnessed. When Moses came down from the mountain, his face still shone with the glory of God so that the people were unable to look at him (Exodus 34:29-35). Later Moses would ascend another mountain, Mount Nebo, where he would be able to see the glory of the Promised Land, but he would never be allowed to enter there because he would die on the mountain (Deuteronomy 34:1-7).

A third dramatic mountaintop experience from the Old testament is that of Elijah and his confrontation and defeat of the prophets of Baal on Mount Carmel (1 Kings 18:19-40). On that occasion, he proved that God was with him and with Israel, and that He was the only true and living God.

In the New Testament, most of the mountaintop experiences recorded involved Jesus.His greatest recorded sermon was preached on a mountain near Capernaum (Matthew 5-7). Although it was not actually a mountain, the hill of Calvary where Jesus suffered and died on the cross (Luke 23:33) is often called "Mount Calvary" by Bible students. From an unnamed mountain peak in Galilee, Jesus delivered the Great Commission to the apostles (Matthew 28:7, 10, 16). He had gone often to pray upon the Mount of Olives, and from a point on that peak between Jerusalem and Bethany, He ascended back to the Father (Luke 24:50; Acts 1:4-12). Our text for this lesson tells us one of the most dramatic and significant mountaintop experiences in the life of Jesus. He shared this experience with three of His closest apostles. The incident recorded here carries important implications for everyone who lives today.

The Witnesses to the Transfiguration (Matthew 17:1)

In the last part of chapter 16, Matthew records our Lord's stunning announcement to the apostles about the death awaiting Him in Jerusalem. Both Matthew and Mark say that "after six days," Jesus went up into the mountain where the Transfiguration occurred. However, Luke says, "And it came to pass about eight days after these sayings, that He took Peter, John and James upon the mountain to pray" (Luke 9:28). There is really no contradiction in these accounts. First, Luke uses the word "about" which proves he was not trying to be precise. Second, Luke was also probably using the Jewish method of reckoning time where a part of the day when expressed was calculated as a whole day. Third, the other two synoptic writers did not count the day of the Lord's dramatic revelation or the day of the Transfiguration but only the six days in between.

Upon what mountain did these events take place? Because none of the writers tell us the exact spot, we cannot know for certain. Some people have suggested Mount Tabor, which was a three-day journey from the last known geographical location of Jesus before this event. The distance from the place where Jesus was near Caesarea Philippi before and after the Transfiguration and the height of Mount Tabor itself, only some 1,800 feet high, seem to preclude the possibility that it was the location. However, it is also known that there was a city or a fortress situated on that mountain in the time of Christ that would certainly have prevented them from going there. Mount Hermon, which was in the area of Caesarea Philippi, and whose snow-covered peak rose to more than 9,000 feet, was the most likely place.

In the previous lesson, we studied about the 12 men Jesus chose to be His special messengers. Out of this group He selected three, Peter, James and John, who would become His closest companions during some of the important events in His life. They are generally referred to as "the inner circle." They were with Him when He raised Jairus' daughter from the dead (Luke 8:41-42, 51-56). They went with Him deeper into the Garden of Gethsemane on the night of His great anguish while the remaining eight stayed some distance behind. These three men were also privileged to witness His glorification on the mountain Peter later calls "holy" (2 Peter 1:18).

Why were Peter, James and John the only ones permitted to witness this majestic scene? Some scholars suggest it was because they were the only ones capable of understanding the Lord's predicament. However, we know from a later statement that this is not true (Luke 9:33). Other people have said it was because they were the first among His disciples, but what about Philip, Andrew and Nathanael? Although it does not explain their exclusive appearance at the other two events mentioned, the reason for it here may have simply been that it was the best way to carry out the Lord's injunction to tell "no one until the Son of Man is risen from the dead" (Matthew 17:9). The more people who saw this happen, the harder it would be to keep it quiet. In any case, it is ironic that these trusted men could not even stay awake through two of the most significant moments of our Lord's life (Luke 9:32; Matthew 26:40, 43, 45).

The Meaning of the Transfiguration (Matthew 17:2)

Luke tells us that Jesus was praying when this incident occurred (Luke 9:29). Matthew informs us that when Jesus was "transfigured before them. His face shone like the sun, and His clothes became as white as the light." Luke says, "And as He prayed, the appearance of His face was altered and His robe became white and glistening" (Luke 9:29). Mark adds that "His clothes became shining, exceedingly white, like snow, such as no launderer on earth can whiten them" (Mark 9:3). These statements prove that His outward appearance was dramatically changed.

The word "transfigured" comes from the Greek word that we get the English word "metamorphosis" from. The word is translated "transformed" in Romans 12:2 and 2 Corinthians 3:18. It means "a change on the outside that comes from the inside." Jesus' glory was not reflected, but it radiated from within (Hebrews 1:3). Seeing Christ in this glorified state so affected Peter and John that both of them referred to the incident many years later (John 1:14; 2 Peter 1:16-18).

Why is the Transfiguration such a significant event? There are many reasons. First, it proved without question to the three apostles that Jesus was divine. For the second time, God spoke out of heaven and declared that He was His Son. There would be only one more time that He did this (John 12:28-30). Second, it announced to them that the old Jewish system, of which Moses and Elijah were representative, was soon to pass and that Jesus was God's only spokesman for the new age (Hebrews 1:1-3). Third, it proved the Resurrection and life after death. Fourth, it showed to these men who were so grieved at the announcement of Jesus' approaching death that His path led to the Cross, but the Cross was His pathway to glory (John 17:1-5, 24).

The Men Who Conversed with Jesus (Matthew 17:3)

As Luke tells us, Peter, James and John were asleep during most of what happened, but when they awoke rather suddenly, they were amazed to see Moses and Elijah talking with Him (Luke 9:32-33). How did they know this was Moses and Elijah? While the text does not specifically tell us, we can be certain that God somehow revealed this fact to them. Recognition comes through other means than just sight. Ask any sightless person. This is certainly an encouragement to us to know that it will be possible to recognize and know many of the great men and women of the Bible and our own precious ones who will be in heaven.

That Moses and Elijah were the two who appeared with Jesus was appropriate. Moses was the great lawgiver of Israel (John 1:17). Yet he wrote that God said, "I will raise up for them a Prophet like you from among their brethren, and will put My words in His mouth, and He shall speak to them all that I command Him" (Deuteronomy 18:18). This scene was a testimony to that fact. Elijah was one of God's greatest prophets, and he was one who did not die but was taken up into heaven in a flaming chariot (2 Kings 2:11-12). The appearance of these men, who represented two of the great historical periods of the Old Testament, signaled that the end of "all the law and the prophets" was at hand (Matthew 5:17-18; Luke 24:44; Romans 10:4; Ephesians 2:14-16; Colossians 2:13-17).

Matthew does not record the content of Jesus' conversation with Moses and Elijah, but Luke's account says that they "spoke of His decease which He was about to accomplish at Jerusalem" (Luke 9:31). Another reason for their appearance must have been to give Jesus support and encouragement as He faced the prospect of death. The word translated "decease" here is also translated "departure" and "exodus" (2 Peter 1:15). For the Christian, death is not a journey into oblivion but is a release from bondage to enjoy the pleasures of our heavenly home (John 14:1-6; 2 Corinthians 5:1-4). Death is merely a transition from a physical state to a spiritual one (Ecclesiastes 12:7; Philippians 1:19-24). However, it is fearful prospect for people who have not gone that way before. Jesus has done for us what Moses and Elijah did for Him and more. He gives us assurance that a person can die and live again and that the grave cannot hold us because He conquered death (1 Corinthians 15:50-58). Because He was victorious over mankind's last enemy, we can share in that victory (1 Corinthians 15:25-26).

Peter's Response to This Heavenly Scene (Matthew 17:4)

From Luke we learn that Peter, James and John awoke from a deep sleep to see the glorious sight of the radiant Christ talking with Moses and Elijah (Luke 9:32). Peter was so overcome with emotion that he said excitedly, "Lord, it is good for us to be here; if You wish, let us build here three tabernacles: one for You, one for Moses, and one for Elijah" (v. 4). The Transfiguration occurred in the Jewish month of *Tishri*, or October, which was the sixth month before the Passover. If that is the case, this was only six months before the Lord's crucifixion. It was during this month that the Feast of Tabernacles or Booths took place, a time when the Jews celebrated their 40-year sojourn in the wilderness (Leviticus 23:33-44). A tabernacle was a tent, and each family who participated lived in a tent during this feast week. Was Peter urging Jesus to allow them to build three tabernacles or tents so they could remain on the mountain to celebrate this memorial feast together? If that was the case, why only three, and not six or four? Also, why did God react so suddenly to Peter's statement and say what He did?

There is another explanation for Peter's intentions. The tabernacle, which was also called the tent of meeting where Jews worshiped in the wilderness, was an elaborate tent (Exodus 25:1-27:21). He may have been suggesting that because fall three men were in a glorified state (Luke 9:32) they were somehow equal and a worship place should be constructed for each one of them.

God's Endorsement of His Son (Matthew 17:5)

In this connection, consider God's rebuke of Peter: "This is my beloved Son in whom I am well pleased. Hear Him!" (Matthew 17:5). The point of this statement is that Jesus, Moses and Elijah were not equals. First, Jesus was God's Son and therefore deity. Second, only Christ is God's spokesman for today. God once spoke through Moses and Elijah, but that time had passed. Jesus is the only "Lawgiver who is able to save and to destroy" (James 4:12).

Whatever Peter's real motive was, we may never know, but we do know it was a foolish request. As Luke says, he spoke "not knowing what he said" (Luke 9:33; Mark 9:6). He was so caught up in the emotion of the moment that he spoke without really thinking it through. We must never allow our emotions to rule our reason.

When God spoke, it was an awesome spectacle. A cloud overshadowed the mountain, and when it was lifted Jesus was alone; Moses and Elijah had disappeared as quickly as they had emerged (Luke 9:36). Although the term is not used in the Bible, this phenomenon of the cloud, which was usually accompanied by a brightness of light and sometimes smoke, is called Shekinah by later Jewish scholars (Exodus 13:21; 16:10; 40:35; Numbers 9:17; Deuteronomy 1:33; 1 Kings 8:10-11; Nehemiah 9:19; Ezekiel 1:4). It always represented to the Jews the presence of God.

The Disciples' Reaction to God's Appearance (Matthew 17:6-13)

The presence of God usually brought forth a fearful reaction. When the disciples heard the voice, "they fell on their faces and were greatly afraid." Jesus comforted them, first with a touch, and then by His presence and words of encouragement. They apparently spent the night there, and as they were coming down from the mountain, He urged them, "Tell the vision to no one until the Son of Man is risen from the dead" (Matthew 17:9). Some people have suggested that the use of the word "vision" here implies this was not an actual occurrence but was simply something that took place in the minds of the apostles. A vision was a specially prepared visual event that may or may not have been actually occurring at that moment.

The disciples were still unsure about the meaning of the appearance of Moses and Elijah. They asked Jesus a question that was connected with the prophecy of Malachi (Malachi 4:5).They must have thought this was the fulfillment of that prophecy. However, Jesus corrected that misunderstanding by reminding them about something that He had told them earlier. This was that John the Baptist was the Elijah who was to come (Matthew 11:14; 17:12). He also reminded them that John the Baptist had been killed and that He would soon suffer the same fate.

Lessons Learned

1. There are many mountaintop experiences in the lives of God's children, but there are also valley experiences.
2. Even Jesus had special friends in whom He confided and with whom He shared significant moments.

3. The Transfiguration served to prove a number of things, but significant among them was that the Old Testament system was soon to vanish away.
4. The Transfiguration also proved that we do not lose our identity after we die and there are more ways to know people that by sight alone.
5. Death is merely a transition from a physical state of being to a spiritual one.
6. Moses and Elijah, as great as they were, were not equal to Jesus Christ because He was divine. Only deity is to be worshiped.

Questions

1. What were the Old Testament mountaintop experiences mentioned in this lesson?
2. What were the mountaintop experiences in the life of Christ mentioned in this lesson?
3. When did the Transfiguration occur, and why is that significant?
4. On what mountain was the Transfiguration thought to have taken place?
5. What three significant events in the life of Christ were Peter, James and John present for?
6. Why were only three of the apostles present?
7. What were these three men doing on two of these special occasions?
8. What does the word "transfiguration" mean?
9. What four significant things are demonstrated by the Transfiguration?
10. What were Moses and Elijah talking about with Jesus?

Lesson 8

The Mission of Jesus

Week of Oct. 25, 1998

Lesson Text

LUKE 5:29-39

(29) Then Levi gave Him a great feast in his own house. And there were a great number of tax collectors and others who sat down with them.

(30) And their scribes and the Pharisees complained against His disciples, saying, "Why do You eat and drink with tax collectors and sinners?"

(31) Jesus answered and said to them, "Those who are well have no need of a physician, but those who are sick.

(32) "I have not come to call the righteous, but sinners, to repentance."

(33) Then they said to Him, "Why do the disciples of John fast often and make prayers, and likewise those of the Pharisees, but Yours eat and drink?"

(34) And He said to them, "Can you make the friends of the bridegroom fast while the bridegroom is with them?

(35) "But the days will come when the bridegroom will be taken away from them; then they will fast in those days."

(36) Then He spoke a parable to them: "No one puts a piece from a new garment on an old one; otherwise the new makes a tear, and also the piece that was taken out of the new does not match the old.

(37) "And no one puts new wine into old wineskins; or else the new wine will burst the wineskins and be spilled, and the wineskins will be ruined.

(38) "But new wine must be put into new wineskins, and both are preserved.

(39) "And no one, having drunk old wine, immediately desires new; for he says, 'The old is better.' "

Introduction

What is the mission of the church? Is its aim worship, benevolence, counseling people in trouble, entertaining or educating the minds of people? Actually, it is none of these things, nor is it any of the myriad of activities modern churches are using to attract new members. People often confuse the mission of the church with the methods it employs to carry out its mission. Jesus used miracles to attract an audience and to confirm His message (Hebrews 2:1- 4). He fed multitudes on two different occasions (Matthew 14:14-23; 15:32-38). He raised three people from the dead that Scripture tells us about – Jairus' daughter, the son of the widow of Nain, Lazarus from Bethany – cast out demons, and cured many different illnesses. All these things were done to aid Him in fulfilling His purpose in coming to Earth. When He defined His mission, He said, "The Son of Man has come to seek and to save that which was lost" (Luke 19:10). Before He ascended to heaven, He assigned the church the responsibility of fulfilling this mission (Matthew 28:18-20; Mark 16:15-16).

Levi the Soul-Winner (Luke 5:29-30)

Whenever a person is truly converted to faith in Christ, he wants to share that knowledge with other people. We saw this in the life of Andrew, Simon Peter's brother, and also in Philip's example. Even the sinful Samaritan woman, once she knew who Jesus was, could not wait to share this good news with the people of her village. Cornelius, the first Gentile convert, called his "relatives and close friends" together when he heard that God's messenger was coming to see him (Acts 10:24). Levi or Matthew seems to be another example of this dynamic in action. When Jesus called him to the ministry, he immediately left everything to follow Him. Just after this incident, he gave a "great feast at his own house."

What was the purpose of this feast? Several suggestions have been given by various commentators. Some people think it was a celebration of his new life. Other people say it was an opportunity for him to make a break with his past life, and still others say it was just to introduce Jesus to his personal friends. One person even suggests that it was to say to Jesus, "Look what I've given up for you!" Luke does tell us that it was given in honor of Christ. The main reason was to honor Jesus but in doing so, notice the audience present. Obviously, Matthew believed in Jesus. He wanted to share this faith with other people, and he gave them an opportunity to be exposed to the power of Jesus words. Whom did he know that needed this message as much as he did? His own kind, other tax collectors, and fellow outcasts certainly did.

The Professional Critics (Luke 5:30)

Jesus said, "The scribes and Pharisees sit in Moses' seat. Therefore whatever they tell you to observe, that observe and do, but do not do according to their works; for they say, and do not do" (Matthew 23:2-3). Following this statement, He began to chastise the scribes and Pharisees for their hypocrisy, calling them blind guides, fools, unclean vessels, whitewashed tombs and a brood of vipers (Matthew 23:16-17, 19, 24-27, 33). Earlier, He had warned the apostles to"beware of the leaven of the Pharisees and Sadducees" (Matthew 16:6). In Jesus' time, these men had come to be looked upon as the spiritual leaders of Israel.

The Pharisees, meaning "separate ones," in particular considered themselves the spiritually elite among God's people and the example that everyone needed to follow. This attitude made them hypercritical of everyone else, and they became professional critics. As Jesus said of them, "They say, and do not do." They were much better at telling other people how to live than they were at living right themselves. They tithed "mint and anise and cumin," which were tiny spices, but they "neglected the weightier matters of the law: justice and mercy and faith" (Matthew 23:23).

Because Jesus did not conform to their mold or graduate from one of their seminaries, the Pharisees rejected Him. They made it their mission as "defenders of the faith" and the "keepers of orthodoxy" to persecute and finally to prosecute Him. Wherever He went, they or their spies were not far away. That is why they were at Matthew's house. They were not there to learn from Jesus. They were there to catch Him in a serious enough error to bring charges against Him before the great Sanhedrin. He was a threat to their power, popularity and position, so they wanted Him dead.

More than any other people among the Jews, these men should have understood Jesus' mission. They were the scholars, teachers and transcribers of the Word of God. However, they too did not know who Jesus was or why He came. This is why they got so angry at Him for eating with the publicans and sinners. Their constant criticism of Him was that "He receives sinners and eats with them" (Luke 15:2; Matthew 9:10-17; Mark 2:15-22).

The Great Physician (Luke 5:31-32)

Jesus is the Great Physician, and He has the cure for the worlds greatest malady, sin. He can heal body, mind and spirit, but the real disease is sin. He answered these critics by saying, "Those who are well do not need a physician, but those who are sick" (Luke 5:31). Who were the well? His statement was aimed at the Pharisees, who were as sinsick as anyone else but considered themselves spiritually strong and healthy. Because they did not realize that they were sinsick, they did not see their need for the Physician of the soul, and they certainly were unwilling to take the prescription from Him that could make them whole.

In the second part of His response, Jesus once again made His real mission clear. He came to call "sinners to repentance" (Luke 5:32), and He was passionate about it. In His first recorded sermons, He said, "Repent, for the kingdom of heaven is as at hand" (Matthew 4:17) and "The time is fulfilled, and the kingdom of God is at hand. Repent, and believe in the gospel" (Mark 1:15).

The Question about Fasting and Jesus' Answer (Luke 5:33-35)

At first glance it might appear that the Pharisees asked the question about fasting in verse 33, but closer observation will show that this may not be the case. The people asking this question made reference to the disciples of the Pharisees. This alone does not rule out the Pharisees. However, in parallel accounts of this incident, Matthew and Mark both record that the question was asked of Jesus by some disciples of John the Baptist (Matthew 9:14; Mark 2:18). John's disciples, perhaps following his austere lifestyle, either fasted as a regular practice, or they were doing so at this time because John had already been beheaded by Herod. Jesus answered their question by telling them a parable.

In beginning this parable, Jesus used the term "bridegroom" in referring to Himself, which John the Baptist had used and with which his disciples would be familiar (John 3:29). The question He posed to them was, "Why should His disciples fast while He was still with them?" In this statement, He pointed out that one of the major reasons that the Jews fasted was for grief or mourning (1 Samuel 31:13; 2 Samuel 1:11-16; 12:16-23; 1 Kings 19:4-8; Psalm 35:13). Other reasons that they fasted for were national penitence (2 Chronicles 20:3; Nehemiah 9:1; Jonah 3:5) and before receiving a revelation from God (Daniel 9:3).

Contrary to what many people believe, Jesus did not condemn the practice of fasting. His words in Matthew 6:16-18 were not a condemnation of fasting in general, but they were a condemnation of the manner in which it was observed by the Pharisees. In fact, although He did not command His disciples to fast, He implied in our text from Luke 5:35 that they would. The grief experienced when He was taken from them would bring forth spontaneous fasting on their part. Because it is not a commandment, there should be no ordinance passed to make it mandatory, but Christians could receive much benefit from the practice.

As Guy N. Woods wrote in the *Gospel Advocate*, "Fasting properly enjoined in, can be a source of spiritual blessing, a discipline of the will and an exercise producing inward strength and power. All of us, on occasion, should resolutely put out of our hearts every semblance of worldly desire and fleshly appetites and with prayer and fasting draw very near to God and claim His support and guidance in life. Such an experience would make us all infinitely stronger, richer in faith and better equipped to live the Christian life" (June 17, 1982; p. 358).

New and Old Garments and New Wine in Old Wineskins (Luke 5:36-39)

The two parables that follow one about the Bridegroom must be understood in light of the immediate context. They were used to combat the ritualism and formalism of Jesus' day concerning fasting. These illustrations came right out of the culture in which the original audience lived. The first one involved using a new piece of material to patch an old garment. This does not work for two reasons: 1. The old garment will tear where it is joined to the newer piece; and 2. As everyone knows, the older material will fade with time, and the newer piece will not match it in color or texture.

The second parable concerned how wine was preserved and stored. Animal skins were used for canteens. The skin was dried, and the leg portion was opened at the bottom to form a spout. After the skin had been used for awhile, it would become dry and brittle and would crack and leak. If new wine was put into one of these old skins, the fermentation process could cause a rupture and a loss of the wine.

Some people today are using this passage to teach that Jesus was saying we must adapt the message of the gospel to our culture or that we must put it into modern dress to make it more palatable to today's society. It is not that we should not present the gospel of Christ in fresh new ways or adapt the terminology to that which people can more readily understand that makes this concept wrong. We can and should adapt the language and illustrations to various cultures, but we must never alter the basic message. It is not to be altered or changed in any way that would pervert its intended meaning (John 12:48; 1 Corinthians 15:1-4; Galatians 1:6-8; Jude 3).

With this parable, Jesus was contrasting the practices of traditional Judaism and those His disciples were to observe. The old wineskins were not the teachings of the Old Testament, but they were the rabbinical traditions that had come to supersede and often directly contradict the divine Word of God (Matthew 15:1-9). Jesus made it abundantly clear that He had not come to reform corrupt Judaism but to fulfill and complete it (Matthew 5:17-20). He brought an entirely new way of thinking, believing and living. The main lesson here is that the new order that Jesus brought does not fit the old man-made mold for fasting. Although fasting was an important part of the old system, the frequent observance of it was purely a human invention.

It is a misapplication of Scripture to teach that this parable refers to changing the message of the gospel at all.; it is teaching the exact opposite. The Pharisees and other teachers of the Law had so perverted it that it was no longer God's message to mankind. Many people today are attempting to do the same thing with the gospel. Perhaps this is why some want a new hermeneutic that would allow for such corruptions of Scripture. Our present one will not allow it, and neither will our Lord (Luke 6:46).

Lessons Learned

1. Jesus said His mission was to "seek and to save the lost."
2. When people are truly converted, it is only natural that they would want to share their faith with other people.

3. We must "beware of the leaven of the Scribes and Pharisees."
4. Jesus is the Great Physician with the only cure for the world's greatest disease, sin.
5. While fasting is not a commandment for Christians, it is a privilege of the Christian life.
6. It is right and proper to adapt the methods of presentation of the gospel, but we must never adapt the message of the gospel to suit the culture.

Questions

1. In what ways did Jesus employ miracles?
2. What is the church's mission?
3. How did Matthew indicate interest in the saving of souls?
4. What significant charges did Jesus make against the Pharisees?
5. Why did the Pharisees despise Jesus so much, and why should they not have supported Him instead?
6. Whom did Jesus say He came to call to repentance?
7. What does Jesus' teaching about fasting mean for Christians?
8. What is the meaning of the parables about the old and new garment and the new wine in old wineskins?
9. What is the greatest danger in changing the message of the gospel?
10. Why do some men seem to want a new hermeneutic?

Lesson 9

The Opposition to Jesus

Week of Nov. 1, 1998

Lesson Text

MARK 7:1-13

(1) Then the Pharisees and some of the scribes came together to Him, having come from Jerusalem.

(2) Now when they saw some of His disciples eat bread with defiled, that is, with unwashed hands, they found fault.

(3) For the Pharisees and all the Jews do not eat unless they wash their hands in a special way, holding the tradition of the elders.

(4) When they come from the marketplace, they do not eat unless they wash. And there are many other things which they have received and hold, like the washing of cups, pitchers, copper vessels, and couches.

(5) Then the Pharisees and scribes asked Him, "Why do Your disciples not walk according to the tradition of the elders, but eat bread with unwashed hands?"

(6) He answered and said to them, "Well did Isaiah prophesy of you hypocrites, as it is written: 'This people honors Me with their lips, But their heart is far from Me.

(7) And in vain they worship Me, Teaching as doctrines the commandments of men.'

(8) "For laying aside the commandment of God, you hold the tradition of men--the washing of pitchers and cups, and many other such things you do."

(9) He said to them, "All too well you reject the commandment of God, that you may keep your tradition.

(10) "For Moses said, 'Honor your father and your mother'; and, 'He who curses father or mother, let him be put to death.'

(11) "But you say, 'If a man says to his father or mother, "Whatever profit you might have received from me is Corban"--' (that is, a gift to God),

(12) "then you no longer let him do anything for his father or his mother,

(13) "making the word of God of no effect through your tradition which you have handed down. And many such things you do."

Introduction

A hot-button word today is "tradition." We constantly hear and read about a traditional service, traditional worship, and traditional songs and prayers as if to say that word is bad. When someone says "You are traditional" or "Your church is a traditional church," it is not meant as a compliment. In fact, it is used in a derogatory way. Tradition is equated with stubbornness, bigotry, being mean-spirited and lacking in love. Tradition means "handed down," but is it a bad word? Traditions are neither good nor bad; they just are. Whether they are bad are good depends upon our attitude toward them and our application of them.

Charles Aebi wrote an excellent article, "We Knew Who We Were," dealing with this very subject. In the first paragraph he wrote: "A friend asked, 'Why are we in churches of Christ so bound by the traditions of the 1950s?' It was not an unusual question; often these days I hear or read the assertion that the church of Christ has to get away from the traditions of the 1950s and do things differently. When asked what is meant by the traditions of the 1950s, the answer usually has to do with our worship or our teaching about salvation. Sometimes it is a matter of the format of worship – number and order of songs and prayers, whether the songs are projected on a screen or a hymnal is used – but often it goes beyond that" (*Gospel Advocate*, August 1997; p. 29).

There are man-made traditions, and there are God-given ones. Both Peter and Paul mention traditions received from men that lead men away from God instead of closer to Him (Colossians 2:8; 1 Peter 1:18). These kinds of traditions must not be allowed to hinder our progress in our service to God. However, God-given, inspired traditions need to be observed. Paul urged the Christians at Corinth to "keep the traditions as I delivered them to you" (1 Corinthians 11:2). To the saints in Thessalonica he said, "stand fast and hold the traditions which you were taught, whether by word or by epistle" (2 Thessalonians 2:15). He also commanded them to "withdraw from every brother who walks disorderly and not according to the traditions which he received from us" (3:6). The only way to determine God-given traditions from those that originated with men is by "rightly dividing the word of truth" (2 Timothy 2:15). In our rush to be nontraditional, we must not abandon the God-given traditions that make us who we are and that will eventually lead us to heaven. There may even be some good reasons to keep certain man-made traditions. However, we must avoid allowing such traditions to rule our worship and service to God. The text for this lesson shows the negative side of keeping man-made traditions.

The Jews received the Law on Mount Sinai through Moses. Originally, the Law meant one of two things: the Ten Commandments or the Pentateuch, the five books of Moses. In the fourth or fifth century before Christ, legal experts called "scribes" came into being. These men had a passion for interpretation. They wanted the great principles of the Law expanded, broken down and amplified until it issued into thousands of rules and regulations. The rabbis divided the Law of Moses, or the *Torah*, into 613 separate decrees of which 365 were considered prohibitions and 248 were positive commandments. Based upon these decrees, they had drawn arbitrary distinctions between what was permitted and what was not permitted. In doing so they had attempted to regulate every facet of a Jew's life. For centuries these rules were not written down, but the people were still expected to observe them. These unwritten laws were called the Oral Law or the Traditions of the Elders, or Fathers. The term "elders" in this context does not refer to the leaders of the synagogue or to the members of the Sanhedrin. The word has reference to the great legal rabbis or legal experts such as Hillel and Shammai, who interpreted the Law. Many of these traditions were later written down by Rabbi Judah the Prince, born in 135 B.C., in organized form and are called the *Mishnah*. These traditions and not God's Law were the cause of the problem in our text.

The Enemies of Truth (Mark 7:1)

This verse shows how desperately the Jewish leaders in Jerusalem wanted to catch Jesus in an error. Certain Pharisees and "some of the scribes" came down from Jerusalem for the sole purpose of trapping Him (Mark 3:6-7; 11:18; John 11:46-53).

The majority of men called lawyers and scribes came from the Pharisaic sect. These men had probably been sent by the Sanhedrin, the body of 70 men, elders of Israel, that operated as a kind of supreme court of the Jews. Most of these men hated Jesus.

Why did they hate Him so much? Several reasons have been advanced: 1. He claimed to be speaking for God; 2. He did not honor their man-made traditions; 3. He associated with publicans and sinners; and 4. He was everything they were not. This last reason may have been the principle one. His humility contrasted with their spiritual showmanship (Matthew 6:1-18; 23:4-7). His sincerity contrasted with their hypocrisy, and His compassion contrasted with their cruelty (vv. 13-30, 33-35).

The Violation (Mark 7:2-4)

When you look closely enough, you can find fault with anyone. These spies from Jerusalem came to find a violation of their laws, and they found it. Jesus had already violated their traditions concerning the Sabbath (Mark 2:23-3:5), and they were anxious to catch Him in another infraction. They saw some of Jesus' disciples eating without washing their hands, an act that transgressed and dishonored an ancient tradition. If they could clearly point out the sinfulness in this matter, then they may have thought they could turn the tide of popular opinion against Him. This incident shows the powerful effects of man-made traditions.

The tradition they chose to capitalize on was not just washing hands before a meal but it was the way in which this was to be done. It did not concern personal hygiene but ceremonial cleansing. The word used here, "*Koinos*" in Greek, means "ceremonially unclean and unfit for service to God." According to their tradition, a person could have used the strongest soap available and scrubbed his hands until they were raw and still be unclean.

The statement in Mark 7:3 proves that the disciples of Jesus were not eating without washing their hands, but they were eating without washing them in the prescribed way. God commanded washings that were more clinical than ceremonial (Leviticus 15:1-33). The rabbis had expanded these commands and had made them more ceremonial than practical. According to their tradition, they had to hold their hands out with the palms slightly tilted upward and have someone pour water over them. It was not just any water that could be used but water that was kept in a sterilized container for this purpose. After this was done, the hands had to be held with the fingers pointing downward. Each hand was then scrubbed with the fist of the other hand. Then water was again poured over the arms from the elbow down to remove any defiled matter. This process was performed before eating and between each course. If a person failed to do this washing in the exact way prescribed, he was subject to an attack by a demon named Shibta, and he would be in danger of poverty and destruction.

Mark points out that these traditions also involved the washing of cups, pots and vessels used for eating. The *Mishna* mentions at least 12 prolonged treatises that explain in detail how different types of vessels were to be made ceremonially clean. To the Pharisees, these rules were the very essence of true spirituality. The traditions meant everything, and the Word of God meant nothing. The Jews said the traditions were "the fence of the Law." The traditions defended the Law instead of the Law defending the traditions. This particular tradition may have occasioned Jesus' comments, "Now you Pharisees make the outside of the cup and the dish clean, but your inward part is full of greed and wickedness" (Luke 11:39; Matthew 23:25-26).

Jesus Answers His Accusers (Mark 7:5-8)

After the Pharisees asked Jesus why His disciples ate without observing the traditional hand washing, He charged them with two indictments. First, He called them hypocrites. He used this term only this once in Mark, but three times in Luke and numerous times in Matthew. There, the term is found mostly in the two major discourses of Jesus, the Sermon on the Mount (chapters 5-7) and in the woes of chapter 23. The word "hypocrite" refers to a person who is acting or wearing two faces. The Greek word for this is *hypo,* which means "a mask." Because the Pharisees acted in a certain way, they believed themselves to be religious. Such an attitude emphasizes the outward behavior and disregards the heart. A Pharisee could hate his fellow man, be full of envy, jealousy, pride and covetousness, but if he observed the outward rituals, he was considered clean.

Jesus answered these critics with a quotation from Isaiah 29:13 and then later added some scriptures from the Law (Exodus 20:12; 21:17; Leviticus 20:9). The content of His remarks was that these Pharisees were merely giving lip service to doing God's will while their hearts were "far from Him." No greater danger exists than allowing man-made religious traditions to be equated with true spirituality. The Sermon on the Mount was directed at this attitude of thinking that as long as a person observed the outward rituals, he was spiritual. The sixth Beatitude says, "Blessed are the pure in heart for they shall see God" (Matthew 5:8). Jesus warned people possessing this wrongful attitude about spirituality that it is what is inside that counts (Matthew 5:21-22, 27-30; 6:1-18, 25-34; 7:1-5, 15-20; 15:10-20).

Second, Jesus charged these Pharisees with trying to make their human traditions equal to, or even superior to God's Holy Word. He made this charge three times (Mark 7:8-9, 13). Instead of listening to God, they had reached a point of trusting in ingenious interpretations, debates and clever arguments. Human cleverness must never be allowed to be the basis of our religious beliefs (Ephesians 4:14; 1 Timothy 6:3-5, 20; 2 Timothy 4:3-4; 2 Peter 2:12-16). What would Jesus say today about the countless human opinions substituted for plain Bible teaching?

Traditions and Real Relationships (Mark 7:9-13)

Traditions affect the people obsessed with them, and they also affect the people closest to them. Jesus showed these Pharisees how their traditions violated God's teaching about honoring their parents. Notice the statements "Moses said … But You say." He was contrasting their perversions of the Law with what the Law actually taught. The command, "Honor your father and your mother" implies more than just being polite to them. It means to provide for them, especially as they grow older. This command was not just given to young children but is applied here to adults as well (cf. Ephesians 6:2-3).

The Jewish rabbis had worked out a neat little system to excuse themselves from this obligation. They took the money they could have used to help their parents and called it *corban*, which Mark tells us meant "dedicated to the temple" (Mark 7:11). A gift that was set aside for God, although not actually given, could not be used for any other purpose according to this tradition. The person might eventually only give a portion of this gift to God but still be free from the obligations to parents. This vow was considered irrevocable.

Jesus shows that the only way to devote something to God is to use it to serve Him and to meet the needs of other people (Mark 7:12). Any rule or regulation that allows a person not to meet a genuine need is a contradiction of God's will. For people not to use what God has blessed them with to bless other people is a clear violation of Scripture (Matthew 25:31-46; Galatians 6:10; 1 Timothy 5:8). Keeping God's commandments is important, but there is no commandment of His that will permit us to shirk our responsibility toward our fellow man.

Lessons Learned

1. Traditions are neither bad nor good, and whether they are depends on our attitude and application of them.
2. God-given traditions must be kept. There may be good reason to keep some man-made ones, but these should never be made law.
3. We must be careful not to allow traditions to become more important than God's Word.
4. Observing outward rituals, as important as some of them may be, can never make a person clean inside.
5. Human wisdom and cleverness cannot be the basis for our beliefs.
6. The only way to devote something to God is to use it for Him and for the needs of other people.

Questions

1. What does the word "tradition" mean?
2. What should be our attitude toward man-made traditions?
3. What did the term "Law"originally mean to the Jews?
4. What was the Oral Law?
5. What is the *Mishnah*?
6. Why did the Jewish rulers hate Jesus so much?
7. What tradition did the disciples of Jesus violate on this occasion?
8. After this incident, with what two things did Jesus charge the scribes and Pharisees with?
9. What is the explanation of the prophecy of Isaiah 29:13?
10. How did the Jewish rabbis get around their responsibility to take care of their aging parents?

Lesson 10

The Betrayal of Jesus

Week of Nov. 8, 1998

Lesson Text

MATTHEW 26:14-16, 47-56

(14) Then one of the twelve, called Judas Iscariot, went to the chief priests

(15) and said, "What are you willing to give me if I deliver Him to you?" And they counted out to him thirty pieces of silver.

(16) So from that time he sought opportunity to betray Him.

(47) And while He was still speaking, behold, Judas, one of the twelve, with a great multitude with swords and clubs, came from the chief priests and elders of the people.

(48) Now His betrayer had given them a sign, saying, "Whomever I kiss, He is the One; seize Him."

(49) Immediately he went up to Jesus and said, "Greetings, Rabbi!" and kissed Him.

(50) But Jesus said to him, "Friend, why have you come?" Then they came and laid hands on Jesus and took Him.

(51) And suddenly, one of those who were with Jesus stretched out his hand and drew his sword, struck the servant of the high priest, and cut off his ear.

(52) But Jesus said to him, "Put your sword in its place, for all who take the sword will perish by the sword.

(53) "Or do you think that I cannot now pray to My Father, and He will provide Me with more than twelve legions of angels?

(54) "How then could the Scriptures be fulfilled, that it must happen thus?"

(55) In that hour Jesus said to the multitudes, "Have you come out, as against a robber, with swords and clubs to take Me? I sat daily with you, teaching in the temple, and you did not seize Me.

(56) "But all this was done that the Scriptures of the prophets might be fulfilled." Then all the disciples forsook Him and fled.

Introduction

The name of Judas Iscariot is infamous. Wherever traitors are spoken of, his name is remembered and despised. No one would call a son by that name. Yet the name means "praise" and is the same as "Judah" in the Hebrew (Genesis 29:35). How did Judas become a betrayer of the Man who had befriended him and the one who came to be his Savior? Was he the pathetic figure portrayed in the rock musical *Jesus Christ Superstar*, who attempted to dissuade his Master from the path of certain destruction when he believed Him to be insane? Or was he merely a victim of circumstances beyond his control and the passive instrument of God's providence? Can we be absolutely certain?

At the time Jesus preached His sermon about the Bread of Life, John records: "From that time many of His disciples went back and walked with Him no more." Jesus turned and asked the Twelve, "Do you also want to go away?" Simon Peter answered Him, "Lord, to whom shall we go? You have the words of Eternal life. Also we have come to believe and know that You are the Christ, the Son of the Living God." In His response to this statement by Peter, which included all of the apostles, Jesus said, "Did I not choose you, the twelve, and one of you is a devil?" Because John's gospel was written so much later than the others, he informs us that Jesus was speaking about "Judas Iscariot, the son of Simon, for it was he who would betray Him" (John 6:66-71). Peter was so sure that all of the Twelve had the same faith in who Jesus was. If that was true and if Judas really believed Jesus was the Christ, how could he have condemned his Lord to death?

Many unanswered questions about Judas exist that we may never know the answers to. In understanding the tragedy of Judas, we must examine closely certain facts about his life revealed in Scripture. First, although the betrayal of Jesus was a prophesied event, we know that Judas was not an unwilling pawn in God's plan of redemption (Psalm 41:9; 55:12-14; Acts 1:25). Second, as the passage from John 6:70 tells us, Jesus chose him to be an apostle. From among the multitudes of disciples who followed Him, Jesus chose only 12 men to be His personal ambassadors. Judas was one of the chosen ones. By the time Jesus made the statement recorded here, He knew that one of the Twelve would betray Him. However, even He may not have known that Judas would be the one until the night it happened (John 13:11).

Judas was not chosen by Jesus because he was a devil, but, as we will see, he became a willing agent of the devil. Third, Judas had received power from the Lord to work miracles just as the other apostles had, and He had most likely used it (Matthew 10:1; Luke 9:1; 10:20). He had also witnessed Jesus perform miracles (Luke 6:16-18). When a person had seen the power of God working through Jesus and through himself, he had to know what he was doing. Judas was not deceived about Jesus' true identity, but he knew exactly who He was when he sold Him to His enemies (Matthew 27:3-4). The main question that remains to be answered is why did he betray the Lord? Our text provides some answers to this question.

Judas Had a Covetous Problem (Matthew 26:6-13)

When Judas went to the chief priest to betray Jesus, by this time in his life it was not out of character for him. Matthew has the meeting of Judas with the chief priests and elders occurring immediately after Jesus was anointed by an unnamed woman who John later identifies her as Mary, the sister of Lazarus, in the home of Simon the leper. Some people have suggested that the reason why Matthew and Mark did not mention her name was out of concern for her safety. John also informs us that the particular ointment she used was a "very costly oil of spikenard" (John 12:3). When this was done, the disciples began to criticize her for the waste (Matthew 26:8). Mark says "Some among them were indignant among themselves." However, John shows us that while some of the disciples may have been involved in this criticism, Judas was the one who initiated it (John 12:4-5).

John also gives us some additional information that provides insight into Judas' character. The main bone of contention was that this valuable perfume could have been sold and the money used to help the poor (John 12:5). Mark said it could have been sold for 300 denarii or shillings (Mark 14:5). To understand how significant an amount this was, Matthew tells us that a denarius was considered a good day's wage (Matthew 20:8-10). So when Judas said, "This could have been sold and the money given to the poor," it may have sounded good to a few other apostles, and they joined in the discussion. John clears the matter up by telling us that it was not because Judas really "cared for the poor" that he did this, but it was because "he was a thief" (John 12:6). When John says he "had the money box," or "had the bag" as the King James version renders it, he meant that Judas was the treasurer for the Lord and His disciples. He handled the money for them and was stealing from their meager resources. This proves Judas was a greedy man who would stop at nothing to increase his fortunes. When a person will steal, he will lie and commit many other sins, including betraying a friend.

Judas Had a Heart Problem (Matthew 26:14-16)

Why was Judas so upset with Mary's generous, unselfish act in the first place? Why did he consider it such an extravagant waste? In the Sermon on the Mount, Jesus said, in warning against laying up treasure on Earth, "For where your treasure is, there will your heart be also" (Matthew 6:21). Paul warned Timothy against covetousness and said, "But those who would be rich fall into temptation and a snare and many foolish and harmful lusts which drown men in destruction and perdition. For the love of money is a root of all kinds of evil, for which some have strayed from the faith in their greediness, and pierced themselves through with many sorrows. Command those who are rich in this present age not to be haughty, nor to trust in uncertain riches but in the living God, who gives us richly all things to enjoy" (1 Timothy 6:9-10, 17). Judas had a problem with greed, but as with all sins, it originated in his heart (Matthew 15:19). He was more concerned with gathering up riches in this world than he was in laying up treasures in heaven.

As further evidence of his spiritual heart condition, note that it was immediately after Mary's gracious gift and our Lord's mild rebuke to him that he went to the chief priests and elders to bargain for Jesus' life. Matthew and Mark say that, "Then one of the twelve, called Judas Iscariot, went to the chief priests" (Matthew 26:14; Mark 14:10). The act of his going to them appears to have been precipitated by the events leading up to it. Because of his greed he became angry, and in his anger, he could not tolerate the gentle reprimand that Jesus had given him. If his heart had been right, he would have accepted the Lord's correction and been grateful (cf. Acts 8:9-24).

Judas Had an Allegiance Problem (Matthew 26:47-50)

Before the events recorded in these verses, a lot of things had transpired. Judas had already conspired with the Jewish leaders to give Jesus up to them for 30 pieces of silver. This was the price to be paid for the life of a slave who had been killed by an animal (Exodus 21:32). This amount was also the very price that Zechariah had prophesied the Messiah would be betrayed for (Zechariah 11:12-13). Although some people question that this prophecy refers specifically to Jesus' betrayal, verse 12 makes it clear that it does, for the prophet tells us the amount of money involved and that it would be used to purchase a potter's field. Matthew records the fulfillment of this prophecy and tells us the potter's field purchased with the defiled money became a burial place for strangers.

Earlier the Jewish leaders had met to discuss how they might capture Jesus to put Him on trial before their council (Matthew 26:3-5; Mark 14:1; Luke 22:2; John 12:10-11). We can only imagine how happy they were to see one of Jesus' own disciples offer to turn him over to them. Luke tells "they were glad" (Luke 22:5). From that point on, Judas sought just the right opportunity to make good his promise to deliver Jesus to His enemies (Matthew 26:16; Mark 14:11; Luke 22:6).

When the time for the Passover came, Jesus assembled with His disciples in an upper room somewhere in Jerusalem (Mark 14:15-16). During this meal, Jesus instituted the Lord's Supper as a memorial of His sacrifice soon to take place on Mount Calvary (Matthew 26:26-29; Mark 14:22-25; Luke 22:17-20). John provides more details about the events as they unfolded. On this occasion, Jesus washed the disciples' feet, including Judas', to teach these proud men a lesson in humility (John 13:3-11). At some point in this instruction He informed them that one of them was going to be His betrayer (John 13:18, 21). The disciples could not believe their ears. Immediately, the finger pointing started. Luke says, "They began to question among themselves, which of them it was who would do this thing" (Luke 22:23). They each asked the Lord, "Is it I?" (Matthew 26:22). Judas even asked the question, most likely to direct attention away from himself because he had already made his deal with the Jewish leaders (Matthew 26:25). It was not as if he really expected a "No" response.

Leonardo da Vinci's famous painting, *The Last Supper,* portrays the disciples sitting in chairs around a table with the Lord at the center as if posing for a picture. The real situation would have been much different. They would have been reclining around a table close to the floor with each man's feet near the next person's face. John adds that Peter motioned to "one of the disciples whom Jesus loved," we believe this one to be John himself, who was leaning on the Lord's breast to ask Him who the betrayer was. He asked Him, "Lord, who is it?" Jesus answered him, "It is he to whom I shall give a piece of bread when I have dipped it" (John 13:23-28). After Jesus had dipped the bread in the sop, He turned and gave it to Judas, who was on the opposite side from this disciple. It was then that John says, "Satan entered him" (John 13:27). Jesus said to him, "What you must do, do quickly." None of the other disciples understood what He meant by this remark. John tells us that they thought Jesus was sending Judas to buy supplies or to give some money to the poor because of the statement he had made about Mary's act of generosity. Judas immediately left the scene, walking out into the night (vv. 28-30).

Because Judas left before the Passover was concluded, he missed out on so many meaningful experiences. He missed the institution of the Lord's Supper where Jesus plainly prophesied His resurrection (Matthew 26:29, 32). He missed the Lord's encouraging words to the disciples in John 14:1-21. He missed the promise Jesus made to send the Holy Spirit to comfort the apostles, to teach and remind them of His words, and to guide them into all truth (vv. 23-27; 16:13-15). He missed the lesson about the vine and the branches about the importance of abiding in Jesus (15:1-17). He missed the Lord's tender prayer for the disciples and His expressed desire that all of His followers be united (17:1-26).

The next time we see Judas is when he entered the Garden of Gethsemane with a mob to betray Jesus into the hands of His enemies. John mentioned that he brought with him an attachment of troops and officers from the chief priests and Pharisees (18:3). Judas apparently came in just in front of the other men, ran to Jesus, and kissed Him repeatedly (Matthew 26:49). Matthew is the only writer to include that Jesus called Judas "friend" and asked him why he had come (Matthew 26:50). Luke adds that Jesus asked Judas, "Are you betraying the Son of Man with a kiss?" (Luke 22:48). John also informs us that Jesus did not wait for the mob to come to Him, but He went to them and asked, "Whom are you seeking?" (John 18:4) When they answered Him, "Jesus of Nazareth," and He said, "I am He," at first they drew back and fell to the ground (vv. 5-6). Jesus again identified Himself to them, and asked them to let the disciples who were with Him go free (vv. 8-9).

At that moment that some of the disciples asked Jesus if He wanted them to "strike with the sword" (Luke 22:49). Without waiting for a response, Peter quickly drew the sword he was carrying and cut off the ear of Malchus, a servant of the high priest. Jesus told him, "Put your sword into its place, for all who take the sword will perish by the sword" (Matthew 26:52), and He healed the servant's ear (Luke 22:51). After these things, John says the soldiers arrested Jesus, bound Him and led Him away to the high priest (John 18:12-13). The disciples fled at this point (Matthew 26:56; Mark 14:50). Then Peter and another disciple, probably John because he was the only writer to mention this, followed the crowd from afar (Matthew 26:58; Mark 14:54; Luke 22:54; John 18:15-16).

Judas Had a Forgiveness Problem (Matthew 27:1-5)

Matthew records that when Judas realized that Jesus "had been condemned," he "was remorseful and brought back the thirty pieces of silver to the chief priests and elders, saying 'I have sinned by betraying innocent blood' " (Matthew 27:3-4). This is the only hint that Judas may have expected Jesus to be freed or that He would do something dramatic to free Himself. When those things did not happen, Judas tried to right the wrong by returning the blood money (v. 6).The Jewish leaders would have no part of that because they had tried too long to capture Jesus without causing a stir among the multitudes. They were not about to release Him now.

Judas repented in that he had a change of heart, but he did not do anything to receive forgiveness from Jesus. Perhaps he thought the deed he had done was so horrible he could not be forgiven. That he did not understand true forgiveness is tragic, because if he had sought it in the right way, he could have received it just as Peter did (John 21:15-19). Instead, he "went and hanged himself" (Matthew 27:5). His body must have hung for days until it began to decompose and then fell to the ground, bursting open (Acts 1:18).

Lessons Learned

1. From Judas we learn that a person can ruin a good name or reputation by a single act.
2. Only Jesus has the words of eternal life.
3. Even faithful followers of Christ can be overcome by Satan, but he cannot do anything to us that we do not allow him to do.
4. The "love of money is a root of all kinds of evil" (1 Timothy 6:10).
5. "For where your treasure is, there your heart will be also" (Matthew 6:21).
6. No person is beyond the forgiveness of God except for the person who will not seek it in the appropriate way.

Questions

1. What did the name “Judas” mean originally?
2. Why did Jesus’ sermon about the Bread of Life have such a negative effect on His followers?
3. What revealing insights into the character of Judas are listed in this lesson?
4. Why was Judas so angered by Mary’s gracious and generous act of anointing Jesus?
5. Why did John call Judas “a thief”?
6. Which prophet foretold the amount given for the betrayal of Jesus and what was to be done with that money?
7. When was the Lord’s Supper instituted?
8. How did Jesus reveal to John who His betrayer would be?
9. What did Judas miss by leaving the Passover meal so early?
10. Who was the man that severed a servant’s ear, and what was the servant’s name?

Lesson 11

The Death of Jesus

Week of Nov. 15, 1998

Lesson Text

MARK 15:22-39

(22) And they brought Him to the place Golgotha, which is translated, Place of a Skull.

(23) Then they gave Him wine mingled with myrrh to drink, but He did not take it.

(24) And when they crucified Him, they divided His garments, casting lots for them to determine what every man should take.

(25) Now it was the third hour, and they crucified Him.

(26) And the inscription of His accusation was written above: THE KING OF THE JEWS.

(27) With Him they also crucified two robbers, one on His right and the other on His left.

(28) So the Scripture was fulfilled which says, "And He was numbered with the transgressors."

(29) And those who passed by blasphemed Him, wagging their heads and saying, "Aha! You who destroy the temple and build it in three days,

(30) "save Yourself, and come down from the cross!"

(31) Likewise the chief priests also, mocking among themselves with the scribes, said, "He saved others; Himself He cannot save.

(32) "Let the Christ, the King of Israel, descend now from the cross, that we may see and believe." Even those who were crucified with Him reviled Him.

(33) Now when the sixth hour had come, there was darkness over the whole land until the ninth hour.

(34) And at the ninth hour Jesus cried out with a loud voice, saying, "Eloi, Eloi, lama sabachthani?" which is translated, "My God, My God, why have You forsaken Me?"

(35) Some of those who stood by, when they heard that, said, "Look, He is calling for Elijah!"

(36) Then someone ran and filled a sponge full of sour wine, put it on a reed, and offered it to Him to drink, saying, "Let Him alone; let us see if Elijah will come to take Him down."

(37) And Jesus cried out with a loud voice, and breathed His last.

(38) Then the veil of the temple was torn in two from top to bottom.

(39) So when the centurion, who stood opposite Him, saw that He cried out like this and breathed His last, he said, "Truly this Man was the Son of God!"

Introduction

It is not entirely correct to say that the four Gospels – Matthew, Mark, Luke and John – contain four accounts of the same story. In fact, there are not four Gospels, but only one presented by four different writers. To have the entire story about Christ, we must put these accounts together in some harmonious relationship. Because these men wrote by inspiration, each man wrote from a different perspective and for a different audience and purpose. This is why we find one writer emphasizing certain aspects of Jesus life and ministry or mentioning certain events, people and places that the other writers do not mention. When the Gospels are understood in this manner, not as four separate works but as four parts of one whole, then the apparent discrepancies can be eliminated. This approach is needed if we are to understand our Lord's crucifixion.

Our last lesson ended with Jesus being led captive to the home of the high priest. From that time to the present text, many important events took place. He was first taken to the house of Annas, who was considered by the Jews to be the official high priest, having been appointed to the office by Quirinius in A.D. 7 (John 18:13). However, although this man was highly esteemed by the Jews, he had been removed from office by Valerius Gratus. He was later replaced by Joseph Caiaphas, a son-in-law, which helps to explain why they got along, about A.D. 18. According to Josephus, he was removed from office by procurator Vitellius in A.D. 36 or 37. This means that Caiaphas was the reigning high priest when Jesus was crucified.

Jesus was taken from Annas to Caiaphas (Matthew 26:57; Mark 14:53; Luke 22:54; John 18:24) and then to Pilate, the Roman governor, or procurator, who did not really want to get involved in the affair (Matthew 27:2; Mark 15:1; Luke 23:1; John 18:28). When he found out Jesus was Galilean, he sent Him to Herod Antipas, the ruler over Galilee (Luke 23:6-12). Herod thought that Pilate did this as a favor to him because he had wanted to see Jesus for sometime. While Pilate apparently had a different objective in mind, this incident healed the breach between these two men that had existed for a long time (Luke 23:12). After Herod allowed his soldiers to place Jesus in a "gorgeous robe mocking Him," he sent Him back to Pilate (Luke 23:11). Pilate questioned Jesus again and then made an attempt to set Him free after twice declaring that he could find "no fault in Him" (Luke 23:4, 14). Pilate's wife urged him, "Have nothing to do with that just Man, for I have suffered many things today in a dream because of Him" (Matthew 27: 19).

Pilate tried to use a tradition of the Roman rulers to release a prisoner of the Jews' choice at Passover. In a move that he may have thought would surely get Jesus freed, he offered to release either Jesus or a murderer and insurrectionist named Barabbas. Incited by their leaders, the people cried for Barabbas to be set free and for Jesus to be crucified (Mark 15:13; Luke 23:17-21). "When Pilate saw that he could not prevail at all, but rather a tumult was rising, he took water and washed his hands before the multitude, saying, 'I am innocent of the blood of this Just person. You see to it' " (Matthew 27:24). The people cried out, "His blood be on us and our children" (v. 25). Pilate finally yielded to pressure and turned Jesus over to the Jews to be crucified after he had first allowed his soldiers to mock and ridicule Him (vv. 26-31).

The Trek to Golgotha (Mark 15:22)

Although there are some minor differences in detail, the accounts about the Crucifixion by Matthew and Mark are similar. In the Greek text, Matthew's account contains 200 words, and Mark's account contains 150 words. Luke's account contains barely 100 words, and John's contains only 70. It is strange, at least to us, that an event of such monumental proportions is given to us in such and abbreviated form.

However, consider the Creation story in Genesis that is related for the most part in one chapter. The fact of brevity only serves to prove inspiration.

Mark's account is often referred to as Peter's Gospel. Early church writers called Mark "Peter's interpreter" and attribute to Peter the words of Mark's gospel (Papias, Eusebius, *Church History III* .39; A.D. 140; *Anti-Marcionite Prologue to Mark*, author unknown, A.D. 160-180; Irenaeus, *Against Heresies III*. I. 1, A.D. 180). After Mark's defection from the first missionary journey with his uncle Barnabas and Paul, he became a dependable servant to both Peter (1 Peter 5:13) and to Paul (2 Timothy 4:11). Paul's comment would place Mark in Rome about the time of the death of both of these apostles. Also, Mark may have been close to Jesus, and he may have been the disciple who fled naked from the Garden of Gethsemane on the night of Jesus' betrayal. He was the only one of the four writers to mention this incident (Mark 14:51-52). This tie would have given Mark much first-hand information as well as Peter's words.

Mark concentrates primarily upon three time periods. In verse 25 he says, "Now it was about the third hour, and they crucified Him." In verse 33 he writes, "Now when the sixth hour had come, there was darkness over the whole land until the ninth hour." The next verse, 34, says, "At the ninth hour Jesus cried out with a loud voice, saying,' Eloi, Eloi lama sabachthani?' Which is translated, 'My God, My God, why have you forsaken Me?' " Obviously these three time periods stuck in Mark's mind for some particular reason, although there were many dramatic events also taking place.

Mark says simply, "Then they brought Him to the place Golgotha, which is translated, Place of the Skull" (Mark 15:22). Two of the others writers, Matthew and John use this name for the place of crucifixion. The name "Golgotha" comes from Aramaic. The Hebrew word is *Golgoleth* which is translated "skull" in Judges 9:53 and 2 Kings 9:35. The Greek word for skull is *kranion*, which in English is "cranium." Why was it called the Place of the Skull? It may be because of a skull-like rock formation in the immediate area or because of skulls that some people claim had been piled there as a reminder to anyone who might break Roman law. Or it could have been named thus simply because it was the place of death.

Luke is the only gospel writer who uses the word "Calvary" (KJV) in reference to this place, and this translation was obviously influenced by Jerome's Latin Vulgate (Luke 23:33). One location in Jerusalem, just outside the city walls, called Gordon's Calvary, bears a skull-like formation in its side. Many people believe it is the place where Jesus was crucified. However, there is also another location, currently inside the city walls, designated The Church of the Holy Sepulchre, where some people believe Jesus died. To know which of these locations, if either, is the exact place is impossible. But we do know Jesus was buried in the tomb of Joseph of Arimathea, and on the Sunday morning following His burial, He was raised from the dead. Mark omits the journey of Jesus through the streets of Jerusalem. Luke tells us, "A great multitude of the people followed Him, and women who also mourned and lamented him" (Luke 23:27). In His reply to these women, Jesus gave both a prediction and a warning about the destruction of Jerusalem by the Romans that occurred in A.D. 69/70 (Luke 23:28-31).

John tells us Jesus left Pilate's hall "bearing His cross" (John 19:17). Historical accounts tell us the Romans made a condemned person carry his cross or at least the cross beam. However, both Matthew (27:32) and Luke (23:26) record that Simon from Cyrene, a place in North Africa, was compelled to bear the cross. While the texts do not tell us, it is reasonable to believe that after the all-night torture and beating Jesus had endured, He was too weak to carry the cross Himself. After falling under its weight, Simon was commandeered to bear it for Him. Mark adds an interesting historical note by telling us that Simon is the father of Alexander and Rufus (Mark 15:21). Why mention these two men if they were not well-known to those who would read this account? Later, Paul urged the Roman Christian to "Greet Rufus, chosen of the Lord, and his mother and mine" (Romans 16:13). Many Bible scholars believe Rufus was Simon's son and that Simon had converted both of them after he himself became a Christian.

The Bitter Cup (Mark 15:23)

When they arrived at Golgotha, Jesus would have stretched his arms over the cross beam, and his hands and feet would have been nailed to the wood (John 20:25; Luke 24:40). The Romans had two ways of making crosses. One method was to have the center pole nailed to the cross beam; the cross with the condemned person on it would be raised then and sent thundering into the hole prepared for it. This would cause excruciating pain as the body swayed and sagged on the nails. The other method was to nail the person's hands to the cross beam and then raise and lower it into a notched tree stump cut for that purpose. Because three men were crucified at that time, it is reasonable that the first method would have been the one employed on this occasion. In that area, it would have been difficult to find three trees together.

Pilate had written an inscription to be placed above the head of Jesus. It said, "This is Jesus of Nazareth, The King of the Jews." Each of the writers appears to have a different inscription, but each one no doubt wrote what he remembered most or else he wrote an abbreviated form (Matthew 27:37; Mark 15:26; John 19:19; Luke 23:38). The Jews objected to the wording, but Pilate said, "What I have written, I have written" (John 19:22). This superscription was written in three languages, Hebrew, Latin and Greek, so that the greatest number of people could read it.

The executioners offered Jesus a bitter mixture of sour wine (Luke 23:36). Some people believe this was done as a humanitarian gesture to dull the senses to help the condemned person bear the pain. But the Romans were not known for their compassion to condemned people, so it is doubtful this was done to make the dying process less severe. In all probability, it was done to keep the person alive longer so the torture could be prolonged. Jesus refused to drink this bitter cup so He could fully taste the cup of anguish (cf. Matthew 26:39, 42). One of the last statements Jesus made just before He died was, "I thirst!" They filled a sponge with this bitter mixture and placed it to His mouth (John 19:28).

Why did He refuse this drink the first time and apparently drink of it the second time it was offered (Matthew 27:48; Mark 15: 36; John 19:29)? Burton Coffman, in his *Commentary on Mark,* does not believe that He drank it (Firm Foundation Publishing House, Austin, 1975; p. 329). However, if He did drink of it, John's account provides us with the possible answer. Right after He took the mixture the second time, John records His sixth utterance from the cross was, "It is finished!" Then "He gave up His spirit" and died (John 19:30). The time had come for Him to "Lay down His life" (10:18), so taking the sour wine at that point in time would not make any difference. His final cry was, "Father, into your hands I commend my spirit" (Luke 23:46).

The Scenes at the Cross (Mark 15:24-33)

Imagine the picture of Jesus suspended on that cross looking down on the people He was dying for and seeing the things He saw. The first words Jesus uttered from the cross were spoken on behalf of sinners: "Father forgive them, for they do not know what they do" (Luke 23:34). He said this while Roman soldiers at His feet were casting lots for the only things He owned on Earth, His garments and a seamless robe (Psalm 22:18; Mark 15:24; John 19:23).

Standing a little distance away were the chief priests and the scribes, who joined the people in mocking Jesus. You can almost hear the tone of their words as they said, "Let the Christ, the King of Israel descend now from the cross that we may see and believe" (Mark 15:32). We know they were not sincere because they had witnessed many miracles from Jesus, and yet they chose not to believe. Nothing He did then, including coming down from the cross, would have convinced them.

Farther away Jesus could perhaps see some of the disciples crouching in the darkness, watching to see what would happen (Matthew 27:55-56; Mark 15:40-41; Luke 23:49). Near the cross was His mother, Mary, along with some of the other women who had followed Him and the "disciple whom Jesus loved" (John 19:25-27). In His dying moments, among His last thoughts were concern for His mother, and so He committed her care to the man He knew would take that responsibility seriously. He said to her and to the "disciple whom he loved," "Woman behold your son. Son, behold your mother" (vv. 26-27).

On either side of Him, there was a thief. At first they both joined in the mockery (Matthew 27:44), but in time one of them had a change of conscience. He began to say to the other man, "Don't you fear God, seeing that we are in the same condemnation? And we indeed justly, for we receive the due reward of our deeds; but this man has done nothing wrong" (Luke 23:40-41). Then this penitent man turned to Jesus and said, "Lord, remember me when You come into Your kingdom" (v. 42). The recorded second statement of Jesus was to this penitent thief: "Assuredly, I say to you, today you will be with Me in Paradise" (v. 43). Was he saved although he was not baptized? First, he may have been baptized (Matthew 3:5; Mark 1:5), but the Great Commission had not yet been given so baptism was not a commandment for salvation. He was saved because "the Son of Man had power on earth to forgive sins" (Mark 2:10).

When Jesus Died (Mark 15:33-39)

When the "sixth hour had come, there was darkness over the land until the ninth hour" (Mark 15:33). For three hours, heaven and Earth were silent. It was probably out of fear on the part of the Lord's enemies that they were silent. They did not know what was going to happen. Some people have suggested that even God refused to look upon this scene and this refusal explains why the heavens were blackened. This conclusion is doubtful in view of God's omnipresence (cf. Psalm 139:7-10). This incident certainly served to illustrate that this was the darkest moment in human history. It was the ninth hour that Jesus cried out in His fourth statement from the cross, asking His Father why He had forsaken Him. Some people near Him thought He was calling for Elijah and said, "Let Him alone; and see if Elijah will come to take Him down" (Mark 15:37). Mark then tells us that "Jesus cried out with a loud voice, and breathed His last" (Mark 15:27) He does not record the words of Jesus. Luke records that it was at this point that He uttered His last statement: "Into your hands I commend My Spirit (Luke 23:46). Matthew says that "He yielded up His Spirit"and that "the veil of the temple was torn in two from top to bottom, and the earth quaked, and the rocks were split (Matthew 27:50-51). The splitting of the temple veil symbolized the end of the Jewish system and the removal of the "middle wall of division between us" (Hebrews 10:19-22; Ephesians 2:14) and "the graves were opened and many bodies of the saints who had fallen asleep were raised and coming out of their graves after His resurrection, they went into the holy city and appeared to many" (Matthew 27:52-53). All of these things moved the centurion in charge of the crucifixion to say, "Truly this was the Son of God" (v. 54).

Lessons Learned

1. There are not four Gospels but actually only four accounts of the same story.
2. Pilate knew that Jesus was innocent and still allowed Him to be crucified.
3. The whole story about the Crucifixion, as monumental as it is, is told in less than 600 words.
4. Mark wrote the account of the Gospel that bears his name, but Peter was the principal source.
5. Jesus left Pilate's hall bearing His cross, but Simon of Cyrene carried it the rest of the way to Golgotha.
6. Jesus refused the numbing potion of sour wine so that He could fully "taste of death for every man."

Questions

1. Why are the four accounts of the gospel different?
2. Why were there two high priests in Jesus time when there was supposed to be only one?
3. What proof do we have that Pilate did not really want to get involved in the trials of Jesus?
4. Why did Pilate's sending Jesus to Herod heal a beach between the two men?
5. What does the brevity of the accounts of the Crucifixion prove?
6. Why do scholars of the Bible refer to Mark as Peter's interpreter, scribe or secretary?
7. What point of distinction does Mark use in relating his story about the Crucifixion?
8. What does the word "Golgotha" mean and why?
9. When Jesus spoke to the women on the road to Golgotha, what future event did He refer to?
10. Can you quote the seven statements Jesus made from the cross in order?

Lesson 12

The Resurrection

Week of
Nov. 22, 1998

Lesson Text

MARK 16:1-13

(1) Now when the Sabbath was past, Mary Magdalene, Mary the mother of James, and Salome bought spices, that they might come and anoint Him.

(2) Very early in the morning, on the first day of the week, they came to the tomb when the sun had risen.

(3) And they said among themselves, "Who will roll away the stone from the door of the tomb for us?"

(4) But when they looked up, they saw that the stone had been rolled away – for it was very large.

(5) And entering the tomb, they saw a young man clothed in a long white robe sitting on the right side; and they were alarmed.

(6)But he said to them, "Do not be alarmed. You seek Jesus of Nazareth, who was crucified. He is risen! He is not here. See the place where they laid Him.

(7) "But go, tell His disciples – and Peter – hat He is going before you into Galilee; there you will see Him, as He said to you."

(8) So they went out quickly and fled from the tomb, for they trembled and were amazed. And they said nothing to anyone, for they were afraid.

(9) Now when He rose early on the first day of the week, He appeared first to Mary Magdalene, out of whom He had cast seven demons.

(10) She went and told those who had been with Him, as they mourned and wept.

(11) And when they heard that He was alive and had been seen by her, they did not believe.

(12) After that, He appeared in another form to two of them as they walked and went into the country.

(13) And they went and told it to the rest, but they did not believe them either.

Introduction

After Jesus died, Joseph of Arimathea and Nicodemus went to Pilate and requested that they be allowed to bury His body. When Pilate consented, they prepared the body for burial in the traditional Jewish way by wrapping it in strips of cloth soaked in a mixture of myrrh and aloes. This was done hastily because of the Jews' preparation day before the Sabbath. Then they buried the body in Joseph's new tomb (John 19:38-42).

If that were the end of the story, we would have every reason to be sad because we would live in a world without hope. Paul told the Corinthian Christians, "If in this life only we have hope in Christ, we are of all men the most pitiable" (1 Corinthians 15:19). Why? Because if Jesus did not rise from the dead, our faith and our preaching are in vain; the apostles and other early Christians who said they saw Him alive after His resurrection were false witnesses. We would still be in our sins, and people who died in the Lord are perished and this world is yet without a Savior (vv.

14-18). In the Roman letter, Paul writes that Jesus was "declared to be the Son of God with power according to the Spirit of holiness, by the resurrection from the dead" (Romans 1:4).

The day Jesus died was literally and figuratively the darkest day in human history. Even the people closest to Him did not believe they would ever see Him alive again, and His disciples hid out in an upper room somewhere in Jerusalem (cf. John 20:19). They did not really believe He would return to life again although they had seen Him raise other people from the dead. Had that been merely an illusion, or were those people really dead to begin with? However, just three days later, their disbelief changed as reports began to circulate that His body was missing from the grave. One by one, His followers began to share amazing stories of having seen Jesus alive. Some people walked with Him and talked with Him; some even ate with Him. It soon became evident that these were not the reports of a few fanatical followers hallucinating because of their deep grief, but Jesus really was alive. That one fact dramatically changes everything.

A Glorious Sunday Morning (Mark 16:1-3)

Early on the Sunday morning after the Crucifixion, Mary Magdalene, Mary the mother of James and Salome, Joanna and some other unnamed women went to the tomb of Jesus to anoint His body properly. This had not been done because of the haste involved to get His body in the ground before the Sabbath began (Luke 24:10). When they began their journey it was dark, but by the time they arrived, the sun was rising (John 20:1; Mark 16:2).

As these women walked to the tomb, they were discussing how they would remove the large stone from the entrance. Neither the women, nor any of the disciples, apparently knew that Pilate had ordered the tomb to be marked with a Roman seal. He had also consented to the fears of the Jewish rulers and placed a guard at the entrance of the tomb to prevent the body from being removed by His disciples (Matthew 27:62-65). They obviously expected Jesus' body still to be in the grave.

He Is Risen Indeed (Mark 16:4-8)

Before the women arrived at the tomb, "there was a great earthquake; for an angel of the Lord descended from heaven, and came and rolled back the stone from the door, and sat on it" (Matthew 28:2). His "countenance was like lightning; and his clothing a white as snow" (v. 3).The sudden appearance of this heavenly messenger so frightened the guards at the door of the tomb that they "shook for fear of him, and became as dead men" (v. 4).

Imagine the surprise of these women when they arrived at the tomb to find the stone rolled away. Luke says that "they were greatly perplexed about this" (Luke 24:4). Mark and Luke make it clear that the women entered the tomb only briefly and encountered an angel. Luke 24:4 says there were two. Why the difference? Because Mark referred only to the one who delivered the message. One of the angels told them Jesus had risen and to "go and tell His disciples and Peter" (Matthew 28:5-7; Mark 16:6-7). Mark says they "trembled and were amazed and afraid" (v. 8). In fact, they were so upset that John tells us they ran away from the tomb and went immediately to tell Peter and John, "They have taken away the Lord out of the tomb, and we do not know where they have laid Him" (John 20:2). Luke adds that these words "seemed to them like idle tales, and they did not believe" (Luke 24:11). Mary returned with Peter and John, who ran on ahead and came to the tomb first and looked inside. John saw the burial cloths that Jesus had been wrapped in lying there, but he did not enter (John 20:4-5). Peter came a little behind him and entered the sepulchre to see the "linen cloths lying there and the handkerchief that had been around his head" folded neatly, laying off by itself (vv. 6-7). The disciples apparently did not remain at the tomb long but quickly left (Luke 24:12; John 20:10).

Although they believed He had been resurrected, the full impact of what had happened had not become clear to them. They were dismayed and in shock. Mary was left behind grieving because she did not really understand what had happened to the Lord's body. She bent over and looked in the tomb again, and this time she saw two angels there who asked her why she was weeping. Once again she expressed her profound grief because the body of Jesus was gone, and she did not know where He had been taken (John 20:12-13).

Neither Mary and the other women, nor Peter and John, knew these men were angels at that time. When Mary turned away from the tomb Jesus was standing behind her, but she did not know who He was and thought He was the caretaker of the garden. The question is often asked why Mary was confused, why she was weeping, and why she did not recognize Jesus. Remember that none of the disciples expected Jesus to rise again. When they discovered His body missing from the tomb, some of them assumed that either it had been moved to another location or someone had stolen it.As for Mary's not recognizing Jesus, she was in deep grief, which explains why she did not fully comprehend the words of the angel. She did not expect to see Him there alive. Also, her eyes were filled with tears. All of these circumstances taken together explain Mary's situation.

More About Mary Magdalene (Mark 16:9-11)

Mary Magdalene is undoubtedly one of the most misunderstood women in the New Testament. She has been called a prostitute; the blasphemous rock musical, *Jesus Christ Superstar,* portrays her chasing after Jesus and trying to seduce Him. Many mistakenly identify her with the woman caught in adultery (John 8:1-11) or with the sinful woman who wept on Jesus' feet, wiped them with her hair, and then kissed and anointed them with fragrant oil (Luke 7:37-38). This is because the first mention of her was after this incident. She was none of these women.

Mary was from Magdala, on the southwestern coast of the Sea of Galilee (Matthew 27:56-57; Mark 15:40-47; Luke 8:2). She loved Jesus, but there was nothing sexual about her love. She had good reason to love Him because He had cast seven demons out of her (Mark 16:9; Luke 8:2). She was a devoted follower of Jesus (Luke 8:2-3) who was one of the last people at the Cross (Matthew 27:56; Mark 15:40; John 19:25) and one of the first at the tomb (Mark 16:1).

Jesus Was Seen by Many Witnesses (Mark 16:12-13)

The incident of Jesus' encounter with two of His disciples on the road is related by Mark in a few words. Luke supplies us with additional information. These two disciples "were traveling that same day to a village called Emmaus, which was about seven miles from Jerusalem" (Luke 24:13). One of them was Cleopas, but we do not know who this man was. No good reason exists to identify him with the Clopas of John 19:25. The other disciple is unnamed, but some people have speculated it was Luke. But this speculation is doubtful because Luke was a Gentile and would not have referred to the Jewish leaders as "our rulers" (Luke 24:20).

These disciples were discussing the events regarding Jesus. As they walked and talked, Jesus appeared to them, but "their eyes were restrained, so that they did not know Him" (Luke 24:16). Because they did not recognize Him, they were at first surprised that He did not seem to know about the events in Jerusalem surrounding the death of Jesus. They talked with Him about the Crucifixion and expressed grave disappointment that Jesus of Nazareth was not the Christ (Luke 24:19-21). Instead of being flattered that they had such strong feelings for Him, Jesus was disappointed that they had not understood the prophecies of the Old Testament (Luke 24:25-26). "Beginning at Moses and all the prophets, He expounded to them in all the Scriptures the things concerning Himself" (Luke 24:27; cf. Numbers 21:9; John 3:14-15; Deuteronomy 18:15; Isaiah 7:14; 9:6- 8; Daniel 2:44; 9:24; Malachi 3:1-2.) After they arrived in Emmaus, they invited Him to eat with them. "He took the bread and blessed and broke it; and gave it to them" (Luke 24:30). There was something in that act that caused their eyes to be opened. They knew instantly who He was. He then vanished from their sight as quickly as He had appeared (Luke 24:31). After He was gone, they went to share this good news with the disciples (Luke 24:33-35).

In all there were 12 post-resurrection appearances of Jesus. Of interest is that whenever a day was mentioned for these appearances, it was always on the first day of the week (Mark 16: 2, 9; Luke 24:1; John 20:1, 19, 26 – it would have been eight days counting from Sunday to Sunday. Jesus first appeared to Mary Magdalene (John 20:15-18), and then to the other women as they were walking home from the tomb (Matthew 28:9-10). From Luke and Paul we learn that He appeared to Peter by himself (Luke 24:34; 1 Corinthians 15:5). He then appeared to the two disciples walking on the road to Emmaus (Luke 24:13-35).When these two disciples went to inform the Eleven, Jesus appeared while they were still there, but Thomas was not present (John 20:19).

The following Sunday, He appeared to all of the Eleven in the Upper Room, behind locked doors (John 20:26). Sometime later, He appeared to seven of the apostles by the Sea of Galilee (John 21:1-2). Matthew indicates that He appeared to all of them on a mountain in Galilee as He had promised, (Matthew 28:7-10, 16). His last appearance to the apostles was just before His ascension from a place on the Mount of Olives near Bethany (Luke 24:50; Acts 1:4-11). Paul tells us that He also appeared to "over five hundred brethren at once" (1 Corinthians 15:6), after which He showed Himself to His brother, James, who later became a leader in the Jerusalem congregation (1 Corinthians 15:7; Acts 15:13; Galatians 1:19; 2:9). Paul adds, "Then last of all He was seen by me also, as by one born out of due time" (1 Corinthians 15:8).

The Resurrection of Jesus is a historical certainty. Luke writes, "He also presented Himself alive after His suffering by many infallible proofs, being seen by them during 40 days and speaking the things concerning the kingdom of God" (Acts 1:3). After stating the negative consequences occurring if Jesus had not been resurrected, Paul wrote, "But now Christ is risen from the dead, and has become the firstfruits of those who have fallen asleep" (1 Corinthians 15:20). As Jesus told Martha, "I am the resurrection and the life. He who believes in Me, though he may die, he shall live. And whosoever lives and believes in Me shall never die. Do you believe this?" (John 11:25-26). Because He was raised, we can say with Paul, "But thanks be to God, who gives us the victory through our Lord Jesus Christ" (1 Corinthians 15:57).

Lessons Learned

1. Our hope in Christ is certain because He was raised from the dead.
2. Jesus proved to His disciples, "with many infallible proofs," that He was not a ghost or a phantom – He was very much a living flesh, blood and bone person.
3. Even Jesus' closest disciples did not believe that He would be raised from the dead.
4. Mary Magdalene was not the immoral person she is often portrayed as being, but she was one of Jesus' most devoted disciples.
5. Jesus used the Old Testament scriptures, just as Peter did on the Day of Pentecost and Philip did with the Eunuch, to open minds of the disciples on the road to Emmaus.
6. There were 12 post-resurrection appearances.

Questions

1. Who were Joseph of Arimathea and Nicodemus?
2. How was Jesus' body prepared for burial?
3. What would be the consequences if Jesus had not been raised from the dead?
4. Why didn't the disciples believe Jesus would be raised form the dead?
5. On what day was Jesus raised, and how can we prove it?
6. How can we harmonize all of the accounts of the Crucifixion that at first seem to be so contradictory?
7. Why did Mary Magdalene not recognize Jesus in the garden Sunday morning?
8. Why did Mary Magdalene love Jesus so much?
9. For what reason did Jesus conceal His true identity from the two disciples on the road to Emmaus?
10. What proof do we have that Jesus was really raised from the dead?

Lesson 13

The Ascension of Jesus

Week of Nov. 29, 1998

Lesson Text

LUKE 24:44-53

(44) Then He said to them, "These are the words which I spoke to you while I was still with you, that all things must be fulfilled which were written in the Law of Moses and the Prophets and the Psalms concerning Me."

(45) And He opened their understanding, that they might comprehend the Scriptures.

(46) Then He said to them, "Thus it is written, and thus it was necessary for the Christ to suffer and to rise from the dead the third day,

(47) "and that repentance and remission of sins should be preached in His name to all nations, beginning at Jerusalem.

(48) "And you are witnesses of these things.

(49) "Behold, I send the Promise of My Father upon you; but tarry in the city of Jerusalem until you are endued with power from on high."

(50) And He led them out as far as Bethany, and He lifted up His hands and blessed them.

(51) Now it came to pass, while He blessed them, that He was parted from them and carried up into heaven.

(52) And they worshiped Him, and returned to Jerusalem with great joy,

(53) and were continually in the temple praising and blessing God. Amen.

Introduction

Quoting from a prophecy by the psalmist, Paul wrote concerning Christ, "When He ascended on high, He led captivity captive, and gave gifts to men" (Ephesians 4:8; Psalm 68:18). In this brief statement, the prophet explains in majestic imagery our Lord's victory march. When a victorious Roman general would return home, he would have a triumphant march through the streets of the capital city. In the procession would be the conquered foes, including the leaders of the opposing army and also the former captives who were now set free. To be able to bestow gifts upon men, Jesus had to receive the power and be in the position to do so. This was accomplished when He re-entered heaven and took the throne to reign over the kingdom of God. On His triumphant return, He "led captivity captive." Mankind had been under the domination of sin and its consequences (death: Romans 5:12) since the Fall. In that sense, all men were captives or slaves to death. By rising from the dead, Jesus took death captive so that it can no longer hold under its power people who belong to Him (John 5:24-29; Romans 5:12-21; 6:9-12, 22-23; Hebrews 2:14-15; Revelation 20:6; 21:8). When He returns, He will defeat this "last enemy" of mankind once and for all time (1 Corinthians 15:26).

Before Jesus returned to the Father, He had one last order of business to attend to. This was to assign the job of carrying out His orders on Earth to men whose duty it would be to fulfill that responsibility. We call this parting charge the Great Commission, which was given first to His apostles but was intended for His church in all ages. The full content of this final message is not recorded in any one place. Jesus delivered various components of this commission at different times during the 40-day period between His resurrection and His ascension.

Matthew's account reveals that these words of Jesus were delivered on an unnamed mountain in Galilee (Matthew 28:18-20). Mark records that these words were delivered by Jesus upon one of His appearances to the apostles in the Upper Room in Jerusalem. This was shortly or immediately before He led them to the Mount of Olives from which He ascended back to Heaven (Mark 16:14-18; Luke 24:50). To determine exactly where Jesus was when the words recorded by Luke were given is difficult; but based upon the context of Luke 24:33-49, it appears to have been while the apostles were still in the Upper Room. John is the only one of the four writers who does not mention any part of this commission. However, Jesus' prayer in John 17 expresses these same ideas (vv. 12-21). To receive the full content of Jesus' commission, we must put together the three accounts supplied by the Holy Spirit.

In his *Commentary on Luke*, Ray Summers says Luke 24:44-49 "more naturally indicates a summary statement representing Jesus' teaching during that 40-day period when he was alternatively with them and away from them" (Word Books, Waco, 1972; p. 333). Burton Coffman writes, "This is a summary of the great commission which was probably given repeatedly during the 40 days prior to the ascension" (*Commentary on Luke*, Firm Foundation Publishing House, Austin, 1975; p. 525). In his *A Commentary on Acts of the Apostles*, J.W. McGarvey wrote, "The items of which it [the Great Commission] is composed are not fully stated by either of the historians, but must be collected from the partial statements of Matthew, Mark, and Luke. Matthew presents three of them … Mark presents five items … Luke simply states that Jesus said, 'Thus it behooved the Christ to suffer, and to rise from the dead the third day, and that repentance and remission of sins should be preached in his name among all nations beginning at Jerusalem.' If we combine all these items, by arranging them in their natural order of succession, we will have the commission fully stated" (Gospel Advocate Co., Nashville, 7th ed.; pp. 10-11). H. Leo Boles says that "Luke omits other appearances of Jesus during the 40 days after his resurrection; He gives here a summary of what Jesus taught the disciples between his resurrection and his ascension" (*New Testament Commentaries: Luke*, Gospel Advocate Co., Nashville, 1 940; p. 475).

It seems clear, then, that we must put all of these statements together to have our Lord's complete charge to the church. In this charge He states the conditions upon which salvation will be rendered. McGarvey's solution is as follows: "In brief, they were commanded to go into all the world, and make disciples of all nations by preaching the gospel to every creature; to immerse all penitent believers into the name of the Father, and of the Son, and of the Holy Spirit, promising such the remission of sins; then teaching them all their duties and privileges, as disciples of Jesus. In the mean time, all were to be assured that he who believed not should be condemned" (p. 11). A study of the Great Commission is important and urgently needed in the church today. Sadly, the Great Commission has become the Great Omission – it is truly the neglected essential.

The Promise Fulfilled (Luke 24:44-45)

After Jesus had proved to the apostles that He had risen from the dead by showing them the wounds in His hands and feet and by eating a meal with them, Luke records that He turned their attention to a promise He had made to them early in His ministry. In the Sermon on the Mount, Jesus said, "Do not think that I came to destroy the Law or the prophets. I did not come to destroy but to fulfill. For assuredly, I say unto you, till heaven and earth pass away, one jot or one tittle will by no means pass from the law till all is fulfilled" (Matthew 5:17-18). He had also told them on numerous occasions about His impending death (Matthew 16:21; 20:17-19; 26:20-24; Mark 8:31; 10:33-34; Luke 18:31-33; John 16:17-22). None of this made a lasting impression upon them because they really did not believe it would ever happen (John 20:9).

In His statement, Jesus made it clear that "all" of the prophecies that were made concerning Him in the Old Testament had been fulfilled. The three divisions of the Old Testament that He mentioned, the Law of Moses, the Prophets and the Psalms, were those recognized by the Jews. They combined the Law with the books that we list as history. They included in the category of Psalms all of the books that we list as poetry. The category of prophecy referred to all 17 books of prophecy. We have divided them into major, the longer works, and minor, the shorter works, prophets. During His personal ministry, Jesus quoted from each one of the three divisions.

After Jesus told them that all the prophecies made about Him in the Old Testament had been fulfilled, "He opened their understanding, that they might comprehend the Scriptures." How did He accomplish this? Most likely it was in the same way in which Lydia's heart was opened as Paul taught her from the Word of God (Acts 16:14). He probably took portions from each of the three divisions He had mentioned and showed how He had fulfilled those prophecies. To conclude this was a miraculous event has no reason. John 14:26, 16:13 and Acts 1:4-8 would appear to preclude an infusion of inspiration by the Holy Spirit at this point. These prophecies were not fulfilled until the Day of Pentecost, when the apostles were baptized in the Holy Spirit (Acts 2:1-4, 22-36).

The Great Commission (Luke 24:46-48)

These verses contain Luke's summary of our Lord's Great Commission. After showing that He was the fulfillment of the Old Testament prophecies pertaining to the Messiah, He explained that this is why it was "necessary"for Him to die and to be raised again from the dead (cf. Psalms 22:1, 16-18; Isaiah 53:1-12; Daniel 9:26-27). Doctrines exist today that imply God could have saved mankind without sacrificing Jesus on the cross. If that is true, then God would be some type of sadistic being and not the One who loved the people of the world so much that He sent His Son to die for them. Jesus knew there was no other way to redeem mankind, and so He submitted Himself to the Father's will (Matthew 27:39-46).

Luke adds repentance to the command to believe and to be baptized for salvation. Jesus was the One who taught, "Unless you repent you will all likewise perish" (Luke 13:3, 5). Luke recorded the words of Peter on the Day of Pentecost, when the people who were convicted of the sin of participating in the death of Christ asked, "Men and brethren, what shall we do?" (Acts 2:37). Peter answered, "Repent and be baptized every one of you in the name of Jesus Christ for the remission of sins and you shall receive the gift of the Holy Spirit" (Acts 2:38). Repentance implies a complete change of life. Repentance is a turning away from sin and a turning of one's life over to God.

The book of Acts is a continuation of Luke's account of the gospel as Acts 1:1 shows. Because of this, we see many parallels in the two accounts. In Luke 24:48, Jesus told the apostles they were witnesses of the events of His life, and they were called to preach to all the world. In Acts 1:8 He told them, "You shall receive power when the Holy Spirit has come upon you; and you shall be witnesses to Me in Jerusalem, and in all Judea and Samaria, and to the end of the earth." In Luke 24:49, Jesus told the apostles that He would send the "promise of My Father upon you" and that when this happened they would be endued with power from on high. This was obviously a reference to the coming of the Holy Spirit. In Acts 1:5 He told them they would be "baptized with the Holy Spirit not many days from now." In verse 8 of the same chapter, He said, "You shall receive power after the Holy Spirit has come upon you"

Luke records that after Jesus had spoken these words, "He led them out as far as Bethany." In Acts 1:12 this was on the Mount of Olives, about a Sabbath Day's journey, or three quarters of a mile, from Jerusalem. As they talked with Him, He lifted up His hands to bless them, and then "He was taken up, and a cloud received Him out of their sight" (v. 9). Luke closes his account by saying that the apostles "returned to Jerusalem with great joy" and that they were "continually in the temple praising and blessing God" (Luke 24:52-53). In Acts he says they were in the Upper Room, along with 109 other people, where they "continued with one accord in prayer and supplication" (1:13-15). These two accounts cannot be contradictory because they were written by the same person. The facts are that the apostles were staying in the Upper Room, but at appropriate times during the 10 days while they were waiting for the promise to come, they went to the temple to pray.

Lessons Learned

1. When Jesus rose from the dead and ascended to the Father, He took death captive; and when he returns again in the clouds of heaven, He will defeat it forever. Therefore Christians should not fear death.
2. The Great Commission was given first to the apostles, but it is the church's responsibility to fulfill it until the end of the world.
3. When all of the accounts of the Lord's final charge to the apostles are taken together, we learn that a person who has received the gospel and believes it must repent and be baptized into Christ for the remission of sins. The Bible also teaches that before a person can be baptized, he must confess his faith that Jesus is the Son of God (Matthew 10:32-33; Romans 10:9-10; Acts 8:37).
4. There are more than 300 prophecies in the Old Testament concerning the Messiah, and Jesus fulfilled all of them.
5. It was necessary for Jesus to die so that He might fulfill the Father's will and complete His plan of redemption.
6. The apostles were eyewitnesses to Jesus' ministry, death, resurrection and ascension. We cannot be witnesses in that sense, but we can bear witness that their testimony was true and share this message with other people.

Questions

1. How can we be certain that the Lord's kingdom is in existence today and is not yet in the future?
2. Why do we know that the Great Commission is our responsibility too?
3. Because confession of faith in Christ is not mentioned in any of the three accounts about our Lord's final instructions to the disciples, how is it included in the plan of salvation?
4. What promise did Jesus make to the apostles before His death concerning the Old Testament prophecies?
5. Can we prove that we are not living under the Old Testament today? How?
6. What does the Bible mean by the word "inspiration"?
7. Can you name some specific doctrines that would deny or nullify the vicarious death of Christ on the cross?
8. What is repentance and what does it require?
9. What two things are promised to people who repent and are baptized (Acts 2:38)?
10. How do we know Luke wrote the book of Acts as well as the Gospel of Luke?

Lesson 1

Creation

Week of
Dec. 6, 1998

Lesson Text

GENESIS 1:1-2, 24-31

(1) In the beginning God created the heavens and the earth.

(2) The earth was without form, and void; and darkness was on the face of the deep. And the Spirit of God was hovering over the face of the waters.

(24) Then God said, "Let the earth bring forth the living creature according to its kind: cattle and creeping thing and beast of the earth, each according to its kind"; and it was so.

(25) And God made the beast of the earth according to its kind, cattle according to its kind, and everything that creeps on the earth according to its kind. And God saw that it was good.

(26) Then God said, "Let Us make man in Our image, according to Our likeness; let them have dominion over the fish of the sea, over the birds of the air, and over the cattle, over all the earth and over every creeping thing that creeps on the earth."

(27) So God created man in His own image; in the image of God He created him; male and female He created them.

(28) Then God blessed them, and God said to them, "Be fruitful and multiply; fill the earth and subdue it; have dominion over the fish of the sea, over the birds of the air, and over every living thing that moves on the earth."

(29) And God said, "See, I have given you every herb that yields seed which is on the face of all the earth, and every tree whose fruit yields seed; to you it shall be for food.

(30) "Also, to every beast of the earth, to every bird of the air, and to everything that creeps on the earth, in which there is life, I have given every green herb for food"; and it was so.

(31) Then God saw everything that He had made, and indeed it was very good. So the evening and the morning were the sixth day.

Introduction

The Bible is the only book to really answer the questions: "Where did we come from?"; "Why are we here?"; and "Where are we going?" The first two of these questions are answered in the first verse of the Bible, "In the beginning God created." Many people deny this statement as truth, but they give no answers to these questions. They opt for big-bang-type theories, spontaneous generation, radical evolution and the idea of man crawling out of some prehistoric primordial soup. All such attempts to explain our existence are purely speculative and have no basis in fact.

The so-called theory of evolution has been one of the most popular ideas about the origins of life on planet Earth. But it is not a theory at all, because it has never advanced beyond the hypothesis stage in the scientific process. For it to be a legitimate theory, it would have to be based upon repeatable, verifiable data. The idea of evolution is based upon several unprovable assumptions. Many people in the scientific community have abandoned this idea altogether, and as more information becomes available, others will follow suit. The tragic thing is that while it is being taught, the faith of many people is being destroyed. If people will only study the facts, they will see that the weight of the evidence supports special creation. Batsell Barrett Baxter, in the book *I Believe Because*, wrote that we do not have to prove God exists; we only have to prove that it is more reasonable to believe in God than it is to reject Him (Baker Book House, Grand Rapids, 1971; p. 22).

God was not limited to evolution when He created this world. He created everything full-grown: the universe, vegetation, animals and mankind. He then blessed this full-grown world and its inhabitants to begin reproducing after its own kind. The Bible says that He accomplished this creation in six days by the word of His mouth (Genesis 1:1-31; Hebrews 11:3; 2 Peter 3:5-7). The abundance of evidence supports that fact. This answers the age-old question, "Which came first – the chicken or the egg?" No life comes into existence today except from pre-existing life. It has been that way since the beginning.

In the Beginning (Genesis 1:1)

This statement is here to tell us about the beginning of all things. It is not here to give us an explanation of when it happened. Before time began, there was eternity. Time is simply a measurement of eternity with infinite duration on either side of it. When this Earth is no more, time will cease to exist, but eternity will go on and on. Time is only important to people who are limited by it. God is not bound by time, clocks or calendars. "With the Lord one day is as a thousand years, and a thousand years as one day" (2 Peter 3:8).

Some of the modern versions of the Bible translate Genesis 1:1, "In the beginning of God creating," or "When God began to create." This may be an attempt to accommodate the exaggerated dates of the evolutionist's geologic timetable. They speak about the beginning of the universe in terms of hundreds of millions to billions of years. The fact is there is no proof to justify these dates. They are pure guesswork. While no one knows exactly when the beginning was, evidence indicates we live on a young Earth. It may be older than theologians have concluded, but it is certainly much younger than some scientists have speculated. Dr. Henry Morris, one of the leading Creation scientists in America, says in *The Genesis Record* that the earth is no more than 10,000 years old, and from a biblical standpoint, it may be much younger than that (Baker Book House, Grand Rapids, 1976; p. 46).

God Created

The name for God in Genesis 1:1 is the Hebrew word *Elohim*. It is a uniplural noun that indicates the plurality of God, or the "Godhead" (Acts 17:29; Romans 1:20; Colossians 2:9). The Hebrew *Shema,* said each Sabbath in the synagogue before the start of the service, says, "Hear, O Israel: The Lord our God, the Lord is one!" (Deuteronomy 6:4). God is one and yet more than one (Matthew 28:19; John 10:30; 1 John 5:7). God is Spirit, a universal Spirit who is equally shared with three distinct persons. God the Father and the Son, whose eternal relationship to deity was the "Word," or in Greek, *logos* (John 1:1-2, 14; 1 John 5:7), and the Holy Spirit (Genesis 1:2). The Holy Spirit is always referred to with proper names, such as the Comforter, or in Greek, *paraclete*, the Spirit of God, the Spirit of Christ or the Spirit of

Truth, and with personal masculine pronouns, such as He, Him and His. All three members of the Godhead were present at, and participated in, the Creation. This explains the use of the plural pronoun "us" and "our" in Genesis 1:26.

The word for "created" in this passage is the Hebrew word *bara*, which is used 48 times in the Old Testament. According to *Vine's Expository Dictionary of Biblical Words,* it refers exclusively to God's creating activity. This word is never used in Scripture to discuss what man creates. Only God can bring something into existence from nothing (Romans 4:17; Hebrews 11:3). Men can only reorder or rearrange the materials that God has provided, but they cannot create new materials out of nothing.

We have two choices. Either this universe and all that is in it came into being through the activity of an infinite, eternal, and omnipotent Creator, or it is the product of lifeless, unintelligent, emotionless matter that somehow came into existence out of nothing. It is a choice between eternal mind or eternal matter. Which is more reasonable and scientific? Paul warned Timothy to "beware the oppositions of science falsely so-called" (1 Timothy 6:20 KJV). Why do some scientists and even some people who say they believe in the Bible subscribe to the view that the universe is millions or billions of years old? The problem originates with the fact that scientists think they know exactly how long it took for the universe to form and then for Earth to become habitable. Because they surmise it would have taken perhaps 3 billion years for the universe to form and then a few million more years for the Earth to become habitable, they began to accept the dates as factual. If you begin with such a concept, then every decision you make is based on that concept. The conclusions drawn then are no more reliable than the facts upon which they are based.

Some Bible believers have accepted the exaggerated dates for the beginning because they have been taught to believe science has proven that these dates are accurate. They do the same thing with evolution. Because they have been taught that evolution has been proven beyond question, they have accepted that God used the process of evolution to bring all life into being. This is called theistic evolution. The Greek word *theos* is English for "God." There are great variations in the dates given by scientists about the age of the earth and the universe. When they talk to laymen, they often get carried away with their millions and billions of years. However, when they are among their peers, they are more guarded. Why? Because they do not know how old the universe or the earth is, and their absolute dates are pure speculation.

Is it necessary to accept the exaggerated dates thrown out by scientists, especially in view of the lack of consensus among them? The answer is an unequivocable no. If under ordinary circumstances, it would have taken billions or millions of years to form the universe and Earth, God just sped up the process and did it instantaneously. God created a full-grown Earth with full-grown people and animals to live upon it and to reproduce (Genesis 1:22, 28). To deny this is to deny the omnipotent power of the supreme God described in the Bible. He can do whatever He wills to do. "For with God nothing will be impossible" (Luke 1:37; cf. Mark 10:27 NKJV).

The Heavens and the Earth

The word "heavens" corresponds to our word "space." Paul speaks about "the third heaven" in 2 Corinthians 12:2. The first heaven would be our atmosphere where the planes and birds fly. The second heaven would be the space above our atmosphere where the space rockets and satellites maneuver, and where the stars and planets abide. The third heaven is the throne room of God, the residence of the angels and our eternal home. What are the first two heavens but a marvelous canopy above our heads and what is the earth but ground beneath our feet? The word "earth" most likely referred to the totality of matter in the universe that was eventually shaped by God into material bodies. The Hebrew word used here is *erets*, which is often translated "ground" or "land." From this we conclude that the material universe was initially a shapeless mass of matter until God formed the earth and the other heavenly bodies, which were not created until the fourth day. The earth was also a shapeless mass, void of any living thing.

The sacred writer then tells us that "darkness was upon the face of the deep." At this time, light had not been created. Darkness results from the absence of light. The "deep" refers to the waters, and most likely means all of the water in the universe. The picture that Moses is presenting to us is one in which the material elements that make up the universe were existing in a watery matrix throughout the darkness of space. The universe was present, but everything was still and dark.

The "Spirit of God," or the Holy Spirit, began to move "upon the face of the waters." Dr. Henry Morris states that the word "moved" can be translated "vibrated" (p. 52). He points out that in the beginning the universe was unenergized and that a prime mover or energizer was necessary. He discusses the fact that energy transmissions are movements of various kinds of waves, such as light and sound. This is true in every case except for nuclear energy, which is involved in the structure of matter itself. He believes the Holy Spirit moved in vibrating motions across the watery matrix described earlier to create energy that was then used to form the shapeless matter into the physical universe. Although there is no uniform agreement about this question, Morris' idea does provide one plausible explanation.

God Said

Throughout the six days of Creation, the emphasis is on what God said: "God said, 'Let there be light'; and there was light" (Genesis 1:3); "God said, 'Let there be a firmament in the midst of the waters, and let it divide the waters from the waters' " (v. 6); "God said, 'Let the waters under the heavens be gathered together into one place, and let the dry land appear'; and it was so" (v. 9); "Then God said, 'Let the earth bring forth grass, the herb that yields seed, and fruit tree that yields fruit according to its kind; whose seed is in itself, on the earth' " (v. 11). This continues with each creating event through the sixth and last day and the creation of mankind (vv. 14, 20, 24, 26). The Hebrew writer declares that "the worlds were framed by the word of God, so that the things that are seen were not made of things which are visible" (11:3).

After pointing out that certain scoffers would deny that God once destroyed all life on Earth with the exception of that which was within the ark, Peter says they are ignorant of the fact that "by the word of God the heavens were of old, and the earth standing out of the water and in the water" (2 Peter 3:5). He then says that "the Heavens and the earth which now exist are kept in store by the same word, reserved unto fire until the day of judgement and the perdition of ungodly men" (v. 7). In the beginning God spoke, and it was so. In the end of all things, He will speak again, and this Earth and all that is on it will be completely burned up (vv. 10-13). Then Earth and time will be no more, and eternity will stretch before us.

God's Crowning Creation – Mankind (Genesis 1:24-31)

On the sixth day of Creation, God made the "cattle, creeping things, and beast of the earth" (v. 24). They were said to have been "brought forth" from the earth, meaning that their bodies were formed from the dust of the ground to which they would return. Once the animals were created, God turned his attention to the creature "made a little lower than the angels" – mankind (Psalm 8:5; Hebrews 2:6-8). He formed man's physical body "out of the dust of the ground," just as He did that of the animals (Genesis 2:7; cf. Ecclesiastes 12:7). However, there is a distinct difference between man and animals. God made man "in His own image" (Genesis 1:27). It is in the spiritual sense that man is like God. God gave man a "living being" (2:7). "The body without the spirit is dead" (James 2:26). The body of man was a lifeless lump of clay until God breathed into it the breath of life. God called the first man "Adam."

After Adam had time to be aware of his loneliness and saw that all other creatures had companions, God made a woman for him (Genesis 2:18). God performed the first surgical operation and removed a rib from Adam's side and used it to fashion a perfect complement for him (v. 22). She was a "helper comparable to him" (v. 20). God then performed the first marriage ceremony when he brought the woman to Adam (vv. 22, 24). Jesus said it was God who said, "For this reason a man shall leave his father and mother and be joined to his wife, and the two shall become one flesh. So then, they are no longer two but one flesh, Therefore what God has joined together, let no man separate " (Matthew 19:4-6). This model of one man and one woman for one lifetime was to be perpetuated forever (vv. 8-9). Adam named his wife "Eve" because he said "she was the mother of all living" (Genesis 3:20).

The psalmist said, "I will praise Thee: for I am fearfully and wonderfully made" (139:14). The human being is the most remarkable and complex organism God has created. Our heart supplies our bodies with food and oxygen through red blood cells beating about 36 million times a year. Barring any complications, it can be expected to work for 70 or more years without needing any repairs. Our eyes are precision lenses that are more accurate than anything man has devised. Our brains are more complex than any computer. We seem to have unlimited storage capacity for information within our brain cells and the ability of instant recall for most of it. In addition to this, our brains can process and store thousands of sights, sounds, smells, feelings and emotions. There is no other explanation for this wonderful creature that is man except for the fact that God made him. It may be hard for some people to believe that God did this, but the alternative is even more unbelievable. If you choose to believe you are the product of evolution from gas out of a murky prehistoric swamp rather than the creation of a loving, caring, giving, all-knowing, omnipotent Creator, then carefully consider the consequences of your decision. As Joshua said, "But as for me and my house, we will serve the Lord" (Joshua 24:15).

Lessons Learned

1. The Bible allows for changes within a species. We see such changes in almost every kind of life. There are many types of horses, cows, pigs, dogs, cats, monkeys and even humans. We do not see, nor can we find any evidence of, the radical crossover of species that evolutionists believe happened. Dogs are dogs, cats are cats, monkeys are monkeys, humans are humans, and never the twain shall

meet. Despite what we have been led to believe, evolution is not scientific. This also includes theistic evolution. Do not limit the omnipotent God to human imagination and speculation.

2. No person really knows when the universe or the Earth began. Theologians do not know because the chronologies in the Bible are not there to determine time; they are there to show relationship. Scientists do not know because no dating method devised so far is 100 percent accurate. This includes the carbon dating methods that are supposed to be the most precise. If this were not the case, we could determine accurately how old certain fossils are. However, most of the evidence, including the oldest living things on Earth, points to a young Earth. When the Earth was created is not really important to those of us living today, but when it ends will be. The mind of man cannot fully comprehend the divine. God is unlike any other being known to us. He had no beginning, and He has no end. He is one Supreme Spirit that exists as three distinct persons in the Godhead. This omnipotent being made us and gave us life. That we are here cannot be denied. If not God, then who? How can people believe in eternal, lifeless, nonintelligent matter and reject the eternal, supreme Mind? How could man exist without God? Do not our intelligence and reason shout the glory of God (Psalm 19:1)?

Questions

1. Which two great questions are answered in Genesis 1:1?
2. How do we know, "Which came first – the chicken or the egg?"
3. What is time?
4. How does the Hebrew noun for God, *Elohim*, help us understand the nature of God?
5. What truth does the Hebrew word *bara* convey?
6. What are the only two real choices we have regarding the origin of life?
7. What is theistic evolution, and why is it not biblical?
8. What did Paul mean by the term "the third heaven?"
9. Upon what is the emphasis placed throughout the six days of Creation?
10. Why did Adam name his wife Eve?

Lesson 2

Consequences

Week of
Dec. 13, 1998

Lesson Text

GENESIS 3:8-19

(8) And they heard the sound of the LORD God walking in the garden in the cool of the day, and Adam and his wife hid themselves from the presence of the LORD God among the trees of the garden.

(9) Then the LORD God called to Adam and said to him, "Where are you?"

(10) So he said, "I heard Your voice in the garden, and I was afraid because I was naked; and I hid myself."

(11) And He said, "Who told you that you were naked? Have you eaten from the tree of which I commanded you that you should not eat?"

(12) Then the man said, "The woman whom You gave to be with me, she gave me of the tree, and I ate."

(13) And the LORD God said to the woman, "What is this you have done?" The woman said, "The serpent deceived me, and I ate."

(14) So the LORD God said to the serpent: "Because you have done this, You are cursed more than all cattle, And more than every beast of the field; On your belly you shall go, And you shall eat dust All the days of your life.

(15) And I will put enmity Between you and the woman, And between your seed and her Seed; He shall bruise your head, And you shall bruise His heel."

(16) To the woman He said: "I will greatly multiply your sorrow and your conception; In pain you shall bring forth children; Your desire shall be for your husband, And he shall rule over you."

(17) Then to Adam He said, "Because you have heeded the voice of your wife, and have eaten from the tree of which I commanded you, saying, 'You shall not eat of it': "Cursed is the ground for your sake; In toil you shall eat of it All the days of your life.

(18) Both thorns and thistles it shall bring forth for you, And you shall eat the herb of the field.

(19) In the sweat of your face you shall eat bread Till you return to the ground, For out of it you were taken; For dust you are, And to dust you shall return."

Introduction

When God had created all things, He saw "that it was very good" (Genesis 1:31). If a good God made a good, perfect world, then how do we explain the presence of evil in it? This is one of the principal questions upon which unbelievers stumble. Did God also create evil? Did He create Satan as he exists today? Why do we have suffering, disease and death? The answer to that question is sin. But where did sin come from? God made us creatures of free will with the right to choose between good and evil. God could have made us robots, programmed to do only good, but He gave us the right to choose to serve or not to serve Him. He wanted us to serve Him completely out of love and devotion and not because we had no choice. If there were no opportunity to do evil, there would be no virtue in doing good.

Eve brought evil and its consequences into the world when she sinned by yielding to Satan's temptation to eat the forbidden fruit and by giving it to Adam, who also yielded (cf. 1 Timothy 2:13-15; James 1:12-16). At no time did she or Adam have to yield. Sin then, as now, was a matter of choice. The regrettable thing is she and Adam chose to believe Satan and not God. Satan accused God of lying, and Eve believed him (Genesis 3:4-5; cf. John 8:44). Satan seduced Eve with the "lust of the eyes, the lust of the flesh, and the pride of life" (Genesis 3:5-6; 1 John 2:15-17). These are the same avenues through which he tempts us today. When sin entered, death was introduced to the world (Romans 5:12). This is the last enemy Jesus Christ will destroy when He returns in the clouds to take the redeemed to heaven (1 Corinthians 15:26; 1 Thessalonians 4:13-18).

The Intimate Relationship Between God and Man Ended

When Adam and Eve consumed the forbidden fruit, their innocence was forever shattered. They realized for the first time they were naked. In the Bible, nudity is associated with three things: innocence, insanity and demonic possession. Once Adam and Eve realized they were naked, they made themselves coverings from leaves. It is not so much that they were ashamed of being naked in the presence of each other, but they realized the shame of nakedness, and they experienced the guilt associated with it. For the first time, they also felt the fear of God. When they heard "the sound of the Lord God walking" in the garden, they hid themselves.

God is pictured as walking in the garden in the cool of the evening. This could be an anthropomorphic expression. There are reasons to believe that it is not, but that it was actually God in human form, a theophany. The word translated "voice" is the Hebrew *qol*. It is translated "sound" in the Revised Standard Version and the New English Bible. The same word is connected with the sound of marching feet in other Old Testament passages (2 Samuel 5:24; 1 Kings 14:6; 2 Kings 6:32). The idea being conveyed is that Adam and Eve heard the footsteps of God walking in the garden. This was apparently not a one-time occurrence but a daily appointment. There had been a intimate relationship between God and mankind before the Fall. This association was broken forever afterwards.

God called out to Adam saying, "Where are you?" (Genesis 3:9). Are we to assume that the omniscient God did not know where Adam and Eve were hiding? The question was not for His benefit but for their benefit; God does not need the information. The series of questions He asked them was to help them understand the depths to which they had fallen by their disobedience. He questions to get us to face facts, to see our sins honestly, and to try to get us to repent of them. This question could also be viewed as an act of grace wherein God gave Adam an opportunity to answer the call voluntarily and come out of hiding and face Him. When Adam came out to face God, he answered that he was naked and therefore was afraid, so he hid himself. After they had consumed the forbidden fruit, the "eyes of them both were opened, and they knew that they were naked" (v. 7). They were ashamed to appear before God in that condition, but they had previously done so many times without any sense of shame. God asked them how they knew they were naked, but He knew the answer to that question too. Then God asked, "Have you eaten from the tree of which I commanded you that you should not eat?" (v. 11).

Adam began a practice that has become an all-too-common excuse – making or playing the blame game. He excused his participation in the sin and first blamed Eve. "The woman … she gave me of the tree, and I ate" (v. 12). Eve did not force him, she did not coerce him and she did not threaten him; all she did was give it to him, and he ate of it. Paul plainly says that while Eve was deceived, "Adam was not deceived" (1 Timothy 2:14). This means he knew exactly what he was doing, and he was not concerned about the consequences.

Ultimately, Adam did not blame only Eve; he blamed God. Look at his statement again: "This woman whom You gave to be with me." In other words, "It's not my fault, God! You are the one who made this woman who caused me to eat the fruit."

The habit of making excuses has become popular. Guilty people today blame their genes, environment, parents, spouses, society, the church and even God – anyone but themselves. Like Adam, they refuse to take personal responsibility for their decisions and actions. Would it have made a difference if Adam had simply said, "It is my fault, God. I did it. I'm responsible. Please, forgive me!"? We will never know, but from what we do know about God's mercy and grace, it certainly could have.

Next, God turned His attentions to Eve, and He asked her, "What is this you have done?' Not to be out done by her husband, or to personally take the blame, she said, 'The serpent deceived me, and I did eat' " (Genesis 3:13). Everything she said was true, but she still was unwilling to acknowledge her guilt. It was the serpent's fault because he had deceived her. Once again, it was ultimately God's fault because He was the One who created the serpent. The serpent did not have anyone else to blame.

The Serpent's Curse (Genesis 3:14-15)

Notice God did not ask the serpent what part he played in all of this. He knew, and God pronounced a curse upon him. There are three parts involved in this curse. First, he would crawl upon his belly and eat dust. There is a possibility that serpents originally walked. Some paleontologists say that certain varieties of snakes appear to have appendages on their skeletons where feet might have been attached. While this is certainly a debatable point, there is the additional fact that the scripture refers to the snake as a "beast," or "wild creature," rather than a "creeping thing," which is the category they were later placed in (1:26, 30; 3:1). God also calls the serpent by the designation of "cattle" (v. 14). Obviously then, this serpent was not like any variety known to us today. Based upon the biblical description, it would have probably resembled one of the larger reptiles, such as alligators or crocodiles.

We must consider who this serpent was. Paul referred to this incident and calls the tempter "the serpent" (2 Corinthians 11:3). In Revelation, John calls Satan "that serpent of old" (12:9; 20:2). Jesus seems to be referring to this incident when He said, "You are of your father the devil … He was a murderer from the beginning, and does not stand in the truth, because there is no truth in him. When he speaks a lie, he speaks of his own resources, for he is a liar, and the father of it" (John 8:44). The devil either disguised himself as a serpent, or he took possession of the serpent and spoke through him. The latter explanation seems to be the correct one, otherwise why was the serpent cursed?

Second, the apparently peaceful coexistence between man and snakes before the Fall was no more. This may help to explain why, in addition to her innocence, Eve was not shocked or afraid when the serpent began to speak to her, and she did not run away. God said to the serpent, "I will put enmity between you and the woman, and between your seed and her Seed" (Genesis 3:15). There is in most people an innate fear of snakes. Why? Only certain species of snakes are poisonous, and some are even helpful in reducing the population of scavengers among smaller animals. Many snakes are also very beautiful creatures. Yet we are generally repulsed by them. People have been taught some phobias but not this one. The only logical explanation is that it goes back to the Fall and the curse God placed upon the serpent.

The third part of the curse upon the serpent is the conflict between its seed and humans. Serpents can harm humans, but humans can dominate and exterminate them. For this reason, serpents would forever be wary of mankind. Experts say that snakes are not naturally aggressive toward humans. They do not attack but simply react to humans out of innate fear. Some snakes, such as the rattler, even give off an audible signal to warn intruders away.

The question arises: "If the devil did it, why was the serpent punished at all?" We may not be able to answer this question satisfactorily. It has been suggested that this was God's way of reminding us of the instrument through which the Fall came as a warning to us about Satan. Some people have said this was a way of saying animals are responsible but not accountable for their actions. In the Law of Moses, God said that when animals harmed humans in any way, they were to be punished (9:5; Exodus 21:28). Other people have suggested this is just God exercising His will. Paul wrote, "Does the potter not have power over the clay, from the same lump to make one vessel for honor and another for dishonor?" (Romans 9:21). However, because the nature of animals was different at that time, it may be that the serpent was culpable in some way.

This second part of God's pronouncement upon the serpent is called the "protevangelium," or the "first announcement of the gospel." It is without a doubt the first of many messianic prophecies. In this statement God referred to the "seed of woman." We know that the seed comes from the man and the egg from the woman. Normally the Bible speaks correctly about "the seed of man" (Genesis 38:9; Leviticus 22:4; Numbers 16:40; Mark 12:20-22; Acts 13:23). As Paul pointed out, God also said "Seed … as of one," and not "seeds, as of many." And he specified this one Seed was Christ (Galatians 3:16). Jesus Christ was the only human born without a human father. The Holy Spirit impregnated the egg in the womb of the virgin Mary with Holy Seed, and the product of that union was both God and man, the Son of God and the Son of Man (Matthew 1:18-25; Luke 1:35-37). Jesus Christ was both fully God and fully man.

When Jesus went to the cross and died, He was "bruised." That is, the blow that was struck by Satan to God's plan of redemption was not a fatal one. He was "wounded for our transgressions," but it did not end His life because He overcame it to live again forever (Isaiah 53:5). Christ's resurrection forever struck a mortal wound to Satan and his designs for this world from which he will never recover. This is the power of the Resurrection in which we also share the victory (1 Corinthians 15:50-57).

God's Curse Upon Eve (Genesis 3:16)

God said to Eve, "I will greatly multiply your sorrow and your conception; in pain shall you bring forth children." From this statement there is the ridiculous notion that childbearing was the curse, but this is not true. God had already blessed the couple to "be fruitful and multiply; fill the earth and subdue it" (1:28). Although we do not read they had any children until after the Fall, this passage indicates that they could have. They lived in a perfect environment before the Fall without any sickness, pain, suffering or death. The curse resulted in the pain experienced during childbirth. The sorrow may be associated with childbearing also, but it could be the sorrow that comes as a result of raising children. Any mother knows what this is like. It is also not true that the sin was the sexual act. God gave sex for pleasure in marriage and for procreation (1 Corinthians 7:1-5, 28, 35-36; Hebrews 13:4).

The unique relationship God had planned for man and woman was also altered forever. A woman's desire "shall be for her husband, and he would rule over her." This is not to be a dictatorial rule. Paul says that a man is to be "the head of his wife" (Ephesians 5:23; cf. 1 Corinthians 11:3). He also says that a wife is to be "subject to her husband" and to "respect them" (Ephesians 5:22, 33; Colossians 3:18). In giving a charge to the husband, He said he is to "love his wife ... as Christ loved the church," and as his "own body" (Ephesians 5:25, 28, 33). This is related to the Fall (1 Timothy 2:11-15).

God's Curse Upon Adam (Genesis 3:17-19)

In listening to Eve, Adam refused to listen to God. God cannot allow such idolatry to go unpunished. If we heed anyone's word and disobey God's Word, then punishment will inevitably follow. In His curse of Adam, God also pronounced a curse upon the ground and all of mankind. First, He said that the ground would bring forth "thorns and thistles." This does not necessarily mean that God invented them to punish man, but it may only mean that before the Fall they were controlled and were in some ways beneficial to mankind. After the Fall, they were allowed to grow unrestrained and to become a hindrance and a nuisance. Today, when ground is neglected, the thorns and thistles take over very quickly. Men now laboriously prepare the ground to produce their food. Although Adam was put in the garden to "tend and to keep it," there must have been little backbreaking work involved (Genesis 2:15). Now there is hard labor and perspiration involved.

Ironically, the same ground out of which man was taken and from which his food is derived will one day claim his mortal remains. Solomon wrote, "the dust shall return to the earth as it was, and the spirit shall return to God who gave it" (Ecclesiastes 12:7). Adam brought death upon all mankind (Romans 5:12-14). Death will one day be no more because the curse will be removed (1 Corinthians 15:25-26, 54-55).

Lessons Learned

1. God made the world good in the beginning. It was corrupted when Adam and Eve sinned. When this happened, they unleashed a series of events that lead mankind ultimately to the grave. Before that, men will know pain and suffering, and they will be acquainted with grief. Their sin was not unavoidable, but it was a matter of choice. The same thing is true today. We have the right to choose to do evil or to do good. God does not condemn us; we condemn ourselves by the choices we make.
2. When God asked Adam where he was, it was not for His benefit. God is omniscient, all-knowing, so He does not need to be told where we are. He asked this question to help Adam understand his situation and the consequences of

his actions. God warns us about the consequences of sin for our benefit. He knows where such actions lead, but He wants us to know it so we can avoid the horrible destination of the wicked.

3. Adam began what has become a national pastime – blaming someone else for our problems. People are no longer willing to take personal responsibility for their sins or failures. It is always easier to blame someone else. "Passing the buck" is a favorite sport for many people. Until a person is ready to assume responsibility for his actions and choices, he is not ready to receive salvation.

Questions

1. Why did God allow Adam and Eve to sin?
2, What avenues of temptation did Satan use on Eve, and how does he use them on us today?
3. What happened initially to Adam and Eve when they ate of the forbidden fruit?
4. How can God's personal presence in the garden be explained?
5. Whom did Adam blame for his sin?
6. Who was the serpent?
7. What are the three parts of the curse upon the serpent?
8. To whom was God referring when He mentioned the Seed of woman?
9. What was Eve's punishment?
10. What was Adam's punishment?

Lesson 3

Renewal

Week of
Dec. 20, 1998

Lesson Text

GENESIS 8:13-22

(13) And it came to pass in the six hundred and first year, in the first month, the first day of the month, that the waters were dried up from the earth; and Noah removed the covering of the ark and looked, and indeed the surface of the ground was dry.

(14) And in the second month, on the 27th day of the month, the earth was dried.

(15) Then God spoke to Noah, saying,

(16) "Go out of the ark, you and your wife, and your sons and your sons' wives with you.

(17) "Bring out with you every living thing of all flesh that is with you: birds and cattle and every creeping thing that creeps on the earth, so that they may abound on the earth, and be fruitful and multiply on the earth."

(18) So Noah went out, and his sons and his wife and his sons' wives with him.

(19) Every animal, every creeping thing, every bird, and whatever creeps on the earth, according to their families, went out of the ark.

(20) Then Noah built an altar to the LORD, and took of every clean animal and of every clean bird, and offered burnt offerings on the altar.

(21) And the LORD smelled a soothing aroma. Then the LORD said in His heart, "I will never again curse the ground for man's sake, although the imagination of man's heart is evil from his youth; nor will I again destroy every living thing as I have done.

(22) "While the earth remains, Seedtime and harvest, Cold and heat, Winter and summer, And day and night Shall not cease."

GENESIS 9:1-7

(1) So God blessed Noah and his sons, and said to them: "Be fruitful and multiply, and fill the earth.

(2) "And the fear of you and the dread of you shall be on every beast of the earth, on every bird of the air, on all that move on the earth, and on all the fish of the sea. They are given into your hand.

(3) "Every moving thing that lives shall be food for you. I have given you all things, even as the green herbs.

(4) "But you shall not eat flesh with its life, that is, its blood.

(5) "Surely for your lifeblood I will demand a reckoning; from the hand of every beast I will require it, and from the hand of man. From the hand of every man's brother I will require the life of man.

(6) "Whoever sheds man's blood, By man his blood shall be shed; For in the image of God He made man.

(7) And as for you, be fruitful and multiply; Bring forth abundantly in the earth And multiply in it."

Introduction

When the population of the earth grew, and the "sons of God" began to intermarry with the sinful element, "the daughters of men," their progeny became exceedingly wicked. They had degenerated into a people whose every thought was evil and whose very existence was to think about more ways to express their sinful desires and attitudes (Romans 1:18-32). The Earth was "corrupt and filled with violence" (Genesis 6:11). God saw that "the wickedness of man was great in the earth," and "He was grieved in His heart" (vv. 5-6). He was sorry He had ever made man. That is why He determined to destroy the Earth and all life on it (v. 7).

As God was contemplating His decision, "Noah found grace in the eyes of the Lord" (v. 8). One person caused God to change His mind about destroying everything He had made. Noah's righteousness stood in stark contrast to the sinfulness of his age. The Hebrew writer says Noah "condemned the world, and became heir of the righteousness which is according to faith" (11:7). God pronounced the sentence of death upon the sinful inhabitants of Earth, so how did Noah condemn the world? He condemned them by living righteously in the midst of their wicked environment. Moses records that he was "a just man and perfect in his generation" (6:9). Noah was not perfect in the sense of absolute sinlessness, but he was so much holier than all of the other people around him that he was, comparatively speaking, perfect in his own generation. In saying he was just, Moses implies that he was observant of all the rules and regulations of God and of society. The word "just" is also a synonym for "righteous."

Noah also condemned the people of the world by preaching to them. Peter calls him "a preacher of righteousness" (2 Peter 2:5). He also tells us that Noah preached during the entire time that He was building the ark (1 Peter 3:20), and he did not make a single convert (Genesis 6:3). How discouraging that must have been. The preacher's job is to sow the seed, and if he faithfully executes that responsibility, God will give the increase (Luke 8:5, 11; 1 Corinthians 3:5-8). Noah was successful in that he saved his family, and that was something to be grateful for.

God Commanded Noah to Build an Ark

To save Noah and his family, God commanded him to build an ark, which was a large boat. The measurements of this boat are given as 300 cubits in length, 50 cubits in width, and 30 cubits in height (Genesis 6:14-16). The average figure for a cubit is 18 inches. If we use this figure, the dimensions of the ark would have been 450 feet long, 75 feet wide, and 45 feet high. It would have contained around 101,250 square feet, which is about the capacity of 500 railroad boxcars. If we take the sheep as an average size animal, it would have taken only 200 boxcars to hold 75,000 of them. Taking into account the eight people aboard and all of the supplies that were needed, only about 60 percent of the total capacity of the ark was used.

The Flood Came

When the ark was completed, on the day that God had specified, Noah and his family entered the ark along with the animals (7:1-3). Once they were safely inside, God shut the door, sealing the inhabitants of the ark inside and keeping the wicked out (v. 16). Once they were inside, "all the fountains of the great deep were broken up, and the windows of heaven were opened" (v. 11). It rained for "forty days and forty nights" (v. 12). Noah and his family remained inside the ark until God permitted them to leave (Genesis 8:15-18).

The Waters of the Flood Dried Up (Genesis 8:13-14)

Noah and his family entered the ark seven days before the Flood began, in accordance with God's command (7:4). This was on the 17th day of the second month. The waters prevailed upon the earth for 150 days (vv. 15-20, 24; 8:3). The Flood ended on the 27th day of the second month one year later.

This was not just a localized flood. The Hebrew word translated "flood" in the Genesis account is used only in reference to the deluge in Noah's time. There are more than 30 expressions in Scripture that indicate it was universal. The Flood covered even the high hills and the mountains under about 15 cubits of water, or about 22 feet. No local flood could have accumulated such a depth and duration of water. Even after the ark came to rest on Mount Ararat, it was another two and one half months before the tops of the mountains could be seen. It took another year before enough land was dry for Noah and his family to leave the ark.

The day after the waters began to recede, the ark came to rest on the peak of Mount Ararat, which is believed to be Mount Massis or Agridagh, which rises some 17,000 feet above sea level. The Ararat mountain range is in modern Turkey. This happened during the seventh month of the Jewish calendar, *Abib*, which is equivalent to April. When the mountaintops became visible (8:5), Noah waited another 40 days and then sent out a raven, which did not return, and then a dove that did (vv. 6-8). The raven is a scavenger and will land anywhere, even upon a dead carcass, but the dove is relatively clean and will not land just anywhere. The text says the "dove found no resting place for the sole of her foot, and she returned into the ark to him" (v. 9). He waited seven more days before sending out another dove, and it also returned holding a freshly picked olive branch in its beak (vv. 10-11). Noah waited yet another seven days and sent out another dove that did not return, proving the waters of the earth had dried up enough so that she could find a permanent habitation. He waited another 29 days and removed the covering from the ark so he could determine for himself if the ground was dry enough. Still, he remained in the ark with his family for another 57 days until God told him they could leave the ark (v. 13).

The text says that "in the second month, on the twenty-seventh day of the month, the earth was dried" (v. 14). As noted earlier, the Flood began on the 17th day of the second month one year previous. This means that Noah and his family were in the ark for 371 days, or for exactly 53 weeks. It was also seven months from the time the ark came to rest on Mount Ararat until they disembarked at God's command.

Noah and His Family Leave The Ark (Genesis 8:15-19)

The first verse of Genesis 8 tells us "God remembered Noah and every living thing, and all the animals that were with him in the ark." This is an anthropomorphic expression because God does not forget. It simply means He remembered where Noah was and how long he had been there. Because of this, He made a strong wind to pass over the earth to begin the drying process. The vaporous canopy that had surrounded the earth and caused it to be watered (1:6-9; 2:5-6) was now gone, and a natural cycle had taken its place. The subterranean waters also ceased to flood the earth and retreated into the caverns beneath the sea.

God told Noah to "Go out of the ark" and to take his family and also the animals with him (8:15-19). The earth had been cleansed and every living thing that was upon it perished, with the exception of the sea creatures and those which were in the ark. God was now ready to repopulate the earth and once more wanted the animals and man to "abound on the earth, and be fruitful and multiply upon the earth" (v. 17; 9:1).

Noah and His Family Begin a New Life (Genesis 8:20-22)

The first thing Noah did after he left the ark was to build an altar so that he could worship God. From the story of Cain and Abel in Genesis 4, we know that sacrifices had already begun to be offered. They were most likely begun by Adam and Eve when they were driven from the garden. It must have been at God's command that they were offered. The Hebrew writer tells us that "by faith Abel offered to God a more excellent sacrifice than Cain" (Hebrews 11:4). Because Paul tells us that "faith comes by hearing … the word of God" (Romans 10:17), at some point He must have specified to them the kind of offering He wanted. Proof of this commandment can be found in the statement that Noah offered the clean animals and birds as a sacrifice (Genesis 8:20). The first mention of clean and unclean animals is in Genesis 7:2. However, these must have been designated by God to be used for sacrifice from the beginning of the practice. This explains why Noah was told to take seven pairs of the clean and only one pair of the unclean. The clean would be used for food for the first time (9:3), and they would also be used for the sacrifices. This would require many more of them than those animals designated unclean. For a more detailed discussion about the varieties of clean and unclean animals, see Leviticus 11.

The text says "And the Lord smelled a soothing aroma" (Genesis 8:21). This is a purely figurative term, meaning only that God approved of Noah's offering. It pleased Him so much that He made a promise never again to curse the ground or destroy mankind or the other living creatures completely. He tells Noah that He will not destroy the earth again with a flood (9:11). It is clear that the next time the Earth will be destroyed by fire (2 Peter 3:9-12).

Have you ever heard the expression that "before the end of time you won't be able to tell one season from another"? This statement has no basis in fact. God declared that with the abrupt changes in climactic conditions after the Flood, there would be clearly defined seasons in evidence. He also asserted that as long as the earth stands these seasons will remain (8:22).

God Established His Covenant with Noah

God promised to establish His covenant, or actually to re-establish His original covenant with mankind, with Noah and his family. This covenant included all life upon the earth. Just as the animals had been included in the judgment upon the earth, they would now share in the provisions of this covenant. The two provisions of the covenant are given in Genesis 9:11. First, He promised never again to destroy all flesh by a flood. Second, He promised not to destroy the earth with a flood. The rainbow was not a part of the covenant, but it was a sign or a symbol of His promise. Some people believe the rainbow existed before this time, but there is no reason to believe this is true. Dr. Henry Morris believes that the atmospheric conditions before the Flood would have made a rainbow impossible. If it had existed before the Flood, what would be the significance of giving it as a symbol afterwards?

Noah entered the ark at the age of 600 (7:6). He lived to be 950 years old, or 350 more years after the Flood. This was longer than any of his ancestors with the exception of his grandfather Methuselah, 969 years, and Jared, 962 years. This means that he would have lived up until the 58th year of Abraham's life.

Lessons Learned

1. Some philosophers and other people believe man is continually getting better. This lesson proves that men without God do not get better. Instead, they get worse. The antediluvians became so sinful that their every thought was wicked. For a clearer picture about men without God, read Romans 1:18-32. These are similar to the conditions that will exist in the last days (2 Timothy 3:1-7). We live in an impersonal world. Often we are made to feel unnecessary. From Noah we learn that one person does matter and can make a difference. God was ready to give up on His divine experiment and forget the whole thing, but Noah restored His faith in mankind. He was so impressed with Noah's life that He decided to give it another try. All of mankind is indebted to Noah for his existence. If Noah could live a godly life in the midst of the wickedness that was all around him, what excuse do we have?
2. Noah preached for 120 years and did not save anyone, anyone, that is, except his family. We should be concerned about reaching as many people as possible with the gospel, just as Noah was faithful to deliver the message God had given to him. However, we must not neglect our family. Salvation should begin at home. We are not responsible if people do not respond to the gospel; we are only responsible for delivering it to them. Remember, the soils in the parable about the sower represent different kinds of hearers. They are responsible for the way they receive the gospel, not the sower.
3. The ark reminds us of the church. There was one door, or means of entrance, into it. Jesus said that He is the only door into the kingdom of God (John 10:7). It is significant that God shut the door. Today He seals those who are His (Ephesians 1:13-14). There was one window for a source of light, just as the Bible is the light for men to see by today (Psalm 119:105; 1 John 1:7). There was only one family saved, and they were inside the ark. God's family today is the church, and only those in His family will be saved (Acts 2:47). Peter tells us that as the waters of the Flood saved Noah and his family, the waters of baptism save the people in the church (1 Peter 3:21). Men say "water does not save you," and there is a sense in which that is true because Jesus is the Savior. But Peter said baptism "saves" us in the same fashion as the floodwaters saved Noah and his family.
4. One lesson that cannot be overlooked is that God is "longsuffering toward us, not willing that any should perish, but that all should come to repentance" (2 Peter 3:9). In the days of Noah, God waited while the ark was being built for 120 years. That is not long on God's time, but on our time it is an extremely long time. This proves once again the patience God has with us. It is not His will that any person be lost (1 Timothy 2:4). However, even God's patience can be exhausted (Genesis 6:3). One day when He can no longer endure the sinfulness of mankind, He will bring an end to this universe.

Questions

1. Who were "the sons of God" and "the daughters of men"?
2. What does the text mean when it says "God repented"?
3. How was Noah a "perfect man"?
4. In what way did Noah condemn the world of his day?
5. What were the dimensions of the ark?
6. How can we prove that the Flood of Noah was not just a localized flood?
7. What was the purpose for Noah sending out the raven and the doves?
8. How long were Noah and his family in the ark, and what does this tell us?
9. What is the significance of the rainbow?
10. How old was Noah when he entered the ark, and how old was he when he died?

Lesson 4

Confusion

Week of
Dec. 27, 1998

Lesson Text

GENESIS 11:1-9

(1) Now the whole earth had one language and one speech.

(2) And it came to pass, as they journeyed from the east, that they found a plain in the land of Shinar, and they dwelt there.

(3) Then they said to one another, "Come, let us make bricks and bake them thoroughly." They had brick for stone, and they had asphalt for mortar.

(4) And they said, "Come, let us build ourselves a city, and a tower whose top is in the heavens; let us make a name for ourselves, lest we be scattered abroad over the face of the whole earth."

(5) But the LORD came down to see the city and the tower which the sons of men had built.

(6) And the LORD said, "Indeed the people are one and they all have one language, and this is what they begin to do; now nothing that they propose to do will be withheld from them.

(7) "Come, let Us go down and there confuse their language, that they may not understand one another's speech."

(8) So the LORD scattered them abroad from there over the face of all the earth, and they ceased building the city.

(9) Therefore its name is called Babel, because there the LORD confused the language of all the earth; and from there the LORD scattered them abroad over the face of all the earth.

Introduction

The question of how men became dispersed upon the earth has long puzzled scientists and theologians alike. Many scientists believe in a great continental divide. They believe that at one time the whole land mass of Earth (Genesis 1:9-10) was connected, and that through a series of turbulent upheavals, such as earthquakes, there was a continental drift. Over time, the earth took its present form, but it is constantly in the process of changing. This view is postulated to explain the dispersion of people across the globe. People of this persuasion who believe in the Bible think this separation came after the division of tongues in Genesis 11. Support for this idea comes from the Hebrew word for "divide" in Genesis 10:5 and 32 in the King James Version.

Other scientists believe that migration took place across land bridges once located at the Bering Strait and the Malaysian Strait. After the Flood, and for centuries to follow, the sea level would have been dramatically lower than it was before because of huge stores of water preserved in ice. People could have also migrated by boat. These ancient people descended from Noah, and they would have inherited knowledge about how to build large ships that could transport men, animals and supplies across oceans of water. None of these views contradict anything taught in Scripture.

While we may not know exactly how people became dispersed on the earth, we do know why. That question is answered in Genesis 11. The division of people was because of God's judgment about sin. Most scholars consulted believe Genesis 10 was recorded after the incident related in chapter 11. It is placed to give us the genealogy of Noah and to explain how the earth became so quickly populated again. The confusion of the tongues came about more than 100 years after the Flood.

Rebellion Against God (Genesis 11:1)

Because the inhabitants of Earth had all emanated from Noah, they were one family and of one language. What language was it? It would be impossible to say for certain, but some people believe it was the Semitic language and some form of Hebrew. The names of people and places in the period before the confusion of tongues all had Hebrew or cognate language meanings. The original language may have been retained by Shem's descendants because it is believed they did not participate in the rebellion at Babel. As this language was passed from generation to generation, there would have been many modifications. Any living language changes over time. For example, the English language has undergone so many changes that it would hardly be recognizable in its original form.

There was certainly nothing wrong with men having a common language. In our modern world, we can see the advantages of a kind of universal language. In China and in Russia many languages are spoken, although most of the people in Russia are taught the Russian language. If you want to see the advantages of a common language, visit India. It has 26 states, and each state has its official language. There are also thousands of dialects. English is spoken by many educated Indians, and Hindi is the most nearly common national language. To function in India, most educated citizens know at least four or five native languages. The problem at Babel was not the common language, it was rebellion. The confusion of tongues was just the way God decided to solve the problem.

Nimrod – The Empire Builder (Genesis 11:2)

Back in Genesis 10:9, we are introduced to the most infamous son of Cush, who was the son of Ham. Perhaps out of bitterness about the Hamite curse (9:25-27), Cush named his youngest son Nimrod, which means "let us rebel." God had said their descendants would be servants to their brethren, but beginning with Nimrod, their attitude was "We'll see about that." Nimrod was called "a mighty hunter" (10:9). What was he a hunter of? He may have gained his prominence by hunting animals, but some people have suggested he was also a hunter of men. The Jerusalem Targum says, "He was powerful in hunting, and in wickedness before the Lord, for he was a hunter of the sons of men, and he said to them, 'Depart from the judgments of the Lord, and adhere to the judgments of Nimrod.' " The Hebrew word for "hunter" can also be translated "tyrant," as it is in many modern translations.

God commanded Noah and his descendants to scatter and multiply on the earth (9:1). Nimrod rebelled against that injunction by creating the first empire or kingdom (10:10-12). Enoch, not to be confused with the righteous son of Jared, was the first to build a city in rebellion to God. Nimrod first settled in the area of Shinar and built cities. He then moved to Assyria and built other cities there. Two of the notable cities he built were Babel, which came to be called Babylon, and Nineveh, which later became the capitol of the Assyrian Empire. It was situated on the upper Tigris River some 200 miles north of Babylon. Some scholars believe that he did not actually build Babel, but that it already existed and he conquered it. Babel originally meant "the gate of the gods," but it came to mean "confusion" after God's judgment there.

Men under Nimrod's leadership moved from the east and settled in Shinar, which is the earlier name of Babylonia. Nimrod apparently wanted the people in cities so they would be easier to control. The events of this chapter must be understood in light of his domination over a large portion of the populated Earth. This is but another indication of his rebellion against God. It can be assumed that Nimrod called his leaders over these cities together, and they jointly made decisions for their people.

The Building of a Tower to Heaven (Genesis 11:3-4)

This was the beginning of brick-making and brick buildings. Before this time, archaeological discoveries have shown that the principal building material was clay bricks that were sun-dried. They were not hardened by baking in a kiln, as was done here. They also used slime or bitumen instead of mortar. This was a tarry mixture found in many pools or asphalt pits in that region. Archaeological digs have uncovered this type of kiln-fired brick and asphalt construction.

The decision to colonize was in rebellion to God's command (v. 4). The people said, "Let us make a name for ourselves, lest we be scattered abroad over the face of the whole Earth." Some people refer to this as the first strong humanist statement. It is an arrogant declaration of rebellion against God. As the first part of the statement indicates, they were apparently motivated by pride.

The purpose of building this tower has been grossly misunderstood. The translation of the King James Version has caused some of the problem. It is not that it is incorrect, but the interpretation some people have given to it is. It reads: "Let us build a tower whose top may reach into heaven." This has been interpreted to mean they wanted to build a tower so they could climb up into heaven where God was, or they thought they might make themselves into gods like Him. The translation, "we will build a tower unto heaven" more accurately conveys the original intent. They did not want to build "a tower into heaven," but they wanted to build "a tower unto heaven." That is, they wanted to build a tower to worship the heavenly bodies: the sun, moon, stars and planets.

This is an apt description of the Babylonian ziggurat, a large pyramid-shaped building. Unlike the Egyptian pyramids, ziggurats were constructed with terraces so they could be climbed like steps. They resembled the South American pyramids. Ziggurats were usually 70 to 160 feet high. Many such structures have been uncovered in that part of the world: at Ezida, Borsippa, and the famous Ziggurat of Sin, the moon-god that was discovered at Ur, Abraham's birthplace. These buildings were places of worship built to honor the deity or deities of the heavens for which the heavenly bodies themselves became a symbol (Romans 1:18-32). Many of the buildings were adorned with drawings of the constellations in the beginning, but eventually birds, beasts and fish were added. Later, idols were introduced into this worship.

These temples may have originally been constructed to worship God, but when the Law was given, He specifically forbade such devotions (Exodus 20:4-6). It is generally conceded that the Babylonians worshiped Jehovah in the beginning, but their worship degenerated into idolatry. Nimrod himself was later deified and became the sun-god Marduk. This may also have been the beginning of the pseudo-science of astrology with its signs of the zodiac. It always was, and still is, superstitious paganism, despite its growing popularity.

These people wanted to build this tower to worship the heavenly bodies and to make a name for themselves. This is what most displeased God. They had defied His command to populate the earth. They had perverted His design of worship given to Adam and handed down through Noah. Their purpose was to exalt themselves and to dethrone God in the hearts and lives of men.

God's Displeasure with Man's Devices (Genesis 11:6-9)

The rebellious people said, "Let us go up," and God said, "Let us go down." This is another figurative expression. God does not need to come down to Earth to investigate the actions of puny mankind. He is omniscient and omnipresent. This language is used only to dramatize God's activity. The situation had advanced to the point that it demanded His immediate attention. It also shows us how small the plans of men are, when they seem so big in their own eyes.

The statement in verse 6 indicates a united front in their rebellion against God. What was the source of their unity? It was their common language. The words, "and this is what they begin to do" (11:6), prove that they had thus far been successful in their building project. If they had completed it, what would they have done next? God had made a covenant not to destroy man completely again, so what could He do? He could block their plans by confusing their language.

Who was God talking to? The same persons He was addressing in Genesis 1 – the two other members of the Godhead. The use of the phrase, "Come let us go down" is seen as a figure of speech that is contrasting the ability of God to fulfill His resolve with that of mankind.

God could and would do whatever He determined to do. Man was and is limited by the will of God in what he may want to accomplish. James warns us against having such a self-reliant attitude (4:13-15).

God confounded their language so they "might not understand one another's speech" (Genesis 11:7). How He did it is not known to us. However, we do know it was not a miracle of the ear, but it was a miracle of the tongue. God plainly said He was going to "confuse their language." The miracle of Pentecost was also not one of the ear but was of the tongue (Acts 2:4, 6-8, 11).

The statement that "they ceased building" (Genesis 11:8) does not preclude any future construction on that site. The city was completed and was named Babylon after the original Babel. This name is forever associated with wickedness and rebellion (Daniel 1-6; Revelation 17-19). Scripture plainly says, "The Lord scattered them abroad over the face of the Earth" (Genesis 11:9). It may be that the confusion of tongues was sufficient enough to accomplish that task, or He may have used some other method. In any case, it was the work of God that dispersed people on the earth, not the work of men.

Lessons Learned

1. As noted in the lesson, a common language is of benefit today in commerce and in human relationships. However, if because of their common language men become rebellious against God, then it is a detriment. Language was not the prob-

lem. They had a problem of the heart. They wanted to dethrone God and enthrone themselves. The solution God employed was the most rapid and successful one He could have employed. When the builders could no longer communicate, their project stopped. Just imagine the scene of people working together, and then suddenly they can no longer understand one another. At first astonishment would be evidenced, then suspicion about each other because they could no longer know what the other person was thinking or planning. The natural thing would then be to group yourselves together with other people who you could understand and go off to settle in another place.

2. Nimrod was the first person to establish a kingdom, and it was in direct rebellion to God's commandment to populate the whole Earth. We cannot know for sure if this was because of the curse placed upon his family but that seems to be the reasonable conclusion. This statement made by Noah may not have been as much a curse as it was a prediction of what would happen to Ham's descendants. At any rate, it seems they were determined to try to prevent that prediction from happening. The extent of Nimrod's rebellion covers the entire Old Testament period. One of the cities he built, Nineveh, was the capitol of the Assyrians, who carried away the Northern Kingdom into captivity, never to be restored. The other prominent city, Babylon, became the capitol of the Babylonian Empire under Nebuchadnezzar. He destroyed Jerusalem and its temple and carried away most of the people of the Southern Kingdom into captivity. Our sins can have far-reaching consequences.
3. The corrupted form of worship developed in Babylon is still with us today. It is seen in the New Age religions, in Eastern mysticism and in pure superstition, such as worshiping pyramids and practicing astrology. Astrology and its practioners are condemned throughout the Old Testament. It is put in the same category with witchcraft and sorcery. Every Christian should avoid such paganism (Revelation 21:8; 22:15).

Questions

1. What are some of the different views about the migration of people on the earth?
2. Who or what was actually responsible for this migration and why?
3. What was the main problem with the people at Babel?
4. What are some of the interpretations of the word "hunter" with reference to Nimrod?
5. What was Nimrod's real sin?
6. Why did the people want to build this tower?
7. What is a ziggurat?
8. Who was Marduk?
9. How do you explain God's statement: "Let us go down?"
10. What was God's intent when He confounded the tongues, and how was it accomplished?

Lesson 5

Peace

Week of
Jan. 3, 1999

Lesson Text

GENESIS 13:1-18

(1) Then Abram went up from Egypt, he and his wife and all that he had, and Lot with him, to the South.

(2) Abram was very rich in livestock, in silver, and in gold.

(3) And he went on his journey from the South as far as Bethel, to the place where his tent had been at the beginning, between Bethel and Ai,

(4) to the place of the altar which he had made there at first. And there Abram called on the name of the LORD.

(5) Lot also, who went with Abram, had flocks and herds and tents.

(6) Now the land was not able to support them, that they might dwell together, for their possessions were so great that they could not dwell together.

(7) And there was strife between the herdsmen of Abram's livestock and the herdsmen of Lot's livestock. The Canaanites and the Perizzites then dwelt in the land.

(8) So Abram said to Lot, "Please let there be no strife between you and me, and between my herdsmen and your herdsmen; for we are brethren.

(9) "Is not the whole land before you? Please separate from me. If you take the left, then I will go to the right; or, if you go to the right, then I will go to the left."

(10) And Lot lifted his eyes and saw all the plain of Jordan, that it was well watered everywhere (before the LORD destroyed Sodom and Gomorrah) like the garden of the LORD, like the land of Egypt as you go toward Zoar.

(11) Then Lot chose for himself all the plain of Jordan, and Lot journeyed east. And they separated from each other.

(12) Abram dwelt in the land of Canaan, and Lot dwelt in the cities of the plain and pitched his tent even as far as Sodom.

(13) But the men of Sodom were exceedingly wicked and sinful against the LORD.

(14) And the LORD said to Abram, after Lot had separated from him: "Lift your eyes now and look from the place where you are--northward, southward, eastward, and westward;

(15) "for all the land which you see I give to you and your descendants forever.

(16) "And I will make your descendants as the dust of the earth; so that if a man could number the dust of the earth, then your descendants also could be numbered.

(17) "Arise, walk in the land through its length and its width, for I give it to you."

(18) Then Abram moved his tent, and went and dwelt by the terebinth trees of Mamre, which are in Hebron, and built an altar there to the LORD.

Introduction

In Genesis 11 one of God greatest servants, the man who came to be known as Abraham, is introduced. He was called "the friend of God" (2 Chronicles 20:7; Isaiah 41:8; James 2:23). This was because of his intimate relationship with Jehovah God. He has also been called the "father of the faithful" (Galatians 3:7). Although he was not always a giant of the faith, he reached a point where God pronounced him righteous solely on the basis of his faith (Genesis 15:6; Romans 4:3, 9; Galatians 3:6). His faith was not just verbalized or mere "heartfelt religion," that is "better felt than told," but it was a living and active faith (Hebrews 11:8-10, 17-19; James 2:21-23).

Terah begat Abram, Nahor and Haran when he was more than 70 years of age (Genesis 11:26). Abram was in all probability not the oldest son. Terah was 205 years old when he died, and Abram was 75 when he left Haran. This would mean that Terah was 130 years old when Abram was born. Abram was mentioned first only because he was the prominent son. Haran was most likely the oldest son, and before Abram and Nahor married, he had moved away to a city that came to bear his name. Nahor married one of Haran's daughters, his own niece, which was permissible under the laws of that day. Abram married a half sister, Sarai, who was the daughter of Terah, but they had different mothers. This would indicate that Terah might have followed the practice of polygamy, which had begun with Lamech (4:19). Of course, his first wife could have already been dead when he married again, but we do not know for certain.

The Home Abram Left Behind

Abram grew up in the Ur of the Chaldees, which was a bustling commercial center located in Mesopotamia. It was bordered by the Persian Gulf on one side and by the Euphrates River on the other. From the archaeological discoveries in the area we know that the city was only four square miles, but it had a population estimated at 300,000. These archaeological finds show that the people of this region were highly civilized and educated. They were proficient in astronomy, math, engraving and weaving. They preserved their ideas in writing on clay tablets.

Ur was also known as a center of idolatry. A large ziggurat in the center of the city was dedicated to Nanna, the moon-god. Joshua plainly says that Terah and his sons had all been idolaters at one time in their lives (Joshua 24:2). It is possible they worshiped Jehovah, too, but they were polytheistic and not monotheistic. We do not know when Abram ceased being an idolater, but it is certain that he had stopped the practice long before God called him. The fact that God called a man from this background is an example of His mercy and grace, and it proves His desire for all sinners to know the joy of salvation.

Although we are not told in Genesis 11 that God called Abram while he lived in Ur, this information is given to us later (Genesis 15:7; Acts 7:2-5). Also, it would appear that it was not Abram's call that precipitated the move to Haran, but it was Terah who initiated it (Genesis 11:31). The reason for the move was because of the untimely death of Haran. Terah took his family there to bury his son and possibly to settle his affairs. Terah's health may not have been good when the move was made because they remained in Haran for 15 more years until his death.

God called Abram for the second time in Haran (12:1). This time He asked two things of him, and in return, He made two promises to him. First, God told Abram to get out of his country, from his kindred and from his father's house. Second, He told him to go to a land that God would show him. In return for his obedience, God promised Abram that He would make him a great nation, bless him and make his name great, and he would be a blessing (Genesis 12:2). Abram obeyed God and left Haran for Canaan at the age of 75.

A Journey of Faith

Ur was 600 miles from Haran. The distance from Haran to Canaan is about 400 miles. This means Abram moved more than 1,000 miles at God's direction, and he did not know where he was going. When he left Haran he took his wife, his nephew Lot and his family, his servants and all of his substance, which could have been considerable. Later, we learn that he was able to amass 318 fighting men from among his household. Moving this large group of people, flocks, herds, possessions and supplies was a mammoth task.

Abram was not in Canaan long until God appeared to him again (Genesis 12:7). God had walked with Adam, Enoch and Noah, and now He appeared to Abram. God appeared to him many times after this in a phenomenon known as theophany, or "God in human form." On this occasion, God promised Abram that his seed would inherit this land as a gift. The Hebrew writer emphasized that he never lived to see the fulfillment of that promise, but he trusted God to keep His word to him (Hebrews 11:8-16). The first thing Abram did after God appeared to him was to build an altar and to worship God out of a thankful heart.

The House of God

When Abram settled near Bethel, he built another altar (Genesis 12:8). Near this site was where Jacob had his vision and gave it the name Bethel, which means "the house of God." Before this, it had been called Luz by the Canaanites (28:19). In the early phase of the judges, the tabernacle was also situated here (Judges 20:18-28; 21:2-4). It had been one of the centers of worship established by Samuel (1 Samuel 7:16). Regrettably, Bethel became one of the two centers of idolatrous worship in the Northern Kingdom under Jeroboam I (1 Kings 12:26-33; 2 Chronicles 13:8-9). The other location was at Dan in the northern part of the kingdom.

Abram and Lot (Genesis 13:1-4)

Abram had disobeyed God by going into Egypt, but still God watched over him. Despite Abram's disobedience and his dishonesty with Pharaoh, God protected him and Sarai. Abram repented and went back to where God had told him He would bless him. When Haran and Terah died, Abram took Haran's son Lot with him to Canaan. Lot also made the journey with him to Egypt, and Abram treated Lot like a son.

Abram was very wealthy (v. 2). It would be unreasonable to assume that he was so only because of the gifts that were bestowed upon him in Egypt. He was already rich before that time, and God blessed him even more in Egypt. He had left Haran with a sizable company and great possessions. However, he was even wealthier now.

Abram felt a compulsion to go to the place where he had erected an altar to God near Bethel. There, he "called upon the name of the Lord" (vv. 3-4). This expression means only the "paying of religious devotion." There would be no reason to mention the altar here except to imply that Abram offered sacrifices there. This phrase is used numerous times in Scripture, and every time it means more than just calling out to God (Acts 22:16; Romans 10:13-17). Some people have suggested that at this time Abram felt the need to thank God for his safe return and to express sorrow for his sins committed in Egypt and ask for forgiveness. While that could be the case, it seems reasonable that he was renewing the intimate relationship he had with God and that this practice continued throughout the rest of his life.

A Problem of Prosperity (Genesis 13:5-7)

By remaining with Abram, Lot also became prosperous (Genesis 13:5). The problem that developed between Lot and his uncle was because of their prosperity. The land where they located at this time could not support both of them. "Their possessions were so great that they could not dwell together" (v. 6). We also know from stories about Isaac and Jacob that water was scarce in that region. It would have been difficult enough to find adequate water supplies, but to find enough for such large flocks and herds was impossible.

In addition to these problems, strife developed between the herdsman of Abram and Lot. This may have been about the short supplies of water and grazing land. Moses also mentioned the fact that the Canaanites and Perizzites dwelled in the land. The Canaanites lived mainly in walled cities. The Perizzites were a nomadic people much like Abram and Lot. The connection between these two events is that if these people saw the friction between Abram and Lot's herdsman, they may have taken advantage of the situation and fought against them and taken their wealth for themselves.

Abram, a Man of Peace (Genesis 13:7-9)

Abram determined to be a peacemaker and not a troublemaker. He did not want strife between himself and Lot. They were brethren by blood (v. 8), but Lot was more than that to Abram. Because Abram had no son, Lot had been like a son to him. In his statement to Lot, Abram's character is revealed in that he mentioned himself first, as if to take the blame for much of the problem.

Abram was the one who God had chosen to be the head of the redemptive nation, not Lot. He was the one to whom God promised the land, and not Lot. He had every right to demand that Lot take his family and belongings and find somewhere else to live. Instead, he conceded to Lot and gave him the right to choose where he would dwell. Abram said, "Is not the whole land before you? Please, separate from me" (v. 9). In other words, "You choose first, and which ever direction you decide to go in, I will go in the opposite direction." Although they parted, Abram still loved Lot and his family. Genesis 14 tells the story about how he rescued them from the five kings from Mesopotamia. Genesis 18 tells the story about Abram pleading with God to spare Sodom and Gomorrah, mainly because Lot lived there.

A Bad Choice Made Out of a Bad Motive (Genesis 13:10-13)

Once again from this incident, we see the progression of sin through the avenues of the "lust of the eyes, the lust of the flesh and the pride of life" (1 John 2:16). Lot was moved by all three of these to choose what he thought was the most fertile land available. We also see in this account the process that led Lot to become trapped in a web of sin. First, he saw the lush green grass around Sodom. Second, he moved his tents towards Sodom. Third, he moved into Sodom (Genesis 14:12). Fourth, he became one of the city leaders (19:1). Fifth, he acknowledged the men of Sodom as brothers (v. 7). Sixth, he offered his virgin daughters to the wicked men of Sodom in an effort to satiate their sexual appetite (v. 8). Seventh, when the angels told him it was time to leave Sodom, "he lingered" until it was almost too late (v. 16).

Lot's choice was made out of greed. He wanted the best for himself regardless of the kindness shown to him by his uncle. Greed can bring out the worst in the best of men. He did not consider the long-range consequences of this choice. His covetous decision led him to lose everything in his life that really mattered.

God Renews His Promise to Abram (Genesis 13:14-18)

After Lot had departed for the plains of Sodom, Abram met with God again. Although Lot had been allowed to choose where he wanted to live, the land belonged to Abram and to his descendants. Lot received a parcel of land in a place that was not really his, and he finally lost it (v. 11). Abram was given the entire land as an inheritance from God. Although he never did own the land as such, it was his by promise so that while he lived it belonged to him.

God said that he would give this land to Abram and to his descendants forever (v. 15). This has often been taken to mean that the Israelites would always own this land. That is not the case. God gave them the land just as He had promised to Abram, but it was conditioned upon their continued faithfulness. They did not remain faithful although God was long-suffering with them for many centuries. He then brought final judgment upon them in A.D. 70 after the promised Seed, Jesus Christ, had come. All of God's promises to Abram were fulfilled. There remains nothing else for the Jews except for the blessings they can find in Christ. The fact that the Jews now control a portion of the old kingdom of Israel in no way nullifies the promise God made that He would scatter them to the four winds and that they would never again become a great nation. Jews now live in most of the nations of the world. Although Israel was given territory in Palestine in 1948 and formed the State of Israel, a person would hardly call that small parcel of land a great nation. They live under the constant threat of annihilation by their Arab neighbors.

Lessons Learned

1. The fact that God chose Abraham from an idolatrous background is a testimony to His mercy and grace. Although we can be certain God did not call Him while he was an idolater, it is still remarkable that he was chosen as the person through whom the Savior of the world would come. Why did He choose such a person? The answer is found in the story of God's visit to Abraham before the destruction of the cities of the plains. God said "I know him" (Genesis 18:19 KJV). God knows not only what we are but also what we have the potential to become. Eventually, He came to see Abraham as a close, intimate friend. Not too many people in Scripture ever had that designation. Our background does not determine our outcome. Neither our environment nor our heredity determine what we can be with God's help.
2. Abraham was not always faithful. He made many mistakes on his spiritual journey, but he was able to learn from them and to rise above them. Abraham persevered and did not give up. When he realized he had made a mistake, he repented and sought God's forgiveness. When we turn to God in humble and sincere repentance, He wipes the slate clean (1 John 1:7-10). We can begin anew, just as Abraham did when he returned to Canaan from Egypt.
3. How can such a sacred place have such a sad end? Bethel was the "house of God," and it became the home of idols. The names of Abraham, Jacob and

Samuel are all associated with this place. How can a once-strong congregation of the Lord's church become digressive? How can people who were once so devoted to the Lord's way be so easily led astray by wolves in sheep's clothing? We once thought we did not need to dwell on the basics, that everyone had heard them many times. Now we have a generation of young people that know little or nothing about our heritage or what we stand for. If we fail to indoctrinate even one generation, apostasy is only a generation away.

4. A choice made in a moment of greed is never a good one. How many people have been taken in by get-rich-quick schemes, lotteries and gambling? No wonder Paul said that "the love of money is the root of all kinds of evil" (1 Timothy 6:10). Lot chose Sodom out of self-serving greed. He did not consider Abraham, his wife, his children or even his future. He moved his family into an ungodly environment that resulted in his losing his home, his wife, and essentially all of his children. Some died in the fire, and two were lost to immoral conduct, of which he was a part. He paid a high price for high living, and he ended up on the low end of life.

Questions

1. Why was Abraham called "the father of the faithful"?
2. Whom did Nahor marry, and whom did Abraham marry?
3. Who was the first polygamist?
4. When and where did God first call Abraham, and when and where did He call him the second time?
5. What did God ask of Abraham in Haran, and what did He promise in return?
6. What was one of the first things Abraham did when he came into Canaan?
7. What does Bethel mean, and what important events happened there?
8. What does "calling on the name of the Lord" mean?
9. What motivated Lot to choose the plains of Sodom?
10. Why did the Israelites lose the Land of Promise?

Lesson 6

Destruction

Week of Jan. 10, 1999

Lesson Text

GENESIS 19:15-29

(15) When the morning dawned, the angels urged Lot to hurry, saying, "Arise, take your wife and your two daughters who are here, lest you be consumed in the punishment of the city."

(16) And while he lingered, the men took hold of his hand, his wife's hand, and the hands of his two daughters, the LORD being merciful to him, and they brought him out and set him outside the city.

(17) So it came to pass, when they had brought them outside, that he said, "Escape for your life! Do not look behind you nor stay anywhere in the plain. Escape to the mountains, lest you be destroyed."

(18) Then Lot said to them, "Please, no, my lords!

(19) "Indeed now, your servant has found favor in your sight, and you have increased your mercy which you have shown me by saving my life; but I cannot escape to the mountains, lest some evil overtake me and I die.

(20) "See now, this city is near enough to flee to, and it is a little one; please let me escape there (is it not a little one?) and my soul shall live."

(21) And he said to him, "See, I have favored you concerning this thing also, in that I will not overthrow this city for which you have spoken.

(22) "Hurry, escape there. For I cannot do anything until you arrive there." Therefore the name of the city was called Zoar.

(23) The sun had risen upon the earth when Lot entered Zoar.

(24) Then the LORD rained brimstone and fire on Sodom and Gomorrah, from the LORD out of the heavens.

(25) So He overthrew those cities, all the plain, all the inhabitants of the cities, and what grew on the ground.

(26) But his wife looked back behind him, and she became a pillar of salt.

(27) And Abraham went early in the morning to the place where he had stood before the LORD.

(28) Then he looked toward Sodom and Gomorrah, and toward all the land of the plain; and he saw, and behold, the smoke of the land which went up like the smoke of a furnace.

(29) And it came to pass, when God destroyed the cities of the plain, that God remembered Abraham, and sent Lot out of the midst of the overthrow, when He overthrew the cities in which Lot had dwelt.

Introduction

The two angels who had been with the Lord on His visit to Abraham at Mamre now came to the second part of their mission. "The two angels came to Sodom" (Genesis 19:1). When they had arrived at Abraham's tent it was day (18:1), but when they arrived at Sodom it was evening (19:1). It was more than 40 miles from Mamre to Sodom. If these men had traveled that distance by foot it would have been a remarkable feat indeed. Even if they had done so over a two-day period, which would have been required, they would have had to travel over some of the hottest territory and the roughest terrain in the world. However, these were not mere men but angels, and they could have made the journey on the same day and in a very short time.

Lot – A Father of a Sinful City

When they arrived, Lot was sitting at the gate. He was now an influential member of the community. The city gate was the place were business was transacted, legal matters were adjudicated and political decisions were made. Lot was likely one of the city leaders, such as a magistrate or city councilman. How could this man find himself among such company? He is called a righteous man by Peter (2 Peter 2:6-8). That means that he was righteous when compared to the people around him. He certainly did not possess the character or the goodness of Abraham.

As the angels approached, Lot rose from his place and met them. He greeted them by bowing with his face to the ground. This was not done to show homage or obedience, because as yet Lot did not know who these men were. Probably partly out of hospitality and partly out of fear of what would happen, Lot invited the men to come to his house. Notice how specific he was in his invitation. He did not know why they were there or how long they intended to stay, but by now he knew Sodom and its citizens. He knew that it would not be safe for strangers to remain there long, so he urged them to stay the night with him and then to leave early in the morning (Genesis 19:2). Perhaps Lot became a city father so that he could be in a position to prevent visitors from being abused by Sodom's perverted citizens. They had intended to spend the night on the street in order to observe firsthand the wickedness of the people, but upon Lot's insistence, they accepted his invitation.

The Sin of Sodom

It was not long until they knew firsthand how wicked this city had become. Even before they could retire for the night, the wicked men, "old and young," of Sodom encircled Lot's house demanding that he send them out so they could "know them carnally" (Genesis 19:4-5) The New English Bible translates it, "Bring them out so that we may have intercourse with them." Sodom and Gomorrah and the three other surrounding cities of the plains had given themselves over to immorality and perversion. Homosexuality was rampant in that time (Romans 1:26-27; Jude 7). It was so prevalent in Sodom that the term "sodomy" has come down to us as a synonym for homosexuality.

Homosexuality is still an abomination to God. Paul says that the Law was given for such lawless persons as "immoral men, for sodomites, for kidnappers, for liars, for perjurers, and if there is any other that is contrary to sound doctrine" (1 Timothy 1:10). In his letter to the Corinthians he wrote, "Do you not know that the unrighteous will not inherit the kingdom of God. Do not be deceived. Neither fornicators, nor idolaters, nor adulterers, nor homosexual, nor sodomites … will inherit the kingdom of God" (1 Corinthians 6:9-10).

As apparent as the sin of homosexuality was in Sodom, it was not the only sin they were guilty of. They were intolerant towards the poor, widows and orphans (Isaiah 1:10-17; 3:9). They were guilty of adultery, lying, condoning evil and encouraging wickedness (Jeremiah 23:14; cf. Romans 1:32). They were also guilty of pride, gluttony, idleness and neglect of the less fortunate. No wonder God said "Their sin is very grave" (Genesis 18:20). God destroyed them as an example to wicked people for all time that they might know the doom of those who rebel against God and His way.

One thing you can say about Lot; he was not a coward. He would not allow a guest in his house to be abused. He went out to the mob, putting his life in jeopardy, and shut the door behind him. Archaeological discoveries have located many houses in that part of the world where the large, heavy doors could not be opened from the outside. Lot attempted to dissuade the men of Sodom from their intended purpose. First, he tried to form a commonality with them by calling them "brethren." He quickly found out how they really felt about him. He was a stranger in their midst. Second, he offered them his virgin daughters so they could have sexual relations with them, but they refused. When the men threatened to harm Lot and attempted to break down the door of his house, the angels reached out and pulled him inside. They then blinded the men of Sodom so they could no longer find the door and grew weary.

The Angels Deliver a Message of Doom (Genesis 19:15-17)

The angels revealed their true identity to Lot and asked him if he had other family in the city. They informed him why they had come and that the city would soon be destroyed. They gave him time to warn his married daughters and their families. Lot tried to encourage his sons-in-law to leave with him, but they thought he was "joking" (v. 14). We can imagine how foolish this must have sounded to such unreligious people. They had no knowledge of God and no fear of His power. The next morning the angels urged Lot to leave with his wife and two unmarried daughters but "he lingered" (v. 16). They had to remove Lot forcibly, his wife and their daughters from the city and take them outside to safety.

The angels then gave them specific instructions. "Escape for your life! Do not look behind you – do not stay anywhere in the plain. Escape to the mountains, lest you be destroyed" (v. 17). Lot lingered until it was almost too late to save his life and then he argued with the angels about fleeing to the mountains. He said he was fearful for his life if he went to the mountains and asked them to allow him to go to Bela, or Zoar, which he said was one of the smaller cities (vv. 19-22). There were two other cities, Admah and Zebolim, which were also destroyed (14:8; 19:25). It is believed that these cities were located at the southern end of the Dead Sea. This area is now under water, but archaeologists have discovered five cites in this area. It is in a valley suggested by the statement "the vale of Sidim." This area is very mountainous, and there are many caves located nearby.

The destruction God rained down upon these four cities was so complete that nothing and no one survived. The brimstone and fire came down from the Lord out of the heavens. The entire process could have been the result of a combined series of earthquakes, volcanic eruptions and explosions. Geologists have found that this area is volcanic in nature and is located upon a fault that extends into Africa. A volcanic explosion in Indonesia in the late 1800s took 36,000 lives. Scientists say it had the force of 30 hydrogen bombs. The eruption of Mount Saint Helens was the largest one in North America in years. According to authorities, it was equal to 500 blasts the size of the bomb dropped on Japan at the end of World War II.

Remember Lot's Wife (Genesis 19:26)

Jesus gave an ominous warning in connection with the destruction of Jerusalem by urging the people to "Remember Lot's wife" (Luke 17:32). Lot, his wife and their two daughters had been warned not to look back. It would appear that Lot's wife was lagging behind. This may have been out of grief for having to leave her home and family. She had children there, possibly even grandchildren, and what about all those mementos that she did not have time to carry with her?

Whatever her reasons, she disobeyed and looked back towards the city. The text suggests it was a long, lingering look. The words, "she became a pillar of salt," are inconclusive as to the time lapse involved. It might have happened instantaneously as a result of divine judgment upon her for disobeying. It could also have been, as some people have suggested, that she was instantly covered with volcanic ash, and over time this formation became covered with salt. Salt deposits and many unusual rock formations are very common in this area. It is safe to say that none of them can be accurately identified as Lot's wife, but we do not deny the historicity of this event. Jesus gave evidence about its authenticity by using it as warning to the people of Jerusalem, but also to us, lest we look back toward a sinful world.

The Scene of Destruction (Genesis 19:27-29)

When Abraham arose early the next morning, he had to see for himself if God had destroyed the cities of the plain. When he looked in the direction of those former fertile fields of Sodom and Gomorrah, all he could see was one huge cloud of billowing smoke rising toward heaven. To him it resembled the smoke from a fiery furnace.

Abraham had asked God not to destroy the righteous with the wicked. Only 10 righteous people could have saved the city of Sodom from destruction. Only three people had survived: Lot and his two daughters. God allowed them to escape because of His feelings for Abraham.

The Aftermath of Sodom (Genesis 19:30-36)

It is ironic that Lot begged the angels to allow him to live in Zoar because he was fearful of living in the mountains. He fled Zoar out of fear and ran to the mountains and dwelt in caves. This once mighty man had fallen from a position of wealth and influence to become a homeless cave dweller. He had little in terms of material things, and all the family he had left was his two daughters.

In their desperate act we see how much these girls had been influenced by their life in Sodom. Fearful that their father would not leave any seed now that their mother was dead, they conspired together to get him drunk and commit incest with him. The text is clear that he was not a willing participant to this transaction because "he knew not when they lay down, or when they rose up" (vv. 33, 35). Both daughters conceived and produced sons whose names were Moab and Ammon. They became the heads of two tribes of people, the Moabites and the Ammonites, who were bitter enemies of the Israelites, and they caused problems for them throughout most of their history in Palestine.

Lessons Learned

1. Lot's downfall began when he looked towards Sodom. He lusted for the fertile plains on which he could graze his large flocks and herds, and he moved into

the neighborhood. He moved into the city, and finally Sodom moved into him. How could he not have known about the sinfulness of this place? It did not become that way overnight, and there had to be signs and warnings. He did not see them because he chose not to look. That failure cost him dearly.

2. Homosexuality is being heavily promoted today by many people. Even some religious people have joined the bandwagon. It does not matter how accepted this alternative lifestyle becomes; it is still a sin. Homosexuals are made, not born. It is a sexual perversion that is against nature. Those people who practice it will not enter heaven. For centuries it has been a symbol of a degenerate society. Homosexuality can be stopped just as any sin can (1 Corinthians 6:11). Every person has to control his or her sexual appetites. If homosexuality can be justified, so can any sexual deviancy.
3. Lot's lingering almost cost him his life. It may have contributed to his wife's death. But he lingered long before this incident. He should have left the city years before. He might be excused for moving into the city by saying he did not really know what these people were like, but after living there for a long time he knew, and he still remained there.
4. Besides the loss of Lot's wife and other family members, perhaps the saddest part of this story is what happened with his two unmarried daughters. They were either children when he moved them into Sodom, or perhaps they had not been born yet. In either case, they had been infected with the disease of sin that was all over Sodom. Otherwise how could they think what they did with their father was acceptable? To his credit, they had to get him drunk because they apparently knew he would not agree to their sinful proposal. People often move their families into ungodly places without any thought to their spiritual welfare. Money is not everything. If you lose your soul, you have lost it all.

Questions

1. What makes scholars believe Lot was one of the city officials?
2. Why did Lot urge the angels to leave the city early in the morning?
3. What were some of the other sins of Sodom?
4. How did Lot show courage, and how did he show cowardice?
5. Why would Lot's sons-in-law not listen to him?
6. Where is it believed that Sodom and Gomorrah are located?
7. How were the cities destroyed?
8. In what context did Jesus use the warning about Lot's wife?
9. Why do we know the incident about Lot's wife is an historical one?
10. What evidence of Sodom's influence upon Lot's daughters do we have?

Lesson 7

Rivalry

Week of
Jan. 17, 1999

Lesson Text

GENESIS 25:19-34

(19) This is the genealogy of Isaac, Abraham's son. Abraham begot Isaac.

(20) Isaac was forty years old when he took Rebekah as wife, the daughter of Bethuel the Syrian of Padan Aram, the sister of Laban the Syrian.

(21) Now Isaac pleaded with the LORD for his wife, because she was barren; and the LORD granted his plea, and Rebekah his wife conceived.

(22) But the children struggled together within her; and she said, "If all is well, why am I like this?" So she went to inquire of the LORD.

(23) And the LORD said to her: "Two nations are in your womb, Two peoples shall be separated from your body; One people shall be stronger than the other, And the older shall serve the younger."

(24) So when her days were fulfilled for her to give birth, indeed there were twins in her womb.

(25) And the first came out red. He was like a hairy garment all over; so they called his name Esau.

(26) Afterward his brother came out, and his hand took hold of Esau's heel; so his name was called Jacob. Isaac was sixty years old when she bore them.

(27) So the boys grew. And Esau was a skillful hunter, a man of the field; but Jacob was a mild man, dwelling in tents.

(28) And Isaac loved Esau because he ate of his game, but Rebekah loved Jacob.

(29) Now Jacob cooked a stew; and Esau came in from the field, and he was weary.

(30) And Esau said to Jacob, "Please feed me with that same red stew, for I am weary." Therefore his name was called Edom.

(31) But Jacob said, "Sell me your birthright as of this day."

(32) And Esau said, "Look, I am about to die; so what is this birthright to me?"

(33) Then Jacob said, "Swear to me as of this day." So he swore to him, and sold his birthright to Jacob.

(34) And Jacob gave Esau bread and stew of lentils; then he ate and drank, arose, and went his way. Thus Esau despised his birthright.

Introduction

In Genesis 23 Moses records the death of Sarah. She was 127 when she died (vv. 1-2). Abraham mourned and wept for his wife, apparently for a number of years. Later Abraham took another wife named Keturah. She is called a concubine in Genesis 25:6 and in 1 Chronicles 1:32 probably because she was never given the status of a true wife as Sarah was. Abraham had a son, Isaac, in his old age with Sarah, and he fathered six other sons by Keturah. It would be difficult to trace the lineage of most of these sons. Jokshan is identified mostly with his sons, Sheba and Dedan, whose names appear frequently in Scripture. Midian was the father of the Midianites, who on various occasions aligned themselves with the Ishmaelites, Moabites and the Amalekites against Israel (Genesis 37:25-36; Numbers 25:1, 6-15; Judges 6:3). The answer as to why may be found in Genesis 25.

Abraham's Gifts to His Sons (Genesis 25:5-6)

Isaac was Abraham's only son by Sarah and the son of promise. When He was preparing to die, Abraham gave the bulk of his fortune to Isaac, and he only gave "gifts" to his other sons (v. 6). If it did not generate bitterness on the part of the sons themselves, it certainly did on the part of the grandsons and their posterity. There was, and still is, conflict between them. We should not accuse Abraham of cruelty to these other sons. According to the laws of that day, they were not owed any inheritance. What he gave them, and it surely was not a meager offering, was a gift out of the goodness of his heart. He gave it to them while he was still living.

Why did he send them away? The only answer is that he was endeavoring to maintain the pure descendants of his son Isaac. This proves he took God's promises for Isaac's lineage very seriously. A sad fact of history is that what he tried to accomplish was undone later when the Israelites failed to carry out God's command to rid the Promised Land of all of the heathens. Many of them eventually intermarried with the heathens and corrupted the worship of God.

The Death of the Patriarch (Genesis 25:7-10)

Abraham lived to be 175 years old. The text says that "he was an old man and full of years" (v. 8). Two statements here illustrate the eternal quality of life. First, "he gave up the ghost," or his spirit. This means his soul separated from his physical body (Ecclesiastes 12:7; James 2:26). Second, he "was gathered to his people" (Genesis 25:8 KJV). In the cave of Machpelah, where his body was buried, only Sarah was buried there at this time. Therefore, being "gathered to his people" meant something more than simply being buried. It implies that he went to where the souls of his people were (Luke 16:19- 31). The soul of man never dies.

There is a touching scene connected with Abraham's death. It would be so even if Isaac were the only son present, but another son is also there, Ishmael. Because Ishmael was one of the sons of a concubine, we can safely assume that he was among those to whom Abraham gave gifts, and the one he sent away to the East (Genesis 25:6). Yet he was there to participate in his father's solemn burial. Despite all that had happened, Ishmael was devoted to Abraham. If there was any hint of bitterness in him, it is not shown here. Ishmael lived to be 137 years old and died 58 years before his brother Isaac. His descendants are given in Genesis 25:12-18 to show God kept His word to Hagar that her son's descendants would become a great nation.

Isaac Prays for a Child (Genesis 25:19-23)

In Genesis 24, after Sarah had died, Isaac was 37 years old and had not married. This fact alone would have created an unusually strong bond between him and his mother. When Sarah died, he almost grieved himself to death for a period of three years (v. 67). Abraham was growing older and thought he would not live too much longer, so he made arrangements for Isaac to be married. He sent his trusted servant, probably Eliezer of Damascus (ch. 15), back to his home in Mesopotamia to seek a wife for Isaac from among his kindred. He wanted to be sure his son's bloodline would not be corrupted by marrying one of the heathen women.

The servant must have been a devoted worshiper of Jehovah because he prayed to Him and asked for His guidance in showing him the woman who would become Isaac's wife. Everything he requested of God was done. When he met Rebekah, who was the daughter of Bethuel and a granddaughter of Nahor, Abraham's brother, he knew she was the one the Lord had chosen. He arranged the marriage with Rebekah's older brother Laban, the father of Rachel and Leah, who later became the father-in-law of Jacob. Why was this not done by her father? Bethuel may have already been deceased, but according to an ancient custom in Mesopotamia, marriages were arranged by the older brother. It was called a "sistership marriage." When the servant returned with Rebekah, the text says that Isaac took her to be "his wife and he loved her. So Isaac was comforted after his mother's death" (24:67).

Isaac was 40 years old when he married Rebekah. At the time of our text, he was 59 and had not had any children because Rebekah was barren. In our modern culture, it may be hard to understand how important it was for a woman to have a child and for a man to have an heir. In that day, a woman's sense of purpose and self-worth was wrapped up in her ability to bear children and especially to give her husband a male heir. We saw this attitude in Sarah. Isaac prayed, actually "pleaded," with God to let Rebekah have children. The Lord heard him and answered his prayer (25:21).

There are many similarities between Isaac's birth and that of his sons. First, both mothers were barren for a considerable period of time and bore children to their husbands late in life. Abraham was 100, and Isaac was 60. Second, both women finally conceived only after divine intervention. Third, in both cases the younger son became the heir of his father's principal wealth and of God's promises.

Rebekah had undoubtedly seen other pregnancies and knew something was different about her pregnancy. You can imagine her concern because she had been barren for so long and then had all of this activity going on inside of her. She must have thought something was desperately wrong. She did not know until she inquired of the Lord that she was carrying twins. The children struggled within her. There is no reason to assume that Jacob and Esau were already fighting in the womb as some people have surmised. It is only natural for babies who have matured sufficiently to struggle in their mother's womb. This is especially true when there are two or more babies crowded together in one womb.

Abortionists would have us believe that infants are not actually alive while they are in their mother's womb. They choose to refer to an unborn child with the biological term fetus. This makes it all right to terminate a baby's life because it is a thing, an object that the mother may choose to eliminate from her body. The Bible proves that unborn babies are considered to be alive and to be a separate human beings from God (Psalm 139:14-16; Ecclesiastes 11:5; Luke 1:44).

Out of her concern, Rebekah went to the Lord and asked Him what was happening. God answered her by informing her that: 1. there were two babies in her womb; 2. they would each be the head of a nation of people; 3. they would be a different types of people; 4. one would be stronger than the other; and 5. the older would serve the younger. There is a perception that God caused this to happen. The Bible does not make this statement. God was clearly making a prediction of what would happen because of His divine knowledge. He did choose Jacob over Esau, but this was not an arbitrary choice (Romans 10:9-14). It was made on the basis of His knowledge about what the nations that came from each of these men would become. He did not make Jacob or Esau what they were, nor did he make the Israelites or the Edomites what they became.

The Birth of Twins (Genesis 25:24-26)

When her nine-month period of gestation was over, Rebekah gave birth to two sons just as God had told her she would. They were twins, but they were not identical. Esau was the first to be born, and he came out red and "hairy like a garment all over," which is known as hypertrichosis and is very common in newborns (v. 25). Esau means "hairy one." The word for "red" was Edom, the name given to the Edomites who descended from Esau. This same word is used to describe the color of the soup that Jacob sold Esau for his birthright (v. 30).

Jacob was the second son to be born, and he came out of his mother's womb holding his brother's heel. His name originally meant "heel-catcher" or "supplanter." This was prophetic in that Jacob did supplant or replace his brother as the rightful heir to the major portion of his father's estate (27:36). However, based upon an ancient Mesopotamian custom, the father was allowed to replace his oldest son with another sons and designate him to be the principal heir. This was also practiced in Israel (1 Chronicles 5:1-2).

As the Twig Is Bent So Grows the Boy (Genesis 25:27-28)

As Rebekah's sons grew, the dramatic differences between them became even more apparent in their manner of life. Psychologists now believe children have a unique personality that is in them before they are born. They also believe that each child has a natural bent, which a wise parent will endeavor to discover. This may be the best explanation of the statement, "Train up a child in the way he should go [that is, according to his natural bent], and when he is old he will not depart from it" (Proverbs 22:6). Esau was an outdoor type, a cunning hunter. That may not have been complimentary in those days. The only other hunter mentioned in Scripture so far was Nimrod, and what was said about him certainly was not complimentary (Genesis 10:9). It may be that Esau exhibited some of the same rebellious nature that this illustrious ancestor did. Several unfavorable characteristics were displayed in him as the story unfolds.

What is said about Jacob is not flattering. The term given for Jacob –"mild man" – can be deceiving. Nothing about him was mild. Although he was not the rough outdoors man that his brother was, he was the stronger personality of the two (25:23). He would become the dominant one. There may have been many things Jacob was involved in besides just housecleaning and cooking (25:27). Both brothers were "tent dwellers," but while Esau was out hunting game, Jacob was home cooking it. Esau could also cook (27:1-4).

The reason for a lot of the heartache that befell this family is given in verse 28: "Isaac loved Esau … but Rebekah loved Jacob." They played favorites. They may have even contributed to the different directions these boys went in. There is no hint that either parent did not love the other child, only that they loved one more than the other. Parents should never show partiality to one child over another. This leads to a serious loss of self-esteem on the part of a child and can result in many problems. Every child is a unique human being, and each needs to be loved for who he or she is.

Once when Esau came in from the field, Jacob was preparing a meal of stew. The King James Version has "pottage," which is a thick vegetable soup or stew made with lentils, a plant belonging to the pea family. This variety gave off a reddish color when cooked. Sometimes they were mixed with meat. Esau was weary or faint, perhaps from hunger. The aroma of the stew was more than he could bear. The original text suggest an impatience in Esau's behavior that is a bad characteristic. He said, "Feed me with that same red stew" (25:30).

Jacob appears to have been the initiator of the idea for Esau to sell him his birthright. Although his mother later assisted him in deceiving his father so he would bestow the birthright on Jacob, he wanted it badly. It meant that he would inherit a double portion of his father's estate; he would become the head of the family, spiritual and material, and he would become the perpetuator of the promises of God. While there can be no doubt about the type of person Esau was, it does not justify Jacob's trickery and deceit. There is nothing to prove at this point that Jacob was more concerned with spiritual matters than Esau was.

Esau was more concerned with the present than he was with the future. He surely was not at the point of malnutrition so that he would die if he had not eaten. The truth of the matter is that at that point his birthright meant nothing to him (v. 34). He sold it for a bowl of soup. How many people today sell their precious inheritance in heaven for far less?

Jacob made Esau take an oath that he forfeit his birthright, and there may have been a written agreement, although none is mentioned. After the agreement was reached, Esau ate and drank, rose and went about his business. He gave no serious thought to what he had done, perhaps because he had no real intention of sticking to the agreement anyway (27:1-4, 30-41).

The Hebrew writer tells us more about Esau's character. He is called "a fornicator or profane person … who for one morsel of food sold his birthright" (12:16-17). Esau did not deserve the precious birthright or to be the heir to God's promises made to Abraham and Isaac. God saw this beforehand, and that is why He chose to bless Jacob instead of Esau.

Lessons Learned

1. The statement about Abraham "being gathered to his people" reveals much about our futures. Although his body was placed lovingly in the crypt or cave of Machpelah, his soul was not there. This statement could be construed as figurative by some people, but it obviously states a spiritual fact: "The body returns to the dust from which it came and the spirit to the God who gave it" (Ecclesiastes 12:7). It is interesting that in his story about the rich man and Lazarus, Jesus referred to paradise as "Abraham's bosom" (Luke 16:19-31; 23:43). Death is only the separation of the soul from the body (James 2:26). It is not annihilation.
2. Even before Jacob and Esau were born, God knew them and what their future held for them and for their posterity (cf. Psalm 139:13-16; Jeremiah 1:5). John the Baptist was no less the forerunner of the Christ while still in his mother's womb (Luke 1:13-17, 41-44). Jesus was no less the Savior while He was still in Mary's womb (Luke 1:26-36). Before the infamous *Roe v. Wade* decision by the U.S. Supreme Court, we knew when life began. Now people say they are confused about the issue. The ambiguity does not come from reading Scripture.

The Bible makes it abundantly clear that life begins at conception (Exodus 21:22-24). To take an innocent life has always been wrong (Genesis 9:5).

3. Jacob and Esau are a clear example of the sin committed by parents who show favoritism. Some people have suggested Rebekah showed favoritism to Jacob because Isaac showed favoritism to Esau because he was the firstborn. It does not matter what their reasons were, it was sin against the boys to make those kinds of distinctions. Children need to be loved, appreciated and respected for their unique personalities. Their own self-worth begins with their concept of how their parents feel toward them. Often these things are passed down through families. Abraham showed favoritism to Isaac over Ishmael. Jacob showed favoritism to Joseph, and it brought heartache, pain and sorrow to his whole family. It is a cycle that must be broken.

Questions

1. Why did Abraham give the bulk of his estate to Isaac, and only give gifts to his other seven sons?
2. Why did Abraham send his other sons away before he died?
3. What lessons about the immortality of the soul can be learned from Abraham's death?
4. How was Rebekah selected to be Isaac's wife?
5. How was the birth of Jacob and Esau similar to Isaac's birth?
6. What predictions did God make concerning Esau and his posterity?
7. What did Jacob's original name (remember God later changed his name to Israel) mean and how was it prophetic?
8. What was the reason for much of the heartache in Isaac and Rebekah's family?
9. What was the real reason Esau sold his birthright?
10. How can God's selection of Jacob over Esau, even before they were born, be explained if Calvinistic predestination is incorrect?

Lesson 8

Integrity

Week of
Jan. 24, 1999

Lesson Text

GENESIS 26:1-16

(1) There was a famine in the land, besides the first famine that was in the days of Abraham. And Isaac went to Abimelech king of the Philistines, in Gerar.

(2) Then the LORD appeared to him and said: "Do not go down to Egypt; live in the land of which I shall tell you.

(3) "Dwell in this land, and I will be with you and bless you; for to you and your descendants I give all these lands, and I will perform the oath which I swore to Abraham your father.

(4) "And I will make your descendants multiply as the stars of heaven; I will give to your descendants all these lands; and in your seed all the nations of the earth shall be blessed;

(5) "because Abraham obeyed My voice and kept My charge, My commandments, My statutes, and My laws."

(6) So Isaac dwelt in Gerar.

(7) And the men of the place asked about his wife. And he said, "She is my sister"; for he was afraid to say, "She is my wife," because he thought, "lest the men of the place kill me for Rebekah, because she is beautiful to behold."

(8) Now it came to pass, when he had been there a long time, that Abimelech king of the Philistines looked through a window, and saw, and there was Isaac, showing endearment to Rebekah his wife.

(9) Then Abimelech called Isaac and said, "Quite obviously she is your wife; so how could you say, 'She is my sister'?" And Isaac said to him, "Because I said, 'Lest I die on account of her.' "

(10) And Abimelech said, "What is this you have done to us? One of the people might soon have lain with your wife, and you would have brought guilt on us."

(11) So Abimelech charged all his people, saying, "He who touches this man or his wife shall surely be put to death."

(12) Then Isaac sowed in that land, and reaped in the same year a hundredfold; and the LORD blessed him.

(13) The man began to prosper, and continued prospering until he became very prosperous;

(14) for he had possessions of flocks and possessions of herds and a great number of servants. So the Philistines envied him.

(15) Now the Philistines had stopped up all the wells which his father's servants had dug in the days of Abraham his father, and they had filled them with earth.

(16) And Abimelech said to Isaac, "Go away from us, for you are much mightier than we."

Introduction

"Like father, like son." How many times have you heard that? It was true often in the Bible. In the previous lesson we saw how the favoritism of the father for one son over another was passed down through three generations. Abraham was not a perfect man. He was human. Just like us, he made mistakes in his life. In many ways, Isaac followed in his father's footsteps. Abraham made the same mistake Isaac did in lying about his relationship to his wife, but he made it twice. The first time was in Egypt (Genesis 12:14). Shortly after he had settled near Negev, a severe famine struck Palestine. Such famines were quite common and usually resulted from droughts. Abraham heard that there was ample food supplies in Egypt, which was blessed with rivers, but the Egyptians also had become quite proficient in irrigation techniques. This provided them with fertile soil, especially near the Nile and its tributaries. This partly explains why they had storehouses full of food when the surrounding nations were starving.

The reason for Abraham going to Egypt was similar to that of the sons of Israel, but their move was providential while Abraham's was not (45:5-9). Notice there is the absence of any statement, suggestion or implication that God had told him to leave and go to Egypt. Someone might say, "The famine was severe, and he and his family might have perished." Would God have told him to go to Canaan and remain there and that he would bless him and then let him die? Abraham went to Egypt because of a lack of faith in God. At that time, he had more faith in men than he did in God. Abraham had a lot of growing to do before he would become the man God knew he could be. Although Abraham made a mess out of everything by lying and jeopardized his wife's morality and Egypt's prosperity, God even blessed him there.

The second time Abraham lied about Sarah being his wife was in Gerar, or Philistia, the same place where Isaac later lied about his relationship to Rebekah (20:1). Out of fear for his life, Abraham said, "She is my sister" (vv. 2, 11). He apparently spread this around broadly, and word came to Abimelech, the king. This name means "my father is king." It is most likely a dynastic or family name, as it is used for future kings also. The king took Sarah, intending to make her one of his wives. Here is one striking difference in the story of Abraham's encounter with Pharaoh, and Isaac's encounter with a later Abimelech. In this account, God actually appeared to this Abimelech in a dream. How much knowledge this heathen king had about God we do not know. Some scholars think that he was a believer, and he does refer to God as "lord" (v. 4). If it is true that he was a believer, his people, the Philistines, certainly were not. God prevented Abimelech from consummating a sexual union with Sarah, and told him that he was a dead man because she was Abraham's wife (vv. 3, 6). Abimelech told God he had done this out of a pure motive because Abraham and Sarah lied about their true relationship (v. 5). God said, "I know that you did this in the integrity of your heart" (v. 6). He then told the king to ask Abraham to pray for him because he was a prophet and to restore Sarah to Abraham or the king would die (v. 7). Abraham prayed for him, and God healed him and his house (v. 17). This is a case where the sinner had more integrity than the saint.

Isaac Followed in His Father's Footsteps – Almost (Genesis 26:1-5)

As noted earlier, the name "Abimelech" was either a family name, a dynastic name or an official title for the Philistine monarchs. This man could not possibly be the same one who was involved in the story of Abraham and Sarah in Genesis 20. There are too many years between them.

There is a difference in the circumstances surrounding the famine in this chapter and the one involved in Abraham's story. Isaac apparently thought he would have better provisions near the seacoast at Gerar, which was the capital city of the Philistines. They were probably living at Beer-lahai-roi at the time (25:11). This was done not against God's will but with His blessing (26:2). God told him if he stayed in the Land of Promise, He would be with him and bless him there. Unlike his father, he heeded God's commandment.

This is the first time Scripture says God appeared to Isaac. He had spoken to Rebekah, but nowhere are we told that He had talked to Isaac, although he may have been present when his father spoke with God. This may have been the case on Mount Moriah when Abraham was preparing to offer Isaac as a sacrifice to God (ch. 22).

God knew that Isaac was prepared to go to Egypt if he had not found adequate provisions in Gerar. That is why He commanded him not to go there. God told him that if he obeyed, He would bless him in the land. For the first time, God renewed the promises He had made to Abraham, applying them this time to Isaac because he was the heir to them. God promised to multiply his seed as stars of "the heaven," to give his "descendants all these lands" and that in his seed "all nations of the earth shall be blessed" (26:4).

Why did God bless Abraham? Some people point out that God blessed him because of his faith, which is true, but they do not include obedience. They say it was by faith alone. This verse plainly says God blessed Abraham because he "obeyed His voice, kept His charge, His commandments, His statutes, and His laws" (v. 5). This confirms what is said later by the writer of Hebrews (11:8-10, 17-20). It also proves there were laws and commandments during the Patriarchal Age, although some people deny this. They were not written down because God spoke to the fathers through various means (1:1).

Isaac's Lie (Genesis 26:6-11)

With God's approval, Isaac remained in Gerar for a long time, and God blessed him there (v. 6). When the men of that place saw Rebekah's beauty, although she was in her 60s, they asked Isaac who she was. He lied and said, "She is my sister" (v. 7). Sarah was Abraham's half sister. His lie was not in saying, "She is my sister," which she was, but it was in denying that she was his wife. Isaac told a lie because Rebekah was his cousin not his sister. She was also his wife. Both Abraham and Isaac lied out of fear for their safety with no consideration given to the dangerous situation in which they placed their wives. In both cases, adultery and pregnancy were a real possibility. Although Isaac displays a lot of integrity later when he dealt with the Philistines, he certainly did not do so on this occasion (vv. 17-22).

There was a time when truth was considered a premium. As Cervantes said, "An honest man's word is as good as his bond." An alarming trend in America and in other parts of the world, indicates that is not true anymore. In some recent polls taken in America, the majority of people said they had lied before and would lie again if it was to their advantage to do so. Phillips Brooks, an early American preacher, said, "Truth is always strong, no matter how weak it looks, and falsehood is always weak, no matter how strong it looks." John Dryden, the English poet, wrote, "Truth is the foundation of all knowledge and the cement of all societies." Perhaps this might help to explain why our society in general is crumbling.

Another major difference exists between this story and the one involving Abraham. In both situations concerning Abraham and Sarah, the monarchs took Sarah into their harem. Here, no one had taken Rebekah to be a wife yet, but there is every reason to believe it would have happened given enough time.

In the King James Version, we are told Abimelech saw Isaac "sporting with his wife" (v. 8). The New King James Version says "Isaac was showing endearment to Rebekah his wife." This is closer to the original text that uses stronger language suggesting he was actually in a loving embrace with her at the time the king saw them.

Abimelech called for Isaac and confronted him with his deceit. All he could answer was that he was afraid for his life. Not only was he unconcerned about his wife's welfare, but also he did not care about the predicament in which he had placed his gracious host. As in the case with Abraham, this heathen king had treated Isaac well. We cannot help being impressed with the moral sensitivity of this king. He had a much higher standard of morality than Isaac gave him credit for. It is a sad day when an unconverted heathen shows more integrity than God's servant. Some people have suggested that it was because he was aware of the relationship his predecessor had with Isaac's father, Abraham.

He might have insisted that Isaac leave the country, but he did not. Despite Isaac's deceit, Abimelech commanded that no one harm him or his wife, promising to execute anyone who did so. The indications are that He did not punish Isaac and protected him.

God Blessed Isaac in Gerar (Genesis 26:12-14)

Up to this time Isaac had been a herder of sheep, living a nomadic lifestyle such as his father before him. This text shows that he spent a considerable amount of time in Gerar. Nomads traveled around continually, seeking grazing pasture. Here, Isaac sowed or engaged in farming pursuits apparently for the first time. It may be he learned a lesson from this famine, and so he restricted his labors to one area. It is interesting that his yield was a hundredfold. This was said to show the prosperity of Isaac. It is interesting that this is the same amount that the good man's field produced in Jesus' parable about the sower (Matthew 13).

As a result of God's blessing, he became very prosperous and powerful. He was already wealthy because he had inherited the major portion of his father's estate. We can only imagine how much wealth he had now. He had more flocks, herds and servants. The result was envy on the part of his Philistine neighbors. The same situation developed in Egypt when the Israelites prospered, and many of their Egyptian neighbors did not (Exodus 1:7). They did not attribute his success to God but perhaps to the king's decree. At any rate, Isaac was a foreigner in their land, and he was taking the wealth they believed belonged to them. It is certain all of his neighbors would not have been prospering as much because God was blessing him. His neighbors decided to do something about it. The wells that Abraham had dug were apparently being used by Isaac. To discourage him so he would move on, the Philistines stopped up the wells so they could not be used.

It is wrong for a rich man to oppress a poor man, but the wise man says it is also wrong for those with less possessions to envy people who have wealth (Proverbs 14:20-21, 31; 23:4-5). It can cause covetousness in their hearts, which is like the sin of idolatry (Colossians 3:5). Even Abimelech eventually urged Isaac to move on because he had become so powerful the king thought he was a threat to him and his people. No doubt many of his subjects had come to him complaining about the prosperity of Isaac in their land. Some of them might have even suggested fighting against Isaac, which would help to explain the king's remark about Isaac's strength compared to his own.

Lessons Learned

1. The prophet Ezekiel said, "The son shall not bear the guilt of the father, nor shall the father bear the guilt of the sons" (18:20). That is unquestionably true. Each person will answer only for himself. It is also true that the son often repeats the sins of the father. There is no more important influence in a son's life than that of his father. In America today, absent fathers are a real problem. A father is his son's first real role model. When that relationship is missing, a boy's education suffers the loss of a vital component. Fathers should not underestimate the power of their presence in their children's lives. Also, they should not mistake the power of being the right kind of example in front of their children.
2. The story of Abraham and Abimelech is a difficult one to understand. Abimelech said to God, "Lord, will you slay a righteous nation too?" He had more integrity in this situation than Abraham, yet Abraham was blessed and Abimelech almost destroyed. Why? How could God bless Abraham in the face of what he had done? How could he punish Abimelech although he was unaware of Abraham and Sarah's deceit? Part of the answer involves the patriarchal promises made to Abraham. God knew Abraham was not a perfect man when He called him, but he was the best man available. We must also remember Abraham was involved in fulfilling this promise with Sarah. God is merciful and gracious to people who are His, despite our sins. John assures us that when we walk in the light and confess our sins to God, He will forgive us our sins and cleanse us from all iniquity (1 John 1:7, 9). This does not apply to people who are not His children.
3. It is a sad day when the unconverted have more integrity than the people of God. The two Abimelechs showed far more integrity than either Abraham or Isaac. God's people must be known as people of integrity. We must always be certain we speak the truth and do it with love. When we give our word, we must be sure to keep it. God, Christ and the church are all judged by our actions. The church must not let the world set our standards.

Questions

1. Why did Abraham go to Egypt, and why was it wrong for him to do so?
2. What does the name "Abimelech" mean?
3. Why was Abimelech not able to consummate a sexual union with Sarah?
4. What are some of the differences in the two stories of Abraham and Isaac and the Abimelechs?
5. Why did God bless Abraham?
6. What alarming trend in America today is mentioned in the lesson?
7. How did Abimelech know that Rebekah was Isaac's wife?
8. What change in occupation did Isaac undergo in Gerar?
9. Why is covetousness like idolatry?
10. What attitude is as bad as that of despising the poor?

Lesson 9

Discovery

Week of
Jan. 31, 1999

Lesson Text

GENESIS 28:10-22

(10) Now Jacob went out from Beersheba and went toward Haran.

(11) So he came to a certain place and stayed there all night, because the sun had set. And he took one of the stones of that place and put it at his head, and he lay down in that place to sleep.

(12) Then he dreamed, and behold, a ladder was set up on the earth, and its top reached to heaven; and there the angels of God were ascending and descending on it.

(13) And behold, the LORD stood above it and said: "I am the LORD God of Abraham your father and the God of Isaac; the land on which you lie I will give to you and your descendants.

(14) "Also your descendants shall be as the dust of the earth; you shall spread abroad to the west and the east, to the north and the south; and in you and in your seed all the families of the earth shall be blessed.

(15) "Behold, I am with you and will keep you wherever you go, and will bring you back to this land; for I will not leave you until I have done what I have spoken to you."

(16) Then Jacob awoke from his sleep and said, "Surely the LORD is in this place, and I did not know it."

(17) And he was afraid and said, "How awesome is this place! This is none other than the house of God, and this is the gate of heaven!"

(18) Then Jacob rose early in the morning, and took the stone that he had put at his head, set it up as a pillar, and poured oil on top of it.

(19) And he called the name of that place Bethel; but the name of that city had been Luz previously.

(20) Then Jacob made a vow, saying, "If God will be with me, and keep me in this way that I am going, and give me bread to eat and clothing to put on,

(21) "so that I come back to my father's house in peace, then the LORD shall be my God.

(22) "And this stone which I have set as a pillar shall be God's house, and of all that You give me I will surely give a tenth to You."

Introduction

After Esau realized Jacob had received his birthright and Isaac's blessing, he swore that he would kill him after his father had died and the days of mourning for him were past (Genesis 27: 41). Esau had apparently made this vow before other people, or else related it to other people, because it came to the attention of his mother, Rebekah. She called for Jacob and related Esau's threat to him and urged him to flee to Mesopotamia to her brother Laban's house and to stay "for a few days until your brother's fury turns away" (vv. 43-44). Rebekah said she would send for him when Esau's anger subsided. She was deceiving herself about how quickly this matter would be resolved. A few days turned into 20 years. As far as we know she never saw her son again, and he was not there when she died. All we know about her after this time is that she was buried in the cave of Machpelah (49:30-31).

Although Rebekah showed favoritism towards Jacob, we cannot doubt the love she had for Esau. Her statement to Jacob that she did not want to be deprived of the company of both of them shows a genuine concern for Esau's welfare (27:45). If he had killed Jacob, his life would also have been taken, and she would have lost both sons. By sending Jacob away, she preserved the lives of both sons, but she was deprived of Jacob's presence for the rest of her life. In one respect, they both were paid back for their deceit.

In appealing to Isaac for him to allow Jacob to leave, Rebekah never mentioned the threat made by Esau. Instead, she used a common fear that both of them shared – Jacob would marry one of the daughters of Heth, a Hittite, as Esau had already done (26:34-35). Apparently these daughters-in-law did not get along too well with Rebekah. She essentially said, "If Jacob also married one of these daughters of the land, I would rather die than face it" (27:46).

Isaac called Jacob before him and charged him not to marry one of the Canaanite women. He told him to go to Padan Aram to Bethuel's, or his grandfather's, house and select a wife from among his kindred. What follows proves Isaac fully understood Jacob was to be the heir to the promises of God. He rehearsed the promises God had given to him and told Jacob the blessing of Abraham would now be passed on to him and to his descendants (28:4). Isaac then sent Jacob away to Padam Aram or Haran, Mesopotamia.

When Esau first married the heathen women, he did not appear to have done so out of rebellion. Issac and Rebekah apparently had not given him the guidance they should have. Did they ever tell him he should not marry a woman who did not fear God? Did they ever explain to him they were a people blessed of God because of his grandfather, Abraham? Did they ever tell him about God's promises to Isaac's descendants? If so, we have no record of it. This may have been the first time Esau realized his father's displeasure about his choice of brides. In what was an attempt to regain his father's favor, he took Mahalath, his cousin, the daughter of Ishmael, as a wife (v. 9). He may have thought by marrying in the family, Isaac would be pleased. He did not realize that Abraham had sent Ishmael away, along with the sons of Keturah, and was not included in the covenant blessing.

Jacob's Flight (Genesis 28:10-11)

Undoubtedly, Beersheba had been Jacob's home for most of his life. This was the first time he had traveled away from home as far as we know. It was not a pleasant journey because he was fleeing from his brother's wrath and facing an uncertain future. Would Esau come after him and try to kill him? Would he have enough supplies to make the journey safely? Nothing is said about any traveling companions. He appears to have been alone at this emotional time in his life. The spoiled mamma's boy now had to walk the road by himself, but all of that was about to change quickly and dramatically. Jacob was about to meet God, and he would begin to walk by faith and not by sight.

It was late in the evening, and the sun had gone down when Jacob came to the place later called Bethel. This would become a sacred place for Jacob and his descendants (35:1). He stopped for a night's rest and lay on the hard ground with a stone for his pillow. This was a common practice in the East, and it probably was more for protection than anything else.

Jacob's Ladder (Genesis 28:12-15)

At this low juncture in Jacob's life, God chose to reveal himself to him. He did so through the medium of a fascinating dream. In this dream Jacob saw a ladder that extended into the heavens. Upon it were angels ascending and descending, indicating God's intense interest in the affairs of Earth. His ministering spirits are continually going to and fro throughout the earth, performing God's service (Psalm 103:20; John 1:51; Hebrews 12:22). The writer of Hebrews said angels are "ministering spirits sent forth to minister for those who will inherit salvation" (1:14).

The Lord stood at the top of the ladder. In what form He appeared to Jacob or how Jacob even knew this was the Lord, we do not know. We do know that he did not see God in His fullness (John 1:18). God's message to him was a renewal of the promises made to Abraham and Isaac. The promises included some additions that were specifically for Jacob's benefit. God told him that he would multiply his seed as the dust of the earth and that they would occupy the entire land of Canaan (Genesis 28:14). Jacob was no longer going to be alone because God promised to be with him wherever he went, and God would bring him back to this land (28:15). He also promised Jacob He would not leave him until He had fulfilled this pledge.

A New Day Dawns in Jacob's Life (Genesis 28:16-18)

Waking from his sleep, Jacob knew this was more than just another dream. He realized the sacredness of this event and of this place. He said, "Surely the Lord is in this place, and I did not know it" (v. 16). His initial reaction to this revelation was one of fear. This was not a dreadful place, a place to be afraid of, but a place to be revered. He saw it as the "house of God," and "the gate of heaven" (v. 17).

This was a holy moment and a time of spiritual awakening for Jacob. He did not build an altar, and he may not even have had an animal for sacrifice, but he could consecrate this place. He took the stone upon which he had slept and placed it upon a pillar and poured oil over it to memorialize this event. This was his way of setting this place apart as sacred. In later Hebrew literature, the pouring out of liquid was symbolic of emptying one's self and devoting one's life to God (Exodus 29:41; Philippians 2:17; 2 Timothy 4:6).

Jacob's Dedication of God's House (Genesis 28:19)

In dedicating this place to God, Jacob renamed it. The nearby city had previously been called Luz. Jacob gave it the name of Bethel, which means "the House of God." Later, he returned to it and built an altar there (Genesis 35:3-7). It was the burial place for Deborah, Rebekah's nurse who had served her since the days before she left her father's house (24:59; 35:8).

The later history of this place, however, was not so noble. Although it was used at one time as a place of worship to Jehovah, Jereboam I forever changed all of that.

It became a center of idolatry where he set up one of the golden calves in his apostate religion (1 Kings 12:29-33; 13:1-15). It was denounced by God's later prophets (Jeremiah 48:13; Hosea 10:15; Amos 3:14; 7:10-13). It was given the contemptuous name of Bethaven by Hosea, which means "house of vanity," or "house of idols" (Hosea 4:15). During Josiah's reforms, its defiled altars were torn down (2 Kings 23:4, 19, 20).

Jacob's Vow (Genesis 28:20-22)

Jacob's statement to God sounds like he is bargaining with God. Jacob was trying to make a deal with God, but he was also affirming his faith in His promises. God had promised to care for him, to be with him, and to bring him safely back to his home again. Because of that, Jacob promised he would worship and honor God alone. God does not need to make deals with His people because all of His blessings are conditioned upon their continued faithfulness.

A part of that worship would consist of Jacob giving God a tenth of all that he would receive. As far as we can tell, there was no written law about tithing at that time. If he knew of it, Jacob may have been inspired by the incident of Abraham giving his tithe to Melchizedek when he returned from the battle with the kings of the East (Genesis 14:18-20). Tithing was made a part of the Law of Moses (Leviticus 27:30-32; Numbers 18:21-24). This provision was done away with, along with the rest of the Law, when Jesus was nailed to the cross (Ephesians 2:13-16; Colossians 2:13-14). Christians are not commanded to tithe because we are not under the Law of Moses. However, does anyone really believe that if the Jews were required to give a tenth Christians living under a more perfect covenant are expected to give less? See Matthew 5:20. We are taught to give, and we are told when, where, what proportion and with what disposition to do so.

The when is "upon the first day of the week" (1 Corinthians 16:2). The where is "when you come together" (11:18, 20, 23). The question is often asked, "What percentage should we give?" God does not deal in percentages today. The proportion is "as we may prosper" (16:2). The disposition is "cheerfully, and sacrificially" (2 Corinthians 8:5, 12-15; 9:6-14).

Lessons Learned

1. Once again we learn the lesson that "Be sure your sin will find you out" (Numbers 32:23). Rebekah was the one who motivated Jacob to deceive his father. She was probably partly responsible for the attitude he had towards Esau. Jacob had to bear the responsibility for what he did. Both of them ended up paying for their sins. Jacob had to leave the mother to whom he was so devoted. He never saw her again. Rebekah saw her son leave, never to return. The son she had not shown much attention to was left to comfort her in her old age, to be there when she died and probably to arrange for her burial. We can be forgiven for our sins, but the consequences will follow us.
2. Esau is a pathetic figure. When he took Mahalath, the daughter of Ishmael, to be one of his wives, he was like a small child trying to win his father's favor. It changed nothing and may have made the situation worse. While he was ultimately responsible for his conduct, we must wonder how much his parent's neglect contributed to his problems. While Isaac gave him love and attention,

he did not give him direction. Rebekah, on the other hand, virtually ignored him while lavishing her attentions on Jacob. Often in our quest to give our children what we did not have, we fail to give them the things that are really important – our time and attention.

3. Angels are very popular today. The bookstores are filled with books about them. You can purchase angels for your clothes, car and home. Most of these things are based on pure superstition. Some of the books are testimonials by people who say they have met, talked to or been served by angels. Despite all the unreliable material out there, angels are real. They are God's ministering servants to Christians. They are the agents of His providence and are working out His will in this world. They are not to be worshiped, but they are to be respected for what they do for us.
4. We are not to give a tenth, but that would a good place to start. The average contribution among all churchgoers is about 2 percent. In the churches of Christ, the average is about $10 per attender. Paul said we are to "purpose in our heart" what we will give (2 Corinthians 9:7). This does not mean to wait until we get to worship and then decide. It means to give thought to our gift before hand. It means to evaluate our prosperity honestly and to give accordingly. The Macedonians gave beyond their ability to give, but they did something more important; "they first gave themselves to the Lord" (8:5). When you give yourself to God, giving your money, your time and your talent is easy.

Questions

1. How long was Jacob away from Canaan?
2. What reason did Rebekah give to Isaac for wanting Jacob to go to Padan Aram?
3. Why may Esau have married Mahalath?
4. What purpose might the rock that Jacob slept on have served besides just being a pillow?
5. How did God reveal himself to Jacob?
6. What did the angels ascending and descending on the ladder Jacob saw illustrate?
7. What were the additional provisions in God's promises that He made to Jacob?
8. Why did Jacob pour oil on the rock he had slept on?
9. What does the name "Bethel" mean, and why did Jacob give it to that place?
10. Why should Christians not tithe, and how should they give?

Lesson 10

Worship

Week of Feb. 7, 1999

Lesson Text

GENESIS 35:1-15

(1) Then God said to Jacob, "Arise, go up to Bethel and dwell there; and make an altar there to God, who appeared to you when you fled from the face of Esau your brother."

(2) And Jacob said to his household and to all who were with him, "Put away the foreign gods that are among you, purify yourselves, and change your garments.

(3) "Then let us arise and go up to Bethel; and I will make an altar there to God, who answered me in the day of my distress and has been with me in the way which I have gone."

(4) So they gave Jacob all the foreign gods which were in their hands, and the earrings which were in their ears; and Jacob hid them under the terebinth tree which was by Shechem.

(5) And they journeyed, and the terror of God was upon the cities that were all around them, and they did not pursue the sons of Jacob.

(6) So Jacob came to Luz (that is, Bethel), which is in the land of Canaan, he and all the people who were with him.

(7) And he built an altar there and called the place El Bethel, because there God appeared to him when he fled from the face of his brother.

(8) Now Deborah, Rebekah's nurse, died, and she was buried below Bethel under the terebinth tree. So the name of it was called Allon Bachuth.

(9) Then God appeared to Jacob again, when he came from Padan Aram, and blessed him.

(10) And God said to him, "Your name is Jacob; your name shall not be called Jacob anymore, but Israel shall be your name." So He called his name Israel.

(11) Also God said to him: "I am God Almighty. Be fruitful and multiply; a nation and a company of nations shall proceed from you, and kings shall come from your body.

(12) "The land which I gave Abraham and Isaac I give to you; and to your descendants after you I give this land."

(13) Then God went up from him in the place where He talked with him.

(14) So Jacob set up a pillar in the place where He talked with him, a pillar of stone; and he poured a drink offering on it, and he poured oil on it.

(15) And Jacob called the name of the place where God spoke with him, Bethel.

Introduction

After the powerful spiritual experience that Jacob had at Bethel, he remained for a few days and then moved on towards Haran. It is here that he would have some of life's most pleasurable experiences but also some of its most bitter lessons. From the time he arrived in Padan Aram, his life was one series of struggles after another. Jacob had lied to and deceived his father, Isaac. Laban, his father-in-law, would lie to and deceive him. There was bitter rivalry between Jacob and his brother Esau. There was equally bitter rivalry between his older sons and Joseph. Jacob also had to deal with the bitter rivalry between his four wives. He and his mother used a goat to deceive his father, and his sons later used a goat to deceive him. He had to flee from his home in Beersheba from the wrath of Esau. He had to flee in the night from Padan Aram from the treachery of Laban. As it is said, "What goes around comes around." How was Jacob able to endure all of it?

One thing remained constant in Jacob's life since his encounter with God at Bethel and that was his faith in God's promises. God had promised to be with him wherever he went. God did not let him down. Being a child of God does not immunize us against the trials and tribulations of the world, but it does give us the antibodies to fight against further infections. In good times and bad, God is there. Christians today have the same wonderful promise of God's constant presence that Jacob had. Jesus promised His disciples that when they were going out to take the gospel to the world, "lo, I am with you always even to the end of the age" (Matthew 28:20). The Hebrew writer adds, "He Himself has said, 'I will never leave you nor forsake you' " (13:5).

One of the most painful experiences any father can endure is when someone hurts his child. Dinah, one of Jacob's daughters by Leah, was raped by Shechem, the son of Hamor "the prince of the country" (Genesis 34:2). Although he was strongly attracted to her and loved her, Hamor committed an unpardonable sin in the eyes of Jacob's sons, Simeon and Levi.

When Hamor came to make peace with Jacob and asked that Shechem be allowed to marry Dinah, Jacob's sons spoke deceitfully to him. They said they could not allow their sister to marry "one who is uncircumcised, for that would be a reproach to us" (v. 14). Hamor and the men of his city agreed to be circumcised. Because they were numerically larger, they anticipated that by intermarrying with Jacob's family all of his wealth would eventually belong to them (v. 23). Their motives were not altogether honorable. When the men of Shechem were recovering from this painful procedure, Levi and Simeon slew all the males of the city with a sword and took Dinah away. Jacob's other sons also participated in the plunder of the city (vv. 25-29).

Jacob was not pleased. He was very angry with them and said, "You have troubled me by making me obnoxious among the inhabitants of the land … and since I am few in number, they may gather together against me and kill me. I shall be destroyed, my household and I" (v. 30). God had promised to be with Jacob and to protect him. He decided it was time for him to move.

Jacob Returns to Bethel (Genesis 35:1)

Genesis 35 is predominantly a chapter about worship. Although it also contains the story of the death and burial of Jacob's beloved Rachel, the only wife he really ever wanted, her nurse, Deborah, and his father, Isaac, God is central in this chapter. His name is mentioned 10 times. One of the names that is used for God in this chapter is "El Shaddai," which means "the almighty God, the all-sufficient One" or "God is all powerful" (v. 11).

Jacob had promised to build an altar at Bethel many years before (28:19-22). At this point, he had been back in Canaan for about 12 years. Although Bethel was only 30 miles from Shechem, he had not yet returned. Jacob had built an altar at Shechem which he called "El Elohe Israel," which means "God, the God of Israel" (33:20), but it was not "the house of God." Bethel was the place where God had so richly blessed Him with the heavenly vision and by bestowing the patriarchal blessing upon him. God told him it was time to go back and build an altar there. Jacob obeyed, but there was something that had to be tended to before he could go back to this holy site.

The Putting Away of Idols (Genesis 35:2-4)

It would appear that up until this time, Jacob had been lax in governing his household. He made a promise to God that if He would deliver Him from his brother, protect him where he was going and bring him home again, He alone would be his God. While he probably adhered to that promise himself, he had not, as the head of his household, demanded that his family and his servants put away their idols. Jacob considered Bethel to be holy ground. He could not allow his household to go there without first consecrating them to God and purifying them in His sight. He commanded them to "Put away your foreign gods … purify yourselves and change your garments" (35:2). Although this was a ceremonial and symbolic act, it did represent a complete break from idolatry for his family.

Verse 3 indicates that Jacob had previously informed his family about Bethel and what had happened there. We wonder what kind of testimony Jacob had presented to his family about God in view of their continued idolatry. How much did his lack of spiritual guidance contribute to the disgraceful behavior of his sons in the previous chapter? What part did it play in the ungodly act of his oldest son that is related later in this same chapter (v. 22)?

Jacob's entire household complied with his request (v. 4). They gave him all of their idols, which surely would have included the ones Rachel stole from her father, Laban, before they left Padan Aram (31:34-35). They also gave him their gold earrings. These might have been surrendered because they were amulets containing small likenesses of the idol worshiped. Jewelry was often used in religious observances (Exodus 32:3; Judges 8:24-27). Jacob buried all of these under "the terebinth [oak] tree at Shechem" (Genesis 35:4). Because the definite article is used, this might have been "the terebinth tree of Moreh," mentioned in Genesis 12:6.

Jacob Safely Returns to Bethel (Genesis 35:5-6)

In the previous chapter, after the terrible deed done by Simeon and Levi, Jacob was fearful of the people of the land and with good reason (34:30). God promised to protect Jacob, and He did. He put the terror of God in the hearts of all the surrounding enemies of Jacob. When the nation of Israel came to Canaan, God put that same fear in the Canaanites (Exodus 15:14-16; Deuteronomy 2:25; Joshua 2:9-11). This made it much easier for them to conquer their enemies. When God's people fear Him and are walking in His will, they need not fear any man (Ecclesiastes 12:13; Matthew 10:28). Jacob's enemies were so fearful that they did not even try to pursue him.

God had brought Jacob safely back to Bethel. Moses reminds us that this city was known as Luz by the local inhabitants. Bethel did not become the common name for it until after Israel had conquered the land of Canaan. Jacob gave it a more expanded title when he had finally built the altar there. He called it "El Bethel," or "the God of Bethel." The place was not as important as the God who hallowed it. We give lip service to the idea that a church building today is not God's house, but we treat it as if it were. Worse yet, we sometimes act as if God is confined to that place. God has always been what makes a place hallowed or sacred (Exodus 3:4-5). Jesus told the woman of Samaria, "Believe me, the hour is coming when you will neither on this mountain [Mount Gerizim, where the Samaritan temple had once stood], nor in Jerusalem [Mount Moriah, where the temple stood], worship the Father … But the hour is coming when the true worshipers will worship the Father in spirit and in truth, for the Father is seeking such to worship Him. God is a spirit, and those who worship Him must worship in spirit and in truth" (John 4:21-24).

The Death of Deborah (Genesis 35:8)

Few women are immortalized in the Old Testament, but this one who is barely known is honored. Deborah was Rebekah's nurse. She was probably the one who nursed her from birth. She came up with her from Padan Aram (24:59). How she came to be with Jacob is unknown to us. This would indicate that Jacob had visited with his father since his return to Canaan. He had known her from his earliest days. She may have even nursed him too and was a second mother to him. Because Rebekah and Isaac were dead, it would only be natural for her to live with Jacob instead of Esau. Jacob had many children who needed the care she provided. Although she was only a servant, Deborah was much loved. Jacob buried her body beneath a terebinth (oak) tree at Bethel. He then gave this place the name "Allon Bachuth," which means "the Oak of Weeping" (35:8).

God Appears to Jacob Again (Genesis 35:9-15)

Earlier, God had reappeared to Abraham and Isaac on a number of occasions to reaffirm His covenant with them. In this section of the text, He does the same to Jacob. On the night Jacob was preparing for his confrontation with Esau, he wrestled with a man. This man was undoubtedly a theophany, or God in the form of a man, because Jacob later said, "I have seen God face to face, and my life is preserved" (32:30; Hosea 12:2). The name Jacob gave to that location, Peniel or Penuel, means "the face of God" (Genesis 32:31). It was at this time that God changed Jacob's name to Israel, which in Hebrew means "to struggle with God" (vv. 27-28). Some people translate it "the one who wrestled with God." It has come down to us to mean "the Prince of God." This time God appeared to Jacob to confirm his new name and to reaffirm His covenant with Jacob.

In addition to telling Jacob that his seed would be as numberless as the dust, He told him "a nation and a company of nations shall proceed from you." And for the first time, He told him that kings would be numbered among his descendants. God also reaffirmed the land promise that all of Canaan would belong to him and to his descendants (35:12). Then the text says that "God went up from him" (v. 13). Jacob erected another pillar there and dedicated that place by pouring oil and a drink offering over it because it was the place where God had talked with him.

Lessons Learned

1. The expression "What goes around comes around" certainly describes the life of Jacob. When his father was old and had poor eyesight, Jacob conspired with his mother to deceive him. When Jacob was old, his sons deceived him about the death of his favorite son, Joseph. They did not have to say anything. They took the blood of a goat and soaked Joseph's prized coat of many colors in it

and sent it to their father and allowed his imagination to take it from there. Seeing the coat, his conclusion was that Joseph had been torn to pieces and devoured by a wild beast. Jacob's grief was instant and prolonged. He wished to die himself (37:31-35). Do you not suppose that during his grief he thought about the deception he and his mother had pulled on Isaac? Because he had become a very godly man, is it not reasonable to believe that he also felt immense sorrow for the terrible things he had done, both to his father and his brother? This was not divine retribution or punishment, but life does have a way of paying us back for the wrongs we commit. Our eternal judgement will rest in the hands of the righteous Judge.

2. Jacob, "the Prince of God," failed his sons, even as his father failed him and his brother. Why do children keep repeating the mistakes of their parents? Should we not learn from other's mistakes? Jacob was a good man, a godly man, or else God would not have blessed him. Our pattern for parenting should be our parents and our Heavenly Father. The guidebook for rearing children should not be the latest parenting author, but the Bible. We will make mistakes, but if we parent our children with love and caring discipline, they will develop into healthy individuals. However, we must not neglect the most important aspect of their training, and that is their religious instruction (Proverbs 22:6; Ephesians 6:4).
3. Although we do not always do what we say we will, God keeps His word. We must remember that His promises are conditional. Israel inhabiting the Promised Land forever was conditioned upon their continued faithfulness. God kept His part of the covenant; they did not keep theirs. Our promise of a heavenly home is conditioned on our initial acceptance of God's gracious gift of salvation in Christ. We receive the benefits of God's grace through faith in Christ, repentance of our sins, a public confession of our faith and by being baptized so that His blood might cleanse us of our sins (John 8:24; Matthew 10:32-33; Romans 10:9-10; Acts 2:38; 8:36-37; 22:16; Ephesians 1:7; Colossians 1:14; Revelation 1:5). Once we have accepted God's offer of salvation through the initial steps, our home in heaven is assured if we continue to live a faithful life (Revelation 2:10; 2 Timothy 4:6-8). That is faithful, not perfect. We cannot live a perfect life, but we can strive for perfection and live a life that is full of faith (Hebrews 6:1).
4. Jacob set up the altar at Bethel to worship "the God of Bethel." The shrine he built was holy only because of the purpose for which it was being used. When we come together, the place in which we meet is not a holy place, but the reason for which we come together is a holy purpose. In this age of entertainment, people want to turn worship into some kind of entertainment extravaganza. Worship is not entertainment. By definition, worship is showing adoration, praise and devotion to God. Should not our worship be such that pleases Him? If our worship is man-centered and not God-centered, it is not true worship (Matthew 15:7-9). To worship God in spirit and in truth means that what we do in our worship is according to the pattern given in the New Testament to the church and that our inner being is involved. We must not make the mistake the Jews made and allow our worship merely to become an external exercise in futility. When their worship became merely rituals, motions and ceremonies, God abhorred it (Isaiah 1:10-15). We must not lose the awe, holiness and wonder of it all (6:1). When we do, our devotion, no matter what we chose to call it, is certainly not worship.

Questions

1. In what ways was Jacob paid back for the sins he had committed?
2. What had remained constant in Jacob's life throughout all of his trials in Padan Aram?
3. What terrible deed had Levi and Simeon done? Why?
4. How long had Jacob been in Canaan before he went back to Bethel?
5. What was one of the principal reasons for his delay in returning to Bethel?
6. Why did the people surrender their earrings along with the idols?
7. How did God protect Jacob and his family when they left Shechem?
8. What does it mean to worship "in spirit and in truth?"
9. When was Jacob's name changed to Israel? Why?
10. What does *El Shaddai* mean?

Lesson 11

Faithfulness

Week of
Feb. 14, 1999

Lesson Text

GENESIS 39:7-23

(7) And it came to pass after these things that his master's wife cast longing eyes on Joseph, and she said, "Lie with me."

(8) But he refused and said to his master's wife, "Look, my master does not know what is with me in the house, and he has committed all that he has to my hand.

(9) "There is no one greater in this house than I, nor has he kept back anything from me but you, because you are his wife. How then can I do this great wickedness, and sin against God?"

(10) So it was, as she spoke to Joseph day by day, that he did not heed her, to lie with her or to be with her.

(11) But it happened about this time, when Joseph went into the house to do his work, and none of the men of the house was inside,

(12) that she caught him by his garment, saying, "Lie with me." But he left his garment in her hand, and fled and ran outside.

(13) And so it was, when she saw that he had left his garment in her hand and fled outside,

(14) that she called to the men of her house and spoke to them, saying, "See, he has brought in to us a Hebrew to mock us. He came in to me to lie with me, and I cried out with a loud voice.

(15) "And it happened, when he heard that I lifted my voice and cried out, that he left his garment with me, and fled and went outside."

(16) So she kept his garment with her until his master came home.

(17) Then she spoke to him with words like these, saying, "The Hebrew servant whom you brought to us came in to me to mock me;

(18) "so it happened, as I lifted my voice and cried out, that he left his garment with me and fled outside."

(19) So it was, when his master heard the words which his wife spoke to him, saying, "Your servant did to me after this manner," that his anger was aroused.

(20) Then Joseph's master took him and put him into the prison, a place where the king's prisoners were confined. And he was there in the prison.

(21) But the LORD was with Joseph and showed him mercy, and He gave him favor in the sight of the keeper of the prison.

(22) And the keeper of the prison committed to Joseph's hand all the prisoners who were in the prison; whatever they did there, it was his doing.

(23) The keeper of the prison did not look into anything that was under Joseph's authority, because the LORD was with him; and whatever he did, the LORD made it prosper.

Introduction

When Jacob's father-in-law, Laban, deceived him by giving him Leah to be his wife instead of Rachel, he set off a chain reaction of events that would forever alter

Hebrew history. Because of the resentment of the two sisters, Jacob had two concubines as each sister tried to outdo the other woman. Rachel was barren and bore Jacob no children (Genesis 29:30-31). Leah had four sons in succession – Reuben, Simeon, Levi, Judah – and she thought that this would make Jacob love her, but it did not (vv. 32-35). As with Sarah before her, Rachel, seeing that she could not have children, brought her handmaiden, Bilhah, to Jacob and insisted that he take her as a wife that she might bear children to her. The strange customs of that day allowed the slave owner to claim a slave's children as their own. Bilhah bore Jacob two more sons, Dan and Naphtali (30:3-8).

When Leah had stopped bearing children she gave Jacob her handmaiden, Zilpah, who quickly bore Jacob two sons, Gad and Asher. Leah bore Jacob two more sons, Issachar and Zebulun, and a daughter named Dinah (vv. 17-21). Rachel had pled with Jacob, "Give me children, or else I die" (v. 1). Jacob became angry with her and answered, "Am I in the place of God who has withheld from you the fruit of the womb" (v. 2). At this time Jacob had 11 children, 10 boys and one girl, and still Rachel had produced no children for her husband. Evidently she had been praying to God for a child because "God remembered Rachel, and He listened to her and opened her womb" (v. 22). The son that was born to her she named Joseph because she said, "God has taken away my reproach" (v. 23). She also said, "The Lord shall add to me another son" (v. 24). Rachel did have another son, but she died giving birth to him. With her dying breath, she named him Ben-Oni, which means "son of my sorrow."

Jacob must have thought this was a great burden for a young man to carry throughout his life – to be tagged with a name that somehow signified he had caused his mother's death. He called him Benjamin instead (35:16-19). Jacob now had 12 sons in all and only one daughter. Each of these sons became the patriarch of a tribe of people, and combined they became the 12 tribes of Israel, or the nation of Israel. Rachel had been the only wife Jacob ever really wanted. When she bore her first son to him, Joseph became the favored son of the favored wife. Not only did Jacob have a favorite son, but he displayed it openly. It created a climate of hostility that culminated in the act of Joseph's brothers selling him into slavery. They hated him, and no brotherly words passed between them. The text says they "could not speak peaceably to him" (37:4). Jacob's partiality for Joseph really reached a boiling point with his other sons when he gave him "a tunic of many colors" (v. 3). This gesture characterized his love for Joseph but proved to the other sons that he was the one Jacob cared about the most.

Joseph the Dreamer

Joseph did not help the situation any by relating two dreams to his father and brothers. One was about sheaves of grain in the field, and the other dream was about stars and planets. In the dreams, Joseph's sheaves and stars were shown obeisance by his brother's and father's stars and sheaves (vv. 5-9). The brothers angrily responded, "Shall you indeed reign over us? Or, shall you indeed have dominion over us" (v. 8). There was nothing wrong with Joseph's dreams because they were sent by God, and they did come true later. However, he would have been wise to have kept them to himself. Did he not know how his brothers already felt about him without adding more fuel to the fire? Joseph was not evil, just young and naive. At any rate, his actions caused an even deeper hatred for him on the part of his brothers.

Joseph Is Sold into Slavery

The brothers moved 50 miles away, toward the territory of Shechem where their lives might be in jeopardy. Although we cannot say for certain why they moved so far away, it seems reasonable to think that they wanted to be as far away from Joseph and their father as they could be. Jacob became worried about his sons, perhaps remembering their slaughter of the Shechemites, and he sent Joseph to see about them. One is made to wonder if Jacob did not know how his favoritism of Joseph had affected his 10 other sons. When Joseph arrived at Shechem, his brothers had moved 20 miles farther away to Dothan where there were several large wells or cisterns for collecting and storing water.

When the brothers saw Joseph coming from a distance, they said, "Look, this dreamer is coming!" (v. 19). They immediately began to conspire to kill him and throw his body in a nearby pit and then tell their father that he had been killed by a wild animal (v. 20). Reuben, hearing their plan, urged them not to "Shed no blood, but cast him into this pit which is in the wilderness, and do not lay a hand upon him" (v. 22). His intent was to return later after the other brothers had left and return Joseph safely to their father. It was not to be, for while he was away a caravan of Ishmaelites passed through, and Joseph's brothers sold him into slavery for 20 shekels of silver (v. 28). The Ishmaelite traders took Joseph to Egypt and sold him on the auction block to Potiphar, the captain of Pharaoh's personal body guard (v. 36). Joseph became a slave in this powerful man's house.

Potiphar's Household Blessed Because of Joseph (Genesis 39:1-6)

"The Lord was with Joseph, and he was a successful man" (39:2). Potiphar was able to see that the Lord was with Joseph and that all he did prospered: "So Joseph found favor in his sight" (v. 4). Being the wise chief executive that he was, Potiphar promoted Joseph to steward or "overseer of his house and all that he had" (vv. 4-5). He turned the management of all of his affairs over to Joseph, and "he did not know what he had except for the bread which he ate" (v. 6). Like the blessed man in Psalm 1, God prospered everything Joseph did (v. 3).

Joseph is a great example of a man who trusted in God through good times and bad. He had every reason to be bitter, to bathe in self-pity and to allow hatred for his brothers and the desire for revenge to eat him alive. Certainly Joseph would rather have been back home in Hebron, but he made the best of bad situation. As tragic as what happened to Joseph was, if he had remained in Hebron with his pampering father, he might not have become the strong individual he turned out to be. Strength of character and conviction comes from adversity (2 Corinthians 12:9-10). Joseph had to experience the pit before he could reach the pinnacle of power. Jesus had to endure the Cross before He could wear the crown. We must first walk in this wilderness before we can rest in heaven.

Potiphar's Wife's Wandering Eyes (Genesis 39:6-9)

To prepare us for what happened later, Moses records that "Joseph was handsome in form and appearance" (v. 6). Potiphar was not the only one in whose eyes Joseph found favor. The text tells us Potiphar's wife "cast longing eyes on Joseph" (v. 7). The promiscuous attitude of the women of Egypt during this period has been well-documented. Aside from speculation concerning any reasons why she might have been interested in other men, it seems that it was considered to be the master's privilege, or in this case the master's wife's privilege, to demand sexual favors from servants. She insisted that Joseph lie with her (v. 7).

Joseph refused on the following grounds: 1. Potiphar had not withheld anything from him, giving him complete control of his entire household and therefore tremendous trust in him; 2. the only thing his master had withheld from him was his wife; and 3. he refused to commit fornication because it was a sin against God (vv. 8-9). Any sin is against oneself, but Paul specifically mentioned fornication as being a sin against our body (1 Corinthians 6:18). It is also a sin against the other person, but ultimately, as with any sin, it is a sin against God.

A Case of Attempted Rape (Genesis 39:10-12)

Potiphar's wife did not quit trying to entice Joseph to have sex with her with just one attempt. His refusal must have heightened her interest in him. Because he had rejected her advances, she may have felt the need to prove to herself that she was still a desirable woman. Among the many reasons usually given for marital infidelity are personal pride, the realization that one is growing older and the fear of the loss of virility. All of these factors contribute to make a person think he is less of a man or a woman. Unless these feelings are recognized for what they are, and the energy is directed in a positive, productive channel, a person may do a terribly foolish thing and throw away in a moment of passion the work and reputation of a lifetime.

The statement "she spoke to Joseph day by day" indicates that she constantly pressured him (v. 10). She may have thought that she could wear down his resistance, but she was wrong. He continued to resist her advances. It would appear that she planned ways for the two of them to be alone so she could exert more pressure on him. Indications are that she had the other servants doing work outside the house because Joseph's work was centered inside (v. 11). This time Potiphar's wife became aggressive with him. She took hold of his garment and tried to pull him onto her bed. Joseph was able to shake free of his cloak and run from the house.

A Woman Scorned (Genesis 39:12-19)

When Potiphar's wife saw that she was left with only Joseph's cloak, she called the other male servants into the house. She may have been concerned about what they would have thought when they saw him running from the house. She immediately began to fabricate a story accusing Joseph of trying to molest her sexually. Although no one heard her call out until she called for them to come inside, she said she had cried out when he attacked her and that is why he fled. The proof of her accusation was the garment Joseph had left behind. Her accusations may have struck a cord with some of these other servants or been seen by them as an opportunity to get even for two reasons. First, Joseph had been elevated rather quickly to the most responsible position in Potiphar's house. That could have left other servants with longer tenures envious of his sudden success. Second, she triumphed by emphasizing that he was a Hebrew. Because she says "us" to the servants, it is reasonable to assume that they were all Egyptians (v. 14).

Potiphar's wife apparently continued to lie on her bed and hold onto Joseph's cloak until her husband returned home that evening (v. 16). She began to relate to him her lie about Joseph's attempt to rape her. The implications are that she continued to nag him about it until it angered him. The words "when he heard the words which his wife spoke to him … his anger was aroused," leave an impression that he was angry with Joseph. However, there may be another explanation. It is known from historical records that a crime such as Joseph was accused of demanded the death penalty. Potiphar was Pharaoh's chief executioner. To dispose of Joseph would have been an easy matter for him. Why did he not do so? Certainly God was with Joseph, and His providence was working out for his good. Potiphar also recognized the power of Joseph's God and may have feared the consequences if he had executed Joseph. But Potiphar had entrusted Joseph with everything he owned, and he had proved himself to be a man of honesty and integrity. Could there also be the possibility that Potiphar did not completely believe his wife but thought he could not afford the courageous stand of telling her so? If that be the case, it could explain why he threw Joseph into jail instead of executing him as a means of placating her.

No Justice for Joseph – Yet (Genesis 39:20-23)

Another indication that Potiphar might not have believed his wife is the fact that Joseph was not placed into the common prison. Instead, he was put into the prison where "the king's prisoners were confined" (v. 20). This was the place where those servants were housed who had angered the king personally or people who were political prisoners. However, there is some question as to whether or not these prisoners were treated any better than other prisoners. After all, the king's baker was taken from this same prison and was hanged (40:22). Also, Psalm 105:16-22 has reference to some inhumane treatment of Joseph while he was in that prison.

Even in prison, "the Lord was with Joseph, and showed him mercy, and He gave him favor in the sight of the keeper of the prison" (Genesis 39:21). Whatever he did there prospered, and the chief jailer saw this. He soon promoted Joseph to a position above all of the other prisoners and let him run the daily affairs of the prison (vv. 2-23). Once again, Joseph had gained such trust in the eyes of another person that he was entrusted with great authority although it was in a prison.

Lessons Learned

1. We can certainly see in the story of Jacob the wisdom of God in not permitting polygamous marriages. There are several polygamous marriages mentioned in Scripture. Lamech, the grandson of Cain, was the first polygamist. Ishmael and Esau were also polygamists, but so were Abraham and Jacob. Of all the polygamous marriages mentioned, none were peaceful. God ordained the marriage relationship, and His model was one man for one woman for one lifetime. Any other arrangement besides that one is deviant. God intended marriage to be a permanent and not a temporary experiment. The only provision he made for dissolution of the marriage was death. He did permit Moses to give a provision for divorce, but this was never God's will. Jesus later amended that original statement by allowing divorce in the case of fornication or martial unfaithfulness on the part of one of the marriage partners (Matthew 19:1-9). God's way is always the best way.

2. If the Lord was with Joseph, then why did all of those terrible things keep happening to him? He was either a slave or in prison for the first 13 years of his life in Egypt. He was 17 when he was sold into slavery, and he was 30-years-old when he was released from prison to become the second highest official in the land. He lived to be 110-years-old. This means he had 13 difficult years, but in return he had 80 very good years. More importantly, he said that God sent him there to preserve the people. We are not promised everything that happens will be good, but we are promised that God will bring good out of everything that happens to us (Romans 8:28).
3. We cannot help but admire Joseph's courageous decision not to commit fornication. He was a young man with normal male appetites, far from his home and family, abused by his brothers and the system. Many people in his position would have said, "Why not! It is a reward for all that I have endured." Not Joseph. Somehow he kept himself from bitterness, resentment, vengeance and fornication. Some people talk as if sexual appetites cannot be controlled, but they can. Abstinence still pays dividends. You will never be sorry when you practice it, but if you fail to, you will have a lifetime of regret. The thing that kept him from falling into any of these sins was his commitment to God. He said, "I cannot do this thing and sin against my God." He believed God was with him and that He was watching over him. He also believed that sometime God would right all the wrongs in his life. His faith was rewarded.

Questions

1. Why did jealousy exist between Leah and Rachel?
2. What did Joseph's dreams imply?
3. Why might Joseph's brothers have moved so far from home?
4. What was Potiphar's position in Egypt?
5. What was the position that Joseph held in Potiphar's house?
6. What does the statement, "She spoke to Joseph day by day," imply?
7. What reasons did Joseph give for not submitting to Potiphar's wife's sexual advances?
8. How did Potiphar's wife prejudice the other servants and her husband against Joseph?
9. What are some of the indications that Potiphar may not have completely believed his wife?
10. What was the position that Joseph was given in the prison?

Lesson 12

Forgiveness

Week of
Feb. 21, 1999

Lesson Text

GENESIS 45:1-15

(1) Then Joseph could not restrain himself before all those who stood by him, and he cried out, "Make everyone go out from me!" So no one stood with him while Joseph made himself known to his brothers.

(2) And he wept aloud, and the Egyptians and the house of Pharaoh heard it.

(3) Then Joseph said to his brothers, "I am Joseph; does my father still live?" But his brothers could not answer him, for they were dismayed in his presence.

(4) And Joseph said to his brothers, "Please come near to me." So they came near. Then he said: "I am Joseph your brother, whom you sold into Egypt.

(5) "But now, do not therefore be grieved or angry with yourselves because you sold me here; for God sent me before you to preserve life.

(6) "For these two years the famine has been in the land, and there are still five years in which there will be neither plowing nor harvesting.

(7) "And God sent me before you to preserve a posterity for you in the earth, and to save your lives by a great deliverance.

(8) "So now it was not you who sent me here, but God; and He has made me a father to Pharaoh, and lord of all his house, and a ruler throughout all the land of Egypt.

(9) "Hurry and go up to my father, and say to him, 'Thus says your son Joseph: "God has made me lord of all Egypt; come down to me, do not tarry.

(10) "You shall dwell in the land of Goshen, and you shall be near to me, you and your children, your children's children, your flocks and your herds, and all that you have.

(11) "There I will provide for you, lest you and your household, and all that you have, come to poverty; for there are still five years of famine." '

(12) "And behold, your eyes and the eyes of my brother Benjamin see that it is my mouth that speaks to you.

(13) "So you shall tell my father of all my glory in Egypt, and of all that you have seen; and you shall hurry and bring my father down here."

(14) Then he fell on his brother Benjamin's neck and wept, and Benjamin wept on his neck.

(15) Moreover he kissed all his brothers and wept over them, and after that his brothers talked with him.

Introduction

Joseph had languished in an Egyptian prison for two years after he had interpreted the king's chief butler's dream. At that time he promised to remember Joseph to the king, but he soon forgot. When Pharaoh had a dream two years later, the butler remembered his promise. Joseph was brought out of prison and interpreted the king's dreams. They essentially contained one message. There would be seven years of abundance, followed by seven years of the worst famine possible. In addition to the interpretation, Joseph proposed a plan to store up grain during the years of plenty in preparation for the years of famine. He suggested the king find a wise man who could implement this plan. Pharaoh's response to Joseph was to say, "Can we find such a one as this, a man in whom is the Spirit of God? … Inasmuch as God has shown you all of this, there is no one as discerning and as wise as you" (Genesis 41:38-39).

Joseph Receives a Promotion

Pharaoh elevated Joseph to the second highest position in Egypt and "set him over all the land of Egypt" (v. 41). He said only in the throne would he be more powerful than Joseph. Joseph's duties would have made him similar to a prime minister today (vv. 40-43). He was given the king's signet ring, giving him the power to act on his behalf and to be able to stamp legal transactions officially. Joseph was also given a royal robe and a gold necklace, indicating the position he held in the king's court. He was transported in the chariot reserved only for royalty. The king commanded that when Joseph passed by, people should bow the knee and pay him homage (v. 43).

Pharaoh gave Joseph an Egyptian name "Zaphnath-paaneah," which means "the provider of food" (v. 45). He also gave him an Egyptian wife named Asenath, who gave Joseph two sons. The first was Manasseh, whose name means "forgetting," implying that God had allowed Joseph to forget his years of hardship (v. 51). The second was Ephraim, whose name means "fruitful," implying that God had made Joseph fruitful in the land of his captivity (v. 52). Despite the polygamous culture of Egypt, as far as we know, Asenath was the only wife Joseph ever had.

The Providence of God

In the last several years, the continent of Africa has been hit hard with prolonged droughts. These have caused severe famines, costing countless lives and millions of dollars in aid. The droughts are near the same geographic area as Egypt. However, the famine in Joseph's time was not a random act of nature. It was by deliberate design to set in motion God's providential plan to save the children of Israel from extinction (41:32). God brought them to Egypt to allow them to flourish and multiply in the most fertile place in Egypt, "the land of Goshen" (47:6). Here, they could thrive in relative obscurity from the warring factions who inhabited Canaan and grow into a mighty nation. They lived there in peace and security until "there arose a new king over Egypt, who did not know Joseph" (Exodus 1:8).

The severe famine Joseph had predicted plagued Egypt and covered "all the face of the earth" (Genesis 41:56). It extended back to Hebron where Joseph's family was still living at that time. Jacob heard there was grain in Egypt, and he sent 10 of his sons to purchase as much as they could. The grain may have been rationed, each person allowed to buy only so much, which may explain why he sent so many of them. Only Benjamin remained behind, as he had come to occupy the favored place once held by Joseph.

God's providence thus brought Joseph's brothers to Egypt. Apparently everyone who purchased grain had to appear before Joseph and explain the extent of their need before they could purchase any grain.

The Brothers Appear Before Joseph

When Joseph's brothers came before him they bowed, fulfilling the prophetic dreams he had so many years before (42:6, 9) They did so two more times (43:26; 44:14). He immediately recognized them, but they did not know who he was. They did not recognize him for several reasons. First, he was 17-year-old kid when they sold him into slavery, and he was now close to 40 years old. He was 30 when he was released from prison; the seven years of plenty had already passed, and they were at least one year into the seven years of famine (45:6). Second, he was wearing Egyptian clothes, and he spoke in the Egyptian language. Third, the position he held certainly would have confused them. Fourth, he spoke harshly to them through an interpreter, and he imprisoned them for three days (42:9-17, 23). Fifth, they thought Joseph was dead, and they did not expect to see him alive and ruling over Egypt (v. 22). One thing he said should have caused some suspicions on their part. When he brought them out of prison the third day, he said, "Do this and live, for I fear God" (v. 18). Egyptians were polytheistic, but Jehovah was not one of their gods.

In their attempts to satisfy this harsh Egyptian ruler, the brothers revealed some important information to Joseph. First, his brother Benjamin was still alive. But how could he be sure Benjamin would not meet the same fate that he had or worse? Second, his father, although aged, was still alive. This news must have warmed Joseph's heart. Joseph needed to have this information confirmed. After all, how could he trust these men when they had treated him so cruelly? He devised a plan that would let him know if these brothers had really changed and what they thought about their younger brother Benjamin. To prove they were honest men, they would have to bring their younger brother back with them when they returned (vv. 20, 33). Joseph took Simeon prisoner and bound him before their eyes to be sure they understood the seriousness of this request. He sent each of the brothers home with sacks of grain. Later, they were to discover that the sacks not only contained the grain but also the money that they had used to purchase it. This only increased their fears (vv. 25-28).

When they returned home, they related all that had happened to Jacob and told him that Simeon had been imprisoned. They also made it clear they could not return to Egypt without Benjamin (vv. 29-35). Jacob would not allow that. He said that Joseph was dead and Simeon was also now dead. This was because they thought he would be executed if they did not return. Reuben even offered to let Jacob kill his two sons if he did not bring Benjamin safely back to Jacob. What grandfather would agree with that offer? Jacob said if anything happened to Benjamin, he would die of grief, and he refused to let them go back to Egypt (vv. 36-38).

The Long Journey Back to Egypt

Although Jacob did not want any of his sons to return to Egypt, he had no choice but to allow them to go. However, he was still insistent Benjamin would not be allowed to go with them until Judah reminded him they could not return without him (43:1-5). Jacob eventually had to consent, or they would all starve to death. He finally realized there was no other way. He had his sons carry presents for Joseph and double the amount of money for the cost of the grain. He thought this might cause this harsh Egyptian ruler to see that they were honest people and then would release Simeon and Benjamin and send all of his sons back home safely (vv. 6-14). This set the stage for the dramatic conclusion of Joseph's plan.

The Revelation (Genesis 45:1-4)

When his nine brothers returned with Benjamin, Joseph had his steward escort them to his house. They were really fearful now because they thought he might be leading them into a trap and would make slaves of them (44:17-18). What irony that these men who had so callously sold their younger brother into slavery were now worried that they might become slaves. None of their fears were to be realized at that point, for Joseph treated them graciously. In addition to that, they must have been shocked when Simeon was brought out to them safe and secure. This meeting was very emotional for Joseph. Seeing his younger brother for the first time, knowing that no similar fate had come to him as had befallen himself, and wanting to embrace Benjamin were more than he could bear. He left the room where they could not see him and wept (vv. 29-31).

The final part of his plan to test his brothers' true nature was now unfolding. Joseph fed them a good meal, allowed them to get a good night's sleep and the next morning sent all of them, including Simeon and Benjamin, on their way. He gave them more grain and once again returned their money. They were assured they could safely return to Egypt any time to do commerce without any of the pressure they had endured on their previous trips. They must have been feeling pretty good about that time. But all of their feelings of joy were soon to vanish and real terror would be struck in their hearts. Joseph had his steward place an expensive cup in the mouth of Benjamin's sack and then sent the steward after them to discover if it had been stolen (44:2, 5). When the steward confronted them, they were so sure that none of them had the cup and were more than willing for their sacks to be searched. The steward did as Joseph had ordered and found the cup in Benjamin's sack. They were shocked and had no explanation for how the cup got into Benjamin's bag. The steward must have had an armed escort to enforce his demands or else Joseph's brothers would not have complied. Although they might all have been set free except for Benjamin, they returned to Joseph's house and once more appeared before him. He acted as if he would allow the rest of them to go home, but Benjamin had to pay for his crime (v. 17).

In one of the longest and most moving speeches by any single person in the Old Testament, Judah pleaded with Joseph to let Benjamin return with them. He made it clear to him that if Benjamin did not return to their father that Jacob would die (v. 29; 42:38). During his defense, Judah referred to Joseph as "my lord" eight times, and 13 times he mentioned his father. He did not know that each time he mentioned his father or Benjamin, he was reaching the very heart of Joseph. Finally, Judah offered to take Benjamin's place and to become Joseph's slave (vv. 33-34).

Joseph listened intently to this dramatic appeal as long as he could without responding or showing any emotion, but when he could contain himself any longer he burst into tears. He ordered everyone out of the room except for his brothers, and then he wept uncontrollably (45:1-2). He revealed to them his true identity. Imagine their shock and surprise and possible doubt. Perhaps in part to help relieve their fears, he asked about Jacob again, but this time he said, "does my father still live?" (v. 3). How could it be that the brother they had sold into slavery 22 years earlier was now before them as a powerful ruler of the most powerful nation in the world? They were so stunned that they did not know how to respond to him.

Joseph Sees God's Plan Clearly (Genesis 45:5-8)

Joseph graciously took much of the pressure off of his brothers by discussing with them what would have been painful for them to acknowledge. They had sold him into bondage, but they should not be "grieved or angry" with themselves because God was behind it and had "sent me before you to preserve life" (v. 5). He explained that the famine was now two years old, but there were still five years remaining and the severity, because of shortages, would become even worse (v. 6) Once more he explained God's providential care that was designed to "preserve a posterity for you in the Earth, and to save your lives by a great deliverance" (v. 7). They did not send him there; God did and had made him "lord of all Egypt" (v. 8).

It is important to remember Joseph did not know these things when he was thrown in that pit, fearing for his life. He did not know this when he was sold into slavery by his brothers. He did not know this when he was accused of rape by Potiphar's wife and when he was thrown into prison. He did not know this when he was languishing in prison, waiting for the man he had befriended to remember him and speak a good word about him to Pharaoh. Joseph realized these things for the first time with his brothers before him. We may not see or understand God's providence, but it is still there, working behind the scenes to bring about His eternal purpose in our lives and in this world. We must cooperate with God's providence by heeding His Word and making ourselves available to "work out our own salvation with fear and trembling" (Philippians 2:12).

Joseph Sent for His Family (Genesis 45:9-13)

Having convinced them that he was really their brother, Joseph ordered them to return to their father's house and bring Jacob back to live with him in Egypt (v. 9). They were to bring all of their families, flocks and herds, and they would be given a place of their own, Goshen, near where Joseph lived. They must do this because the famine was severe, and supplies would run out. In Egypt he could ensure their safety and survival, but in Palestine he could not (vv. 10-11).

Joseph told them he knew they now knew who he was. This was enough for them to give their father assurances that he was alive and that he wanted them to come to Egypt (v. 13). He then urged them to make haste and return and bring their father with them. What a joyous reunion that was, when Jacob finally saw his son again (46:30).

A Portrait of Forgiveness (Genesis 45:14-15)

Joseph did what he had longed to do from the first time he laid eyes on his younger brother. He fell on Benjamin's neck, and they both wept unashamedly (v. 14). In a show of pure love and forgiveness, he also embraced the brothers who had treated him so cruelly 22 years earlier. Back then they did not concern themselves with the fact that he would probably die in captivity. Now, when their fate was in his hands, there was only mercy and pardon. Can you imagine how they must have felt?

Although we cannot know exactly what they discussed, the text says, "his brothers talked with him" (v. 15). They may have discussed their families, wives, children and grandchildren. They may have talked about their father and told Joseph about his health. But was there nothing more important to talk about than what they had done to him. We cannot be certain, but many scholars believe there were words of deep remorse and genuine repentance. That would certainly be a logical conclusion. This scene closes with a dysfunctional family healed by the grace and mercy of one of its most abused members.

Lessons Learned

1. In Joseph's forgiveness of his brothers, we learn something about the grace and forgiveness of God. As Paul said, it is "not by works of righteousness which we have done, but according to His mercy He saved us, through the washing of regeneration and renewing of the Holy Spirit" (Titus 3:5). They did not deserve forgiveness, but still Joseph gave it to them. That is grace – something needed but not deserved.
2. One thing that stands out is the trickery and deceit Joseph used in bringing his brothers to repentance. How can such conduct be justified? We can be sure this was not God's design. However, from a purely human standpoint, Joseph knew what his brothers had been before. He had to reassure himself that his younger brother and his father were safe and secure. If he had revealed himself immediately, he might never have known for sure what they were like. The end does not justify the means. Two wrongs never make a right. Wrong is wrong, and Joseph was wrong to do what he did, but it certainly proved to him that his brothers had undergone a dramatic change since their ill treatment of him. He also knew they loved their younger brother and their father enough to give their lives for either of them. In the end, God's will prevailed despite his and their wrongdoing.

Questions

1. How long was Joseph in Egypt before he was elevated to the high position he received?
2. What did the Egyptian name Pharaoh gave to Joseph mean?
3. Why did Joseph's brothers have to come to Egypt?
4. What two important things did the brothers reveal to Joseph in their first defense before him?
5. Why did Joseph's brothers not recognize him?
6. Why would Jacob not let Benjamin go to Egypt although Simeon might be killed?
7. What did the brothers think when they returned to Egypt and were ushered into Joseph's house?
8. How did Joseph trap them?
9. What arguments did Judah make to Joseph to try and get Benjamin released?
10. How did Joseph finally convince them of his true identity?

Lesson 13

Reunion

Week of
Feb. 28, 1999

Lesson Text

GENESIS 46:28-34

(28) Then he sent Judah before him to Joseph, to point out before him the way to Goshen. And they came to the land of Goshen.

(29) So Joseph made ready his chariot and went up to Goshen to meet his father Israel; and he presented himself to him, and fell on his neck and wept on his neck a good while.

(30) And Israel said to Joseph, "Now let me die, since I have seen your face, because you are still alive."

(31) Then Joseph said to his brothers and to his father's household, "I will go up and tell Pharaoh, and say to him, 'My brothers and those of my father's house, who were in the land of Canaan, have come to me.

(32) 'And the men are shepherds, for their occupation has been to feed livestock; and they have brought their flocks, their herds, and all that they have.'

(33) "So it shall be, when Pharaoh calls you and says, 'What is your occupation?'

(34) "that you shall say, 'Your servants' occupation has been with livestock from our youth even till now, both we and also our fathers,' that you may dwell in the land of Goshen; for every shepherd is an abomination to the Egyptians."

GENESIS 47:1-12

(1) Then Joseph went and told Pharaoh, and said, "My father and my brothers, their flocks and their herds and all that they possess, have come from the land of Canaan; and indeed they are in the land of Goshen."

(2) And he took five men from among his brothers and presented them to Pharaoh.

(3) Then Pharaoh said to his brothers, "What is your occupation?" And they said to Pharaoh, "Your servants are shepherds, both we and also our fathers."

(4) And they said to Pharaoh, "We have come to dwell in the land, because your servants have no pasture for their flocks, for the famine is severe in the land of Canaan. Now therefore, please let your servants dwell in the land of Goshen."

(5) Then Pharaoh spoke to Joseph, saying, "Your father and your brothers have come to you.

(6) "The land of Egypt is before you. Have your father and brothers dwell in the best of the land; let them dwell in the land of Goshen. And if you know any competent men among them, then make them chief herdsmen over my livestock."

(7) Then Joseph brought in his father Jacob and set him before Pharaoh; and Jacob blessed Pharaoh.

(8) Pharaoh said to Jacob, "How old are you?

(9) And Jacob said to Pharaoh, "The days of the years of my pilgrimage are one hundred and thirty years; few and evil have been the days of the years of my life, and they have not attained to the days of the years of the life of my fathers in the days of their pilgrimage."

(10) So Jacob blessed Pharaoh, and went out from before Pharaoh.

(11) And Joseph situated his father and his brothers, and gave them a possession in the land of Egypt, in the best of the land, in the land of Rameses, as Pharaoh had commanded.
(12) Then Joseph provided his father, his brothers, and all his father's household with bread, according to the number in their families.

Introduction

Put yourself in Jacob's place for a few moments. Twenty-two years earlier he had been deceived by his 10 older sons into believing that his favorite son was dead. They showed him the prized coat of many colors stained with blood. He had no reason to believe otherwise. Although he had almost grieved himself to death over that loss, he had finally come to accept it and had gone on with his life. He also appears to have lavished the affection he felt for Joseph on his youngest son, Benjamin, the second son of his favorite wife, Rachel. Now the same men who had convinced him Joseph was dead tell him that he is not only alive but also one of the most powerful men in the world. Would you believe it? He did not either (Genesis 45:26). However, when he saw the carts that Joseph had sent to bring him to Egypt, "the spirit of Jacob, their father, revived … and Israel said, 'It is enough. Joseph my son is alive. I will go see him before I die' " (vv. 27-28).

Before he departed Palestine for Egypt, Jacob went up to Beersheba and offered sacrifices to God. He must have wanted to be certain this was the will of God. How long it had been since God had talked with him we do not know, but He spoke to him again that night in a vision. He assured Jacob this was His will, and He would be with him there and bless him. God also promised Jacob that He would make of him "a great nation there … and … also surely bring him up again" (46:3-4). Convinced now that God was with him, Jacob proceeded to make the journey to Egypt in the company of all of his family (vv. 5-7).

Moving this group of people was no easy task. We are told there were 66 people who made the journey with Jacob. When Joseph's family is added to that number, in all there were 70 of Jacob's family in Egypt (46:26-27). In Stephen's stirring message before he was stoned to death, he said the number of people was 75 (Acts 7:14). How do we account for the discrepancy? Some scholars believe that he added the five grandsons of Joseph to this number as was done in the Greek Septuagint. This would make 75 and would then include "all of Jacob's kindred." The point of this figure is to show how dramatically the children of Israel grew while in Egypt, proving that God was watching over them and blessing them.

A Time of Rejoicing and Reunion (Genesis 46:28-34)

What a reunion that must have been. It reminds us about the story of the prodigal son returning to his father's house (Luke 15:11-24). On that occasion, the son was spiritually dead; by his return and repentance, he was made alive again. This time, the son was thought to be physically dead, but he was very much alive. Both fathers rejoiced at the restoration of their sons to them.

Jacob had sent Judah ahead to prepare the way for them and to lead them to the land of Goshen where Joseph had indicated they were to settle (Genesis 46:28). Judah is clearly in a position of leadership after demonstrating his strength of character. Although Goshen had been designated by Joseph as the place where they would reside, Pharaoh had not yet given his endorsement to that proposal. His willingness to do so proves the trust he placed in Joseph (47:6).

When told his father had arrived in Goshen, Joseph went up to meet with him. The text says that when they met, they each fell on the other's neck and "wept ... a good while" (46:29). We can be sure that it was a good while because Jacob thought Joseph was dead, and Joseph did not know for years whether Jacob was still alive. Jacob told Joseph that he could now die in peace because he had seen his face and knew he was indeed alive (v. 30). Joseph informed his father that he must now make Pharaoh aware that he had moved his family to Egypt.

Some people accuse Joseph of deception so that he might secure the fertile land of Goshen, the fertile crescent of Egypt, for his family. There was no deception intended. Joseph knew what the Egyptians thought about foreigners, especially shepherds. Their hatred of shepherds, possibly because they were ruled over for centuries by the Hyksos, or Shepherd Kings, has been well-documented. Joseph's plan served a twofold purpose – it allowed the Israelites to maintain their national and spiritual distinctiveness and removed them from the sight of most Egyptians. The land of Goshen was as far away as a person could go and still be in Egypt. It was just before one enters the Arabian Desert and was nearest to Canaan.

Joseph Appeals to Pharaoh (Genesis 47:1-2)

Joseph was a powerful man in Egypt, but even he could not make a decision of this magnitude without the king's approval. To have done so might have resulted in charges of partiality on the part of Joseph. This could have spelled trouble for him and for Pharaoh. Remember, they were still in the throes of a severe famine which would be accompanied by an economic depression. The Egyptians would not take kindly to these foreign sheepherders coming in and taking some prime land from them. Although the land of Goshen was some of the most fertile land in Egypt, because of its location, it was not a desirable place for most Egyptians to live.

To accompany him in his meeting with Pharaoh, Joseph took five of his brothers. The purpose may not at first be clear, but in addition to shepherds being disliked by Egyptians, they were not much of a real threat either. Which of the brothers Joseph selected we are not told, but being the wise and discerning man that he was, we can be sure he chose the ones who would make the best impression on the king.

The King Approves Joseph's Plan (Genesis 47:3-6)

Why did Pharaoh ask them the question about their occupation? The answer has been partially given above, but another part of the answer can be found in verse 6. He wanted to know what kind of jobs they did so they could be employed in Egypt. A question that is asked of resident aliens coming into any country is "What kind of work do you qualify for?" Few nations want to take in people who are not going to be productive citizens.

The brothers informed Pharaoh that they were sojourners in the land. This implied they did not want to take anything away from anyone else. They were not going to be permanent dwellers there; they were only there because of the severity of the famine in their land. To have remained in Palestine would have caused death to their animals and possibly to themselves. They then asked Pharaoh if they could continue to live in the land of Goshen. The king not only acceded to their request but also told them that because they were Joseph's family the whole land of Egypt was before them. He also invited some of them to tend his flocks.

The Pharaoh Meets the Patriarch (Genesis 47:7-10)

Joseph then brought his father, Jacob, in to meet Pharaoh for the first time. He may have bowed before the monarch in customary fashion as some people insist he did, but the text does not indicate that. We are told he pronounced a blessing upon the king. He was the physical and spiritual head of his family. In the Patriarchal Age, the fathers functioned as a priest for their families (see Job 1:5). In Genesis 14:17-24, we are told about Abraham offering tithes to Melchizedek because he was "a priest of the Most High God." The writer of Hebrews refers to this incident and says that "the least was blessed of the greater" (7:6-10). Jacob blessed Pharaoh, who was his superior in the world, but Jacob was superior to Pharaoh in God's spiritual kingdom because he was chosen to father and to lead his people. He blessed Pharaoh again, or perhaps said a blessing before he departed from the king's presence (Genesis 47:10).

The king inquired about Jacob's age, which would indicate that he appeared aged. He told the king that he was 130-years-old. He would live only 17 more years for a total of 147 years (v. 28). This may seem like a long time to us, but considering the age of the other patriarchs before him, it was not long at all. His grandfather, Abraham, lived to be 175 years of age, and his father, Isaac, lived to be 180.

Jacob also said that his days were evil. This does not mean that he was evil, but is similar to the statement of Job: "Man who is born of woman is of few days and full of trouble" (14:1). Jacob's last few years in Egypt were undoubtedly the happiest of his life. His family was at peace at last, and he was able to enjoy them fully for the first time in his life.

Pharaoh was a pagan ruler who worshiped a multitude of gods, but God used him to serve, and in effect, save His people (Proverbs 21:1). God can, has, and may again use unbelieving rulers such as this Pharaoh, the one in Moses' time, Nebuchadnezzar, Cyrus and Augustus to carry out His will (Ezra 1:1; Isaiah 44:28; Jeremiah 25:9; 27:6; Luke 2:1).

Jacob and His Sons Settle in Goshen (Genesis 47:11-12)

Joseph placed his family in Goshen, "giving them possession," meaning that he deeded that land to them. Being in his position, he had full authority from Pharaoh to do so (v. 11). This place is called "the land of Ramses" only here in the Old Testament. The Septuagint has it also in 46:28. This is a notation by Moses as to the name by which this area would later be called (Exodus 1:11; 12:37; Numbers 33:3, 5). The name was changed by Ramses II, 1290-1224 B.C., to honor himself.

Joseph "nourished his family" (Genesis 47:12 KJV) or supplied them with the necessary nourishment, not just in their first settlement but as long it was needed. Five years remained before the famine would be over, and it would take at least one year to recover from those bad years. The people of Egypt would sacrifice for their benefit without knowing it. While they grew poorer, the children of Israel grew stronger in number. When they departed from Egypt 430 year later, they numbered 2 million. Truly God had fulfilled His promise to Jacob.

Lessons Learned

1. Although Jacob was sure that Joseph was alive and he wanted him to come to Egypt, he would not move until he had consulted God. James tells us that we should not make any moves without being sure it is God's will (4:13-16). God will not appear to us in a vision today, but we can seek His will in the Bible. We can also pray that He will help us to understand what His will is and to be guided by it. The more we study His Word, and the more we ask for His direction, the clearer His will for our lives will become.
2. What a wonderful picture of reunion this story presents. If you have ever been away from a loved one for a long period of time or if you are in family that has reunions frequently, you know how meaningful these can be. Paul tells us about a grand reunion that will take place one day when Jesus returns in the clouds of heaven. He will bring the souls of the saved with Him and the righteous living will be caught up to meet them in the air, "and so shall we ever be with the Lord" (1 Thessalonians 4:13-18). What a wonderful day of rejoicing and reunion that will be.
3. This story brings up again the question about God's use of heathen people to accomplish His purposes. Although He used them in the sense that He brought them along with His purpose, at no time did they lose their free will. God used this Pharaoh to bless Israel in this way because apparently he was a man of compassion and generosity. He used the Pharaoh in Moses' day because he was the exact opposite. God did not make either of them who and what they were. God raised up Nebuchadnezzar to punish Judah, but He did not make him who he was. Judas was used by Satan to betray Christ, but he also fulfilled God's will in the process. He was able to be used in that way because he was a greedy man with a covetous heart. God did not make him that way. We are predestined, but it is not individuals that are predestined. All Christians are predestined to be conformed to the image of God's son. That is, God has predestined or predetermined the life we must live to reach heaven.

Questions

1. What finally convinced Jacob that Joseph was really alive?
2. What assurance did Jacob seek before he would make the journey to Egypt?
3. How many people did Jacob take with him to Egypt, and what was the total number of his family that left there?
4. Who were the Hyksos?
5. Why did Egyptians hate shepherds so much?
6. Where was Goshen, and why was it not desirable to Egyptians?
7. How many brothers did Joseph take with him to meet Pharaoh? Why?
8. What was Pharaoh's question to Joseph's brothers, and why did he ask it?
9. What does the word "sojourner" suggest?
10. Why did Jacob bless Pharaoh?

Lesson 1

James Profiled

Week of
March 7, 1999

Lesson Text

ACTS 15:13-21

(13) And after they had become silent, James answered, saying, "Men and brethren, listen to me:

(14) "Simon has declared how God at the first visited the Gentiles to take out of them a people for His name.

(15) "And with this the words of the prophets agree, just as it is written:

(16) 'After this I will return And will rebuild the tabernacle of David, which has fallen down; I will rebuild its ruins, And I will set it up;

(17) So that the rest of mankind may seek the LORD, Even all the Gentiles who are called by My name, Says the LORD who does all these things.'

(18) "Known to God from eternity are all His works.

(19) "Therefore I judge that we should not trouble those from among the Gentiles who are turning to God,

(20) "but that we write to them to abstain from things polluted by idols, from sexual immorality, from things strangled, and from blood.

(21) "For Moses has had throughout many generations those who preach him in every city, being read in the synagogues every Sabbath."

Introduction

The author of the volume called James tells us only that he was "a servant of God, and of the Lord Jesus Christ." Several men by the name of James are referred to in the New Testament. It was a popular name and is equivalent to the Hebrew name Jacob. So just who was the writer of this book? We can rule out James, an apostle, the son of Zebedee and the brother of John, because he was the first apostle to be martyred for the faith. He was killed by Herod in A.D. 44 long before this epistle is believed to have been written (Acts 12:1-2). James, the son of Alphaeus, called "the less," was another one of the apostles who wore this name (Matthew 10:3; Acts 1:13), but little is known about him. Another James, even more obscure than the previous person mentioned, was the father of Judas (Luke 6:16). This apostle was no doubt so designated to distinguish him from Judas Iscariot. The man many people consider the most likely candidate to be the author of this book was James, the brother of our Lord (Matthew 13:55).

As far as we know from Scripture and as noted in an earlier lesson, Jesus was raised in a normal family as any boy of His time would have been. We do know that contrary to a popular religious tradition, Mary did not remain a virgin for the rest of her life after she bore Jesus. She and Joseph had four other sons: James, Joses, Judas (Jude) and Simon, and more than one daughter (Matthew 13:55-56; Mark 6:3). Although we cannot know for certain from what is revealed in the Gospels, it appears that Jesus was not raised as a half brother to His siblings. Every indication is that He was treated just like his brothers and sisters and that they never knew until they were grown that He was unique. It was not until His death and resurrection that any of His family other than His mother believed on Him (John 7:5; Mark 3:31-35). Notice that none of Mary's other children were with her at the Cross, but they were with her in the Upper Room (Acts 1:14).

How did James, who had shown such lack of faith in Jesus, suddenly become a disciple? He certainly had many opportunities to be convinced. He was with Jesus when He performed His first miracle at Cana of Galilee (John 2:1, 12). He left there and went with the disciples to Capernaum, where Jesus performed some miracles (Matthew 4:13-16; Luke 4:23). James may have also been present when Jesus visited the synagogue in Nazareth and was rejected by the hometown folks (Matthew 13:53-58). On another occasion, he came in the company of his mother and brothers to see Jesus where He was preaching and performing miracles (Mark 3:31-35; Luke 8:19-21). With his brothers, he once even tried to persuade Jesus to leave Galilee and go to Judea. They were perhaps fearful for His life (John 7:3-5, 10); they also thought he was "out of His mind" (Mark 3:21). However, none of the events alone appears to have converted James.

Yet we find James, as well as his other brothers, in the company of the disciples in Jerusalem, awaiting the fulfillment of our Lord's promise (Acts 1:6-8, 14). Apparently by this time, He, along with his brothers, had become a believer. We can point to one watershed event in his life that most likely brought about his conversion. Paul tells us that after Jesus' resurrection, among other people Jesus appeared to, was James (1 Corinthians 15:7), the man he calls "the Lord's brother" (Galatians 1:19). From that moment on, there was a dramatic change in this former skeptic's life. He became a Christian and a prominent leader in the church at Jerusalem (Acts 21:18; Galatians 1:18-19; 2:9, 12). The church historian Eusebius writes that James was called "the Just" because of his deep sincerity and honesty. The same writer also tells us that he spent so much time on his knees in prayer that they became "hard and worn, like a camel's." A strong tradition says that James was martyred in A.D. 62 when he was cast down from the pinnacle of the temple. He then was either beaten to death or stoned under orders from Ananias, or Ananus, the most corrupt man ever to serve as high priest.

Although we have little substantial scriptural evidence that James was an elder in the Jerusalem church, some people interpret Acts 21:18 to imply that supposition. However, there can be no doubt about his prominence and influence. He was among the first to whom Peter sent word after he was released from prison (Acts 12:17). He was prominent on Paul's first visit to Jerusalem (Galatians 1:19), and 14 years later Paul calls him "a pillar" of the church there (Galatians 2:1, 9). It was to James that Paul went upon his arrival with the bounty from the Gentile churches for the poor Jewish Christians (Acts 21:18; Galatians 2:9-10). James also appears to have "presided" over the so-called "Jerusalem council" (Acts 15:13). It is at this point that we find him in our text for this lesson. Here we learn much about James and his message.

James: A Reasonable Man (Acts 15:13-14)

As noted earlier, James appears to have taken center stage in the discussions about the Gentiles' relationship to the Law. This does not mean that he was in any sense the leader of the Jerusalem congregation. He did not even allow himself to name drop when writing his book, and he does not refer to himself as the Lord's brother but as "a servant of God, and of the Lord Jesus Christ." That the people would have respect for him is only natural; he was known for his piety and for the fact that he was the brother of Jesus.

James accepted the testimony of Peter regarding the conversion of the Gentiles. This was the second time that Peter had related this information to at least most of this illustrious group (Acts 11:1-18; 15:7-11). The main point, as James saw it, was that God had accepted the Gentiles as well as the Jews. As Peter had said, "we believe that through the grace of our Lord Jesus Christ we shall be saved in the same manner as they" (Acts 15:11).

James Knew the Bible (Acts 15:15-18)

James was astute enough to know that the hardliners among the Jewish Christians would not accept the contemporary testimony alone that pointed to God's acceptance of the Gentiles. In his explanation, he shows clear understanding of the Old Testament prophets and how to use them to correct error. Although James uses only one prophecy, he plainly said "the prophets agree" with what Peter had said. There are numerous prophecies that teach this same truth (Genesis 12:1-3; Isaiah 2:2-4; 49:6; 54:13; Jeremiah 31:31-35; Hosea 1:10; 2:23; Micah 4:1-14). The prophecy James quoted from Amos 9:11-12 proves that God had intended from "eternity" to save "all," Jews and Gentiles, "who are called by My name" (Acts 15:17-18).

Amos' prophecy referred to the "tabernacle of David," an obvious reference to the worship place of the Jews until the temple of Solomon was built. It speaks of this tabernacle as "fallen down" and in "ruins" (Acts 15:14-17), and it foretells that the time would come when Jews and Gentiles would worship God together in a new tabernacle. This prophecy is fulfilled in the body or church of Jesus Christ (Ephesians 2:12-16).

James Was Free from Prejudice (Acts 15:19-20)

After hearing the testimony of Peter, Paul and Barnabas and considering the teaching of God's Word, James urged his Jewish brethren not to impose the burden of the Law on Gentiles. He understood that the Law was uniquely given to them and that it was never intended to govern anyone else's acceptance with God.

The Jews had been privileged to have the Law of Moses. It was meant to prepare them for the coming of the Messiah (Galatians 3:19-25). It had been read from the synagogues every Sabbath for centuries. Therefore, they should have understood its broader implications. Jews did not have to lose respect for it, but neither should they have expected everyone else to observe it. It was only through Christ that all men would be saved.

James was willing only to place upon the Gentile Christians the minimal prohibitions required under the Law that would make fellowship between Jews and Gentiles acceptable. Gentiles would not be required to submit to the covenant seal of circumcision. Nor would they be required to keep the feast days, the holy days, to observe the sacrifices or the peculiar dietary restrictions (Acts 15:24). They were not Jews, and observing these outward rituals would not make them such.

In verse 20, James spells out in brief the four restrictions that Gentiles, as well as Jews, would be required to observe. Some people conclude from James' statement in verse 19 that he was giving a personal opinion. However, if it was an opinion, it was an inspired one. Verse 28 proves that although James may have spoken these words and may have even recorded them they were inspired by the Holy Spirit (2 Peter 1:19-21). In this inspired injunction there are four essential parts: 1. abstaining from things offered to idols; 2. sexual immorality, or fornication; 3. not eating animals that had been strangled because of the difficulty of draining all of the blood from them; and 4. refrain from consuming blood in any form. This is not, however, a prohibition against blood transfusions. There is a difference in consuming blood through the mouth and receiving it in the veins.

While it is possible to show that these principles were condemned under the Law (Genesis 9:4; Exodus 20:14; Leviticus 3:17; 7:26; 17:10-14; Deuteronomy 5:18), there were other good reasons for their prohibition among Gentile Christians. All of these four things mentioned were common practices among Gentiles as parts of their idolatrous worship. This was one reason that they were considered unclean by the Jews. They ate the meat offered to idols and also drank the blood. Ritual prostitution of both males and females was a frequent feature at the idol temples, and sexual orgies were regular fare.

Lessons Learned

1. From Jesus' brothers and sisters, we can learn that people often fail to appreciate what is right before them.
2. James believed because he saw Jesus after His resurrection, but "we walk by faith and not by sight" (2 Corinthians 5:7). Jesus said, "Blessed are those who have not seen and yet have believed" (John 20:29).
3. The greatest skeptics can become the grandest saints.
4. From the example of the Jerusalem council, a gathering of church leaders to solve a mutual problem, we learn how to resolve conflict between congregations.
5. James may have been *a* bishop (elder) of the Jerusalem church, but he was never *the* bishop of Jerusalem or Judea.
6. Jews and Gentiles are saved the same way – by believing and obeying the gospel.
7. God's plan from before the world began was to unite all men unto Himself in one church.
8. The Law was a covenant between God and Israel; it never included the Gentiles.

Questions

1. What is the equivalent Hebrew name for James?
2. Why was James, the Lord's brother, considered to be the best candidate for the author of the book that bears that name?
3. What reasons are given in this lesson for why James should have been a believer before Jesus was resurrected?
4. What do many people consider to be the main reason why James became a believer?
5. What position did James hold in the Jerusalem church?
6. What feature of the book shows James' humility (if he was the author)?
7. What was the main point of Peter's position?
8. How did James gain support of the hardliners among the Jewish Christians?
9. In what way was the prophecy concerning David's tabernacle fulfilled?
10. What was James' conclusion regarding Gentiles and the Law?

Lesson 2

Faith Tested

Week of March 14, 1999

Lesson Text

JAMES 1:1-18

(1) James, a bondservant of God and of the Lord Jesus Christ, To the twelve tribes which are scattered abroad: Greetings.

(2) My brethren, count it all joy when you fall into various trials,

(3) knowing that the testing of your faith produces patience.

(4) But let patience have its perfect work, that you may be perfect and complete, lacking nothing.

(5) If any of you lacks wisdom, let him ask of God, who gives to all liberally and without reproach, and it will be given to him.

(6) But let him ask in faith, with no doubting, for he who doubts is like a wave of the sea driven and tossed by the wind.

(7) For let not that man suppose that he will receive anything from the Lord;

(8) he is a double-minded man, unstable in all his ways.

(9) Let the lowly brother glory in his exaltation,

(10) but the rich in his humiliation, because as a flower of the field he will pass away.

(11) For no sooner has the sun risen with a burning heat than it withers the grass; its flower falls, and its beautiful appearance perishes. So the rich man also will fade away in his pursuits.

(12) Blessed is the man who endures temptation; for when he has been approved, he will receive the crown of life which the Lord has promised to those who love Him.

(13) Let no one say when he is tempted, "I am tempted by God"; for God cannot be tempted by evil, nor does He Himself tempt anyone.

(14) But each one is tempted when he is drawn away by his own desires and enticed.

(15) Then, when desire has conceived, it gives birth to sin; and sin, when it is full-grown, brings forth death.

(16) Do not be deceived, my beloved brethren.

(17) Every good gift and every perfect gift is from above, and comes down from the Father of lights, with whom there is no variation or shadow of turning.

(18) Of His own will He brought us forth by the word of truth, that we might be a kind of firstfruits of His creatures.

Introduction

The book of James is a practical guide to living the Christian life. It might be called applied Christianity. Yet contrary to what some commentators say, it is also a doctrinal book. It is not possible to live a practical Christian life without an understanding of doctrine. The book is not doctrinal in the sense that Romans or Galatians would be. The name of Christ is only mentioned twice, the third member of the Godhead, the Holy Spirit, is never referred to, the Cross is never mentioned, nor is the Resurrection. However, interspersed within its explanation of simple faith in action is the doctrinal foundation that undergirds each truth presented. James realized the need for both doctrine and application, and so through the Spirit's guidance he wove the two together into a strong fabric of faith.

That this little book could be the source of so much controversy is hard to believe. Martin Luther wanted to leave it out of his translation of the Bible. His words for it was that "it is a right strawy epistle." He believed it was a forgery because he perceived that it contradicted his belief in "salvation by faith alone." He believed James contradicted Paul on the matter of faith and works, and therefore his book could not be a genuinely inspired work. Many people since Luther have expressed similar doubts. Are these concerns really justified?

The problem Martin Luther and these later critics have is that James does not support their unbiblical doctrine of faith only. It is they who make an imagined difference between the teaching of Paul and James regarding faith, works and salvation. There is no contradiction between them at all for they are approaching the subject from a different standpoint. In Romans, Paul endeavors to show that salvation is by "grace through faith." James teaches the same thing but shows that the faith that saves is an active faith. Dead faith never saved anyone, and it never will (James 2:20-26). Faith is the blood of a spiritual life, and good works are the respiration that keeps it flowing. If you stop practicing your faith, it will die. One writer said, "Faith is the root; works are the fruit." If you have the root, you will bear the fruit. As Jesus said in John 15:5, "He who abides in Me, and I in him, bears much fruit; for without Me you can do nothing."

Would you know a real Christian if you saw one? The word "Christian" is thrown around so lightly today. We hear all the time about some person passing away who obviously never lived for Christ, but maybe did some good things in his life being called a Christian. This term has even been used to describe people who lived ungodly lifestyles simply because they were considered good by the world's standards. James shows us what a real Christian is and how he is supposed to live. Originally, he was addressing Jewish Christians who were scattered throughout the Roman world (James 1:1). All Christians were experiencing persecution by the time this epistle was penned, A.D. 45-62, but Jewish Christians were hardest hit because they got it from both sides. They were constantly treated with hostility by Gentiles because they were Jews, and they were sorely mistreated by Jews because they were Christians. On orders from Claudius, the Roman emperor, Jews were driven out of Rome, from their homeland and also from Jerusalem. How should Christians live in such circumstances? James gives us some inspired answers to this question.

Confronting Trials (James 1:2-4)

One truth is clearly evident in James' statement – even as Christians trial will come to us (James 1:2; Job 14:1; Psalms 34:19; 2 Corinthians 4:8-9). James does not question that Christians will "fall into various trials." He assumes that we will and says "when" and then tells us how to deal with them. These trials are not temptations, which he discusses later in verses 12-15. They are the trying or testing of our faith that come upon us from without. James plainly says that in verse 3.

One of the hardest questions to answer in regard to God is, "Why do bad things happen to good people?" It is the age-old question about a good God and the problem of evil. The Old Testament book of Job deals with this subject. However, do not expect to go there finding any answers to this question, for what God does with Job is essentially to say, "You're just going to have to trust me." That is what it basically comes down to. We cannot answer all of the questions about "Why?" We cannot solve all of the theological riddles. We cannot answer all of the deep mysteries about God. We have to trust God enough to believe that He will do what is right. As Moses told the children of Israel, "The secret things belong to the Lord our God, but those things which are revealed belong to us and to our children forever, that we may do all the words of this law" (Deuteronomy 29:29).

God did not promise us a rose garden without problems. Anyone who has tried to raise roses can tell you it takes a lot of effort to grow a beautiful garden. Along with the beauty and fragrance of the flower, we have to deal with the thorns. Christians are not immune to troubles, trials and tribulations. In fact, Jesus said exactly the opposite. He said, "These things I have spoken to you, that in Me you may have peace. In this world you will have tribulation; but be of good cheer, I have overcome the world" (John 16:33). Paul adds, "Yes, and all who desire to live godly in Christ Jesus will suffer persecution" (2 Timothy 3:12). Trials of faith will come, so how do we handle them?

The first thing James tells us to do is to "count it all joy" or "rejoice." All of us have dealt with trials, and we can testify they are not fun. How can James tell us to celebrate such difficult times? Am I to say when trials come my way, "Boy, this feels good!"? No, in fact James gives us the reason for rejoicing – "the testing of your faith produces patience" (James 1:3). The writer of Hebrews writing about a similar subject said, "Now no chastening seems to be joyful for the present, but painful; nevertheless, afterward it yields the peaceable fruit of righteousness to those who have been trained by it" (Hebrews 12:11). Spiritually speaking, where there is no pain there is no gain. If all of life was one big amusement park, we would never grow spiritually. It is through meeting and overcoming trials that we grow stronger and are enabled to confront them effectively in the future.

Our faith trials produce patience. This does not mean that we passively accept anything that happens to us. Instead, we aggressively pursue the goal despite any trials we encounter. We learn from them to "wait upon the Lord." We do not learn patience by reading a book, listening to a sermon or even by praying. It is only through life's testing that we come to learn to trust God. He wants us to learn patience because this opens the door to all other blessings. It takes patient endurance to "be faithful unto death" and to receive "the crown of life" (Revelations 2:10; Hebrews 6:12; 10:36). In the end, patient endurance perfects or completes us so as to produce a stable Christian character (Romans 5:3-4).

Coveting Wisdom (James 2:5-8)

Have you not heard or used yourself the phrase, "That person has a lot of book knowledge, but no common sense"? What we call "common sense" Solomon calls "wisdom." The book of Proverbs is about the pursuit of wisdom (Proverbs 2:6-8; 4:5-6; 10:5, 13; 12:8). Wisdom is a quality to be sought after, and once it is found it is a treasure of great value. Wisdom is not just knowledge or a lot of facts in the head. It is the application of that knowledge and those facts to a person's life. Because wisdom is so important, how do we gain it?

Is wisdom merely a byproduct of age and experience? A person may accumulate wisdom by living a long time. However, a person may be wise in his youth and foolish in his old age. Does it simply come through the trial-and-error method? James informs us that wisdom is not merely a byproduct of a lot of failed experiments. It is the result of careful, disciplined, difficult and diligent effort. Wisdom is not a thing that can be taught. You can teach someone facts, but it is impossible to teach a person how to exercise wisdom in the use of that information. Wisdom, rather, is a thing to grasp. James provides us with the necessary steps to achieve wisdom.

First, we must be aware of our need for wisdom and be willing to ask for it. So often people think they are wise because they are intelligent, well-educated or older. Such people will never seek wisdom because they think they already possess it.

Second, we must be cognizant of its origin. James tells us that the source of true wisdom is God. Just as He gives to us "every good gift and every perfect gift" (James 1:17), He will not withhold wisdom from His children who ask for it. In fact, He will give it to us liberally and will not reproach, chide or punish us for asking. James says if we ask, we will receive.

One great barrier to our receiving the wisdom we ask God for is a lack of faith. If we ask but harbor doubts that God will provide, we are like the uncertain sea waves that are stirred about with the wind. The word "doubt" suggests being at odds with one's self (Matthew 21:21; Mark 11:23; Romans 4:20; 14:23;), hesitation (Acts 10:20) or wavering. A person who approaches the Lord on these conditions should not expect to receive anything from Him.

The doubter who asks God for wisdom is a double-minded person. As David Roper wrote in *Practical Christianity: Studies in the Book of James*, this "doesn't mean twice as smart" (Gospel Advocate Company, Nashville, 1987; p. 21). It refers to a person who is teetering on the brink of faith and faithlessness – at one point wanting to trust, but not able to surrender completely. Such a person is unstable in all his ways. Doubters are like corked bottles floating in the ocean at the mercy of the tides. Paul describes this type of person in the Ephesian letter as being "tossed to and fro and carried about with every wind of doctrine, by the trickery of men, in the cunning craftiness of deceitful plotting" (4:14). Instability and insecurity go hand in hand.

Convicting Pride (James 1:9-11)

In addition to the persecution by the Roman government and by the Jewish authorities, it appears from the context of James that poorer Christians were even having to endure mistreatment from their wealthier brothers and sisters in Christ (2:1-9, 14-16; 5:1-6). However, the poor need not be ashamed, nor should the wealthy be haughty. Christianity elevates the poor and humbles the rich. The kingdom of God is the place where "The rich and the poor have this in common, the Lord is the maker of them all" (Proverbs 22:2).

There are two things that should humble the wealthy, and they are the brevity of life and the certainty of death. Notice first that James says just like the "flower of the field" the rich too "will pass away" (James 1:10). James says later that the brevity of life is like "a vapor that appears for a little time and then vanishes away" (4:14). Death is the great equalizer. It knows no strangers, and treats all men, rich and poor, with impartiality. We will not escape it. "And as it is appointed for men to die once, but after this the judgment" (Hebrews 9:27).

Conquering Temptation (James 1:12-18)

"Blessed" is a word meaning "happy," or explicitly, "more than happy." Phrases beginning with this word are called beatitudes because they introduce attitudes that a person who would be happy should possess. There are numerous such statements in the Bible. Some are found in Psalms, in the Prophets, in Revelation, and the best known are those with which Jesus began the Sermon on the Mount.

James tells us several things about temptation. First, temptation will come (1:12). He says that if a person would be happy he must endure temptation. Why did he not say defeat it, or destroy it? The answer is simple. We must learn to endure temptation because as long as we live in the flesh, we will be tempted. Paul reminds us that "No temptation has overtaken you, except such as is common to man" (1 Corinthians 10:13). Remember that after Satan had tempted Jesus in the wilderness, he left Him only for "a season" (Luke 4:13 KJV). He will flee if we resist him (James 4:7), but you can be sure he only does so to lick his wounds and to wait for another opportunity to attack us (1 Peter 5:8).

James uses the word "proved," or tested, in connection with overcoming temptation. Although different from the trials he mentioned earlier, he still views these as a test of our faith. The word in the original also means "approved." This person has stood the test and has been proven genuine. Because of that, he will receive "the crown of life which the Lord has promised to those who love Him" (James 1:12).

Second, James tells us that temptation does not come from God (1:13). He is not the tempter; Satan is (Job 1:9-12; Matthew 4:3; 1 Thessalonians 3:5). God can do everything, but there are things He cannot do. He cannot lie (Titus 1:2), He cannot deny Himself (2 Timothy 2:13), and He cannot tempt mankind with evil, nor can He be tempted to sin.

Third, we must accept personal responsibility for our sins (1:14). We cannot blame God when we are tempted because it is our desires, or lusts, that cause us to sin. The words "drawn away" and "enticed" used here are hunting and fishing terms. Satan knows that we cannot all be tempted in the same way. Just as a fisherman has different lures for different kinds of fish, Satan has a special lure for each of us. For the same reason, he also uses different types of bait in his traps.

Fourth, there is a natural progression in temptation. First, there is desire. Second, when desire becomes strong enough, it produces sin. Third, when sin is full grown, it results in spiritual death. Therefore James says we must not be "deceived" about the source of our sins (1:16).

God does not give us bad things; He gives us only good things (1:17). Every good gift that we have comes from Him. God's basic nature is love, and this does not change (1 John 4:8). He is a loving Father who only wants to give good things to His children (Matthew 7:7-11). To illustrate this point, James tells us that instead of tempting us to sin, God gives us salvation from sin (1:18).

Lessons Learned

1. James is book about applied Christianity and yet it is also doctrinal in nature.
2. James teaches that salvation is by faith but it is an active living faith, not a dead one.

3. Trials will come to us although we are Christians.
4. We should rejoice in trials because when we overcome them we become stronger.
5. If we lack wisdom, God will give it to us if we ask Him.
6. The great barrier to receiving wisdom is a lack of faith.
7. If we do not believe that God desires to hear and answer our prayers, then we are wasting our time praying.
8. Two things should humble the rich: the brevity of life and the fact of death.

Questions

1. Why did Martin Luther reject the book of James?
2. How can Paul and James' teachings about faith, works and salvation be harmonized?
3. Why did Jews have it especially rough during the persecution of Christians?
4. How are trials beneficial to us?
5. What is the difference between wisdom and knowledge?
6. How does wisdom come?
7. Who is a double-minded person?
8. What four things did James tell us about temptation?
9. How did James describe life?
10. What four things does the Bible tell us that God cannot do?

Lesson 3

Religion Defined

Week of March 21, 1999

Lesson Text

James 1:19-27

(19) So then, my beloved brethren, let every man be swift to hear, slow to speak, slow to wrath;

(20) for the wrath of man does not produce the righteousness of God.

(21) Therefore lay aside all filthiness and overflow of wickedness, and receive with meekness the implanted word, which is able to save your souls.

(22) But be doers of the word, and not hearers only, deceiving yourselves.

(23) For if anyone is a hearer of the word and not a doer, he is like a man observing his natural face in a mirror;

(24) for he observes himself, goes away, and immediately forgets what kind of man he was.

(25) But he who looks into the perfect law of liberty and continues in it, and is not a forgetful hearer but a doer of the work, this one will be blessed in what he does.

(26) If anyone among you thinks he is religious, and does not bridle his tongue but deceives his own heart, this one's religion is useless.

(27) Pure and undefiled religion before God and the Father is this: to visit orphans and widows in their trouble, and to keep oneself unspotted from the world.

Introduction

The last lesson ended with James telling us that we have been "brought forth," an expression stating that we have been "brought (born) into the family of God." He tells us in brief how this was done. It was "by the word of truth," but just how is this accomplished? Jesus told Nicodemus that for us to enter the kingdom of heaven, we must be "born again" (John 3:3-6). He was not talking about physical birth, and He clearly indicated this to his late night visitor (John 3:7-8). Jesus explained that spiritual birth is not a visible phenomenon, but although we cannot see it happening, we can see the results. How does spiritual birth occur?

The Word of God is like a seed planted in the mind (Luke 8:11). The mind is like the womb of a woman. When the seed is implanted in the fertile soil of an honest heart, conception begins (James 1:21). A new life is taking shape as the sincere person learns more about God's truth. Once that emerging life is truly converted to the fact that it is lost in sin and believes that Jesus is the Son of God and the Savior, he should be willing to accept the conditions of God to be saved. When the conditions of faith, repentance of sins, and public confession of Christ have been met, then birth is ready to take place in baptism. Peter says, "Having been born again, not of corruptible seed but incorruptible, through the word of God which lives and abides forever" (1 Peter 1:23). At that point, a new baby has been brought into the family of God (2 Corinthians 5:17). If that baby receives the proper nurture and nourishment, it will grow to maturity (1 Peter 2:2; Ephesians 4:12-15). When spiritual growth does not occur, it can have tragic consequences (1 Corinthians 3:1-3; Hebrews 5:12-14).

James says that once we are born into the family of God we are "a kind of first fruit." After God passed through Egypt and all of the firstborn of Egypt died, God told Moses that the firstborn of Israel were to be consecrated to Him (Exodus 13:1-2; Numbers 18:12; Deuteronomy 18:4). All Christians are like the firstborn to God, and they are to dedicate their lives to His service. Therefore, our goal should be to become mature saints in God's household so that we can be most effective in doing His will.

One of the main themes of the book of James is spiritual maturity. In this text, we find some of the marks of spiritual maturity that will exist in the life of any spiritually mature person. This lesson examines those traits.

A Patient Listener (James 1:19-21)

The first thing a spiritually mature person will do is be quick to receive God's Word because he has seen its power. He will not close his ears to it (Matthew 13:13-16); he will be ready and eager to receive "every word that proceeds from the mouth of God" (Matthew 4:4). Before we can hear, we must be willing to listen. If we do not listen, we cannot learn. Jesus said, "He who has ears to hear, let him hear" (Matthew 13:9). This principle is often repeated in Scripture (Mark 4:24; Luke 8:18; Revelation 1:3; 2:7, 11, 17, 29; 3:6, 13, 22). Faith cannot be produced or strengthened in a heart that does not desire to receive the Word of God (Romans 10:17).

A second response we should make to the Word of God is to be "slow to speak." As much as we need to listen to God's Word, we must be also slow to answer. This does not mean being slow of speech, as Moses declared himself to be (Exodus 4:10). It means being slow to begin speaking. As the wise man said, "In the multitude of words sin is not lacking, but he who restrains his lips is wise" (Proverbs 10:19). He adds, "He who has knowledge spares his words, and a man of understanding is of a calm spirit" (Proverbs 17:27). We have been blessed with two ears and one mouth showing the wisdom of listening twice as much as we speak. Talking a lot is not a sign of intelligence, but it is a mark of immaturity. The Pharisees wanted to be heard "for their much speaking" (Matthew 6:7 KJV). Spiritually mature people listen to God carefully, and then they are equally careful in being sure that they follow through with His will.

The third response James says we should have towards the Word of God is to be "slow to wrath." When we hear God's Word, it can result in several types of responses. As an old preacher was fond of saying, "It can make you mad, sad or glad." This is certainly true. Jesus' parable of the sower teaches the truth that men have different ways of receiving the Word (Matthew 13:3-9, 18-23). If a person becomes angry upon hearing the Truth, his heart is not prepared to receive it. In times of anger, we often lose our power to reason properly. Jeremiah tells the story about a king who became so angry at God's Word that he cut it to pieces and burned it in a fire (Jeremiah 36:22-23). His anger did not change the Truth. People often become angry when God's Truth is taught about such subjects as marriage, divorce and remarriage, fornication, immodesty, drinking alcohol, foul language and so on. Their anger does not change the Truth. Paul asked, "Have I therefore become your enemy because I tell you the truth?"(Galatians 4:16). When someone tells us the truth, they are our friend whether we realize it or not (Ephesians 4:15). James closes this thought by saying, "For the wrath of man does not produce the righteousness of God."

A patient listener will make appropriate changes in his life based upon what he hears. Two things are involved: 1. putting off, and 2. taking in. When the Word of God has been received, we should rid our lives of all things not in keeping with it. The idea is that we must find sin repulsive. As long as we find sin attractive, we will never give it up. James mentions two things that must be put off. First, there is "filthiness," which refers to outwardly expressed moral uncleanliness. Second, there is the "overflow of wickedness." This suggests sin that comes from within. When a person's heart is filled with wickedness, it will soon overflow like a cesspool spewing its horrid contents everywhere. Jesus said, "For out of the heart proceed evil thoughts, murders, adulteries, fornications, thefts, false witness, blasphemies" (Matthew 15:19). Ridding our hearts of these negative influences is essential to receiving "with meekness the implanted (engrafted, KJV) word, which is able to save your souls" (James 1:21). God's Word cannot dwell where sin abounds (Romans 6:1-2).

A Productive Doer (James 1:22-25)

Jesus told the story about two sons who were told to perform a certain task. One said, "I will not," but then had a change of heart and went and did as his father asked him. The second said, "I go, sir," but then he did not do it (Matthew 21:28-30). Then Jesus asked, "Which of the two did the will of his father?" (Matthew 21:31) Only the "doers of the word" are pleasing to God. People who "say and do not do" (Matthew 23:3) are deceiving themselves (James 1:22). They are like a person beholding himself in a mirror and then walking away and forgetting what he looked like. Impossible, you say. Have you really looked at yourself in the mirror in the morning? That is, before you have been to the cosmetic counter and splashed, sprayed and slickered? If you like what you see in the mirror in the morning, then maybe you are not seeing too well. What if you went out looking like that? You would not do it unless you forgot what you looked like.

James is saying that God's Word is like a mirror to the soul (1:25; 1 Corinthians 13:12). The person who sees his reflection in this mirror and does not forget what he looked like will change his image to conform to the image of God's Son (Romans 8:29). The result will be a blessing to that person's life. He will be like the fruitful tree, "That brings forth its fruit in its season, whose leaf also shall not wither; and whatever he does shall proper" (Psalm 1:3).

The gospel of Christ is "the perfect law of liberty." Many people believe the terms "law" and "liberty" are mutually exclusive, but James here shows they are not. Christians are under the "law of Christ" (Galatians 6:2). It is perfect because it is complete (2 Peter 1:3; Jude 3). It is the "law of liberty" because it makes us free (John 8:32, 36).

A Practitioner of Faith (James 1:26-27)

In the process of being doers and not hearers only, a spiritually mature person will practice what he preaches. The first thing he will do is bridle his tongue. James has a lot to say about the tongue (1:19; 2:12; 3:1-18; 4:11-12). Christians are not rash with their tongues but will speak words of encouragement, exhortation and edification to others (Colossians 4:6). If a person does not bridle his tongue, he is deceiving himself, and his religion is empty and worthless. In the next verse, James contrasts this useless religion with that which is worthwhile.

True religion will possess two qualities: 1. it will be "pure;" having no admixture of falsity in it; and 2. it will be "undefiled," or faultless; free from pollution. This evaluation is not that of the world, for men accept all kinds of religion, but this is God's evaluation. In the end only His approval matters.

What does this pure and undefiled religion require? James mentions here only two things, but they are in a sense inclusive. They are service and separation. Once we have seen ourselves for what we are and have cleaned up our spiritual lives, we need to see other people's needs and serve them. The word here is "visit," but we learn from James 2:14-16 that it involves more than paying a social call. It means going to the widows and orphans with the intent of supplying their need. Unless we do that, our religion is vain, empty and useless.

The second requirement James gives for pure and undefiled religion is separation. The spiritually mature person will keep himself "unspotted from the world." Later, James warns that "friendship with the world is enmity with God" (James 4:4). John warns us "do not love the world or the things in the world. If anyone loves the world, the love of the Father is not in him" (1 John 2:15). Too many Christians, like Demas, "love this present world" (2 Timothy 4:10). We cannot take ourselves out of this world, and we are to be salt and light in the world, but we must remember we are not citizens of this world. Our home is in heaven (John 17:14; Matthew 5:13-16; Ephesians 2:19).

Lessons Learned

1. Christians have been conceived by "the word of truth."
2. The new birth does not take place until baptism.
3. One of the main themes of James is spiritual maturity.
4. Before we give up sin, we must find it repulsive.
5. Christians are to be "doers of the word and not hearers only."
6. Christians must be practitioners of their faith.

Questions

1. Can you explain the new birth as outlined in this lesson?
2. How are Christians like a kind of "first fruit" unto God?
3. What three responses does James say we should make to the Word of God?
4. What two changes will a patient listener make in his or her life?
5. What are "filthiness" and the "overflow of wickedness?"
6. Why is ridding our lives of negative influences essential?
7. How is the Word of God like a mirror?
8. What is the "perfect law of liberty" and why is it called that?
9. What two things will spiritually mature people do in practicing their faith?
10. What two qualities will true religion possess?

Lesson 4

Partiality Rebuked

Week of
March 28, 1999

Lesson Text

JAMES 2:1-13

(1) My brethren, do not hold the faith of our Lord Jesus Christ, the Lord of glory, with partiality.

(2) For if there should come into your assembly a man with gold rings, in fine apparel, and there should also come in a poor man in filthy clothes,

(3) and you pay attention to the one wearing the fine clothes and say to him, "You sit here in a good place," and say to the poor man, "You stand there," or, "Sit here at my footstool,"

(4) have you not shown partiality among yourselves, and become judges with evil thoughts?

(5) Listen, my beloved brethren: Has God not chosen the poor of this world to be rich in faith and heirs of the kingdom which He promised to those who love Him?

(6) But you have dishonored the poor man. Do not the rich oppress you and drag you into the courts?

(7) Do they not blaspheme that noble name by which you are called?

(8) If you really fulfill the royal law according to the Scripture, "You shall love your neighbor as yourself," you do well;

(9) but if you show partiality, you commit sin, and are convicted by the law as transgressors.

(10) For whoever shall keep the whole law, and yet stumble in one point, he is guilty of all.

(11) For He who said, "Do not commit adultery," also said, "Do not murder." Now if you do not commit adultery, but you do murder, you have become a transgressor of the law.

(12) So speak and so do as those who will be judged by the law of liberty.

(13) For judgment is without mercy to the one who has shown no mercy. Mercy triumphs over judgment.

Introduction

Obviously, partiality on the part of some Jewish Christians was a problem among the people to whom James wrote. It appears to have been a socially accepted sin in those days. James wanted his readers to know this was no small matter, but it was serious business. Despite the fact that we may hold prejudices, most of us resent it when prejudice is directed toward us. Only when we become the target of such slander do the meanness and baseness of such attitudes really comes home to us. The result of such attitudes is that we can become snobs almost without realizing it. Intellectually, we may think, "I've got a degree, look at me"; financially, we may say, "I make big bucks; I am somebody"; or as to status, we may say, "My house is bigger than your house" or "my car is better than yours." What does a degree have to do with the intelligence of an individual? Why is the house someone lives in more important than the people who live in it or why is the car one drives more important than the person who drives it?

One common criticism often heard about churches is that they are cliquish. It is wonderful for Christians to have close friends, and it is good when they belong to the same congregation. It is hard not to be closer to some people than we are to other people. As is often pointed out, even Jesus had Peter, James and John. However, when we consciously or unconsciously exclude certain people from our inner circle, it is wrong. In fact, James plainly says it is sin. So in chapter 2, he devotes 13 verses to denouncing this practice, appealing to some basic doctrines of our faith.

He Appealed to the Lordship of Christ (James 2:1-4)

James begins this chapter by saying, "My brethren." This expression has special significance here because he is writing to Jews, his brothers in the flesh, who are now also his brothers in Christ. If we understand the fatherhood of God and the brotherhood of mankind, then it should remove all prejudice from our hearts. Certainly within the family of God there should be no partiality or preferential treatment shown. All are brothers and sisters of the same Father and in the same family, and we should love one another.

Next, James says, "hold not the faith of our Lord Jesus Christ, the Lord of Glory, with partiality." He was not talking about the faith Christ had, but rather, the faith that we have in Him. James wants us to know and to believe who Jesus is. By referring to Him as "the Lord of Glory," a term usually reserved for the Father, he emphasizes His deity. What kind of faith do we have in Christ? Do we see Him only as a mere mortal man – even if a good one, or do we see Him as the divine Son of the only true and living God? If He is our Lord, He is the absolute Ruler and Sovereign of our lives. Do we see Him as our Lord and Master? What we believe about Jesus affects the way we treat other people.

Why should we not show partiality? Because it is contrary to everything that Jesus taught and stood for. Jesus taught, "Do not judge according to appearance, but judge with righteous judgement" (John 7:24). He practiced what he preached and was never a respecter of persons. Even His enemies admitted that about Him (Matthew 22:16; Mark 12:14; Luke 20:21). James is saying that we need to look at all people through the eyes of Jesus. If people are Christians, they are our brothers and sisters in the Lord. Even if they are not Christians, they still deserve our utmost consideration and respect because they are made in the image of God, and Jesus died for them.

James does not leave the matter purely on theoretical grounds, but he gives us a concrete example of what he is talking abut when he says we should not show partiality. This illustration sounds similar to the parable Jesus told about a Pharisee and a publican who went up to the temple to pray. The scene is at a service where two men, one rich and the other poor, have gone up to worship. The rich man was wearing fine bright apparel with his fingers covered by rings. He was obviously making a show of his prosperity. In contrast, the poor man came in wearing maybe the only clothes he had. They may have been in need of repair, retaining odor, but they may have been the best he had. What would we do if this man came in one Sunday and sat down beside us during worship service?

Notice what happened when these two men went to worship. When the finely dressed man came in, the usher directed him to the best seat in the house. Whoever was leading him to his seat was more concerned with cash than character. But when the poor man came in, he was told "stand in the corner, or sit on the floor." Let me ask you, would you return to a congregation like that? Do you think this poor man ever did?

James concludes his story by saying, "Have you not shown partiality among yourselves, and become judges with evil thoughts?" (James 2:4). The Greek word for "partiality" is one that means "judging by outward appearances" or only by "face value." This kind of judgment is evil because it separates brethren from one another; it nullifies our Christian example; it hinders our evangelistic outreach; and it will damn our souls.

He Appealed to the Impartiality of God (James 2:5-7)

The second major argument James makes for not showing partiality is that God is not partial. When Peter preached the gospel to Cornelius and his family, the Holy Spirit came upon them even as he spoke. This prompted the apostle to say, "In truth I perceive that God shows no partiality. But in every nation whoever fears Him and works righteousness is accepted by Him" (Acts 10:34-35).

In speaking about the same subject, God's acceptance of Gentiles as well as Jews, Paul wrote, "For there is no partiality with God" (Romans 2:11). In writing about a Christian master's responsibility to his servants, he said, "And you, masters, do the same thing to them, giving up threatening, knowing that your own Master also is in heaven, and there is no partiality with Him" (Ephesians 6:9).

Paul also told the Colossian Christians that "He who does wrong will be repaid for what he has done, and there is no partiality" (Colossians 3:25). Peter adds that because God "without partiality judges according to each one's work, conduct yourselves throughout the time of your stay here in fear" (1 Peter 1:17). These scriptures prove that God judges all people without showing partiality to any one person. Because God is not partial in His dealings with us, neither should His people be partial in their relationships with other people.

It seems contradictory that after establishing the principle of God's impartiality James says, "Has God not chosen the poor of this world to be rich in faith and heirs of the kingdom which He promised to those who love him?" (James 2:5). He is not saying that God gives preferential treatment to the poor. The word "chosen" is used in Scripture in the sense of someone being responsive to God's call. Paul said, "Not many wise according to the flesh, not many mighty, not many noble are called" (1 Corinthians 1:26). It was said about Jesus that "the common people heard Him gladly" (Mark 12:37). God's choice of the poor was not an arbitrary selection, but it was because of the fact that they were mostly the ones who chose to come to Him. In contrast to God's treatment of the poor, by the example James used, these Jewish Christians had "dishonored the poor man" (James 2:6).

James finishes his argument by essentially saying that it was not wise in the first place for them to show partiality to the rich non-Christians, because they were the very people who were making their lives miserable. It made no sense for them to show preferential treatment to people who were persecuting them. These rich people perverted justice, meaning they had the best justice money could buy. They also blasphemed the noble name of Christ by which Christians are called.

He Appealed to the Inspired Scriptures (James 2:8-11)

The third argument James makes against partiality is that it is contrary to God's inspired Word. To prove that God's Word condemns showing partiality, James reaches back to the Old Testament. The Law of Moses taught, "you shall love your neighbor as yourself: I am the Lord" (Leviticus 19:18). This commandment was given special attention by Jesus when He said it was second in importance only to the command that says, "You shall love the Lord your God with all your heart, with all your soul, and with all your mind" (Matthew 22:37-38). Mark and Luke add that you should also love God "with all your strength" (Mark 12:30; Luke 10:27). James calls "love your neighbor" the royal law (James 2:8). Why does he call it that? It could be simply because it was given first by God and then reaffirmed by our King Jesus (John 13:34-35). It may also be because of the lofty position it is given by the Lord. Paul writes that "Love is the fulfillment of the law" (Romans 13:10). In either case, the inspired writer tells us we would do well to keep it.

Some people think James was using a rhetorical device by asking a question that he anticipated some of his readers would be asking: "Why should we keep the royal law?" His response was that "if you show partiality, you commit sin, and are convicted by the law as transgressors"(James 2:9). Then he said that even if a person kept the "whole law, and yet stumbled in one point he was guilty of all" (v. 10). Does this mean that if we commit one sin, we might just as well commit them all? Not at all. What he is saying is that we cannot pick and choose our sins and think that some sins are less significant or less important than other sins. Under our system of justice, how many laws would you have to break to be a lawbreaker? Would not just one be sufficient? The same thing is true under God's law. If we are stopped for speeding, it would do no good to point out to the officer that we are not a thief, a murderer or an adulterer. Yet how many people will try to use this argument with God on the Day of Judgment? (Matthew 7:21-23).

It is worthwhile to see why people guilty of the sin of partiality would be guilty of the whole law. It is the basic attitude of their heart. Whenever people willfully and flagrantly disobey one command of God, they show the disposition of heart to disobey all of them if the opportunity presented itself. Thus, the deliberate violator of one of God's laws is guilty of breaking all of them. Because this is true, we need to examine our attitude towards God's Word. We cannot approach it cafeteria-style, taking what we like and discarding the rest. It is all or nothing.

The Certainty of Judgment (James 2:12-13)

The fourth and last argument James makes relative to the sin of showing partiality is that we "Will be judged by the law of liberty" (James 2:12). He is saying that Christians need to act like people who will stand in judgment and give and answer to God for their conduct. If we expect to receive God's mercy on that occasion, then we must extend it to other people now. Jesus reveals the positive side of mercy when he says "Blessed are the merciful, for they shall obtain mercy" (Matthew 5:7). James here shows the negative side: "For judgment is without mercy to the one who has shown no mercy" (James 2:13).

James ends this discussion by saying, "Mercy triumphs over judgment." One translation says,"Mercy glories in the face of judgment" (*The Centenary Translation: The New Testament in Modern English*). Another translation says, "Mercy may laugh in the face of judgment" (PMET). The meaning is that because of God's mercy, we do not need to fear the Judgment because it takes up where our human nature fails us. The person who shows mercy to other people, in particular by not showing partiality to the rich over the poor, can rejoice in the prospect of Judgment because he can know he will receive mercy from God on that day.

Lessons Learned

1. For Christians to show a decided preference for one group of people over another within the family of God is sinful.
2. What we believe about the nature and position of Christ determines how we treat other people.
3. Because God and Jesus show no partiality in making salvation available to all people, neither should we.
4. All people can come to God on the call of the gospel, but many more common people will respond than the great, wealthy and powerful ones will.
5. God's inspired Word condemns showing preferences based on outward criteria alone.
6. If we expect to receive mercy on Judgment Day, then we must be merciful to people while in this life.

Questions

1. Is it wrong for Christians to have special friends? Why or why not?
2. Does Jesus condemn all kinds of judgment? Explain your answer.
3. Why is judging by outward appearances wrong?
4. What does James mean by saying, "God has chosen the poor …"?
5. Why does it make no sense for Christians to show partiality to non-Christians who are rich?
6. What name does James give to the commandment to "love thy neighbor as yourself"?
7. How can we be guilty of breaking the whole law with one violation?
8. Are any sins greater than others?
9. Why show mercy to people?
10. What will we be judged by on the Day of Judgment?

Lesson 5

Faith and Works Required

Week of April 4, 1999

Lesson Text

James 2:14-26

(14) What does it profit, my brethren, if someone says he has faith but does not have works? Can faith save him?

(15) If a brother or sister is naked and destitute of daily food,

(16) and one of you says to them, "Depart in peace, be warmed and filled," but you do not give them the things which are needed for the body, what does it profit?

(17) Thus also faith by itself, if it does not have works, is dead.

(18) But someone will say, "You have faith, and I have works." Show me your faith without your works, and I will show you my faith by my works.

(19) You believe that there is one God. You do well. Even the demons believe--and tremble!

(20) But do you want to know, O foolish man, that faith without works is dead?

(21) Was not Abraham our father justified by works when he offered Isaac his son on the altar?

(22) Do you see that faith was working together with his works, and by works faith was made perfect?

(23) And the Scripture was fulfilled which says, "Abraham believed God, and it was accounted to him for righteousness." And he was called the friend of God.

(24) You see then that a man is justified by works, and not by faith only.

(25) Likewise, was not Rahab the harlot also justified by works when she received the messengers and sent them out another way?

(26) For as the body without the spirit is dead, so faith without works is dead also.

Introduction

Recent polls indicate that the majority of people in America claim to read the Bible regularly, but an almost equal number say that it has little to do with the way they live their lives. This is a dramatic illustration of people divorcing their faith from their actions. Many lives, and even the life of our nation, are seriously jeopardized because too many people have separated their convictions from their conduct.

It is one thing to say we have faith, but when that faith is not translated into positive behavior, it is like trying to live without breathing or eating. James' thoughts can be summarized with one question: "If a person says that he has faith, but then does not demonstrate it in their life, what value is there in that faith?" It is easy to be confused about this point. We can sit in worship service and sing, pray, listen, partake of the Lord's Supper and give of our financial resources and believe that because we do these things, we are a Christian. Certainly a Christian will do these things, but these things alone do not mean we are Christian. When faith is separated from these activities, they mean absolutely nothing to the person performing them.

This is the theme that James is dealing with in our text. He has several things to say about the value of faith without works.

Faith Without Works Is Unprofitable (James 2:14-17)

In James 1, we noted that "saying" and not "doing" are deceptive (v. 22). It was also brought out that "pure and undefiled religion" includes "visiting the orphans and the widows in their trouble" (James 1:27). At that time, the point was made that to visit means more than just making a social call. It involves going to see a person with the intent of relieving his distress. That idea is expanded upon in these verses.

James first presents the principle in 2:14; faith without works is unprofitable. Then he illustrates his point: "If a brother or sister is naked and destitute of daily food, and one of you says to them, 'Depart in peace, be warmed and filled,' but you do not give them the things which are needed for the body, what does it profit?" Most any Christian would answer, "They did not profit that needy person at all." Yet how many times do we hear a sermon that convicts us of the need to be actively involved in the Lord's work, and we resolve to take immediate action? Then once we have left the service, we forget the promise we made. Unless we translate these good intentions into positive practices, what good are they?

It is said that the expression "Depart in peace. Amen!" was the traditional way of ending the Lord's Supper. If that is true, James is showing us just how easy it is to fall into the deceptive trap of coming together under the power of the gospel, making all kinds of resolutions, only to leave them behind when we walk out of the building. If we do, we are like the Levite and the priest in Jesus' story about the good Samaritan who walked by on the other side when they saw the man who was left for dead. We should strive to be like the Samaritan whose faith cost him something.

James concludes this thought with the statement "Thus faith by itself, if it does not have works, is dead." How do we know when someone has died? We check for vital signs, heartbeat, respiration, eye movement and so on. If these signs are not present, the person is presumed dead. Works are the vital signs of living faith. When your faith quits working, you die spiritually.

Faith Without Works Cannot Be Validated (James 2:18)

Simply put, the point is, "How do you prove your faith is genuine?" Anyone can say, "Oh, I have faith." Fine. Now it is show-and-tell time. If polls can be believed, more than 90 percent of the people in this nation claim to believe in God or in a supreme being. If this statistic is true, why is there so much crime, drug addiction, child, spousal and elder abuse, homosexuality, abortion, poverty and declining church attendance? To claim to be a Christian and not accept the responsibilities that go with it create a contradiction that God will not allow.

Christianity is a show-me religion. James says,"You show me yours, and I'll show you mine." If our faith is genuine, it will be validated by evidence. Works are the proof that faith is real. Without works, faith cannot be seen by other people. Jesus told his disciples, "If you have faith as a mustard seed, you will say to this mountain, 'Move from here to there,' and it will move; and nothing will be impossible for you" (Matthew 17:20). Paul, alluding to this statement, wrote, "Though I have all faith, so that I could remove mountains, but have not love, I am nothing" (1 Corinthians 13:2). How many of us are not convicted by this statement?

Faith Without Works Cannot Save (James 2:19-20)

This illustration strikes a fatal blow to the doctrine of "salvation by faith only." If mental assent or pure intellectual faith would save you, why would these demons not be saved? James may have had reference here to the incident involving the Gadarene demoniacs (Matthew 8:28-32). These demons confessed that Jesus was the "Son of God" and that they were fearful of Him (v. 29). Who would say they were saved on the basis of that confession alone? Yet many preachers and teachers will tell people today who want to be saved, "Believe on the Lord Jesus Christ, and you will be saved." This is a misapplication of Acts 16:31. This man was a heathen and did not know what to believe before Paul "spoke the word of the Lord to him" (Acts 16:32). There is no scripture that teaches that merely confessing faith in Christ by itself is enough for a person to be saved.

What good does it do to say, "I believe in God," even if it is faith in the true God, if a person does not act upon that faith? Even to think such is foolish. The writer of Hebrews plainly says, "Without faith it is impossible to please Him, for he who comes to God must believe that He is, and that He is a rewarder of those who diligently seek Him" (Hebrews 11:6).

Faith Without Works Cannot Justify (James 2:21-25)

Justification is one of the great doctrines of the Christian faith. It is not salvation, but it is the result of salvation. It is the act during which God pronounces a sinner righteous. This is not something the sinner does for himself, for he cannot, but it is something only God can do for us. We can know we are justified because we have God's word on it (Romans 5:1-11). How do other people know we are justified? James supplies us with the answer to this question and an illustration.

As James so often does in his book, he has stated a principle, "faith without works is dead," and then he provides us with two illustrations to demonstrate that principle. The two people he refers to are as different as daylight and darkness. One of his illustrations is about a man of faith and the other is about a woman of the world.

The first illustration is about Abraham, "The father of the faithful." He was brought into a right relationship with God when he believed in Him. He proved the value of his faith when God asked him to offer up his son Isaac, the son of promise, on an altar of sacrifice. If Abraham had failed there, he would have shown to God and to the world that his faith was just empty words. What actions must we take? What things must we do to prove our faith is genuine? James says, "by works faith was made perfect (or complete)."

The verse from Genesis 15:6, "[Abraham] believed in the Lord, and He accounted it to him for righteousness," is referred to several times in the New Testament (Romans 4:3, 22; Galatians 3:6; James 2:23). It is always in the context of the actions that Abraham took to demonstrate that his faith was alive and genuine.

The second illustration concerns Rahab, a prostitute who lived on the wall of Jericho. Although she was a heathen, she demonstrated her faith in God by what she said and by what she did. She hid the spies of Israel when they would surely have been discovered. Then she asked them to spare her family when Israel took the city of Jericho. With this contrasting illustration, James shows us that God does not accept the father of the faithful anymore than He does a woman of poor reputation when they both have saving faith.

Faith Without Works Is Dead (James 2:26)

During the final week before His crucifixion, Jesus saw a fig tree alongside the road as He returned to the city of Jerusalem from Bethany. As He approached it, He found that it had no fruit on it although the leaves were present. He cursed the tree saying, "Let no fruit grow on you ever again" (Matthew 21:19). It died immediately, to the amazement of His disciples. Why did Jesus kill the tree? Because if it was bearing no fruit, it was not fulfilling its purpose. Any grove grower knows that when a tree is unproductive, you cut it down to make room for a productive tree.

Just as the body is dead without the spirit, faith without works is dead. When faith is dead, a person is spiritually dead. Death is separation. Physically, it is separation of the soul from the body (Ecclesiastes 12:7; James 2:26). Spiritually, it is the separation of a soul from God (2 Thessalonians 1:9). We can be dead spiritually even while we live (Romans 6:6-8, 23; Ephesians 2:1; Colossians 2:13; Revelation 3:1). It can be because of overt sin, or it can be the result of the gross neglect of our spiritual growth.

Much has been written today to demonstrate the healthy benefits of physical exercise. However, many a couch potato has found comfort in Paul's statement to Timothy: "bodily exercise profits a little" (1 Timothy 4:8). However, Paul was not condemning physical exercise; he was merely stating that it does not have the advantages of spiritual exercise. The benefits of spiritual exercise are experienced in this life, and they can make a difference in where we spend eternity.

People who regularly exercise will normally live longer than people who do not. The same is true spiritually. If you fail to exercise your spirit through prayer, reading and meditating on God's Word, faithful attendance at worship services and by practicing good works, you will die spiritually.

There are a couple of things we must do when considering James' comment: "For as the body without the spirit is dead, so faith without works is dead also" (2:26). First, remember the kinds of works he is discussing. He is talking about good works, as the text clearly indicates. He is talking specifically about acts of benevolence, but the principle is certainly broader and includes any act of service performed in the name of Christ (John 13:14-15; Colossians 3:17). These works do not save us, but they are clear evidence of a living, vibrant faith that does save us (Galatians 5:6). Second, we must never believe that these works, or any works of human merit, are the cause of our salvation. We are not saved by works of human merit. We do not in any sense earn our salvation. It is a gift from God, the result of His amazing grace (Ephesians 2:8-9). We must accept that gift through faith and obedience, and people who do not will be lost.

Someone might ask, "But what about baptism?" Jesus' answer to that question is, "He who believes and is baptized will be saved; but he who does not believe will be condemned" (Mark 16:16). It is a shame what we have done to baptism by putting it in the category of a human work of merit. It is not. It is a work of God, just as faith is (John 6:29). Have you ever noticed that every requirement God has made for salvation but one is spoken of in the active voice? For example, we "must believe, repent and confess," but when we speak about baptism, note the change in voice. We must "be baptized," which is passive voice.

Think about what happens in baptism. We submit ourselves to another person who then immerses us beneath the water and raises us up again. The important thing, however, is not what the person doing the baptism does or even the person being baptized but God's activity in the matter. What good would it do to be plunged beneath the water if God was not involved in that process? When we comply with the conditions He has given for us to receive the gift of salvation, then the blood of Christ cleanses us of our sins (Ephesians 1:7; Colossians 1:14; Revelation 1:5). We are not earning our salvation, but merely accepting God's gracious offer upon His terms.

Lessons Learned

1. No value is found in a faith that is not practiced.
2. We can go through all of the prescribed acts of worship "decently and in order" and deceive ourselves into thinking we have done all that God requires.
3. "Justification" is a legal term that refers to the act of God pronouncing us righteous.
4. Baptism is not a work of human merit, but it is a work of God.
5. Without God's activity, such as cleansing us with Christ's blood and forgiving our sins, baptism would be a meaningless act.
6. There is no scripture that teaches that faith alone saves us.

Questions

1. What dramatic illustration of people divorcing their faith from their actions is in this lesson?
2. Can you summarize James' thoughts with one question?
3. What principle does James present in 2:14?
4. How can you tell if a person has died spiritually?
5. In what way can we prove our faith is genuine?
6. How should Jesus' statement about mountain-moving faith be interpreted?
7. What two illustrations does James give from the Old Testament and what is their purpose?
8. Why did Paul say, "Bodily exercise profits a little"?
9. What kind of works is James discussing?
10. How do you define a work of human merit?

Lesson 6

Speech Controlled

Week of April 11, 1999

Lesson Text

JAMES 3:1-12

(1) My brethren, let not many of you become teachers, knowing that we shall receive a stricter judgment.

(2) For we all stumble in many things. If anyone does not stumble in word, he is a perfect man, able also to bridle the whole body.

(3) Indeed, we put bits in horses' mouths that they may obey us, and we turn their whole body.

(4) Look also at ships: although they are so large and are driven by fierce winds, they are turned by a very small rudder wherever the pilot desires.

(5) Even so the tongue is a little member and boasts great things. See how great a forest a little fire kindles!

(6) And the tongue is a fire, a world of iniquity. The tongue is so set among our members that it defiles the whole body, and sets on fire the course of nature; and it is set on fire by hell.

(7) For every kind of beast and bird, of reptile and creature of the sea, is tamed and has been tamed by mankind.

(8) But no man can tame the tongue. It is an unruly evil, full of deadly poison.

(9) With it we bless our God and Father, and with it we curse men, who have been made in the similitude of God.

(10) Out of the same mouth proceed blessing and cursing. My brethren, these things ought not to be so.

(11) Does a spring send forth fresh water and bitter from the same opening?

(12) Can a fig tree, my brethren, bear olives, or a grapevine bear figs? Thus no spring yields both salt water and fresh.

Introduction

In chapter one, James stressed the importance of proper speech (1:26). In chapter two, he emphasized that Christianity is more than a lot of talk because we must back up our talk with our actions (2:14-26). To clear up any misunderstandings about what we say not being important, in this chapter James gives us a lesson about the proper use of the tongue.

The Christians to whom James wrote were undoubtedly having a serious problem with the sins of the tongue. James has already told them to "be swift to hear, slow to speak, slow to wrath" (1:19). He also told them that the Christian who does not "bridle his tongue" is not really religious no matter what he says (v. 26). He adds that we should speak and act as people who will stand in judgment before Christ (2:12).

Our tongues are a powerful force for either good or evil. Solomon wrote that, "Death and life are in the power of the tongue" (Proverbs 18:21). It can build up or it can destroy. In his letter to the Colossian Christians, Paul wrote, "Let your speech always be with grace, seasoned with salt, that you may know how you ought to answer each one" (Colossians 4:6). To the congregation at Ephesus he wrote, "Let no corrupt word proceed out of your mouth, but what is good for necessary edification, that it may impart grace to the hearers" (Ephesians 4:29). We all need to keep our tongues from evil. In this text, James gives us five ways we need to do this.

The Responsibility to Guard the Tongue (James 3:1-2)

James begins his lesson on the tongue by giving a warning to teachers. This seems to be a strange place to begin a discussion about the dangers of the tongue. Also, it seems strange that he would be telling people not to be teachers. If he means this literally, then he would contradict some plain teaching of Scripture. Jesus assigned all Christians the responsibility for being teachers (Matthew 28:18-20; Mark 16:15-16). The writer of Hebrews condemns some people who had been Christians for many years and had not matured to the point where they could teach other people the gospel (Hebrews 5:12-14). Why would James turn around then and tell people not to become teachers?

James is talking about people who teach the word publicly, as in a classroom situation. Every Christian is to be a teacher, but not every one is required to be a classroom teacher. Everyone does not have that ability. As Paul wrote, "God has set the members, each one of them, in the body just as He pleased. … Now you are the body of Christ, and members individually" (1 Corinthians 12:18, 27). Then he mentioned several responsibilities within the body that God had appointed to demonstrate that there is a job suited to each person's unique ability.

The warning is not against teaching, but it is against a person accepting that responsibility without knowing what is involved. That person should not become a preacher for the wrong reason. In the Jewish religion, out of which the earliest Christians came, the rabbis, or teachers, held a position of great honor. Some of them were highly paid for their services. Although this was not done to this extreme in early churches of Christ, teachers were held in very high esteem. Because of this, there was always the danger that some men would desire to teach only for the glory or the money they might receive (Philippians 1:15-20; 1 Timothy 3:3).

Being a teacher of God's Word has great rewards in this life and in the one to come, but it also carries great responsibilities. Because of this someone might say, "I'll just escape this strict judgment by not teaching publicly." That will not solve the problem, because if a person has the potential to be a teacher and does not do it, God will still hold him accountable.

The Responsibility to Guide the Tongue (James 3:3-4)

In making this point, James uses two common illustrations of that day. First, he talked about the method of guiding horses. The horse is about 1,000 pounds of bone, muscle and sinew. In contrast, the bridle is small, a few ounces of steel fashioned to fit into the horse's mouth. Because a horse's mouth is so tender, this small piece of metal can cause this large animal to go in any direction the rider desires.

The ships of that age were extremely small compared to the large, ocean-going vessels of our time. However, there were rather large ships even then. The one Paul sailed on to Rome was loaded with a large cargo and 276 people (Acts 27:37). No matter how large they were, these ships were maneuvered by a very small rudder controlled by a small helm or wheel in comparison to their total size. Much power resides in small things.

The Responsibility to Control the Tongue (James 3:5-6)

In contrast to the large horse and the gigantic ships, the tongue is a "little member" but "it boasts great things" (James 3:5). Think about how small the tongue is in relation to other parts of the body. It only weighs a few ounces in a body that weighs many pounds. Despite its size, James says it is a powerful force that can start an uncontrollable forest fire. Fire is a great blessing, but when it goes out of control, it is a curse. Every year in our nation forest fires destroy millions of dollars worth of property, and many lives are lost. The tongue is like that fire, which when controlled can be a great blessing to humanity; but when it is out of control, it can destroy in mere seconds what it took a lifetime to build.

Notice the other figures James employs to demonstrate the strength of this little member. First, he says "it is a world of iniquity" (James 3:6). The world contains more than 5.5 billion people, in addition to the thousands of animals, the huge buildings of our large cities, the land mass itself, and the great bodies of water. Yet the writer says the tongue is like the world, but it is one that is filled with all kinds of iniquity – like a sewer that spews its filth in every corner of the globe.

Second, James tells us that the tongue "defiles the whole body" (James 3:6). Every sin that can be named is tied to the tongue. However, we must remember that Jesus said, "Not what goes into the mouth defiles a man; but what comes out of the mouth, this defiles a man. … But those things which proceed out of the mouth come from the heart, and they defile a man. For out of the heart proceed evil thoughts, murders, adulteries, fornications, thefts, false witness, blasphemies" (Matthew 15:11, 18-19).

Third, the writer says that "it is set on fire by hell" (James 3:6). The word for "hell" used here is the Greek word *gehenna,* which refers to the "eternal fire" of that terrible place. When James wants to convey how horrible the tongue could be, he uses the most dreadful symbol he can conceive of – the eternal abode of the damned. Let us not be deceived; when we use our tongues for hurting rather than helping, for discouraging instead of lifting up, for breaking hearts rather than healing them, our tongue is not being controlled by God but by Satan.

The Responsibility to Tame the Tongue (James 3:7-8)

Men have been able to domesticate and tame almost every animal that we know about. James mentions four classifications of animals that cover all types: beast, birds, reptiles, or creeping things and sea creatures (James 3:7). Think about some trained animals you have seen. The massive elephants weighing several tons can be made to stand on a small platform or do other tricks. Ferocious lions and tigers can be made to jump through hoops and even rings of fire. Considering their natural fear of fire, this is truly amazing. Bears ride bicycles. Killer whales can be tamed to lick a person's face. However, "no man can tame the tongue" (James 3:8).

The tongue is like a deadly, venomous serpent whose bite can instantly paralyze and then kill. The tongue can be used for lying and gossip. Of the 18 sins of the tongue mentioned in the Bible, gossip is mentioned more than any other. While the tongue can be used for such negative things, it can also be used for positive ones. Nick Young counted 20 negative things the tongue can do and 20 positive ones. On the negative side, consider how Adolph Hitler's venomous rhetoric inflamed an entire nation and caused otherwise reasonable men to commit some of the most horrible atrocities of war. As David Roper wrote in his book *Practical Christianity: Studies in the Book of James*, "For every word in Hitler's book, *Mein Kampf*, 125 lives were lost in World War II" (p. 61). From the positive standpoint, consider how many millions of people have been influenced for good by the few recorded words of Jesus Christ the Son of God.

Because no man can tame the tongue, shall we give up trying? For that matter, how can God hold us responsible for controlling our tongues when it is impossible to do so? The most important part of this statement is "no man can tame the tongue." What man cannot do alone, he can do with God's help (Matthew 19:26; Philippians 4:13). There is help from above for people who sincerely want to control this unruly member. We need to do all that we can to control our tongues but this is impossible without God's help.

The Responsibility to Be Consistent with Our Tongue (James 3:9-12)

Look at this sad scene: a person praising and adoring God with his tongue and then cursing or invoking evil at his brother or sister with that same instrument. This must have been a common occurrence in his day, or James would not have mentioned it. Unfortunately, it is all too common today. The writer thunders, "these things ought not to be so" (James 3: 10).

While men may be inconsistent with their tongues, nature teaches us lessons about being consistent. Streams do not provide both sweet and bitter water. Fig trees do not produce olive berries; neither can a grape vine produce figs. Do not try to play games by talking about grafting in different kinds of branches, because James is talking about what is natural. In the unfettered world of nature there are no two-flavored streams or two-fruited trees. Regrettably, there are two-faced men and women. Maybe when some people talk in ways they should not, they are just doing what comes naturally – at least for them.

Lessons Learned

1. Unless we bridle our tongues, our religion is not true but is in vain.
2. Our tongue is a powerful force that can be used for good or evil.
3. People who teach publicly have a serious responsibility because souls are at stake – their own and those of their students.
4. Every Christian should be a teacher, but not everyone has to teach publicly.
5. The tongue is a "little member," but it can cause a person to be condemned.
6. Gossip is the sin of the tongue that is mentioned most often in Scripture.
7. With our tongues we can destroy with a word what it took a lifetime to build – a reputation, a career, a good name or a family.

Questions

1. What did James discuss relative to the tongue in chapters one and two?
2. Why did James insist that some people should "not be teachers"?
3. What point was Paul making in the passage from 1 Corinthians 12:18, 27?
4. What was the main point of Jesus' parable about the talents?
5. What are two of the real dangers for people who preach or teach publicly?
6. What truth was James trying to convey with his illustrations of the horse and the ship?
7. How is the tongue like a fire?
8. How is the tongue a "world of iniquity?"
9. How can the tongue, as small as it is, defile the whole body?
10. Why can men not tame their tongue?

Lesson 7

Wisdom Practiced

Week of April 18, 1999

Lesson text

JAMES 3:13-18

(13) Who is wise and understanding among you? Let him show by good conduct that his works are done in the meekness of wisdom.

(14) But if you have bitter envy and self-seeking in your hearts, do not boast and lie against the truth.

(15) This wisdom does not descend from above, but is earthly, sensual, demonic.

(16) For where envy and self-seeking exist, confusion and every evil thing are there.

(17) But the wisdom that is from above is first pure, then peaceable, gentle, willing to yield, full of mercy and good fruits, without partiality and without hypocrisy.

(18) Now the fruit of righteousness is sown in peace by those who make peace.

Introduction

In James 1:5-8 we learned that if any person sincerely wants wisdom and asks God in sincerity, He will help him to attain it. We also learned that wisdom is not knowledge but is the understanding of how to use that knowledge appropriately. With knowledge we learn how to take things apart, but with wisdom we learn how to put them together again by a practical relating of God's truth to everyday life.

People today desire many things, but for most of them wisdom is not included. They want fame, fortune, big homes, fancy cars, expensive jewelry and any other amenities that come with a so-called successful life. If they prayed, it would be for these material things and not for wisdom. In doing this they deny themselves the very thing they need most, and in many cases, it is that which would lead them to the accumulation of the other things mentioned.

It is hoped that all Christians will desire wisdom above all else. Not so that they might gain wealth, power or success but so they might better serve God and His church. Having told us how to gain wisdom, James now tells us that there are two kinds – the wisdom that comes from God in request to prayer and the wisdom of the world. In this lesson we will see why we should covet the former and painstakingly avoid the latter.

How Do You Know You Are Wise? (James 3:13)

It is conceded by most scholars that James' remarks here are directed towards the same people he addressed in verse 1 – the public teachers of the word. A. T. Robertson, in *Word Pictures in the New Testament,* notes that two different Greek words are used here. The word translated "wise" is *sophos*, which "is used for the practical teacher." The second word translated "understanding" is *epistemon,* which is the word "for an expert, a skilled and scientific person with a tone of superiority." (Baker Book House, Grand Rapids, 1933; p. 45). However, we cannot rule out the general application of this verse for all Christians.

We have all encountered teachers who had a head full of book knowledge but who seemed to lack the ability to make a practical application of that knowledge to normal life. There are also those teachers who can move an audience to tears with their stirring oratory but have a problem practicing what they preach. Their speeches are demonstrations of technique, mere performances; they are not genuinely felt from the heart. It is not enough to stand before an audience of starving people and say something; we must have something to say that will fill their souls with spiritual food.

Simply put, James asks, "How do you tell a wise person from an unwise one?" He then contrasts the two kinds of wisdom that, in effect, answer this question. The first contrast is implied, although not specifically stated: "If a person is wise, then it will show by his or her behavior and good works done in humility." Have you not seen those teachers who were arrogant, egotistical and intimidating? Yet they were poor communicators and even worse examples. Then there are those teachers who have education and intelligence along with humility. Their words are believable because they obviously practice them.

In the next few verses, James presents the primary contrast between two kinds of wisdom. The first is the wisdom of the world. The second is the wisdom that comes from God. In the remainder of this study, we will examine both of these in the hope that we will seek only that wisdom that comes from above.

The Wisdom of the World (James 3:14-16)

James tells us a number of things about worldly wisdom: First, its nature; second, its origin; and third, its results. Notice the characteristics that James gives about this kind of wisdom. The first is "bitter envy." Why did he not just say "envy?" The bitterness grows out of uncontrolled envy. The person being described is one who tends toward being suspicious, resistant and given to rivalry. When people see someone who has something they want and think in their hearts they deserve, they began to devise ways they can have it. If they are foiled in their attempts to obtain what they desire, they become even more bitter and angry.

Following on the heels of "bitter envy" is its second cousin, "self-seeking" or "selfish ambition." These are self-promoters who love to be seen and heard (Matthew 6:1-18; 23:1-7). They will run over anyone who interrupts their climb to the top. They love to boast about their accomplishments and become envious when other people's good qualities or works are being praised. Paul wrote to the Philippians about certain preachers who had this characteristic and said that they taught Christ out of "envy and strife" and "from selfish ambition," rather than from pure motives (Philippians 1:15-16). Later in this same book, as if writing to these same preachers, Paul says,"Let nothing be done through selfish ambition or conceit, but in lowliness of mind let each esteem others better than himself" (Philippians 2:3).

The third characteristic of worldly wisdom James mentions is "deceit." He urges his readers not to "lie against the truth" (James 3:14). He is talking about a tendency to twist the truth. When a person boasts, he will usually end up lying. In his *Commentary on James,* Guy N. Woods wrote, "It thus really means to boast of one's affairs to the hurt of another. … It is, alas, all too often true that one person pushes himself upward by propelling another in the opposite direction downward; and it is this disposition which James so straitly condemns here and throughout the Epistle" (Gospel Advocate Company, Nashville, 1964; p. 185)

If anyone could have bragged about his accomplishments, Paul could have. However, in writing to defend his apostleship he said, "But he who glories (boasts), let him glory in the Lord" (2 Corinthians 10:17). We need to have this attitude about our achievements and let the Lord praise us in the Day of Judgment.

Next, James discusses the origin of worldly wisdom. First, he says that it is "earthly" (James 3:15). This means that people possessing this kind of wisdom view everything from an earthly perspective. Anyone who is enamored with the wisdom of this world should consider where it has led men in the past. Paul, in writing to the Romans Christians, said, "Because although they knew God, they did not glorify Him as God, nor were thankful, but became futile in their thoughts, and their foolish hearts were darkened. Professing to be wise, they became fools, and changed the glory of the incorruptible God into an image made like corruptible man – and birds and four-footed animals and creeping things" (Romans 1:21-23). To the Corinthian church he wrote, "The world through wisdom did not know God, it pleased God through the foolishness of the message preached to save those who believe. For Jews request after a sign, and Greeks seek after wisdom; but we preach Christ crucified, to the Jews a stumbling block and to the Greeks foolishness, but to those who are called, both Jews and Greeks, Christ the power of God and the wisdom of God. Because the foolishness of God is wiser than men, and the weakness of God is stronger than men" (1 Corinthians 1:21-25). The wisdom of the world will come to naught, but the wisdom of God will last forever (v. 19).

The second thing James says about the origin of worldly wisdom is that it is "sensual" (James 3:15). The Greek word here is *psukikos* and refers to that which is "natural" or is of "nature." This means that it is the opposite of that which is spiritual. Men naturally have wisdom in them that does not originate from God. Where then does it come from? James answers this question with the next descriptive word.

He says this wisdom is demonic. This term implies that such wisdom originates with Satan. From the fall of mankind, Satan has pitted his wisdom against that of God. Remember that he told Eve the forbidden fruit would make her "wise" (Genesis 3:5-6). Ever since that time, men have believed his lies and have substituted his wisdom that is earthly for that true wisdom that comes directly from God.

What are the results for people who choose worldly wisdom? James gives us two consequences for possessing it. The first is that there is "confusion" (James 3:16). The wisdom of the world has given us atheistic evolution, abortion, euthanasia, cloning and many other kinds of dubious scientific experimentation – most of which go against the wisdom of God and result in confusion, even among many believers. When we are given so much conflicting information by so-called experts, how are we to know what to believe? Once again, we must rely on God's Word. It is not one truth, some truth, a truth among many, but it is the Truth (John 17:17). It is that Truth that sets us free (John 8:32, 36).

Second, James tells us that where worldly wisdom exists there is "every evil thing" (James 3:16). When we open the lid of human wisdom, it is like opening a Pandora's box of every kind of evil imaginable. Before the Flood, we read that "the wickedness of man was great in the earth, and that every intent of the thoughts of his heart was only evil continually" (Genesis 6:5). Men left to themselves without the restraints placed upon them by the wisdom of God do not become better, but instead they become worse.

The Wisdom from Above (James 3:17-18)

The wisdom that comes from God is "first pure" (v. 17). The use of the word "first" here does not mean just first in a list of things, but it refers to that which is first in importance.The word "pure" means "free from defilement, not contaminated," and that which is clean. It does not refer only to moral purity, but also to purity of motive. Jesus promised that the "pure in heart ... shall see God" (Matthew 5:8).

The second characteristic James mentions about godly wisdom is "peaceable" (James 3:17). Jesus said, "Blessed are the peacemakers, for they shall be called sons of God" (Matthew 5:9). Worldly wisdom produces "bitter envy, self-seeking, boasting, lying against the truth," but the wisdom of God brings peace and goodwill among men. It is not peace at any price, which grows out of a spirit of compromise, but peace that grows out of strong conviction. James will tell us in the next chapter that a Christian cannot be a friend of the world (4:4). We should not seek peace with the world but peace with our fellow man and with God, based upon His wisdom.

The third characteristic of godly wisdom is "gentleness" (3:17). The Greek word used here, *epieikes,* is hard to define. It has been rendered "fair, equitable, tolerant, or moderate." Other people suggest that it carries the idea of "reasonableness" or "graciousness" and "the absence of bad manners and a quick temper." Guy N. Woods writes that "some assume they are strong in argument only if they are violent in argument. Some seek to make up in thunder what they lack in lightning, but it should be remembered that it is the lightning that kills!" (p. 193.)

A fourth characteristic of the wisdom from God is that it is "willing to yield" or "easily entreated." The term here is actually a combination of two Greek words that mean that a person is "easy to persuade." Such people are not stubborn or obstinate but are easy to find cooperation with because they are open and conciliatory.

The fifth characteristic of godly wisdom is being "full of mercy." In the Sermon on the Mount, Jesus said, "Blessed are the merciful, for they shall obtain mercy" (Matthew 5:7). Later, He adds the degree of mercy we should possess when He said, "Therefore be merciful, just as your Father also is merciful" (Luke 6:36). The parable about the unforgiving servant deals with the attitude of a person who lacked mercy and the consequences of his actions (Matthew 18:21-35). Unless we extend mercy to other people, we will not receive it on the Day of Judgment.

The sixth characteristic of godly wisdom is bearing "good fruit" (James 3:17). Jesus said,"He who abides in Me, and I in him, bears much fruit" (John 15:5). Paul wrote that "the fruit of the Spirit is love, joy, peace, longsuffering, kindness, goodness, faithfulness, gentleness and self-control" (Galatians 5:22-23). These fruits are the product of a person living a Spirit-led life (Galatians 5:16-18). Because true wisdom comes from God (James 1:5), people who are Spirit-led are people who live according to God's revealed will.

The seventh characteristic of godly wisdom is being "without partiality" (3:17). The original Greek word used here is *adiakritos,* variously translated "impartial," "consistent," "unwavering" and "decisive." The main thought here seems to be that the person possessing godly wisdom does not vacillate but is one with absolute fidelity to truth. Many people who think they are open-minded simply do not have any conviction. People having godly wisdom take their stand for what is right and do not falter.

"[W]ithout hypocrisy" is the eighth characteristic of godly wisdom. People who possess this wisdom from above are sincere people. They are not two-faced; they say what they mean and mean what they say. True wisdom is completely honest and never deceptive.

What are the results of possessing the wisdom that comes from God? James says people who have it will bear "the fruit of righteousness," which is "sown in peace by those who make peace" (James 3:18). Peace is the proper environment in which righteousness can grow. Before righteousness can grow in the heart there must be peace in the soul. Notice the contrast between this verse and the results of worldly wisdom in verse 16. In that environment nothing good can grow. Let us cultivate good ground within us so that we can produce the fruit of righteousness in our lives.

Lessons Learned

1. We learn how to put wisdom and knowledge together to relate God's Truth to everyday life.
2. Many people mistakenly equate success with the accumulation of material things.
3. Self-promoters will run over anyone to reach the top.
4. If we have reason to boast, it should be about the Lord and what He has done.
5. People possessing worldly wisdom view all things from an earthly perspective.
6. Unless we extend mercy to other people, we will not receive mercy from God.

Questions

1. Who was James particularly addressing in this text?
2. What three things does James tell us about worldly wisdom?
3. What does the statement to "be against the truth" mean?
4. How is worldly wisdom demonic?
5. What are two consequences of possessing worldly wisdom?
6. What does James mean by saying that the wisdom from God is "pure?"
7. What is the meaning of the statement "willing to yield?"
8. What does it mean in this text to be "without partiality?"
9. What are the results of possessing the wisdom that comes from God?
10. Where is a proper environment for righteousness to grow?

Lesson 8

Arrogance Forbidden

Week of April 25, 1999

Lesson Text

JAMES 4:1-17

(1) Where do wars and fights come from among you? Do they not come from your desires for pleasure that war in your members?

(2)You lust and do not have. You murder and covet and cannot obtain. You fight and war. Yet you do not have because you do not ask.

(3) You ask and do not receive, because you ask amiss, that you may spend it on your pleasures.

(4) Adulterers and adulteresses! Do you not know that friendship with the world is enmity with God? Whoever therefore wants to be a friend of the world makes himself an enemy of God.

(5) Or do you think that the Scripture says in vain, "The Spirit who dwells in us yearns jealously"?

(6) But He gives more grace. Therefore He says: "God resists the proud, But gives grace to the humble."

(7) Therefore submit to God. Resist the devil and he will flee from you.

(8) Draw near to God and He will draw near to you. Cleanse your hands, you sinners; and purify your hearts, you double-minded.

(9) Lament and mourn and weep! Let your laughter be turned to mourning and your joy to gloom.

(10) Humble yourselves in the sight of the Lord, and He will lift you up.

(11) Do not speak evil of one another, brethren. He who speaks evil of a brother and judges his brother, speaks evil of the law and judges the law. But if you judge the law, you are not a doer of the law but a judge.

(12) There is one Lawgiver, who is able to save and to destroy. Who are you to judge another?

(13) Come now, you who say, "Today or tomorrow we will go to such and such a city, spend a year there, buy and sell, and make a profit";

(14) whereas you do not know what will happen tomorrow. For what is your life? It is even a vapor that appears for a little time and then vanishes away.

(15) Instead you ought to say, "If the Lord wills, we shall live and do this or that."

(16) But now you boast in your arrogance. All such boasting is evil.

(17) Therefore, to him who knows to do good and does not do it, to him it is sin.

Introduction

Chapter and verse divisions in our modern Bibles were added by men long after the inspired Word was delivered to us. The chapter break between chapters three and four is an example of where there should not have been a break. James is continuing the thought he began in chapter three about the evil effects of a loose tongue. The wagging tongue results from a heavy dose of worldly wisdom, and in chapter four we see some more results of putting it into practice.

Family Feud was a popular TV game show on which two families, often contrived, were pitted against each other in a battle of wits and wisdom. The winning family went home with lots of great prizes. The losers went home with consolation prizes. It was loads of fun. However, real family feuds are not pretty.

That is what James is talking about in verse 1 – family fusses and fights. He writes, "Where do wars and fights come from among you?" There is nothing worse than holy wars, and this does not mean the Crusades. It refers to wars among people who should be living holy lives. It has to do with fights concerning congregations. Battles between members of the same family of faith. Is there anything worse?

What is at the root of the problem? The answer to this question is arrogance (James 4:16). In today's text, James tells us the results of arrogance.

Arrogance Results in Fights Among Brethren (James 4:1-3)

Church conflict is not new. Corinth had a lot of factious people (1 Corinthians 1:10-16); some of them were taking their brethren to court to settle personal disputes (6:1-8). The divisions in the Galatian church were so deep that Paul warned them that if they continued to fight among themselves they would be consumed (Galatians 5:15). He had to admonish the Ephesian Christians to "keep the unity of the Spirit in the bond of peace" (Ephesians 4:3). Even Paul's beloved Philippi had to be urged to "fulfill my joy by being like-minded, having the same love, being of one accord, of one mind. Let nothing be done through selfish ambition or conceit, but in lowliness of mind let each esteem others better than himself" (Philippians 2:2-3). Such a flagrant lack of brotherly love is shameful as well as sinful. What causes it?

James' answer is "your desires for pleasure that war in your members" (James 4:1). The word for "pleasures," or passions, in this text denotes lust and desire. It is the Greek word *hedonon,* from which we get the word "hedonist." It carries with it the idea of an evil desire for gratification of the flesh. This selfish desire is the source of the sin of division among brethren, but the place where it is exercised is within the heart of the individual (3:14). When James uses the term "your members," he does not mean the members of the local congregation but the lustful person's bodily members. The conflict is an inside job, basically a problem of the heart.

Notice what this "evil desire" within the heart causes. James accuses the original recipients of this letter of "lust," "covetousness" and "murder." In chapter 1, James said temptation begins with lust, which conceives sin, which if uncorrected leads to spiritual death (James 1:14-15). The picture here is of a person who sees another person having something he wants, then lusting after it until that desire becomes covetousness, or evil desire. Once that happens, this person becomes guilty of murder in the sense that Jesus condemns it in the Sermon on the Mount (Matthew 5:21-22). While He condemns the actual physical act of murder, He emphasizes that a person can also commit murder in the heart. If a person hates another person to the extent that he would kill that person if he thought he could get away with it, or even go through the act in their mind, he is guilty of murder.

When the heart is full of sinful desire, it interferes with a person's prayer life. This is done in two ways. First, sin keeps a person from praying at all. A bitter fountain cannot send forth sweet water. A person filled with hate, who spends his time fighting and warring with other people has no time to pray. He is denied God's blessings because he fails to ask for them. Second, even when he does pray, his selfish prayers are not answered. Is it wrong to pray for something we want and need personally? No, for Jesus said, God "knows the things you have need of before you ask Him" (Matthew 6:8). But He still wants us to ask. He added, "Ask, and it will be given to you; seek, and you will find; knock, and it will be opened to you. For everyone who asks receives, and he who seeks finds, and to him who knocks it will be opened" (7:7-8). What James condemns is prayers that are merely expressions of a person's inward and selfish evil desires. God will not answer such prayers.

Arrogance Results in Worldliness (James 4:4a)

What is worldliness? Most of us would define worldliness as being guilty of specific sins such as drunkenness, adultery, fornication, homosexuality, filthy language "and such like" (Galatians 5:21 KJV). However, the term actually means "love of the world or worldly things." An excellent definition of worldliness is too much of the world in us. When the Christian is in the world, it can be a good thing (Matthew 5:13-16), but when the world is in the Christian, it is not good (John 17:11, 14).

Worldliness prevents a person from heeding God's Word and from being productive. In the parable about the sower, Jesus said some seed "fell among thorns, and the thorns sprang up and choked them" (Matthew 13:7). In explaining this parable to His disciples, He said, "He who received seed among the thorns is he who hears the word, and the cares of this world and the deceitfulness of riches choke the word, and he becomes unfruitful" (v. 22).

Worldliness allows a person to be deceived. It distorts our affections, our vision and our desires. John writes that we should "not love the world or the things in the world … [nor] all that is in the world – the lust of the flesh, the lust of the eyes, and the pride of life" (1 John 2:15-16). The person who is thus affected tries to hold onto the world with one hand and God with the other. No matter how spiritual this person perceives himself to be, he is not a friend of God.

Arrogance Results in Alienation from God (James 4:4-10)

Having said that "Whoever wants to be a friend of the world makes himself an enemy of God," James shows us the consequences of such an illicit love affair. First, it causes alienation of affection. This person is guilty of being a spiritual adulterer (James 4:4; Jeremiah 3:1-5; Ezekiel 23; Hosea 1-2). He is giving his affection to another paramour instead of to God. Exodus 20:5 says that our God is a jealous God. When God sees one of His children having a love affair with the world, it breaks His heart. He wants, and deserves, us to love Him with all of our heart, soul, strength and mind (Matthew 22:37-38; Luke 10:27).

This alienation of affection leads to a failure to submit to God. James urges that we not be too proud to admit our need for God. Why? Because God "resists the proud, But gives grace to the humble" (James 4:6). When we submit to God and resist the devil and his worldly allurement, we cause the devil to flee. However, he has not left forever. Upon the first sign of weakness, he will move back in and try to take over. Only we can make him leave again by putting up the proper resistance. If we are only playing games, Satan will know it and break through our defenses.

Whenever we sincerely draw near to God, as Paul said, "He is not far from each one of us" (Acts 17:27). What it amounts to is saying yes to God and no to Satan. God wants to live in us, but He will not share His residence with our archenemy the devil. Satan does not mind divided loyalties, but God does (James 4:5). How then do we rid our lives of Satan's influence? James provides the answer.

It begins with a good housecleaning. There are some positive steps that should be taken. First, "cleanse your hands, you sinners" (v. 8). Christians should have "clean hands and a pure heart." However, James is using figurative language here to describe the need we have to cleanse our lives of any moral impurity. Second, he said, "purify your hearts, you double-minded" (v. 8). Remember that James 1:8 says, "a double-minded man is unstable in all of his ways." "You cannot serve God and mammon" at the same time (Matthew 6:24). Third, we must truly be sorrowful for our sins (James 4:9). "Godly sorrow produces repentance to salvation" (2 Corinthians 7:10). Sin is not something to laugh about; it is something to "mourn and weep" about (James 4:9). When Isaiah saw the Lord, he also saw how sinful he and his people were, and he said, "Woe is me, for I am undone! Because I am a man of unclean lips, and I dwell in the midst of a people of unclean lips" (Isaiah 6:5). God sent an angel to take a hot coal from the altar of incense within the temple, and he touched Isaiah's mouth and said to the prophet, "Behold, this has touched your lips; Your iniquity is taken away, and your sin purged" (v. 7). When we see our sin in contrast to the holiness of God, we will want to rid ourselves of this filth. Fourth, James says, "Humble yourselves in the sight of the Lord and He will lift you up" (James 4:10).

Arrogance Results in Hasty Judgments (James 4:11-12)

James first says, "Do not speak evil of one another" (James 4:11). The Greek word used here literally means "do not slander" or "do not defame another's character" (2 Corinthians 12:20; 1 Peter 2:1). Arrogance leads us to be hypercritical about the mistakes of other people. These people were apparently self-righteous and intolerant of the sins of others and believed they were not guilty of sin (Romans 2:1-10). Finding fault leads to judging.

The word for "judge" in this text means "pronounce condemnation on another." Jesus condemns judgment of other people (Matthew 7:1-5). However, He does not condemn all kinds of judgment, because He said, "judge with righteous judgement" (John 7:24). This means we are to judge only by God's righteous standard and not our own (Romans 1:32) We must not make judgments from the wrong motivation, based on the wrong criteria, from someone else's motives or from incomplete or incorrect information. It is this kind of judgment that James forbids here (James 4:11).

A good reason not to judge other people is because when we do we "speak evil of the law and judge the law" (James 4:11). What law does James refer to? It is not the Law of Moses, for James tells us that "There is one Lawgiver, who is able to save and to destroy" (v. 12). He is talking about Jesus Christ. The law to which he refers is the "law of Christ" (Galatians 6:2). It is the same one he mentioned earlier, calling it "the perfect law of liberty" (James 1:25). Because he is talking about judging our neighbor, he could have meant the portion of the law of Christ he has called "the royal law ... You shall love your neighbor as yourself" (2:8). After stating this law, Paul wrote that "Love does no harm to a neighbor; therefore love is the fulfillment of the law" (Romans 13:8-10). James makes a statement in this connection that Paul made earlier. "Who are you to judge another?" (James 4:12). We should be very careful in our judgments about other people because the Lord will be the Judge of us all (Romans 14:10-13).

Arrogance Results in Leaving God Out of Our Plans (James 4:13-16)

What was the sin of the rich farmer in Jesus' parable? He was not, as far as we know, an adulterer, a murderer, an extortioner or a drunkard, nor was he guilty of any of the other deadly sins. He had an "I" problem, and he failed to include God in his plans (Luke 12:16-21). James warns against this same sin.

Arrogance leads us to believe we are in control of our lives, so we fail to acknowledge God. How often are you guilty of saying, "Tomorrow I will do this or that"? It is foolish to make such boasts. James calls it "evil" (James 4:16). Why? He supplies us with some answers. First, because of the uncertainty of life. Who of us knows what tomorrow will bring? We are incapable of seeing into the future, and therefore we must depend on Him who holds the future in His hands. Second, because of the brevity of life. Look at all of the figures used in Scripture to describe life. It is "grass which grows up: In the morning it flourishes ... In the evening it is cut down and withers" (Psalm 90:5-6). It is "swifter than a weaver's shuttle" (Job 7:6) and a "cloud [that] disappears and vanishes away" (v. 9). Job also describes our days like a "shadow" (8:9). However, there is no better description than the one James gives us here: "It is even a vapor that appears for a little time and then vanishes away" (James 4:14). Just like the morning fog that is chased away by the heat of the sun, our lives suddenly appear on the scene of history and then just as quickly dissipate. Can you not understand, then, how foolish it is for us to bet on tomorrow?

What we should do instead is live for the Lord each second of every day. We do not have to say, "If the Lord wills" (James 4:15) before we do everything, but this always should be the attitude of our hearts. Whether we honor God in this way while we live, what we eventually do with our life will be according to His will (Philippians 2:9-11). It is far better to do His will while the choice is ours.

Arrogance Results in a Failure to Do Good (James 2:17)

This verse can be looked upon as a summary statement for all that James has said in this text. In this chapter, He has urged people to stop doing bad and to start doing good. He is not talking to people who do not know God's will. Note that he says, "to him who knows." They know it, but they do not obey it. Their sin is not from ignorance, but it is a deliberately defiant act. What the Bible says about deliberate sin should make us all shudder (Hebrews 6:4-6; 10:26-31; 2 Peter 2:19-21). The greatest sin of people today is failing to practice what they know from God's Truth. We know more than we are willing to do. It is not that we do not know; it is that we do not care.

Lessons Learned

1. There is nothing worse than fights between members of the family of faith.
2. The source of the sin of division is selfish, evil desire.

3. Jesus condemns the overt act of sin but also the root cause, which begins in the heart.
4. Sinful desire affects our prayer life.
5. It is not wrong to ask God for things we genuinely need, but it is wrong to ask for anything out of a selfish, evil desire.
6. Worldliness is too much of the world in us.

Questions

1. What does the Greek word *hedonon* mean?
2. What were some of the factious people in Corinth doing?
3. Where does the conflict problem arise?
4. How does evil desires affect our prayer life?
5. How does worldliness keep a person from heeding God's Word?
6. How does worldliness deceive us?
7. What happens when we resist Satan?
8. How do we rid our lives of Satan's influence?
9. What type of judgment does Jesus condemn?
10. What kind of judgment does Jesus command?

Lesson 9

Patience Advised

Week of
May 2, 1999

Lesson Text

JAMES 5:1-12

(1) Come now, you rich, weep and howl for your miseries that are coming upon you!

(2) Your riches are corrupted, and your garments are moth-eaten.

(3) Your gold and silver are corroded, and their corrosion will be a witness against you and will eat your flesh like fire. You have heaped up treasure in the last days.

(4) Indeed the wages of the laborers who mowed your fields, which you kept back by fraud, cry out; and the cries of the reapers have reached the ears of the Lord of Sabaoth.

(5) You have lived on the earth in pleasure and luxury; you have fattened your hearts as in a day of slaughter.

(6) You have condemned, you have murdered the just; he does not resist you.

(7) Therefore be patient, brethren, until the coming of the Lord. See how the farmer waits for the precious fruit of the earth, waiting patiently for it until it receives the early and latter rain.

(8) You also be patient. Establish your hearts, for the coming of the Lord is at hand.

(9) Do not grumble against one another, brethren, lest you be condemned. Behold, the Judge is standing at the door!

(10) My brethren, take the prophets, who spoke in the name of the Lord, as an example of suffering and patience.

(11) Indeed we count them blessed who endure. You have heard of the perseverance of Job and seen the end intended by the Lord--that the Lord is very compassionate and merciful.

(12) But above all, my brethren, do not swear, either by heaven or by earth or with any other oath. But let your "Yes," be "Yes," and your "No," "No," lest you fall into judgment.

Introduction

The theme of this text is patience in view of the imminent return of Christ (James 5:7-8). The word "imminent" is not to be confused with immediate. It means "impending" or "something that could happen at anytime." Some commentators say the early Christians believed that Jesus was returning immediately, or within a few short years of His ascension. This was not the case. Instead, they understood "you know neither the day nor the hour in which the Son of Man is coming" (Matthew 25:13). That is why Jesus encouraged them to "Watch therefore, for you do not know what hour your Lord is coming" (Matthew 24:42). For this reason, they lived with the glorious expectation that Jesus could come at anytime; therefore they needed always to be ready. Christians in every age, including our own, should live with this hope in their hearts.

After warning that "the day of the Lord will come as a thief in the night" (2 Peter 3:10), Peter asked, "Since all these things will be dissolved, what manner of persons ought you to be in holy conduct and godliness?" (v. 11). In other words, "Because Jesus could come at any moment, how should we live?" James was particularly concerned about the way certain wealthy Christians were living and treating poorer people.

Some people have accused the Bible of having an anti-rich bias. There have been those people who have taught that poverty is holier than prosperity, but this is a misapplication of Scripture. Jesus said, "it is hard for a rich man to enter the kingdom of heaven" (Matthew 19:23). He said "hard," but He did not say "impossible." That is why he used the illustration of the camel going through the eye of a needle. It was to show the difficulty involved. Paul warned against the "love of money" (1 Timothy 6:6-10) but gave instructions to the rich for the proper use of wealth (vv. 17-19). Joseph of Arimathea and Nicodemus, who were secret disciples of Jesus, were both most likely wealthy men (John 19:38-39). Some of the early Christians were prominent individuals, both men and women (Acts 16:14-15; 17:12; 18:8). Philemon was a wealthy friend of Paul. It is not the having or not having wealth that is important; it is how it was obtained and how it is being used.

James addresses two subjects in this text. The first is the treatment by the wealthy of people who were poor, which was dealt with partially in James 1:27 and in chapter 2. The second subject is the need for people who were mistreated by the rich to be patient and await God's judgment upon the people who oppressed them (1:2-4).

Warnings to the Rich (James 5:1-3)

James has never sounded more like an Old Testament prophet than he does here. His words are reminiscent of Amos, the "country prophet," when he denounced the extravagant lifestyles of Israel's rich and famous (Amos 6:1-8). James warns these rich, who then lived in the lap of luxury, that they would soon "weep and howl for the miseries that are coming upon you" (James 5:1). This is unquestionably a reference to the destruction of Jerusalem by the armies of the Roman general Titus, which happened only a few years after these words were penned in A.D. 70. More than a million people were killed in the siege of the city and its aftermath, but the wealthy received wrath from their Romans conquerors. They were stripped of their money and power, and many were tortured before being killed (*Josephus Jewish Wars V*, x 424 ff.; xiii, 550 ff).

These people had done what Jesus warned against. They had laid up "treasures on earth, where moth and rust destroy and where thieves break in and steal" instead of "lay[ing] up … treasures in heaven" (Matthew 6:19-20). Notice the similarity of His statement to that of James (James 5:2-3). Then, as now, a person's wealth was not just the currency he had, but it was determined by a number of factors. Look at the graphic language he uses: "corrupted riches," "corroded gold and silver" and "moth eaten garments." What better way to describe the "deceitfulness of riches" (Matthew 13:22)? So much of our time is spent in the acquisition of wealth and the things it will buy, but when life is over for us here, we leave all of this behind. The only thing we will have to show for our lives at the Judgment will be the treasures we have laid up in heaven.

The sin of these people was not in being rich. James lists a number of their transgressions. First among them was they "heaped up treasure." That is, they hoarded their wealth. The richest man in the world today is American entrepreneur Bill Gates. He is one of the founders and the chairman of Microsoft, the leading software company in the world. Gates is worth almost $40 billion. His wealth continues to grow, and yet he has so far refrained from the generous philanthropy that has been customary with many other super-rich people. Although he says he has given away 500 million dollars to different causes in which he believes, this is a very small portion of the enormous fortune he has amassed. He says his intention is to give all of it away before he dies. The point here is not to condemn Gates but only to ask how much wealth does a person have to hoard before he is satisfied? Also, why don't people who have more money than they could ever spend use it for humanitarian purposes? This was the situation with the rich people James was addressing. They had more money than they could ever use themselves, but they wanted more and continued to hoard all they received. Their money will be a witness against them, and all who are like them, in the Day of Judgment.

Other Sins of the Abusive Rich (James 5:4-6)

In these verses James discusses some more sins of these abusive rich. First, they stole from or defrauded the poor laborers who mowed their fields (James 5:4). This probably refers to their shortchanging or deliberately holding back the wages of these people. Second, they cheated the reapers who harvested their grain. Both of the these groups "cried out" against their abusive employers. Their cries had reached the "ears of the Lord of Sabaoth" (v. 4). The title used here for God is not "Lord of the Sabbath," but of "Sabaoth," meaning "hosts." While it is only used here and in Romans 9:29 in the New Testament, it is used 282 times in the Old Testament. It has reference to the fact that God fought on the side of His people with His host of angels and gave them victory in battle (Joshua 5:13-15; 1 Samuel 15:1-3; 2 Samuel 5:10-12; 2 Kings 6:17-23; Isaiah 2:10-21; Psalm 59:1-5). He would surely bring retribution upon these abusive rich for their treatment of the poor.

They stole the money from these poor laborers so they could live in "pleasure and luxury" (James 5:5). The description is that of people living an excessively self-indulgent, wasteful and even lascivious life from their ill-gotten gains. However, what they were actually doing was "fattening" themselves up for the "day of slaughter" (v. 5). Just like animals waiting to be sacrificed, they were growing increasingly fatter on the blood, sweat and tears of the poor. While this day of slaughter may certainly describe the destruction of Jerusalem in A.D. 70, the words "and will eat your flesh like fire" (James 5:3) would include the final Judgment (Matthew 25:31-46; Revelation 20:10-15). Some of these rich people may have even managed to escape the first judgment against Israel, but they would not escape the second one involving all mankind.

Third, these abusive, wealthy people stole from the people who worked for them and had people condemned and murdered the just, so they could take what belonged to them (James 5:6). The word "condemned" suggests a legal sentence of death imposed upon an innocent person. One of the flagrant sins of the wealthy Jews was perverting justice for their gain (Proverbs 17:23; 31:5; Ecclesiastes 5:8; Isaiah 1:17; Micah 3:9; Zechariah 8:16).

Some commentators believe "the just" ("the righteous one" ASV) here has reference to Jesus Christ. The wealthy Jewish leaders were certainly in the forefront of having Jesus condemned, but this interpretation does not fit the context here. It is talking about the poor, defenseless, righteous persons who could not afford, nor did they have the power to protect themselves from their wealthy oppressors (James 5:6).

Advice to the Oppressed (James 5:7-11)

How is a Christian supposed to handle oppression? The natural reaction to mistreatment is the desire for vengeance. This is not the Christian approach. Jesus said, "Whoever slaps you on your right cheek, turn the other to him also … love your enemies, bless those who curse you, do good to those who hate you, and pray for those who spitefully use you and persecute you" (Matthew 5:39, 44). " 'Vengeance is mine, I will repay', says the Lord" (Deuteronomy 32:35; Hebrews 10:30). We must not get into the retaliation game. That being true, how do we deal with mistreatment?

First, James says "be patient" (James 5:7, 8). The Greek word here is actually a combination of two words: *makros,* meaning "a long way, or far," and *thumos,* which means "passion, heat, rage or anger." This gives us the expression "long-suffering." A person who is patient is not a person with a quick temper. An angry, impatient person will never be able to learn the lessons God wants him to know.

As an illustration of what he means by being patient, James mentions farmers. An impatient person cannot be a farmer, for he must plow in hope, wait in faith and harvest with thanksgiving. Farmers know it takes time to grow a harvest. So they wait for the precious fruit of the earth to be watered by the gentle rains from God (Matthew 5:45). When the rains do not come and the droughts dry up the crops, what good would it do to become impatient and ill-tempered? The abused poor must learn to wait patiently for "the coming of the Lord"(James 5:7) at Judgment Day, when all wrongs will be righted, and people who oppress them will be punished.

Second, they needed to "establish (strengthen, NASB)" their hearts. The idea here is that these people bore a heavy burden and needed to be supported in bearing it. Why did they need to be strengthened? Because the Lord's coming was "at hand (nigh)" (James 5:8). He adds, "Behold, and the Judge is standing at the door" (James v. 9). The implication is that the Lord's return was very close. However, as noted before, it means only that it is an imminent event that could happen at anytime.

Third, they needed not to "grumble against one another" (v. 9). This phrase literally means "do not groan in complaint against a brother." When people exist under the stress of oppression, they may direct their anger toward the people who are closest to them. Such complaining might draw the attention of other people and lead to the condemnation of another Christian. It serves no useful purpose, and could result in the complainer's being judged by God.

To illustrate the kind of patience he meant, James uses two illustrations from the Old Testament. The first was the prophets (v. 10). No men or women ever suffered more for their faithfulness to God. They were mocked, scourged, chained and imprisoned, stoned, sawn in two, beheaded and forced to wander about in skins, being destitute, afflicted and tormented (Hebrews 11:36-37). Despite whatever they endured, they remained committed to God and accepted their fate with grace.

The second illustration was that of Job. This suffering servant persevered in the face of unrelenting temptation by Satan, which included the loss of family, fortune, friends and health. Yet he "did not sin nor charge God with wrong" (Job 1:22). In the end, Job was blessed far beyond what he had ever experienced before (42:12-

17). Why do the righteous like Job suffer? We are unable to answer that question completely, but we do know that although God allows it to happen, He intends for us to prosper (Romans 8:28; Hebrews 12:7-11). God is "compassionate and merciful" (James 5:11) and wants only to "give good gifts to those who ask Him" (Matthew 7:11; James 1:17).

Last of all, James advises the persecuted people not to "swear, either by heaven or by earth or with any other oath" (5:12). Whether James remembered this teaching from the Lord or if it was given to him by the Holy Spirit, it was exactly what Jesus taught in the Sermon on the Mount (Matthew 5:33-37). Jesus plainly said, "do not swear at all" (Matthew 5:34). The idea of letting our yes be yes and our no be no (James 5:12) simply means to let our word be our bond. If a person tells the truth, then he can swear by no greater oath than his word. Christians must be people of unquestionable honesty and integrity.

Lessons Learned

1. We should expect that Jesus could return at anytime, but it is foolish to try to set a date.
2. The Bible does not have an anti-rich bias, but it makes salvation available to all people, rich and poor, based on the same conditions.
3. Most of our life is spent in the pursuit of those things that perish with using.
4. Although we may be persecuted, we should reject the desire for revenge.
5. When Jesus returns for the Judgment, all wrongs will be righted.
6. Christians must be honest and upright in all of their dealings and relationships.

Questions

1. What is the difference between imminent and immediate?
2. What was the purpose of Jesus' statement about the camel going through the eye of a needle?
3. What are some of the names of the rich persons who were believers of Christ?
4. What two subjects does James cover in the text for this lesson?
5. What was the "first among" the sins of the wealthy people James condemned in this study?
6. What did James mean by saying that their money would be a witness against them?
7. What is the meaning of the title, "Lord of the Sabaoth?"
8. Why did these rich people steal from their poor laborers?
9. What does the phrase, "condemned and murdered the just" imply?
10. How does James tell the persecuted Christians to deal with their abuse?

Lesson 10

Prayer Urged

Week of May 9, 1999

Lesson Text

JAMES 5:13-20

(13) Is anyone among you suffering? Let him pray. Is anyone cheerful? Let him sing psalms.

(14) Is anyone among you sick? Let him call for the elders of the church, and let them pray over him, anointing him with oil in the name of the Lord.

(15) And the prayer of faith will save the sick, and the Lord will raise him up. And if he has committed sins, he will be forgiven.

(16) Confess your trespasses to one another, and pray for one another, that you may be healed. The effective, fervent prayer of a righteous man avails much.

(17) Elijah was a man with a nature like ours, and he prayed earnestly that it would not rain; and it did not rain on the land for three years and six months.

(18) And he prayed again, and the heaven gave rain, and the earth produced its fruit.

(19) Brethren, if anyone among you wanders from the truth, and someone turns him back,

(20) let him know that he who turns a sinner from the error of his way will save a soul from death and cover a multitude of sins.

Introduction

The subject of today's text is prayer, mentioned seven times in James 5:13-18. This is obviously a continuation of the previous section, encouraging people who were oppressed. Christians are urged to "pray without ceasing" (1 Thessalonians 5:17), "everywhere" (1 Timothy 2:8), in "everything" (Philippians 4:6) and "always" (Luke 18:1). Our motto today seems to be "when all else fails, pray." James tells these Christians their motto ought to be "pray before doing anything else." There may be many things we can do besides pray, but there is no better thing we can do than pray.

This passage is the subject of much controversy. Some religious organizations and preachers insist that the teaching here about "praying over the sick and anointing them with oil" is still to be practiced today. Is this text one that we should observe today and, if so, in what way? Charlatans who claim to possess the gift of healing are abundant and milk ignorant people out of millions of dollars. Testimonies of people who say they have witnessed actual healings or have been healed themselves are also abundant. What are we to make of such claims? How is prayer involved in healing? How does modern medicine fit into this picture? How is sin related to illness? In today's lesson, we will endeavor to answer these questions.

What Is a Christian to Do? (James 5:13)

James discusses two sets of circumstances in which all Christians sooner or later find themselves, and he tells us how we should react to each one. First, when we are suffering, we should pray. The word for "suffering" here is a Greek word that means "in distress." This distress can be caused by mental illness, emotional anguish or physical affliction. What are we to do in such cases? James' answer is to pray. In this place he does not promise healing, and that is not even the reason for praying at this point. The purpose for prayer here is to help us endure. God sometimes chooses not to remove an affliction but instead uses it to strengthen us (2 Corinthians 12:7-9; Philippians 2:25-27; 1 Timothy 5:23; 2 Timothy 4:20; 1 Peter 2;24).

Second, when we are "cheerful (merry, KJV; happy, WTNT)," we should "sing psalms." It is not that we should not pray when we are happy or that we should not sing when we are afflicted. These are the most natural reactions to these two different sets of circumstances. The most natural thing in the world is to sing when we are happy, and the most natural thing to do when we are troubled is to pray. Singing and praying were important parts of the worship of the early church, and they should be today (1 Corinthians 14:15).

While James is not thinking primarily about congregational singing here, it is important to note that a form of the same Greek verb, *psallo*, is used here and in those passages where congregational singing is obviously intended (1 Corinthians 14:15; Ephesians 5:19; Colossians 3:16). In Ephesians 5:18-19, Paul urges these Christians not to "be drunk with wine, in which is dissipation; but be filled with the Spirit, speaking to one another in psalms and hymns and spiritual songs, singing and making melody in your heart to the Lord." In the letter to the Galatians, Paul said one of the fruits of the Spirit is joy. When a person is filled with the Spirit, his joy will be expressed in song.

Sickness, Sin and the Saint (James 5:14-16)

Before dealing with the particulars of this text, let us first analyze what it says. First, if a person, we know he means Christians because he says "among you," was sick, he was to call for the "elders of the church." The elders were to anoint that person with oil "In the name of the Lord." When this was done, health would then be restored and any sins would be forgiven this person. This is what the text says, but how do we interpret it?

Obviously, this text does not mean all types of sickness should be handled in this way. If it referred to all sick Christians, then all of them would have been healed. Saints were frequently sick and some died. We must also acknowledge that it is not God's will that all sicknesses be healed. Paul, who possessed the gift of healing (Acts 20:7-12; 28:7-9), left his friend and brother Trophimus sick at Miletus. Epaphroditus, a beloved fellow laborer with Paul, almost died while he was ministering to the apostle. Timothy, Paul's spiritual son, had a stomach problem and other "frequent infirmities" (Acts 9:32-43; Philippians 2:19-30; 1 Timothy 5:23). The sickness James mentions in this text must be of a special kind.

Let us begin by asking, "What kind of sickness was this?" It would be more appropriate to ask, "Where did this illness originate?" We must realize that there are two causes of sickness. Some illnesses are directly related to sin in a person's life (1 Corinthians 11:30). For example, a person may become drunk and be in an automobile accident that paralyzes the person for life. King David would be a good biblical example (2 Samuel 11 and 12; Psalm 32:3-4).

Then there are those sicknesses that an individual is not personally responsible for. These may result from the sins or mistakes of another person. For example, the person mentioned above may have caused an accident that injures an innocent person. Such illnesses may also be caused by the fact that we live in a sin-cursed world. When sin entered the world, death was introduced to humanity (Romans 5:12). Along with death, there came those factors that cause death to occur: sickness, disease, plagues, drought, famine, floods and so on. The individual has no influence over these factors, and these factors are totally impartial. Two examples of this type of sickness from the Bible would be Job in the Old Testament and the man born blind in the New Testament (Job 2:7-8; John 9:1-38).

The text would indicate that this person was sick because of some sin he had committed. This conclusion is drawn from the statements in James 5:15-16. The Greek text says, "if he has been committed sins" (v. 15). His sickness is serious enough that he cannot go to the church to receive forgiveness, so the church must come to him in the form of the elders.

When the elders arrive, they should do two things: first, anoint the sick person with oil; second, pray over the sick person calling on or invoking the name of the Lord for his healing (James 5:14). Why were the elders to be called? The situation being described was one that transpired during the miraculous period when the gift of healing was available (Mark 16:17-20; 1 Corinthians 12:9). The elders were the spiritual leaders of the local congregation (Acts 14:23; 20:17-28; Philippians 1:1; 1 Timothy 3:1-7; Titus 1:5). While it cannot be proven absolutely, it seems that the elders would have been the logical persons upon whom the apostles would have laid their hands and imparted to them spiritual gifts.

Why were the elders to "anoint with oil"? The oil that was used in most cases was olive oil, which was in abundance in Palestine, although it was sometimes mixed with other ingredients. The anointing of oil was associated with two things in Scripture. The first was ceremonial (Leviticus 8:10-12; 10:7; 21:10; 1 Samuel 10:1-9; 15:17; 16:13; 1 Kings 1:32-40), and the second was medicinal (Psalm 23:5; Isaiah 1:6; Jeremiah 8:22; 46:11; Mark 6:13; Luke 10:34). While some people want to make the purpose here to be medicinal (Jay Adams, *Competent to Counsel*, Presbyterian and Reformed Publishing Company, Phillipsburg, 1970; pp. 107-108), if it is related to the miraculous period, it is surely ceremonial. As Guy Woods wrote, "It appears quite clear here that the use of the oil was symbolic, and not medicinal; and thus served as a token of the power of God by which the healing was accomplished." (p. 301.)

Although the interpretation given here is believed to be the most accurate and true to the text, there are still some applications that should be made for the church today. First, it is always good to pray for the sick. God is still the One who heals, although He may do it through different means today. God has blessed us with modern medical marvels, and we should use them and be thankful for them. Second, it seems to be appropriate for the elders to be the ones who do the praying at the sickbed because they are the spiritual leaders and pastors of the church. We most often call for the preacher, and it is all right to do so, but shouldn't the elders be involved? It is also right for all members to pray for the sick. Third, confessing our sins to one another and praying for forgiveness is still a worthwhile endeavor. This is what we do when erring Christians respond to the invitation of the Lord, asking for prayers of forgiveness. Should specific sins be confessed? While that may be helpful for certain people who make a public commitment to leave a particular sin behind, there does not appear to be any reason to confess them to the church. They should always be confessed to God (1 John 1:9).

James concludes this section by saying that "the effective fervent prayer of a righteous man avails much." That is still true today (Matthew 7:7-11; John 9:31; 1 Peter 3:12; 1 John 5:14-15). Having stated this principle, James gives us an example about what he means.

God Still Hears and Answers Prayer (James 5:17-18)

In making his point, James calls upon an Old Testament illustration that would have been well-known to the Jewish Christians he was writing. Elijah was one of their most revered prophets. Although the circumstances of his praying for it not to rain are not clearly explained, it obviously refers to the period when King Ahab attempted to make Baalism the dominant religion in the northern kingdom. Elijah said, "As the Lord God of Israel lives, before whom I stand, there shall not be dew nor rain these years, except at my word" (1 Kings 17:1). Then he was commanded by God to hide out near the Brook Cherith and afterward at Zarephath (vv. 2-3, 9-10). After much time had passed (James 5:17), God told him to, "Go present yourself to Ahab, and I will send rain on the earth" (1 Kings 18:1). This was done after Elijah defeated the prophets of Baal on Mount Carmel (vv. 36-45).

Elijah was a righteous man of God. He prayed to God and He heard and answered his prayer. However, let us not miss one of the main points of James' illustration. He says, "Elijah was a man with a nature like ours." In other words, Elijah was a man just like we are. If God heard and answered his prayer, He will hear and answer our prayers also (James 1:5). As James has already pointed out, our prayers should always be "If the Lord wills" (James 4:15; 1 John 5:14-15).

Prayer and Restoring the Erring (James 5:19-20)

There is a definite connection between these verses and those that precede it. James is still concerned with the person who is sick because of sin. He could be referring to the same person mentioned in verses 14-15. The specific sins that this person may have committed could be that of "wandering from the truth." The Truth is God's Word (John 17:17). Whenever a person gets too far from it they are subject to slip or backslide (Hebrews 2:1-2). The consequences of wandering are "sin" and possibly "spiritual death" (James 5:20).

When we know a brother or sister is guilty of sin, we should go to them and warn them about the consequences of their actions. This should be done in "the spirit of gentleness, considering yourself lest you also be tempted" (Galatians 6:1). It should always be in a humble, kind attitude, and never arrogant or haughty. Our attitude should be, "There but for the grace of God go I." If that sinful brother or sister hears us and turns back, or repents, we have "saved a soul from death and covered a multitude of sins." This is one of the clearest statements in the Bible to show that a child of God can sin and be lost (Acts 1:25; 8:13-24; 1 Corinthians 10:12; Galatians 5:4; Hebrews 6:4-6; 2 Peter 2:19-22). The privilege to pray and have sins forgiven is only available for a child of God (1 John 1:7-2:2). All other people must first "repent and be baptized for the forgiveness of sins" (Acts 2:38).

Lessons Learned

1. A Christian's motto ought to be "pray before doing anything else."
2. When we are suffering, prayer should be the first thing we do.
3. Singing and praying should still be important parts of a Christian's life and worship.
4. Some illnesses can be caused by sin, but all illness is not related to personal sin.
5. The only purpose for pouring oil over someone's body today would be medicinal.
6. Confessing our sins and praying for one another, although not the specific nature of them, is still a worthwhile endeavor.
7. We should always confess our sins to God, even the "secret sins" (Psalm 19:12 KJV).

Questions

1. What is the main subject of this text?
2. Is it wrong to pray when we are happy or to sing when we are sad?
3. Who were the sick mentioned in this text to call for and why?
4. How does the answer to the above help us understand the nature of the sin in question?
5. What were the two purposes of the anointing with oil in biblical times?
6. Why is it still appropriate today to call for the elders of the congregation when a person is sick?
7. What is the main purpose of James' use of Elijah as an example for us?
8. What happens when a person goes too far from the Truth?
9. What are the ultimate consequences of wandering from God?
10. What is one of the clearest statements in Scripture concerning the fact that a child of God can sin so as to be lost eternally?

Lesson 11

Paul Remembers

Week of May 16, 1999

Lesson Text

PHILEMON 1-7

(1) Paul, a prisoner of Christ Jesus, and Timothy our brother, To Philemon our beloved friend and fellow laborer,

(2) to the beloved Apphia, Archippus our fellow soldier, and to the church in your house:

(3) Grace to you and peace from God our Father and the Lord Jesus Christ.

(4) I thank my God, making mention of you always in my prayers,

(5) hearing of your love and faith which you have toward the Lord Jesus and toward all the saints,

(6) that the sharing of your faith may become effective by the acknowledgment of every good thing which is in you in Christ Jesus.

(7) For we have great joy and consolation in your love, because the hearts of the saints have been refreshed by you, brother.

Introduction

This little one-chapter book is one of the most interesting in the New Testament. Of the 13 epistles we know Paul wrote, this is the shortest one, consisting of only 25 verses. It is one of the letters of Paul that is classed as personal. He wrote many such letters, most of which are unknown to us, and often made reference to them. Why then does this particular one appear in the canon of Scripture? There are three good reasons for its inclusion.

First, it contains information concerning the relationship of Christian slave owners and their slaves who were their brothers and sisters in the family of God. It is estimated there were more than 60 million slaves in the Roman Empire at this time. Paul had written that "There is neither Jew nor Greek, there is neither slave nor free, there is neither male nor female; for you are all one in Christ Jesus" (Galatians 3:28). How, then, were Christian slave owners to treat their slaves who were also Christians? This book gives us an answer to this question.

Second, in verse 2 it is obvious that this personal letter was to be read to the church. Paul greets the church that met in Philemon's house. One view among scholars is that it was also written to be read in the churches at Laodicea and Colossae, and it may have been the letter referred to by Paul in the Colossian epistle (Colossians 4:16)

Third, we can be assured that it is in the New Testament because it belongs there. God inspired the writing of the Bible (2 Timothy 3:16; 2 Peter 1:19-21). He is powerful enough to retain what He desires to be contained in His word and to delete what He does not choose to retain (John 20:30-31; 21:24-25).

The historical context of this epistle is important for understanding its purpose. When Paul was in prison in Rome (Philemon 1, 13), he received a visit from Epaphras. He was most likely a convert during Paul's three-year ministry in Ephesus.

He was a citizen of Colossae, a city of Asia Minor located on the western border of Phrygia, astride the Lycus River. Epaphras was one of the key figures in founding the church in Colossae under Paul's direction. He appears to have been their preacher, and he also preached in Hierapolis and Laodicea (Colossians 1:7; 4:12-13).

Epaphras brought some disturbing news to Paul concerning some unsettling doctrines that were being taught in the church at Colossae. The problem was basically religious syncretism, which is a blend of contradictory beliefs. It probably stemmed from the diverse religious and ethnic backgrounds of the people in the Lycus River valley area. Hierapolis harbored a famous shrine to the goddess Cybelle. This region was also a center for Eastern and European religions, the mystic religions, the philosophies of the Stoics and Epicureans and other intellectual religions.

While Paul was in Rome, he came into contact with a runaway slave named Onesimus and converted him to Christ. His master Philemon was a wealthy Colossian who had been converted by Paul in Ephesus. A congregation of the church met in Philemon's house. Apphia, "the beloved," is most likely Philemon's wife. Archippus "our fellow soldier" may have been Philemon's son and the preacher for the church that met in their home (Philemon 2).

Paul had encouraged Onesimus to go home and had either already written or was in the process of writing a letter of explanation to Philemon. He encouraged Philemon to accept Onesimus back, not just as a slave but as a brother in Christ. This in itself was a revolutionary idea for that time, which was around A.D. 60-63.

Upon receiving the disturbing news from Epaphras, Paul wrote a second letter to the church at Colossae. It was designed to refute the heretical teaching that had been reported to Him and to establish the truth of the gospel. Out of concern that this heresy might spread, Paul also wrote another epistle that some call "the circular letter" (Colossians 4:16). This was in all probability a general epistle that was intended to be read by all of the churches in the area. Paul sent these letters by Tychicus, accompanied by Onesimus, who was returning to Philemon with the letter Paul had written to him (Ephesians 6:21; Colossians 4:7-9). Epaphras stayed on in Rome to assist Paul (vv. 12-13).

Paul Remembers Close Ties with Fellow Christians (Philemon 1-3)

Much of the question of where this epistle was penned hinges upon the meaning of Paul's statement here. Was he actually a prisoner in Rome, or was this one of those times that Paul referred to himself as a prisoner of Christ and the gospel? While this verse may be interpreted in other ways, verse 13 clearly states Paul's current situation. He was in chains and was being administered to by other people, notably Onesimus. Timothy was also in Paul's company, and among other things, he ministered to the apostle while he was a prisoner in Rome (2 Timothy 4:13, 21). Although he was in chains, Paul was able to minister to all who came to him (Acts 28:16-31). He later wrote to the Philippian Christians that his confinement "actually turned out for the furtherance of the gospel" (Philippians 1:12).

Philemon's name means "affectionate" or "beloved." In those days, names were extremely significant. As in the case of Saul of Tarsus, when a person became a Christian, he often took a new name suited to his new life in Christ. This may have been the case with Philemon.

In addition to Paul's obvious love for Philemon, he also had love for his wife, Apphia, and for his son, Archippus. Most scholars agree as to the identity of these two people. They were part of the house church that met in their home, and as noted earlier, Archippus was most likely the preacher for this congregation. House churches were common in those days (Romans 16:5, 10-11; 1 Corinthians 16:19; Colossians 4:15). In fact, according to Newport J. D. White in *Expositors Greek New Testament,* there is no evidence that any church buildings existed among the Lord's people up until the third century A.D. (William B. Eerdmans Publishing Company, Grand Rapids, 1967; p. 212). We should note of the lack of importance that meeting houses took in those days when compared to today. The building is not holy. The purpose for which we come together makes it so when we are gathered to worship God. The building is not the church; the people are. This needs to be straight in our minds.

Paul begins with a traditional greeting (Philemon 3). However, we can be sure that this was said with deep feeling, and it was not just done out of habit. It has been suggested that the admonition for God to grant "grace and peace" to Philemon would strengthen Paul's case in asking of him to show the same consideration to Onesimus.

Paul's Thanksgiving Prayer (Philemon 4)

This statement may have applied to other people as well, but it specifically refers to Philemon. Following it, Paul mentions many reasons why he was thankful for his friend. Considering the status of Philemon, one great truth emerges here – no person who is serving God is outside the need for, or the reach of, prayer (John 9:31).

We also see the need to pray more often. Can you imagine what Paul's prayer list looked like (Ephesians 1:16; Philippians 1:3-4; Colossians 1:3; 1 Thessalonians 1:2-3; 2 Timothy 1:3-4)? His example ought to bring all of us to our knees in a humble prayer for forgiveness. If Paul took the time to pray for all of these people who were dear to him, should we not also find the time? "I am praying for you" should be more than just an expression. We should mean it and practice it regularly. Jimmy Allen once wrote, "The majority of our prayerless people have not rejected prayer on theological grounds – they have simply neglected it" (*The Need for Revival*, 1973; p. 23).

Paul's Reasons for Commending Philemon (Philemon 5-7)

Philemon was first and foremost a faithful Christian. Paul mentions his love and faith in the Lord Jesus and his love "towards all the saints." His faith and love was the source of all of his benevolent activity. Without this relationship with the Savior, his relationship with the brethren would have been meaningless. No testimony is more powerful about a person's faith than seeing his love in action. It is also beneficial in promoting unity and harmony among brethren. It can break down any barriers and resolve all types of differences.

Philemon had faith and proved it by his actions, and he shared his faith with other people. Paul had called him "a fellow laborer" (v. 1). This would indicate that he was active in spreading the gospel and in making converts to Christ. It was Paul's hope that other people could learn from this man to use the "good thing which is in you in Christ Jesus" (v. 6).

Some commentators believe this verse applies specifically to Philemon's generosity in material matters. Paul had written to the Corinthians that there should be a sharing of the burden of the whole group based upon a person's ability to perform (2 Corinthians 8:13-15). In the Galatian letter, Paul wrote, "Let him who is taught the word share in all good things with him who teaches" (6:6). This sharing is taken to mean financial support. It is thought that Paul is encouraging in other people the kind of generosity that Philemon was noted for.

In verse 7 in particular, we see that Philemon was liberal in his gifts to his brothers in Christ. It supplied their physical needs and served to bring joy to Paul's heart (v. 20) that one of his sons in the gospel would have such a Christian spirit. Philemon's gracious acts and deeds "refreshed the hearts of the saints." His generosity is almost certain to have had other positive benefits. In Paul's second letter to the Corinthians, he told them that their generosity had "supplie[d] the needs of the saints" but it had also "abound[ed] through many thanksgivings to God" (2 Corinthians 9:12). This means that people inside and outside of the church glorified God for their "liberal sharing with them and all men" (2 Corinthians 9:13). Jesus had said, "Let you light so shine before men, that they may see your good works and glorify your Father in heaven" (Matthew 5:16).

Paul closes this verse with the tender and affectionate address "brother." There is not a more endearing term in the Greek than this one. It has the same warmth in the English language, but it is used so often that it loses its true meaning. This shows the affection that Paul had for this man and that he in turn had for the apostle.

Lessons Learned

1. The term "inspiration," meaning "God breathed," implies God gave the message and also overruled in it being recorded.
2. Our relationship to Christ does not change our circumstances.
3. God can use even a bad situation such as Paul's imprisonment to accomplish some good result.
4. No Christian is outside of the need or the reach of prayer (John 9:31).
5. When we say, "I am praying for you," we should mean it and do it.
6. There is no greater testimony to our faith than for other people to see our love in action.

Questions

1. What are three good reasons for the inclusion of Philemon in the New Testament canon?
2. Who may have been a central figure in establishing the church at Colossae?
3. What was the Colossian problem?
4. Why was the Colossian letter written?
5. What proof do we have that Paul was in prison when he wrote Philemon?
6. What does the name Philemon mean?
7. What does the name Onesimus mean?
8. When was the first evidence that Christians owned church buildings?
9. Why have many Christians quit praying?
10. What purpose did Philemon's gift serve?

Lesson 12

Paul Appeals

Week of May 23, 1999

Lesson Text

PHILEMON 8-16

(8) Therefore, though I might be very bold in Christ to command you what is fitting,

(9) yet for love's sake I rather appeal to you--being such a one as Paul, the aged, and now also a prisoner of Jesus Christ--

(10) I appeal to you for my son Onesimus, whom I have begotten while in my chains,

(11) who once was unprofitable to you, but now is profitable to you and to me.

(12) I am sending him back. You therefore receive him, that is, my own heart,

(13) whom I wished to keep with me, that on your behalf he might minister to me in my chains for the gospel.

(14) But without your consent I wanted to do nothing, that your good deed might not be by compulsion, as it were, but voluntary.

(15) For perhaps he departed for a while for this purpose, that you might receive him forever,

(16) no longer as a slave but more than a slave--a beloved brother, especially to me but how much more to you, both in the flesh and in the Lord.

Introduction

Paul's entire purpose from the beginning of this epistle was to appeal to the heart of Philemon to receive his runaway slave back without punishing him. Slaves were chattel that could be auctioned off like animals. Roman law sided with the masters and gave them the absolute power of life and death over their slaves. William Barclay described the conditions under which slaves in the Roman Empire lived: "A slave was not a person; he was a living tool. A master had absolute power over his slaves. He could box their ears or condemn them to hard labor making them, for instance, work in chains upon his lands in the country, or in a sort of prison-factory or he may punish them with blows of the rod, the lash, or the knot; he can brand them upon the forehead, if they are thieves or runaways, or, in the end, if they prove irreclaimable, he can crucify them" (*The Letter to Timothy, Titus and Philemon*, Westminister Press, Philadelphia, 1975; p. 270).

If Onesimus returned home without the endorsement and support of Paul, he could have been beaten, branded in the forehead or even sentenced to death. Yet as a fugitive he was in constant danger of being discovered. His only hope to stay alive was to stay on the run. However, when he met Paul and was converted to Christ, it changed everything for him. He willingly stayed with the apostle and loyally served him. This was until they both knew that he had to return home to make things right with his master. Freedom in Christ does not mean freedom from responsibility or from the consequences of our actions before we became Christians. Onesimus was now right in the sight of God, but he needed to make things right with Philemon.

When Onesimus left home he was a fugitive and probably a thief. Paul had said, "if he owes anything, put that on my account" (Philemon 18). This seems to indicate that he took something belonging to his master when he left. He may have taken whatever it was to finance his escape, but even so, it was wrong. He now knew it, and he wanted to make amends so much that he was willing to take the considerable risk in returning, not knowing how he would be received. This shows the true meaning of repentance as well as the power of the gospel to transform lives (Romans 1:16). It had transformed the murderous Saul of Tarsus into Paul, the ambassador of peace (1 Timothy 1:12-15). Using that same transforming power, Paul had changed Onesimus, a fugitive and possibly a thief, into a person of honesty and integrity. This change is noted in his name.

As stated in the previous lesson, names were distinctive in New Testament times. The name Onesimus means "profitable" or "useful." Was this the runaway slave's original name, or was it changed to describe more accurately his present character? We cannot know the answer to this question for certain, but we do know that Paul was saying that Onesimus was now a changed individual. He was not the same person he had been when he ran away from Philemon's home. This is the principle appeal Paul makes to Philemon based on a number of factors that we will examine in this lesson.

Be Motivated by Love (Philemon 8-9)

The word translated "command" in the New King James Version is also translated "enjoin" (Philemon 8). Both words carry the assertion of the right to demand compliance. The word "appeal" can also be translated "beseech," "implore" or "beg" (v. 9). Paul could have said, "By right of the authority of my apostolic office, I command you to forgive, accept and free your slave, Onesimus." Instead, he chose to appeal to this brother on the basis of the love they had for one another and by the love for which Philemon was well-known.

Paul refers to himself as the "aged," but with one slight variation this word, *presbutes*, could be translated "ambassador," *presbeutes;* only one letter difference from the previous word. It is rendered this way in the marginal notation of the Revised Standard Version. Many people seem to prefer this translation because they do not believe Paul was an old man at the time. However, if we are correct in the approximate time of the writing of this book, he would have been in his 60s, and this would certainly have qualified him for the appellation "old man." He may have been using this designation to appeal once more to the heart of his friend, as if to say "I am now getting older, and I don't know how much time I have left, please do this one thing for me." All of this would have been done with absolute sincerity.

Paul once again refers to himself as a "prisoner of Jesus Christ." He could have done so to soften his request even more. It emphasizes that all Christians are slaves to the same Master (Romans 14:4). Onesimus was a slave to Philemon, but Philemon, Paul and Onesimus were all "slaves" of Jesus Christ (Romans 6:13-23).

Be Motivated by Relationship (Philemon 10-13)

Until this point, Paul has not specifically stated his reason for writing to his friend. He was saying, in essence, "I am not writing for myself, but for my son, Onesimus, whom I have begotten in my imprisonment." This would surely have hit home with Philemon because he was also a convert of Paul. Because Paul had "begotten [them] through the gospel" (1 Corinthians 4:15), they were brothers in the family of God (1 Timothy 3:15). Because they were sons of the same spiritual Father, how should one brother treat another?

We cannot be certain how Onesimus had cheated Philemon. As mentioned, it could have been outright theft of money or property. It might also have been embezzlement, the loss of revenue because his absence or simply the loss of the value of one slave. Whatever the real wrong committed by Onesimus against Philemon, he had justification for being bitter towards his slave.

Paul disarms Philemon with the statement that many scholars believe is a play on the name Onesimus, which as we have indicated means "profitable." Where he had been very unprofitable to Philemon, he had become profitable to Paul. He would also now be profitable to Philemon because he was now a Christian (Philemon 11).

You can almost sense Paul's anguish as he tells Philemon, "I am sending him back" (v. 12). The reason for Paul's concern is not so much about the slave's future because he was confident in what Philemon's reaction would be, but he had come to love Onesimus as deeply as he loved his master. That is why Paul asked, "receive him, that is my own heart." The most likely meaning is "receive him back even as you would me, or one of my own." Another reason for his concern could have been that if slave hunters found Onesimus on his journey home, they would have been extremely brutal with him. They would just as soon to have delivered him back to Philemon dead as alive.

In addition to his love for Onesimus, there is another reason why Paul found it difficult to send him home. It was a very personal reason. He was a minister to Paul in his time of need. Philemon was not there and perhaps could not be, but Onesimus could fulfill what he was unable to supply and would have if he could. The service he rendered was not just to Paul, but it was also for the benefit of the gospel that Philemon also served.

Be Motivated by a Higher Purpose (Philemon 14-16)

It has been pointed out that in making this appeal in the manner indicated in verse 14, Paul was doing so based on an advocacy clause in Roman law. A runaway slave was protected under this provision if a friend of his master supported him in his desire to return home. The friend then became an advocate or mediator, asking for the good graces and understanding of the master. J. Sidlow Baxter, in "The Pastoral Epistles," explains, "There were even some instances where the master not only accepted the slave back but adopted the slave into his family" (*Explore the Book*, Zondervan Publishing House, Grand Rapids, 1966; pp. 253-254).

Whether Paul used this provision in Roman law or not, we cannot say with certainty, but we do know that he appealed to a higher motive. Whatever Philemon did, Paul wanted him to be motivated out of his own sense of fairness. The decision was his to make. Onesimus had done wrong in running away and perhaps taking what belonged to his master, so he had to go back and face the consequences no matter what they were. However, in his statement Paul affirms his faith that Philemon would be motivated by his desire to perform a "good deed" and not just because he was compelled to do so. When given the opportunity to decide, Paul knew he would "voluntarily" make the right choice (Philemon 14).

Providence may have also played a role in this outcome. Paul says that Onesimus may have runaway "for this purpose." That is, so he could come under the power of the gospel and be saved eternally. It is important to note that although Paul is an apostle with spiritual powers of discernment, even he was unable always to know exactly how God's providence worked. This always is much easier to detect from the vantage point of time and experience (Genesis 45:1-8). Although we can be absolutely certain that God works through providence today in all our lives, we must avoid being dogmatic as to how, where and when He does so.

If Onesimus had returned home before becoming a Christian, Philemon would have had him for a while, but eventually they would be separated at death. Now that he was a Christian, they could be together forever in heaven. If we will not know each other in heaven, how would this thought be consoling? Heaven will be "richer, fuller, deeper" because we will be with people we have known and loved and with whom we have shared life and experiences in this world. We will know them and they will know us. We will be able to share with them experiences that happened since last we were together. This is part of what makes heaven appealing. Brother Marshal Keeble said, "If I'm going to lose my mind when I get to heaven, I couldn't enjoy it."

Onesimus had run away as a slave; his status in that regard had not changed. Christianity does not change the circumstances of our life, but it forever changes our outlook on life. In writing to the church at Corinth, Paul had said, "Let each one remain in the same calling in which he was called. Were you called while a slave? Do not be concerned about it; but if you can be made free, rather use it. For he who is called in the Lord while a slave is the Lord's freedman. Likewise he who is called while free is Christ's slave. You were bought at a price; do not become slaves of men. Brethren, let each one remain with God in that state in which he was called" (1 Corinthians 7:20-24; cf. 1 Corinthians 6:20).

Onesimus was still a slave, but as Paul said, he was "more than a slave," he was "a beloved brother." Beloved by Paul, but there is surely the implication that he should be loved equally as much by Philemon also.

Lessons Learned

1. Becoming a Christian changes our relationships but not our circumstances.
2. Freedom in Christ does not mean freedom from responsibility or from the consequences of our actions.
3. True repentance initiates a desire to make things right.
4. We are all either slaves "of sin leading to death, or of obedience leading to righteousness" (Romans 6:16).
5. Paul was an apostle, but he was not always sure how or where God's providence worked.
6. Although we can be sure God's providence does work, we cannot always know how or when.
7. We will know each other in heaven.

Questions

1. What treatment might Onesimus have received had he gone home without Paul's endorsement?
2. How do we know Onesimus had really changed?

3. What was Paul willing to do to make things right for Onesimus with Philemon?
4. On what basis did Paul appeal to Philemon?
5. In what way was Onesimus Paul's son?
6. Why was Paul concerned about Onesimus returning?
7. What was the advocacy clause in Roman law that Paul could have used in making his appeal?
8. How did Paul want Philemon to be motivated to receive Onesimus back kindly?
9. How did Paul believe God's providence had worked in this situation?
10. What does Paul mean by the statement, "Let each one remain in the same calling in which he was called" (1 Corinthians 7:20)?

Lesson 13

Paul Proposes

Week of May 30, 1999

Lesson Text

PHILEMON 17-25

(17) If then you count me as a partner, receive him as you would me.

(18) But if he has wronged you or owes anything, put that on my account.

(19) I, Paul, am writing with my own hand. I will repay--not to mention to you that you owe me even your own self besides.

(20) Yes, brother, let me have joy from you in the Lord; refresh my heart in the Lord.

(21) Having confidence in your obedience, I write to you, knowing that you will do even more than I say.

(22) But, meanwhile, also prepare a guest room for me, for I trust that through your prayers I shall be granted to you.

(23) Epaphras, my fellow prisoner in Christ Jesus, greets you,

(24) as do Mark, Aristarchus, Demas, Luke, my fellow laborers.

(25) The grace of our Lord Jesus Christ be with your spirit. Amen.

Introduction

By Roman law, Philemon was under no obligation to receive Onesimus back as anything other than a runaway slave. However, he was under obligation to Paul and, more importantly, to God. No one understood this obligation more than Paul did. In writing to the Christians in Rome, explaining why he wanted to "have some fruit among you," he said, "I am a debtor both to Greeks and to barbarians, both to wise and to unwise" (Romans 1:13-14). Paul knew what his salvation meant (1 Timothy 1:12-15), and he desired that everyone else, regardless of nationality or social standing, share that with him.

Philemon may have been the master and Onesimus the slave, but he too had "sinned and fall[en] short of the glory of God" (Romans 3:23). Had it not been for Paul reaching out to him, he would have been lost. He was a recipient through Paul of the amazing grace of God. How could he now turn his back on another rescued soul? In today's text we see Paul making further appeals to Philemon on behalf of Onesimus. Let us examine in this lesson these new foundations for this appeal.

An Appeal Based on a Common Interest (Philemon 17)

Once more we see Paul appealing to Philemon on a higher purpose, that is he and the apostle were "partners" in the work of the Lord. Although the word "partner," *koinonon*, can refer to worldly enterprises, it most certainly applies here to their being partners in the faith (1 Corinthians 1:9; Philippians 1:5). Philemon was not just a Christian, but he had been instrumental in starting a congregation in his home. In this way, he had demonstrated his love for the cause of Christ. He was involved through this means of reaching lost souls. Therefore, he was an active partner with

Paul in fulfilling our Lord's Great Commission. Even so, now Onesimus was not just a brother in Christ, but he was also a "fellow worker" (1 Corinthians 3:9) in the kingdom of God. He had been aiding Paul in the ministry in addition to ministering to Paul.

For the second time Paul urges Philemon to receive Onesimus back "as you would me" (Philemon 12, 17). Paul invokes once more the feelings of deep emotion that he knew Philemon had for him. The connection Paul makes here with himself also increases the value that he placed on the life of Onesimus. It also accentuated the new relationship that now existed between Philemon and his runaway slave.

An Appeal Based on a Debt Owed (Philemon 18-19)

The word "if" leaves the impression that Onesimus may not have "wronged" Philemon, and some people have clearly interpreted it that way. However, it can also be understood as Paul not knowing for certain that the wrong had been done but having reasonable suspicions that this was the case. While it is certainly possible that Onesimus had confessed his wrong to Paul, it is equally probable that the apostle knew this instinctively. Paul surely knew that no slave could escape and make it all the way to Rome without money. Where did the money Onesimus had used for this purpose come from? He also knew that many slaves were guilty of robbing from their masters. After his release from this first imprisonment, he wrote to Titus to "exhort bondservants [slaves KJV] to be obedient to their own masters, to be well pleasing in all things, not answering back, not pilfering, but showing all good fidelity, that they may adorn the doctrine of God our Savior in all things" (Titus 2:9-10).

Being a Christian did not relieve Onesimus from repaying this debt. Someone had to meet this obligation. Whatever Onesimus had done or might have taken, Paul told his brother Philemon, "put that on my account" (Philemon 18). Paul either had the financial resources to repay Onesimus' debt, or he had the means to get it. Remember that at this time, Paul was a prisoner in Rome. Paul lived on the good graces of other people (1 Corinthians 9:6-14; 2 Corinthians 11:5-9; Philippians 4:15-18), but he was by no means a pauper. Felix, the corrupt Roman-appointed governor in Judea, thought that Paul had money or had access to it. This is why he kept him imprisoned so long, hoping to receive a bribe from him (Acts 24:26). Even in Rome, he was on house arrest in his rented home. Paul was able and willing to repay Onesimus' debt if Philemon required it.

How much did Paul desire for Onesimus to be received back with grace and forgiveness? The simple statement that begins verse 19 illustrates the depth of his concern. He said, "I, Paul, am writing with my own hand. I will repay." Paul may have written this entire letter himself. It was not customary for Paul to write his letters. He dictated to other people who wrote them down, but he often wrote the salutations himself (Romans 16:22; 1 Corinthians 16:21; Colossians 4:18; 2 Thessalonians 3:17). Why he did not write his letters is purely a matter of speculation. Some people have suggested that he had a crippling disease, such as rheumatoid arthritis, that made writing extremely difficult and painful. Although we do not know the real reason, this small gesture, as insignificant as it may seem, would have indicated to Philemon how deeply sincere Paul was in his request.

Paul's remark, "I will repay," has the effect of saying, "This is my promissory note. You can depend on me to pay the debt in full." Then he does something that seems uncharacteristic for Paul. Throughout this letter he has been reminding Philemon about their personal relationship and supplying him with good reasons why he should accept Onesimus back graciously as a brother in Christ. Now he tells this beloved brother, "You owe me even your own self besides." This does not seem to be the way to win friends and influence people. But again, it shows how deeply Paul loved Onesimus and how much he wanted Philemon to see the depth of this love.

Some people have interpreted Paul's comment to imply that there was some financial debt owed by Philemon to Paul. That hardly seems likely, and if anything, the reverse would probably have been the case. It refers to the spiritual obligation Philemon had towards Paul. The apostle was a firm believer in the principle of reciprocity when it came to spiritual debts whether they were owed to God (Philemon 6; 2 Corinthians 8:7-9) or to men (1 Timothy 5:4).

An Appeal Based on an Opportunity (Philemon 20)

Paul wrote to the Galatian Christians, "Therefore, as we have opportunity, let us do good to all, especially to those who are of the household of faith" (Galatians 6:10). Many of those people Paul had converted were given opportunities later in life to do good to him (Romans 16:3-12, 21; 2 Timothy 4:9-13, 20-21). How many times had Philemon been afforded this chance? This may have been the one and only time he would have an occasion to be able to do something for Paul personally. The New King James Version says, "Let me have joy from you in the Lord;" The Revised Standard Version says, "Yes, brother, I want some benefit from you." The word translated "benefit" ("profit," *The New Testament* by Henry Alford) is the Greek word *onaimen*, which is the verb form of the name Onesimus, "beneficial" or "profitable." Some people see in this another occasion when Paul uses a double meaning. They suggest that the benefit Paul actually wanted was Onesimus himself.

The prepositional phrase "in the Lord" is revealing. As a human being with the emotional involvement he had, Philemon may not have been able to overcome those feelings enough to forgive Onesimus by himself. However, if he did so with the help of Christ who had forgiven and befriended him, he could render the same grace to the slave.

An Appeal Based on Need (Philemon 20)

We sometimes think about the great characters of the Bible as people who are almost superhuman. However, they were just people with extraordinary opportunities who rose to meet the challenge of faith that fell to them. They had the same frailties, weaknesses and temptations we all face. Paul was one of God's heroes of the faith and perhaps the greatest missionary who ever lived. While it may be hard to think of him really needing anything, he often expressed this human trait.

In this verse, he urges Philemon to "refresh my heart in the Lord." Paul was asking him to bestow upon him personally the grace he had shown to many other people (v. 7). He urges him once more to place this matter in the context of their relationship in the Lord. Some people see this as an appeal once more to include Onesimus in this request because Paul had said he is "my own heart" (v. 12). However, the request appears to be more personal than that. Paul is in prison. It is true, as stated earlier, that he was in his rented house, but he was still shackled, chained (v. 10) and under guard 24 hours a day. Although there were friends such as Onesimus who "refreshed his spirit," the circumstances alone had to overwhelm him on occasions with depression. Philemon was afforded an opportunity to do a good deed and actually lift the heart of his beloved Paul. The apostle knew this man would do what was right.

An Appeal Based on Character (Philemon 21)

We can arrive at the conclusion based on some of Paul's appeals and the words he employs that he is concerned Philemon will not do the right thing. This is hardly ever in question. Note again the many complimentary remarks he makes about his friend (v. 5-7). Paul was never in serious doubt that Philemon would do the right thing. Here that point is made clear: "Having confidence in your obedience." The word translated "confidence" can be rendered "persuaded," or "convinced" (Philippians 1:25; 2:24). Some scholars see this as another indication Paul's admonishing Philemon with his apostolic authority, but the exact nuance is unclear. The only thing we can be sure of is that he is expecting Philemon's positive response to his letter.

Paul expected Philemon's compliance with his request, and he knew that this beloved brother would do even more than he wanted. He knew this brother's heart and attributes to him the same sacrificing spirit he did to the Macedonians (2 Corinthians 8:3-5). There were many things Philemon might do beyond what Paul requested. He could have given Onesimus the opportunity to become more involved in evangelistic endeavors or reviewed his entire relationship with the runaway and accept him as family, or he could have become an advocate for more humane treatment of other slaves. What he did we cannot be sure, but there was certainly more he could do than that which was asked.

An Appeal from Hope (Philemon 22)

Based upon this verse and others elsewhere (Ephesians 6:18-22; Philippians 1:19-20; Colossians 4:7-9), some scholars have concluded that Paul was certain that he was going to be released soon. They believe that Paul was given this message from the Lord. That could be the case, but the last part of the verse lends itself more not to knowledge but to a fervent hope and expectation of release. His request to Philemon was for that purpose, and he promised to visit him when that happened.

Was this a veiled threat as some see it? Was it an implication that Paul was saying, "I asking this of you, but I'm coming soon to make sure that you have complied." That interpretation hardly seems to fit the context of the former verse. Paul had deep love for both Philemon and Onesimus, and it is only natural that he would want to see these two brothers as soon as possible. He did not really want Onesimus to return, but he knew it was the right thing for him to do. It would warm his heart to witness in person the love and forgiveness that he fully expected Philemon to bestow upon Onesimus.

In closing this personal letter, Paul asked, as he often did, for the grace of Christ to be with this brother and to strengthen his spirit (Galatians 6:18; Ephesians 6:24; Philippians 4:23; Colossians 4:18; 1 Thessalonians 5:28; 2 Thessalonians 3:18; 2 Timothy 4:22;). This was more than a mere salutation. As an apostle, Paul was asking the Lord to bestow upon Philemon his unmerited love and favor.

Conclusion

Paul did not write an appendage to this letter for us or a second letter informing us about the outcome of his request to Philemon. History does not record definitively what happened. There is one possible answer found in the writing of Ignatius, one of the early church fathers who wrote about 50 years after the letter to Philemon was penned, a letter to the Ephesians, addressing their wonderful bishop named Onesimus. William Barclay wrote that Ignatius makes exactly the same pun as Paul made – he is Onesimus by name and Onesimus by nature, the profitable one to Christ. It may well be that the runaway slave had become with the passing years the great bishop of Ephesus (*The Letters to Timothy, Titus, Philemon,* The Westminister Press, Philadelphia, 1975; p. 275.)

It is impossible to be dogmatic and say that this referred to the Onesimus of Philemon, but if it did, it would provide an excellent example about the power of grace and forgiveness that made it possible for a former runaway slave to become a leader in the church of our Lord.

Lessons Learned

1. Every Christian is under obligation to God and to the lost.
2. All of us have "sinned and come short of the glory of God."
3. There is no one minister in the church, but all Christians are ministers.
4. Being a Christian does not relieve us of the obligation to repay our debts.
5. As we have "opportunity, let us do good unto all men, especially those of the household of faith."
6. Great Bible characters were just people given extraordinary opportunities from God.

Questions

1. Why did Paul want to go to Rome (Romans 1:11-16)?
2. What does the word "partner" in this text imply about Philemon?
3. How does Paul accentuate the new relationship between Philemon and Onesimus?
4. In what ways could Paul have know that Onesimus may have stolen from Philemon other than God giving him that information?
5. What scriptural evidence exists of Paul's potential financial condition?
6. What might be indicated by Paul's statement, "I am writing with my own hand?"
7. What is a possible rendering of the word "benefit?"
8. Why was Paul asking Philemon to "refresh my heart in the Lord?"
9. What was the true character of Philemon?
10. How did Paul expect Philemon to respond to his request?

Lesson 1

I Will Pray

Week of
June 6, 1999

Lesson Text

MATTHEW 6:5-15

(5) And when you pray, you shall not be like the hypocrites. For they love to pray standing in the synagogues and on the corners of the streets, that they may be seen by men. Assuredly, I say to you, they have their reward.

(6) But you, when you pray, go into your room, and when you have shut your door, pray to your Father who is in the secret place; and your Father who sees in secret will reward you openly.

(7) And when you pray, do not use vain repetitions as the heathen do. For they think that they will be heard for their many words.

(8) Therefore do not be like them. For your Father knows the things you have need of before you ask Him.

(9) In this manner, therefore, pray: Our Father in heaven, Hallowed be Your name.

(10) Your kingdom come. Your will be done On earth as it is in heaven.

(11) Give us this day our daily bread.

(12) And forgive us our debts, As we forgive our debtors.

(13) And do not lead us into temptation, But deliver us from the evil one. For Yours is the kingdom and the power and the glory forever. Amen.

(14) For if you forgive men their trespasses, your heavenly Father will also forgive you.

(15) But if you do not forgive men their trespasses, neither will your Father forgive your trespasses.

Introduction

The man who does not know how to pray is in the same category as the man who does not pray. Many of our people no longer pray for numerous reasons. As simple as it sounds, many people do not pray because they do not know how. No one has ever taught them how. Some people do not pray because they no longer believe God hears or answers prayers. They search in anguish for evidence that even one of their prayers has been answered. Finding none, they stop praying. As Jimmy Allen wrote, "Some of our people have not quit praying for theological reasons; they have just quit praying."

The powerlessness often seen in the modern church is largely because of a lack of prayer. We pray in worship services – we have at least two or three prayers during the service in addition to the traditional ones at the Lord's Supper. The difficult question we should ask is, why do we pray during the service? Is it because we need to have prayers in our worship service to make it scriptural? Is it because we have always done it that way? Are prayers merely time fillers? Or do we pray because we sincerely believe in the God who hears and responds to the prayers of His children? How we answer this question is extremely important.

Recently, a congregation had a prayer meeting and spent the entire service only praying. Does that sound strange? There was a time when the midweek service was called a prayer meeting. Now we call them Bible studies. There is nothing wrong with having Bible study, but do we need to study more than we need to pray? Do we need to allow God to talk to us more than we need to talk with Him?

Prayer is vitally important, and the church needs to do more of it. The sermon usually takes up the major portion of our worship service. Sometimes we devote all or a large portion of a service to singing, but how often do we devote that much time to praying? Christians also need to pray individually. It is time that we implore, as the Lord's disciples did on one occasion, "Lord, teach us to pray" (Luke 11:1).

In Matthew 6, Jesus provides His disciples with an example of how to pray. Often called the Lord's Prayer, it is not a personal prayer of our Lord, as is true of His prayer in the Upper Room (John 17:1-26) or His prayer in the Garden of Gethsemane on the night of His betrayal (Matthew 26:36-44). As indicated in the passage from Luke 11:1-4, it was given in brief form in response to the disciples' request that He teach them to pray as John the Baptist taught his disciples to pray. It seems more appropriate, therefore, to refer to it as the Lord's prayer of example or the Lord's model prayer. Some people choose to call it the disciple's prayer. No matter what you choose to call it, there is value in studying it to learn from Jesus how to pray. When you really examine it, you are struck with a number of important points about proper prayer.

Brevity

The first thing that stands out about this prayer is how brief it is. In Matthew's account it encompasses only 65 words. Luke's account in chapter 11 contains only 37 words. It takes only a few seconds to read, and yet volumes could not contain the depth of thought found here. In these few words, Jesus included all of the things that are really needed in our lives. There is certainly a lesson here for men who lead prayers in public.

In Matthew 6:5-8, Jesus condemned the prayers of the hypocritical Jewish leaders because they loved to pray in public forums. They would seek out the most conspicuous places in the synagogues where they were sure to be seen. One of their favorite places to sound out long, boring, repetitive prayers was on the busy street corners. They did this to be seen by men. Jesus said, "Assuredly, I say to you, they have their reward" (v. 5). He also warned, "Therefore do not be like them" (v. 8).

Jesus was not condemning public prayers. In His prayer life, Jesus prayed publicly at His baptism (Luke 3:21), before the multitudes (9:16), and while He was on the cross (23:34). He also prayed in private on the Mount of Transfiguration (9:28) and in the Garden of Gethsemane where He repeated the same words three times (Matthew 26:39, 42, 44), indicating He did not condemn repetition in prayers. He prayed all night before the selection of the 12 apostles (Luke 6:12), indicating He did not condemn long prayers; He condemned long public prayers containing meaningless, repetitive phrases designed to elevate the person who prayed. If we follow His example, our public prayers will be shorter, and our private prayers will be longer.

Reverence (Matthew 6:9)

Often we hear about the God of the Old Testament and the God of the New Testament as if they are two separate beings. There is only one God, as the *Shema* declares, "Hear, O Israel: The Lord our God is one! You shall love the Lord your

God with all your heart, with all your soul, and with all your strength" (Deuteronomy 6:4-5). The *Shema* is the first Hebrew word in these verses, and it is the Jewish confession of faith. However, we must admit that men generally did not know God as a Father during that period. The term "Father" was used in the Old Testament 16 times in reference to God , but it was in relationship to the nation of Israel and not to the individual. No passage in the Old Testament clearly represents God as a personal, loving Father.

The Law of Moses revealed the mind of God. Jesus revealed to us God's heart. God is the powerful Creator of Genesis. He is the fearful God of Exodus who wrote His Law on Mount Sinai in stone. He is the warrior God in Joshua who led His people into battle, securing the land of Canaan. He is the God of the prophets who pleaded with His people to repent and return to Him. But He is also the same God who humbled Himself and entered the womb of the virgin Mary in the person of His Son. He is the same servant God who through His Son washed the disciples' feet during the Passover feast in John 13. He is the same sacrificing God who in Christ offered Himself for us on Calvary (2 Corinthians 5:19). He is the same God who is our Father in heaven (Luke 11:2).

Not everyone can pray this prayer sincerely because God is not his or her spiritual Father. Paul told the Athenians that they were the offspring of God (Acts 17:28-29). He meant this in the sense that God has given all of us life, so we are begotten of Him through physical birth. He is not, however, our spiritual Father unless we have been born again into His family (John 3:3, 5). God can only be addressed as Father by people who are His spiritual children. The use of the personal pronoun "our" proves there is a distinction. The reason most prayers are not answered is because they are said by unredeemed tongues. When we can go to God and say, "Abba, Father," He will answer our prayers (Matthew 7:7-11; Romans 8:14-17).

Jesus said, "Hallowed be Your name" (Matthew 6:9). The word "hallowed" is an archaic English word translated from a form of the Greek *hagiazo*, which means "holy." Our God is holy (Leviticus 19:2; Isaiah 6:3). We should hold God's name in reverence (Psalm 111:9 KJV). The third commandment said "You shall not take the name of the Lord your God in vain, for the Lord will not hold him guiltless who takes His name in vain" (Exodus 20:7; Deuteronomy 5:11 NKJV). Twice in Leviticus, Moses wrote that we should not "profane the name of [our] God: I am the Lord" (18:21; 19:12). The Law has been done away with, but that principle was not abolished, as Jesus' example prayer clearly demonstrates. God's name has become such a common profane expression that many people do not even realize what they are saying. When you see it used in that way, it is usually spelled with a little "g." That does not solve the problem. God's name is holy, and it should be held in deepest reverence.

Simplicity (Matthew 6:10-13)

Simple phrases and expressions are prominent in this prayer. None of the eloquence often heard in modern prayers is present. The prayer is absent of pious platitudes that, in Jesus' words, are part of the hypocrites prayers. It contains simple language, simple statements and simple requests.

First, there is a prayer for the kingdom. The kingdom had not yet come at that time, so it was appropriate to pray, "Your kingdom come." That phrase would not be appropriate today. The kingdom was brought into the world on the Day of Pentecost after Christ's ascension. After that time, it is always spoken of in the present tense (1 Corinthians 15:24-25; Colossians 1:13; Revelation 1:9). Peter's sermon on that occasion makes it clear that the kingdom has come and that Jesus is reigning over it now (Acts 2:29-36). We can and should pray for the borders of the kingdom to be enlarged. It is also appropriate to pray that other people will accept the rule and reign of Christ in their hearts and lives (Luke 17:20-21).

Another thing we should pray for is that the will of God be done on Earth as it is done in heaven. Many prayers go unanswered because they are outside the will of God (James 4:1-3; 1 John 5:14-15). One of the main purposes of prayer is to ask that we might accept the will of God for our lives and do it. Anything that is according to His will, He will do. Some people say this is too narrow and too limited. It is as narrow as the ocean is to a row boat. It is wide open. God wants what we would want for ourselves, if we had the wisdom to really know what we needed. He wants us to be fed, clothed, healthy and joyful lives. This is His will for our lives; therefore, we can boldly approach Him and ask for these things, knowing that He desires for us to have them (Hebrews 4:16). As we saturate ourselves with the Word of God, we become more knowledgeable about what His will is and how we should increasingly pray in accordance with it.

Next there is a request for daily bread. The word translated "daily" in the Greek New Testament occurs only in this place. Although there is some discussion among scholars as to its accurate meaning, we can say it is right and proper to ask God for our daily food. If we should not worry about tomorrow (Matthew 6:34), then why not be content with God's blessings today? God wants to supply all of our needs (Philippians 4:19). He did not say desires, wants or lusts, but the specified needs. Jesus promised the same thing in the Sermon on the Mount (Matthew 6:25-34).

There is then a request for forgiveness (6:12). Strangely, this is the only part of the prayer that Jesus commented upon in Matthew's account. Jesus said we should ask for forgiveness but only as we are willing to forgive those people who have sinned against us. He later makes the statement that God forgives people who forgive other people (v. 14). As sinners saved by the grace of God, we should be more than willing to extend that same courtesy to other human beings.

The next request is one for God's protection. Jesus said to ask "do not lead us into temptation, But deliver us from the evil one" (v. 13). James says that "God cannot be tempted by evil, nor does He Himself tempt anyone" (1:13). He does not tempt us to do evil, although He does allow us to be tested. However, He will "not allow you to be tempted beyond what you are able, but with the temptation will also make the way of escape, that you may be able to bear it" (1 Corinthians 10:13). "[T]he Lord knows how to deliver the godly out of temptation" (2 Peter 2:9). He will guide us if we are open to His leading through the Spirit-inspired Word (Galatians 5:16, 18, 25).

Sincerity (Matthew 6:13)

Our Lord begins this prayer with petition and ends it with praise. There is no hesitation on His part in asking for God's blessings. There is absolute faith and confidence in the One to whom He was praying. Remember this is not His personal prayer, but it is His example to us of how our prayers should be said. In Luke's account, after giving the example prayer, Jesus illustrates the principle with two parables. The first is the parable of the friend at midnight (11:5-8), and the second is about a father and his children (vv. 11-13). Jesus is saying that praying to God is as simple as asking a friend for help in a time of need or a child asking his father for something he needs. How many fathers would refuse a reasonable request that was in that child's best interest? God wants to bless His children with every "good gift" (James 1:17), both spiritual (Ephesians 1:3) and material (Matthew 6:25-34; 7:7-11). The sad thing is that "you do not have because you do not ask" (James 4:2).

This statement recognizes the sovereignty of God. He is omnipotent, and His kingdom and power are eternal. Our main purpose in life is to bring glory and honor to His name (Matthew 5:16). At this time He has given His Son all authority over all things (28:18), both in heaven and on Earth, the only exception being Himself (1 Corinthians 15:24-28; Philippians 2:9-11). God deserves such praise, but the Son deserves it also (Revelation 5:9-13).

Prayer can make the difference in living a life of power and strength or leading a life of defeat and failure. Let us be a praying people. Let us be people whose lives demonstrate our sincere belief that God still hears and answers prayers.

Lessons Learned

1. The man who does not pray is no better off than the man who does not know how.
2. The church today is often powerless because it is prayerless.
3. The model prayer is not our Lord's personal prayer, but it was given as an example for His disciples to follow.
4. The model prayer consists of only 65 words, and it can be said in 15 seconds.
5. Jesus did not condemn public prayers, only prayers that are hypocritical.
6. If we follow Christ's example, it seems that our public prayers will be shorter and our private prayers will be longer.

Questions

1. What are some of the reasons why Christians do not pray?
2. Why should we pray in worship services?
3. Why is it inappropriate to call the model prayer the Lord's Prayer?
4. Why did Jesus condemn the hypocrites' prayers?
5. In what kinds of places and on what occasions did Jesus pray?
6. What is the *Shema*?
7. Why can all people not sincerely pray, "Our Father who is in Heaven?"
8. What does it mean to take God's name in vain?
9. Why is it not appropriate today to pray, "Thy kingdom come"?
10. What did Jesus teach us about forgiveness in this prayer?

Lesson 2

I Will Sing

Week of
June 13, 1999

Lesson Text

PSALM 40:1-12, 16

(1) I waited patiently for the Lord; And He inclined to me, And heard my cry.

(2) He also brought me up out of a horrible pit, Out of the miry clay, And set my feet upon a rock, And established my steps.

(3) He has put a new song in my mouth – Praise to our God; Many will see it and fear, And will trust in the Lord.

(4) Blessed is that man who makes the Lord his trust, And does not respect the proud, nor such as turn aside to lies.

(5) Many, O Lord my God, are Your wonderful works Which You have done; And Your thoughts toward us Cannot be recounted to You in order; If I would declare and speak of them, They are more than can be numbered.

(6) Sacrifice and offering You did not desire; My ears You have opened. Burnt offering and sin offering You did not require.

(7) Then I said, "Behold, I come; In the scroll of the book it is written of me.

(8) I delight to do Your will, O my God, And Your law is within my heart."

(9) I have proclaimed the good news of righteousness In the great assembly; Indeed, I do not restrain my lips, O Lord, You Yourself know.

(10) I have not hidden Your righteousness within my heart; I have declared Your faithfulness and Your salvation; I have not concealed Your lovingkindness and Your truth From the great assembly.

(11) Do not withhold Your tender mercies from me, O Lord; Let Your loving kindness and Your truth continually preserve me.

(12) For innumerable evils have surrounded me; My iniquities have overtaken me, so that I am not able to look up; They are more than the hairs of my head; Therefore my heart fails me.

(16) Let all those who seek You rejoice and be glad in You; Let such as love Your salvation say continually, "The Lord be magnified!"

Introduction

A discussion about the Psalms is an ideal place to emphasize the distinct difference between the worship of God under the Old Testament and that which is required of Christians in this age. Many religious people appeal to the Psalms to support the use of mechanical instruments of music in worship today. They reason that if God permitted or even condoned their use in the Old Testament, He would certainly not object to their use in the church in this age.

To support their contention, they insist that the Greek noun for psalm, *psalmos*, and its corresponding verb form, *psallein*, include the use of an instrument. It is not a matter of debate that the Israelites used instruments in their worship to God. They brought instruments with them when they were released from Egypt, and the instruments were used in the tabernacle worship during the period of wandering in the wilderness. These were later used even more extensively in Solomon's temple. However, musical instruments were retained in the outer courts of the temple; they were never permitted in the holy place.

The synagogue form of worship that developed during the Babylonian captivity excluded the use of instruments. One reason often given for their exclusion is that the rabbis during that period associated instruments of music with revelry and heathen idolatrous festivals. The fact that they were not used is important because the worship of the early church was modeled after the synagogue form and not that of the temple. The chanting, not actual singing as we think of it, was done without the aid of any instrument. This practice continued in the early church until about the middle of the seventh century. The Catholic Church was the first to include their use, and Protestant churches eventually followed. However, most Protestant denominations in America refrained from using instruments until the mid- to late-19th century (J. Porter Wilhite, *History and Mysteries of Religion Through the Ages*, Lambert Book House, Shreveport, 1971; pp. 173-177).

Prohibiting the use of mechanical instruments in the worship of the New Testament church has nothing to do with mere tradition, nor is it fostered by a desire just to be different from other religious people who sanction their use. This refusal is based upon what we sincerely believe is the teaching of the New Testament regarding the worship of God in this age. There is no direct command, approved apostolic example or necessary inference to justify the use of instruments. The New Testament is silent when it comes to their use in the worship of the early church. Every reference to music in worship in the New Testament involves only vocal music (Romans 15:9; 1 Corinthians 14:15; Ephesians 5:19; Colossians 3:16; Hebrews 2:12). There is the possible exception of Revelation 5:8-9 and 14:2-3, which describe worship taking place in heaven, not on Earth, and are highly symbolic.

Whether instruments were used in worship in the Old Testament has nothing to do with their use in the Christian Age because the Law has been taken away in its entirety (Ephesians 2:12-16; Colossians 2:14; Hebrews 8:1-10:39). Under the Law, the worship of God had become stale – a chore or a meaningless ritual (Isaiah 1:13-15; Malachi 1:7-8, 10-14). The New Testament form of worship with its provision for singing with the spirit (the inner person or the heart) and with understanding (the mind or intellect) involves and fulfills the needs of the total person.

Why we sing is as important as how we sing. In far too many instances singing has become simply a way to fill the time between the sermon and the Lord's Supper. Many worshipers mouth the words without any thought of their significance. In many congregations, singing has become entertainment rather than an integral part of the whole service. This lesson serves to answer the question about why we sing. We will first examine David's reasons for singing as outlined in Psalm 40, and then we will examine some of the reasons why the early church sang.

David Sang Because God Heard His Prayers (Psalm 40:1)

David is called "the sweet psalmist of Israel" (2 Samuel 23:1). Taken into Saul's court at a young age to be the king's personal musician, David used his songs to soothe the savage beast of depression within Saul's breast on many occasions. However, it is not that role that gave him this title but his talent for writing songs, developed while tending his father's flocks on the hillsides of Bethlehem. He was the principal author and compiler of the book of Psalms, which became the hymn book for the temple. In Psalm 40, we learn many of the reasons why David sang praises to God.

First, David rejoiced because God heard him (Psalm 40:1). The expression "I waited patiently" implies that he waited for a long time before God answered him. The literal rendering would be "waiting, I waited." We need to learn patience in prayer. Jesus taught this in His parables about the friend at midnight (Luke 11:5-8) and the unjust judge (18:1-6). Both parables, spoken in the context of prayer, teach us that God does not always answer right away, but He always answers His children's prayers.

The blind man Jesus healed in John 9, when confronted by the rulers of the Jews and told Jesus was a sinner, said, "Now we know that God does not hear sinners; but if anyone is a worshiper of God and does His will, He hears him" (John 9:31). In response to this statement it is often said the blind man said this and not Jesus. The man may have been blind, but he knew the Old Testament Scriptures, and he based his statement upon them (Psalms 34:16; 66:18; Proverbs 15:8; 28:9; Isaiah 1:15; 59:1-2). This same truth is repeated in the New Testament (John 15:6-7; James 5:16; 1 Peter 3:12; 1 John 3:22-24). We may argue the question of whether God hears the prayer of a sinner, but we cannot argue the fact that God hears His children, and He always answers their prayers. He may say "yes," "no" or "wait a while," but He always answers – in His own time and on time. People who are not children of God cannot sincerely pray, "Our Father in heaven."

David Sang Because God Delivered Him (Psalm 40:2-3)

A second reason David praised God was because God saved him. Some people think these words were written during his days as a fugitive from Saul. Other people think it was during his flight from his rebellious son Absalom. Still other people believe that they were written after the poet had been blessed with recovery from illness. However, there can be no doubt as to the prophetic nature of verses 6-8, because they are repeated in Hebrews 10:5-9 referring to Christ. It may be that David's words in verses 2-3 are referring to the moral mudslide into which he sank during his escapade with Bathsheba. At any rate, he rejoiced because God had lifted him from the sinking sand and set his feet on the solid rock of his salvation. Because of this fact, he had a new song to sing, a song of praise and thanksgiving.

Christians have the same reason for singing praise to God. The redeemed of Revelation 14:3 sang "a new song before the throne." It was the song of salvation. When we understand that we are saved by the blood of the Lamb, we too will sing the song of salvation. The hymn "Amazing Grace" takes on special meaning when we make its message personal.

David Sang Because of God's Blessings Upon His People (Psalm 40:5-10, 16)

Next, David praises God for His "wonderful works" that were too numerous to count. Worship, by its very definition, is God-centered and not man-centered. In the original language the word meant one worthy of worship. It means to "praise," to "adore," to "pay homage or reverence to deity." Worship is an opportunity to return our thanksgiving and praise to God for all He has done for us. It is the one opportunity we have collectively as the church to say, "Thank You, God. Thank You, Jesus. You are so good to us." It is not coming to God and saying, "Fill me up again." Certainly worship that is directed to God will fill the true worshiper with love, joy and peace, but these are byproducts of our spiritual devotion and not the aim of it.

In essence Paul asked the Corinthians, "When you come together to worship, why are you here?" (1 Corinthians 11). This is a good question that needs to be asked today of people who desire to make worship appealing to the masses instead of pleasing to God. When you come to worship, is it to praise God or please yourself? Have you really been to worship lately?

Because of all that God had done for him, David enthusiastically wanted to share that with other people. Notice his words: "If I would declare and speak of them, They are more than can be numbered. … I have proclaimed the good news of righteousness In the great assembly. … Indeed, I do not restrain my lips. … I have not hidden Your righteousness within my heart; I have declared Your faithfulness and Your salvation; I have not concealed your lovingkindness and your truth" (Psalm 40:5, 9-10). David did this in his songs.

When we sing today, we are "speaking to one another in psalms and hymns and spiritual songs" (Ephesians 5:19). In effect, we are praising Him for His "wonderful works." We are telling other people what He has done and is doing for us.

In verse 16, David closes out this Psalm by expressing his desire that people who seek God will rejoice and be glad in Him alone. He wanted them to praise and magnify God for His salvation.

Why Did the Early Christians Sing?

Early Christians sang to edify one another (Ephesians 5:19; Colossians 3:16). Unless their words were understandable, there was no edification (1 Corinthians 14:12, 15, 26-28). The worship of the Corinthians must have been confusing. Some people were speaking in tongues when there was no one present to interpret, while others were singing or praying. Why have a hymnal? Why have a song leader? Why do we sing the same song at the same time? It is to avoid the problems this church experienced. This is why Paul said, "Let all things be done decently and in order" (v. 40).

Early Christians sang to praise God (Hebrews 2:12). In this case, their praise was the fulfillment of prophecy (Psalm 22:22). God is praised for His grace in saving the Gentiles along with the Jews in Christ and making them brothers in His family (Hebrews 2:9-11). Isaiah had prophesied that when the Gentiles saw God's righteousness, His people would "be called by a new name, Which the mouth of the Lord will name" (Isaiah 62:2). That new name is "Christian" (Acts 11:26; 26:28; 1 Peter 4:16).

Gentile Christians certainly have reason to rejoice. Before Christ came we were "aliens from the commonwealth of Israel and strangers from the covenants of promise, having no hope and without God in the world. But now in Christ Jesus you who once were far off have been brought near by the blood of Christ" (Ephesians 2:12-13).

Early Christians sang when they were happy (James 5:13). To a Christian, singing is as natural as breathing. It used to be that when Christians got together, they would break out in a song. This is a practice that should be continued. We have so many reasons to be grateful to God.

Lessons Learned

1. God permitted instruments of music in the Old Testament, but their use then is no justification for their presence in Christian worship.
2. Although instruments were used in the outer courts of the temple, they were never permitted in the holy place or in the synagogues.
3. There is no direct command, approved apostolic example or necessary inference that would justify the use of instruments in the worship of God today.
4. Singing is an integral part of worship and is not merely an entertainment form.
5. David sang because God had heard his prayer, and delivered him from death and had blessed His people in numerous ways.
6. Early Christians sang to edify one another, to praise God for His salvation and to express their joy.

Questions

1. Where did the Jews get the practice of using instruments in their worship?
2. What is the significance of the fact that instruments of music were never used in the synagogue?
3. Who first introduced musical instruments into the worship of God in the Christian Age?
4. What kind of music was used in the early church, based upon the Scriptures concerning their form of worship?
5. Why does the use of instruments in worship in the Old Testament not justify their use in the church today?
6. Why was David called "the sweet psalmist of Israel"?
7. What does the expression "I waited" in Psalm 40:1 imply?
8. What lesson is taught in the parables about the friend at midnight and the unjust judge?
9. Who said, "We know that God does not hear sinners"? Why?
10. What does the word "worship" mean?.

Lesson 3

Confession

Week of
June 20, 1999

Lesson Text

PSALM 51:1-14

(1) Have mercy upon me, O God, According to Your lovingkindness; According to the multitude of Your tender mercies, Blot out my transgressions.

(2) Wash me thoroughly from my iniquity, And cleanse me from my sin.

(3) For I acknowledge my transgressions, And my sin is always before me.

(4) Against You, You only, have I sinned, And done this evil in Your sight – That You may be found just when You speak, And blameless when You judge.

(5) Behold, I was brought forth in iniquity, And in sin my mother conceived me.

(6) Behold, You desire truth in the inward parts, And in the hidden part You will make me to know wisdom.

(7) Purge me with hyssop, and I shall be clean; Wash me, and I shall be whiter than snow.

(8) Make me hear joy and gladness, That the bones You have broken may rejoice.

(9) Hide Your face from my sins, And blot out all my iniquities.

(10) Create in me a clean heart, O God, And renew a steadfast spirit within me.

(11) Do not cast me away from Your presence, And do not take Your Holy Spirit from me.

(12) Restore to me the joy of Your salvation, And uphold me by Your generous Spirit.

(13) Then I will teach transgressors Your ways, And sinners shall be converted to You.

(14) Deliver me from the guilt of bloodshed, O God, The God of my salvation, And my tongue shall sing aloud of Your righteousness.

Introduction

When Samuel delivered the message to Saul that God had rejected him from being king over Israel, the prophet told him that "the Lord sought for Himself a man after His own heart" (1 Samuel 13:14). Paul, speaking in the synagogue at Antioch of Pisidia, said, "And when He had removed him [Saul], He raised up for them David as king, to whom also He gave testimony and said, 'I have found David the son of Jesse, a man after My own heart, who will do all My will'" (Acts 13:22). This was God's early estimation of the shepherd boy who would become king.

After David had been king for a time, one evening he could not sleep and walked on the rooftop of his palace. Looking out over the city, he saw a beautiful young woman bathing on a nearby roof. He should have gone inside or at least directed his gaze in another direction. Instead he continued to look, lingered and then lusted (James 1:14-15). He inquired and found out that the beautiful young woman was Bathsheba, the daughter of Eliam, the wife of Uriah the Hittite. Eliam was the son of Ahitophel (2 Samuel 23:34), a trusted advisor to David (2 Samuel 16:20-21). Uriah was one of David's 30 mighty men of valor (2 Samuel 23:23, 39). However, none of this mattered to David. All that mattered to him was he saw something he wanted, and he had the power to get it.

The text suggests that Bathsheba was not a completely willing participant in what happened. It says, "Then David sent messengers, and took her; and she came to him, and he lay with her, for she was cleansed from her impurity" (2 Samuel 11:4). The phrase "took her" implies that she may have been forced or coerced into going with these men. Note also the phrase "he lay with her." She may have thought that she had no choice and consented to the affair. What other reaction should have been expected when the most powerful man in your nation, your king, calls for you? After their sexual encounter, the statement is made that "she returned to her house" (v. 4). That is the way most affairs end.

David was caught in a trap of his own making. He only wanted casual sex and was not interested in a long-term commitment, but pregnancy resulted. How long did it take Bathsheba to realize she was pregnant? Did she wait two or three months before finally admitting to herself that the unthinkable had happened? What emotions she must have felt – fear, panic, dread – as she sent word to David that she was pregnant.

David's response to the news is very revealing. He was not shocked or troubled. To him there was a simple solution to the problem. David suffered from a disease shared by many other powerful people; he thought he could control everything. He manipulated people as skillfully as he managed armies. He simply called for Uriah to come home, received this loyal soldier for a few moments of polite conversation and then urged him to go home to his wife. Uriah and Bathsheba would sleep together. Then she would announce to him later that she was pregnant, and everyone would live happily ever after. But it was not to be so. David had not counted on one thing in his scheme: the honor of Uriah. He was such a loyal soldier that he refused to find pleasure with his wife while his comrades were still out in the field risking their lives in combat. This went on for two nights, and so David was forced to come up with another plan. He sent a letter to his commander, Joab, telling him to "set Uriah in the forefront of the hottest battle, and retreat from him, that he may be struck down and die" (v. 15). This was no momentary crime of passion; it was premeditated murder.

When Bathsheba heard the news of Uriah's death, "she mourned for her husband" (v. 26). We have every reason to believe her grief was genuine. After allowing her a respectable period of mourning, David brought Bathsheba to the palace and took her to be one of his wives. In his own mind that was the end of the matter. Their baby would be born, and no one would be the wiser. "But the thing that David had done displeased the Lord" (v. 27). What happens to "a man after God's own heart," when he forgets about God?

Almost one year passed from the time of David's sin to the visit from Nathan the prophet. Nathan told David a parable about a poor man who had only one ewe lamb which he loved dearly and cared for tenderly. A rich neighbor who owned many sheep took the poor man's one single lamb and prepared it for a wayfarer's meal. David's reaction to such an atrocious act was moral outrage. How could anyone do such a terrible thing? In his anger, David pronounced the death sentence upon the man guilty of such a deed. Imagine his stunned expression when Nathan pointed his finger straight at him and said, "You are the man!" (12:7). He was exposed, and his soul was bared before all who heard. He had to sit and listen as Nathan spelled out one by one the horrible crimes he had committed. David cried out, "I have sinned."

His sincerity cannot be questioned because Nathan said, "The Lord has also put away your sin; you shall not die" (v. 13). We can almost hear David breathe a sign of relief, but that would have been premature. God was not through with him yet. David was forgiven for his sin, but as with all sins, the consequences followed him through the rest of his life. No man ever paid a higher price for his sin than David.

It was after Nathan had exposed his sin, and David had repented, that he penned the words of Psalm 51. In this very personal penitential confession, David revealed his true heart. We can understand why God loved him so much. We also learn from it how a truly penitent person should react.

A Sincere Penitent's Confession (Psalm 51:1-6)

Where once David had felt that God was the Shepherd of his soul, that he had only to ask and he would receive, he now begs for mercy. The term "have mercy" means to "be gracious." Unlike many transgressors, he does not plead innocence and seek forgiveness based upon it, but instead he appeals to God's "steadfast love" and "abundant mercy." He does not blame his heredity, his environment or other people, but he assumes full responsibility. In effect he throws himself upon the mercy of the court of justice, and he awaits the verdict.

When Nathan stirred the conscience of this "man after God's own heart," David knew instantly how guilty he was. He felt filthy and needed to be cleansed, and he asked the only One who could give it to him. "Blot out" means to erase, literally to "scratch off" as if permanently removing it from a record book. In this same connection he urged God to "wash me." This implies to scrub as one would wash his or her clothes by "trampling them under foot on the rocks." He further added, "cleanse me." David saw his sin as being like the disease of leprosy. The word here carries more the concept of ceremonial cleansing involving the inner man more than merely the outward act.

What was the horrible spot David wanted removed? He used three different terms to describe his crimes. The first is "transgression," which refers to "deliberately crossing over a boundary line." This sin was willful. David knew he was doing wrong at the time. Adultery and murder were both condemned in the Law and were punishable by death (Exodus 21:12-15; Leviticus 20:10). The second term is "iniquity," which means "perverseness." Last of all, he calls his acts simply by the word "sin." This word means "going beyond; missing the mark; falling short." These terms are most likely used to show that David realizes the all-encompassing nature of his sin.

Why should God forgive him? Think of all the horrible things he had done in his sin with Bathsheba. God could forgive him only because he confessed. For a full year he had tried to hide his sin, and He had apparently done a good job as far as people were concerned. But he could not hide it from God or from himself. "I acknowledge my transgression" means he is owning it, saying, "It is mine." Often today sinners blame their parents, teachers, society, heredity, anything and anyone but themselves. David accepted responsibility for his own sin. That is the first step toward forgiveness.

David was shadowed by a ghost for the whole year. The spirit that haunted him was the reminder of his sin which he said was "ever before me." The wording suggests that its pursuit was relentless. It may have slipped back into his consciousness during quiet times when he was trying to be alone with his thoughts, or it might have invaded his dreams. He could have had momentary flashbacks throughout the day. There was no peace to be found until he finally owned up to what he had done.

"Against You, You only have I sinned," David cried. Had he not also sinned against his trusted counselor Ahitophel? He certainly had sinned against Uriah. Even though Bathsheba was a participant in the sin, did he not also sin against her? What about the people he was chosen by God to rule over? Should he not have been expected as God's anointed to provide moral, spiritual and political leadership? Why then did he say he had only sinned against God? Did he not understand the broader implications and the far-reaching consequences of what he had done? At this point, David realized what all of us should, and that is that ultimately all sin is against God.

When a child of God sins, far greater damage is done to the name of God and the cause of Christ than when a non-Christian sins. His children indict God when they transgress. How can a holy God allow such transgressions from one of His own, especially one in the position of David? God did not allow it. He had spoken against the very sins David was guilty of, and he would be judged by the righteous standard of the Holy God.

A troubling issue for many is the questions raised by David's statements in verse 5. Some use this verse to teach the doctrine of inherited sin, and they say that we are born totally depraved. In order to get around this, some have interpreted it to mean that David's mother committed adultery or fornication. This does not solve the problem. We have no proof that David's mother was guilty of either adultery or fornication. Instead we understand that she bore her husband Jesse four sons within the confines of marriage (1 Samuel 16:3-13). Neither of these interpretations is valid from the context of the passage itself. David takes personal responsibility for his sin in the previous verses and in those that follow.

How are we then to interpret this passage? It is simply a poetic device used to demonstrate that David realized that from his birth he was subject to sin. He was born into a world surrounded by sin. Rather than blaming his environment for his sin, David shows that he is a sinner not by nature or nurture but by choice. As verse 6 shows, this is what God desires from any child of His who sins – the recognition of and an acceptance of one's own guilt. Only then can He cleanse us of our sins.

A Prayer for Cleansing (Psalm 51:7-9)

Once more David pleads with God to cleanse him of sin. This was a figure taken from the ceremonies of the Aaronic priesthood. The hyssop was a herb grown in Palestine used in the ceremonial cleansing for leprosy and for sin (Leviticus 14:4-6; Numbers 19:6,18). No doubt it is the latter to which David refers here. He wanted to be clean, "whiter than snow."

Why did it take a year for David to recognize and to repent of his sin? Why did it take God one year before he sent Nathan to David with his parable? Some people, especially proud people, have to be broken before they can be fixed. David was a proud man, which made him try to hide his sin and to fail to acknowledge it. During that year of waiting, David was wrestling with his own conscience as shown in the verses that follow. His words indicate brokenness and depression over his act and the distance that has developed between himself and the God to whom he had felt so close. Now he feels unworthy to even approach Him. Like Isaiah the prophet, he was able to see his own sinfulness in contrast to the sinlessness of the Holy God (Isaiah 6:1-7).

A Promise of Consecration (Psalm 51:10-14)

David did not ask for a heart bypass operation. He asked instead for a heart transplant. He felt that his old heart, the thinking, reasoning, feeling part of man's mind, had become so corrupt that it was beyond repair. The word for "create" here is the Hebrew word *bara* which refers to the action of God. Only God can create. Man can manipulate preexisting materials, move molecules around or manufacture from matter already available, but he cannot create. David realizes that what he is asking is something only God can do. He cannot do it for himself.

David asks for a new heart and for a renewed spirit. Where once he had been steadfast and loyal to God and had been blessed for it, he had become an unstable sinner. He knew he was on shaky ground and wanted to be restored to the steadfastness he was known for before his fall. He felt filthy and undeserving of God's companionship. Because he had been God's man on the throne, at one time He was directed by His Holy Spirit. Although he felt so unworthy, he asked God not to let the Spirit depart from him. David knew the Holy Spirit would not dwell where sin abided (Genesis 6:3; 1 Samuel 16:14; Ephesians 4:30; 1 Thessalonians 5:19).

Had David agonized over his sin during that year of waiting? How deeply did he feel his alienation from God? There can be no doubt from the words of verse 12, "Restore unto me the joy of my salvation." Much of the depression of Christians comes from the knowledge of unconfessed sin in their lives. It may be deep within the subconscious gnawing away at our conscious mind, but its constant presence leaves us, like David, with an unsettled feeling.

Once he was purged from his own sin, David promised God he would "teach transgressors Your ways, And sinners shall be converted to You" (v. 13). He could not do it before his own sin was forgiven. Those who knew of his sins would not listen. They would call him a hypocrite. We may sin by doing terrible things and afterward feel that God can no longer use us because we are tainted. It is not good that Christians sin, but once we are restored we can "strengthen the brethren" (Luke 22:32).

Another thing that is affected when our lives are infected with sin is our worship to God. David could not sing God's praises because of the guilt he carried. Imagine, the voice of the sweet singer of Israel was silent. He longed to sing to God and know that God accepted his worship once again. Christians cannot worship God acceptably when their hearts are not right with God and with their brethren (Matthew 5:23-24; 18:15-20; Acts 8:18-24; 1 Peter 3:12).

Lessons Learned

1. An idle mind is the devil's workshop.
2. No man is above the law of God.
3. It is possible to deceive ourselves about our sins.
4. God sees our sins although others may not.
5. When we sin, we should not blame our heredity, our environment or other people, but instead we should assume full responsibility.
6. The only way to be relieved of the pressure brought on by a guilty conscience is to repent and to ask God for forgiveness.

Questions

1. How could David be "a man after God's own heart" and do the terrible things he did?
2. Why was David's sin so reprehensible?
3. How did David seek to rectify his sin?
4. Why did David's plans for Uriah and Bathsheba fail?
5. What was David's hope when he took Bathsheba to be one of his wives?
6. What was David's initial reaction to Nathan's parable?
7. Which figures used by the poet speak of the cleansing of sin?
8. What three words does David use to describe his sinful actions?
9. How could David say he had sinned only against God?
10. Does Psalm 51:5 teach inherited sin or total hereditary depravity? Explain your answer.

Lesson 4

Reverence

Week of
June 27, 1999

Lesson Text

PSALM 8:1-9

(1) O Lord, our Lord, How excellent is Your name in all the earth, Who have set Your glory above the heavens!

(2) Out of the mouth of babes and nursing infants You have ordained strength, Because of Your enemies, That You may silence the enemy and the avenger.

(3) When I consider Your heavens, the work of Your fingers, The moon and the stars, which You have ordained,

(4) What is man that You are mindful of him, And the son of man that You visit him?

(5) For You have made him a little lower than the angels, And You have crowned him with glory and honor.

(6) You have made him to have dominion over the works of Your hands; You have put all things under his feet,

(7) All sheep and oxen – Even the beasts of the field,

(8) The birds of the air, And the fish of the sea That pass through the paths of the seas.

(9) O Lord, our Lord, How excellent is Your name in all the earth!

Introduction

Who has not stared up into the heavens on a clear night and become awestruck by the spectacle of it all? When you seriously contemplate how this universe operates, you know God is real. No other reasonable explanation for the marvelous symmetry, the delicate balance and the incredible unity of our universe exists except for the fact that, "In the beginning God created the heavens and the earth" (Genesis 1:1).

If you can, imagine a young shepherd boy tending his sheep out in the open spaces on the hillsides of Bethlehem. The night is clear, the sky is cloudless and all of the heavenly bodies are radiantly visible. He gazes up into the heavens and is so emotionally moved by the splendor he sees that he writes about his feelings at the moment. That shepherd is David, the boy who would become king over God's people, Israel. This would have been almost 3,000 years ago, when men were not so knowledgeable in their understanding about this world's existence and how it operates. David had no telescopes; the Hubble Telescope had not been dreamed of yet. There were no sophisticated observatories to inform him of the slightest movements of distant stars and planets. What science existed was very backward, and it provided little help in solving the riddles of the universe. When you consider all of this, it is remarkable that David demonstrated such a comprehension of this complicated mystery.

How was David able to know so much about this universe and how it works? He was inspired of God and wrote as the Holy Spirit moved him to write (2 Timothy 3:16-17; 2 Peter 1:19-21). His words are majestic and beautifully poetic. There is more to these nine short verses than mere sentimentality, for in them David discusses the wonders of God's creation. He also talks about how man, the crowning glory of God's creation, fits into His divine plan for this world.

In this reverential psalm, three distinct contrasts compose the content. The first contrast is in the glory of God, as seen in His creation of the heavens, contrasted with the frailty of humanity. Could anything be more defenseless than a little baby? Yet even babies declare the greatness of God. The second contrast is that of the greatness of this vast universe compared to the smallness of mankind. What is man but a miniscule speck on this terrestrial ball? You have only to fly on a plane and look down to the earth below to realize how insignificant we really are. Despite this fact, we are extremely significant to God. The third and last contrast is in the position of man compared with that of the lower creatures. They are servants, and we are masters. Why is that so? It is not because of our strength, our survival instincts, our cunning or even our intelligence. It is because God has given mankind "dominion over the works of [His] hands" (Psalm 8:6; Genesis 1:28).

How Great Is Our God (Psalm 8:1)

David begins this song of praise with an exclamation about the greatness of God. He begins by using the covenant name for God, Jehovah or *Yahweh*, and then reinforces it with the more general term for Lord, *Adonai*, which means "master, owner or ruler." The excellency of His name is seen in that the Jews would not even speak the covenant name for God.

David emphasizes that God's name is "excellent in all the earth." How can that be when more than a billion Muslims worship Allah, millions of Buddhists bow to a statue, and millions of Hindus worship thousands of gods, including cows, monkeys, elephants and even rats? The answer is found here in the last part of this verse: "Who have set your glory above the heavens!" In Psalm 19, David declares that there are eloquent witnesses to God's glory if men would open their eyes, ears and minds and look at, listen to and try to understand them. He is saying that the heavens continually preach a silent but eloquent sermon proving the greatness of God. In every part of the earth and in every tongue, men can and do receive this heavenly broadcast. Does not a radiant, star-spangled night silently, yet loudly, sing the praises of the God who is behind it all?

Mankind may not accept this heavenly testimony to God's glory, and some people may have "worshiped and served the creature rather than the Creator, who is blessed forever" (Romans 1:25). In David's words they are fools and "they are corrupt" (Psalm 14:1). It is not reasonable or scientific to deny the existence of a Creator when every created thing cries out His being. Who but a fool would doubt God's evidence that is apparent everywhere?

The Glory of the Infinite God and the Frailty of Finite Man (Psalm 8:2)

Against the backdrop of God's greatness revealed in the vastness of the heavens, David contrasts the frailty of human nature. The universe shouts the excellency of His name, and the cries of little infants declare His majesty. Even the enemies of God, doubters, skeptics and scoffers, cannot question His power when they seriously consider the miracle of birth.

A baby is such a helpless creature. Left on its own it could not survive. In the first several years of a child's life, it is completely dependent on its parents for all of its needs. From the moment of conception, a baby enters a hostile environment whose very defenses are a threat to its existence. For nine months of its development, it is protected only by a few inches of its mother's flesh while swimming in a pool. The fact that it can survive in that world is a testimony to its viability. In its weakness, it is made strong.

Despite the frailty of the human infant, there is no greater testimony to the existence of God. The multitude of babies born each day on Earth are a veritable army of God whose voices combine to drown the feeble cries of His enemies. God does not need a great army of soldiers with powerful weapons of destruction to put to flight His foes. In His great wisdom, He uses the weakest of the weak to humble the mighty. Even the hardest heart softens at the whimper of a child, and grown adults babble gibberish in a child's presence. As insignificant as these simple acts may be, they give testimony to the reverence of mankind in the face of such an unquestionable evidence of power. Who but God can make a tree or create a child to climb it?

The Greatness of the Universe; The Smallness of Man (Psalm 8:3-4)

In poetic form, David declares that the heavens were "the work of Your fingers, The moon and the stars, which You have ordained." The Hebrew writer says, "By faith we understand that the worlds were framed by the word of God, so that the things which are seen were not made of things which are visible" (Hebrews 11:3). After speaking about God's creation of the "heavens and the earth," Peter says that they are "preserved by the same word" (2 Peter 3:7).

As David says in Psalm 19:1, "The heavens declare the glory of God; And the firmament shows His handiwork." The moon is the great night light that testifies to the existence of its larger companion, the sun, which rules the day. The moon is approximately 238,857 miles from Earth. Although it is not that large when compared to Earth, there is no sighted person on this planet who cannot see its light on a clear night. It has a tremendous effect upon the waters of Earth and controls the great sea tides. The sun is 93 million miles away, but nothing on this planet escapes its heat. Just a few minutes under the sun's rays and a person with a light complexion can be severely burned. The Earth itself is a rocket, speeding through the heavens at more than 1,000 miles an hour, held there by an unseen hand. Its inner core is molten lava on which its outer crust constantly floats. God has only to speak the word and these tremendous forces can explode in a cascade of volcanic fire.

Today, men debate how many worlds there may be in this universe and whether life exists on any other planets. Such speculations are no longer the domain of science fiction writers and inquisitive minds. Amazingly such people will accept the infinity of space but will deny the infinite God who created it. If the mind can conceive an infinite universe, why cannot it comprehend an infinite Creator?

When you consider this marvelous universe and the greatness of the God who created it, "What is man that You are mindful of him, And the son of man that You visit him?" (Psalm 8:4). The words "mindful of" suggest continuous care and concern for our welfare and well-being. This statement obviously refers to mankind in general, but it also indicates His interest in the individual. More than 5.6 billion people live on Earth today. When you consider how many people there are, how can God be concerned with each one? However, Jesus said, "Are not two sparrows sold for a copper coin? And not one of them falls to the ground apart from your Father's will. But the very hairs of your head are all numbered. Do not fear therefore; you are of more value than many sparrows" (Matthew 10:29-30). Jesus had earlier stated in the Sermon on the Mount that God feeds the fowls of the air which neither sow nor reap, and adds, "Are you not of more value than they?" (6:26). It does not matter how many people live on the earth, God is mindful of each of us. Considering the greatness of God and all that He is able to do, why would He be so concerned about puny mankind? Why would He honor us so? The simple answer is because He loves us.

David tells us what God's love and grace have caused Him to do for us. First, He visits us. This phrase would suggest more than mere concern and implies that He also constantly intervenes on behalf of mankind. When God visits men, something dramatic happens. He visited Sarah at an old age, and she conceived and brought forth the promised son Isaac into the world (Genesis 21:1). Upon the birth of his son John the Baptist, Zacharias praised God for having "visited and redeemed His people" (Luke 1:68). God then visited mankind in the person of His Son (John 1:1, 14; Philippians 2:5-8). He is not a God who created this world and went off to let it run down on its own. He is still actively involved in the affairs of men (Acts 17:28).

Second, He made us "a little lower than the angels" (Psalm 8:5). Angels are a higher order of being, created to be special servants. Angels are higher than men but lower than deity (Hebrews 1:3-4, 13; 2:7-10, 16-18). We are just below them, but they are serving us, not the other way around. They are ministers of the providence of God. Presently, they are engaged in a ministry to Christians, "those who will inherit salvation" (Hebrews 1:14). When we read about angels in Scripture, we are astounded with all the marvelous things they can do. The world today is enamored with angels. You cannot go anywhere without seeing supposed likenesses of them in figurines, pictures and on book covers. Some people wrongly worship them – the practice is condemned (Colossians 2:18). Even the angels themselves forbade the apostle John to worship them (Revelation 19:10; 22:8-9).

Third, He has "crowned him [mankind] with glory and honor" (Psalm 8:5). This text is applied to Christ in the Hebrew letter (2:6-8), but here it clearly refers to mankind. The expression "son of man" (Psalm 8:4) does not refer to Jesus but to the "son of Adam." Jesus called himself "the Son of man" to identify with us. This is why the writer of Hebrews uses this passage in referring to Him, for He too was made a man, "a little lower than the angels."

The word "crowned" is used here metaphorically, not literally. Mankind has been clothed and adorned with glory and marks of honor, which is not too far removed from the splendor of the heavenly host. He was created "in the image of God" (Genesis 1:27). Man was given an exalted position in relation to the created Earth. He is master of all things and over the earthly creatures.

Man's Dominion (Psalm 8:6-9)

Man has been given "dominion over the works of [God's] hands" (Psalm 8:6). To have dominion means to exercise authority or control over someone or something. This is undoubtedly a reference to Genesis 1:28; God told man to have "dominion over every living thing that moves on the earth." Adam was placed in the garden as a caretaker "to tend and keep it" (2:15). Everything God made upon the earth was given to his hand. Mankind is still the caretaker of God's world. All Christians should be environmentalists in the sense that they are concerned about their world and how they will leave it for future generations.

The creatures that man has been given dominion over are not exclusive categories but are intended to be representative of all the animal kingdom. We have control over domesticated animals, wild beasts, fowl and all the creatures that live in the sea (Psalm 8:7-8).

The last part of verse 8 is one example of scientific foreknowledge. Matthew Fontaine Maury, "the pathfinder of the seas," and the founder of the science of oceanography, is honored and respected throughout the world. Once, when he was sick, his son was reading Psalm 8 to him. When his son read the end of verse 8, "And the fish of the sea That pass through the paths of the seas," Maury told him to stop and read it again. He said, "If the Word of God says there are paths in the sea, they must be there. I will find them." In a few years he had charted all of the major lanes of the sea that are still used by oceangoing vessels today.

Considering the greatness of God, and all that He had done for man, David could only end this song of praise the way he had begun it: "Oh Lord, our Lord, How excellent is Your name in all the earth!" (v. 9).

Lessons Learned

1. David was the principal author and compiler of the Psalms.
2. "The heavens declare the glory of God; And the firmament shows His handiwork" (Psalm 19:1).
3. It is not reasonable or scientific to deny the existence of God when all created things cry out to His being.
4. The greatest witness to the existence of God is the miracle of birth.
5. God spoke this universe into existence, and His Word keeps it today.
6. God has given mankind an exalted position within His creation.

Questions

1. How did David know so much about how this universe operates?
2. What are the three contrasts in Psalm 8?
3. What does the Hebrew word *Adonai* mean?
4. How do the heavens proclaim the glory of God?
5. How can a baby testify about God's existence?
6. What does the writer mean when he says the heavens are "the work of Your fingers?"
7. What do the words "mindful of" suggest?
8. How does God demonstrate His love for mankind, according to Psalm 8?
9. What does the word "crowned" mean in this psalm when referring to man?
10. What does having dominion mean?

Lesson 5

Trust

Week of July 4, 1999

Lesson Text

PSALM 23:1-6

(1) The Lord is my shepherd; I shall not want.

(2) He makes me to lie down in green pastures; He leads me beside the still waters.

(3) He restores my soul; He leads me in the paths of righteousness For His name's sake.

(4) Yea, though I walk through the valley of the shadow of death, I will fear no evil; For You are with me; Your rod and Your staff, they comfort me.

(5) You prepare a table before me in the presence of my enemies; You anoint my head with oil; My cup runs over.

(6) Surely goodness and mercy shall follow me All the days of my life; And I will dwell in the house of the Lord Forever.

Introduction

Psalm 23 is very short, containing only six verses and 118 words, and can be memorized quickly. Most people who grew up attending Bible class know it by heart. No psalm is better known or more loved than this one. Charles Allen wrote, "The power of this psalm is not in memorizing the words, but it is in thinking the thoughts it contains." Unfortunately, it has become associated with death, and it is used more frequently at funerals than any other passage of Scripture. However, it is not a psalm about death but a psalm about life. It presents a positive, happy and faith-filled approach to life. It was not written just to provide comfort during the dark hours of grief, but it was written as a source of strength and power for daily living.

The song of the shepherd may have been composed by David while he was a boy, tending to his father's sheep in the field near Bethlehem. Some scholars say this was the same field where almost 1,000 years later angels appeared to shepherds "living out in the fields, keeping watch over their flock by night" (Luke 2:8). An angel announced to these men the greatest event in the history of the world: "I bring you good tidings of great joy which will be to all people. For there is born to you this day in the city of David a Savior, who is Christ the Lord" (vv. 10-11). After the angel's message, the shepherds left their flocks and went and found Joseph and Mary in a stable with the infant Son of God lying in a feeding trough for animals. Is it not fitting that the announcement about the birth of the Shepherd of our Souls should be made to humble shepherds in the performance of their duty?

There are many figures used in Scripture to describe God's love for His people. None is more consoling than the picture of the loving Shepherd (Psalm 77:20; 78:52; 95:7; 100:3; Isaiah 40:11). Jesus must have loved Psalm 23, because He used this same imagery to describe Himself as the Good Shepherd who would lay down His life for His sheep (John 10:11-12, 14-16). As we study this beautiful psalm, let us not think about it as having been written for people living thousands of years ago in a faraway land and of a strange tongue, but let us try to see within it our experiences as we endeavor daily to walk with Christ.

The Shepherd's Providence (Psalm 23:1)

The relationship of a shepherd to his sheep in ancient Palestine was unique. He literally lived with his sheep throughout the long months of grazing. He was solely responsible for providing their sustenance. He constantly sought adequate pasture in desolate places and water in regions where it was often scarce. The shepherd also had to be strong enough to fend off the natural enemies of his defenseless sheep. Lions, bears and wolves roamed this area in David's time. David was renowned for his exploits while a shepherd. His slaying of a lion and a bear while watching his sheep prepared him for his battle with the Philistine giant, Goliath (1 Samuel 17:12-58). The shepherd had to minister to the wounds of his sheep and protect them from the onslaught of harsh winter weather.

Much of the captivating power of Psalm 23 is the personal nature of its message. It becomes personal when we use the pronoun "my." What a difference there is in saying "The Lord is a Shepherd," or "The Lord is their Shepherd," than saying "The Lord is *my* Shepherd." This is exactly where the psalmist places his emphasis. When we say "my child," "my wife/husband" or "my loved one who has died," we understand how deeply personal the emotions and feelings connected with each of these expressions are. It is true in the affairs of this world and true in the family of God. The word "my" makes a world of difference. It can make all the difference between everlasting life and eternal punishment if we can say, in truth, "The Lord is my Shepherd."

Is the Lord really your Shepherd, or are you outside the fold because you have not submitted yourself to His leadership? If God is my Shepherd, then I have no needs that He cannot supply if they are in my best interest and in harmony with His will. "I shall not want" (v. 1). If we have food, clothing and shelter, we can survive and should be content (1 Timothy 6:8). Many millions of people in this world do not have even these basic necessities, while in America we live in the midst of plenty. It is true that thousands of people, even in our nation, suffer from want. David said in another psalm, "I have been young, and now am old; Yet I have not seen the righteous forsaken, Nor his descendants begging bread" (37:25). A person may go without luxuries, but if he is a faithful child of God, he will be provided for in some way (Ephesians 4:28; 1 Thessalonians 4:11; 2 Thessalonians 3:10; James 1:27; 2:15-16).

The Shepherd's Provisions (Psalm 23:2)

This statement refers to a well-fed and fully contented flock. Sheep will not lie down in green pastures unless they are completely satisfied. The scene here is one of a pasture of lush green grass, but the sheep have full stomachs so they lie down completely satisfied. The grass can be thought of as the Word of God that nourishes and strengthens us spiritually. Here, our spiritual hunger can be satiated because there is more food within the Bible than we can possibly consume.

Sheep are nervous creatures, and because of this they will not drink from a turbulent or noisy body of water. They will only drink from a quiet, still stream or pool. If the shepherd cannot find such a water source, he will often dam up and section off a larger stream to provide places where his sheep can drink their fill. These still waters remind us of the fountain of prayer. There, we can quiet our anxious spirits by communing with God and wash off the dust from the road of life from our hearts.

The emphasis of the psalm is on the word "still." This word brings to mind thoughts of peace, quietness, serenity and calmness. Jesus said, "Therefore I say to you, do not worry about your life, what you will eat or what you will drink; nor about your body, what you will put on. Is not life more than food and the body more than clothing?" (Matthew 6:25). To this, Paul adds, "Be anxious for nothing, but in everything by prayer and supplication, with thanksgiving, let your requests be made known to God" (Philippians 4:6-7).

The Shepherd's Protection (Psalm 23:3-5)

In that time, Palestine was dotted with private fields and gardens that were usually not fenced but were often marked with a pile of stones at each edge. If a sheep wandered onto this property, it could legally be forfeited to the land's owner. For this reason, the shepherd had to be very familiar with the surroundings. He also had to be constantly alert to any sheep that might be straying onto private property.

Just as sheep will sometimes wander away from the fold, it is a common experience in our Christian lives to stray from the path of righteousness (Isaiah 53:6; Romans 3:23). Our Shepherd will not let us wander too far away without seeking us and trying to restore and bring us back home. In Jesus' parable about the lost sheep, He told of a shepherd who had 100 sheep, and only one of them strayed away. Although he was concerned about all of his sheep, he left the 99 and went off in search of the one that was lost (Matthew 18:11-14; Luke 15:4-7).

What assurance that is for us. The night is never too dark or the shepherd too weary to go in search of a wandering sheep. Picture the shepherd leaving the safety and security of his camp as he searches for the sheep gone astray. He goes forth calling its name until he hears its cries (John 10:14, 27). It may have stumbled over a shallow cliff or gotten caught in some briars. The shepherd gently frees the sheep from its prison and bears it home in his arms, rejoicing that he has found the one sheep that went astray. The sheep is not berated for wandering away, but it is welcomed back with tears of joy.

The Good Shepherd also seeks to restore His sheep who stray from the fold. We can never wander too far for Him not to be concerned about our welfare. He constantly calls us through the gospel. His blood frees us from the thorns of this world that threaten to engulf us, and He lifts us from the depths to which we may have sunk into the safety of His everlasting arms. Like the prodigal son (Luke 15:11-32), the returning wanderer is not chastised for his foolishness but is received back with love and forgiveness.

Sheep are not dumb animals, but they can easily become preoccupied when grazing and wander away in search of greener pastures. They are unable to recognize the danger until they have gone too far to find their way home. Christians can easily wander from God because they do not know the danger signs to look for. There are some definite signs of drifting, such as losing the joy of serving Christ, ceasing to pray, neglecting our devotional life, missing the assemblies of the saints and no longer enjoying the fellowship of our brothers and sisters in the Lord. If we are not careful, we will fail to recognize these signs until we have wandered so far that it will be "impossible ... to renew them again to repentance" (Hebrews 6:4-6).

Once the shepherd has rescued the wandering sheep and restored it to the fold, he watches more closely to see that it walks "in the paths of righteousness" (Psalm 23:3). Why does he do this? "For His name's sake." He has his reputation to protect. He has the confidence and trust of the sheep to preserve. When our Shepherd rescues us from the allurement of the world and the enslavement of sin, He will put our feet back on the paths of righteousness where it is safe, secure and good for us.

The expression "He leads me" is important. The shepherd never stands behind his sheep, commanding them to go forward, but he is always out in front calling on them to follow him. This points out the leadership style of Jesus (John 10:4). He is not a driver; He is always a leader who walks in front of His sheep, showing them the way. When we see through the eyes of faith the confident form of our Savior ahead of us, we can follow without fear. The writer to the Hebrews tells us that there is no form of temptation or test in life that we will ever encounter that Jesus has not already met and successfully overcome (4:15). He knows the way and can lead us around them. There is no danger lurking around the corner that He does not understand and can protect us from. We are encouraged to follow a calm, confident leadership that says, "Do not hesitate or be discouraged. Come, follow Me."

The phrase "the valley of the shadow of death" means more than just facing the actual physical experience of death. Palestinian shepherds for years described an actual path through the mountain range leading down from Jerusalem to the Dead Sea. It was a narrow and treacherous journey where one wrong step could mean death. It was foreboding, but the sheep were not afraid to take it as long as the shepherd was in front leading them.

Many dark places exist through which we are compelled to pass in this life. Some of these are disappointment, loneliness, rejection, serious illnesses or death. The physical death of someone we love or even the prospect of our own imminent death is certainly the worst of these. This valley is so narrow that it must be walked in single file. No matter how long we have been with a loved one, when it comes time for him to walk this lonesome valley, we cannot go with him. When it comes our time to make this journey, we will walk it alone unless Jesus has been our Shepherd. If so, He will go through that narrow passage with us and escort us safely to the other side.

The shepherds who knew about this valley of the shadow in Palestine described it as a path along which wild animals or robbers could lurk behind every boulder to attack and steal, kill and destroy. Yet the sheep did not fear because the shepherd's rod and staff protected them. With the staff he could rescue a fallen sheep from a ledge below, and with the rod he could beat off predators. These two instruments serve to represent our Shepherd's care and protection over His spiritual flock. This does not mean that no harm will come to us, but if it does He will be there to aid, to assist and to heal our wounds.

The fields of that day were treacherous places with many natural enemies of the defenseless sheep. There were many thorns and thistles, noxious weeds and snakes. Before allowing the sheep to graze in a new field, the shepherd would go through and remove all of the hidden dangers. He would make a peaceful banquet table spread before the sheep in the midst of their enemies.

When the sheep would become bruised or cut from the rocks, the shepherd would tenderly pour oil into its wounds to help promote healing. No wonder the psalmist said, "My cup runs over" (v. 5). Everything the sheep needed was supplied by the shepherd. Our cups of blessing are also running over (Ephesians 1:3). Yet we often are like the Israelites who griped and complained that things were not better for them. We often do not know how to appreciate what we have until we lose it. Let us always be grateful for God's blessings.

The Shepherd's Promise (Psalm 23:6)

The Old Testament was written mostly in Hebrew, with some portions in Aramaic, and had no punctuation. This was added much later by people who translated the Bible into modern languages. Often punctuation is not placed where it naturally seems to belong. That is the case here. A natural pause seems to follow the word "Surely." The Revised Standard Version places the word "Only" in the footnotes as an alternative translation. The writer is saying that because the Good Shepherd leads him and provides all of his needs, then "For sure, or for certain, goodness and mercy will follow him all the days of His life."

If it can truly be said of us that "The Lord is my shepherd," then, and only then, will we "dwell in the house of the Lord Forever" (vv. 1, 6). This can only be true with people who have heard the voice of the Son of God in this life and have voluntarily chosen to follow Him. If we are not following Him, and are following the voice of another shepherd, then heaven will not be our eternal home. If you cannot say for certain that Jesus is your Shepherd, then you need to be sure that you are following Him and that you are in His sheepfold.

Lessons Learned

1. This is not a psalm about death but a psalm about life.
2. Jesus used the same imagery in His parable about the good shepherd (John 10).
3. There is a world of difference in saying "The Lord is *a* or *their* Shepherd" and saying "The Lord is *my* Shepherd.
4. We have no real need that our Shepherd cannot supply.
5. The still waters remind us of the fountain of prayer where we can drink from the living waters and quiet our anxious souls.
6. The green pastures remind us of the Word of God, which is ample food for our souls.
7. The Shepherd will not let us wander off without seeking to find us and trying to restore us to the fold.
8. There are many danger signs that we may be drifting, such as not praying or reading the Bible, missing assemblies and no longer finding joy in Christian fellowship.

Questions

1. What did Charles Allen say was the power of Psalm 23?
2. How should the study of this psalm be approached?
3. What are some of the ways that the shepherd protected his sheep?
4. How can we know that the Lord is our Shepherd?
5. How does the expression "still waters" relate to a Christian's prayer life?
6. In what way did the shepherd "prepare a table before" his sheep?
7. What is one common experience of the Christian life?
8. How is the sheep's wandering similar to that of a Christian?
9. Why does the shepherd lead the sheep in "the paths of righteousness"?
10. How does the expression "He leads me" illustrate the leadership style of Jesus?

Lesson 6

Praise

Week of July 11, 1999

Lesson Text

ACTS 16:19-40

(19) But when her masters saw that their hope of profit was gone, they seized Paul and Silas and dragged them into the marketplace to the authorities.

(20) And they brought them to the magistrates, and said, "These men, being Jews, exceedingly trouble our city;

(21) and they teach customs which are not lawful for us, being Romans, to receive or observe."

(22) Then the multitude rose up together against them; and the magistrates tore off their clothes and commanded them to be beaten with rods.

(23) And when they had laid many stripes on them, they threw them into prison, commanding the jailer to keep them securely.

(24) Having received such a charge, he put them into the inner prison and fastened their feet in the stocks.

(25) But at midnight Paul and Silas were praying and singing hymns to God, and the prisoners were listening to them.

(26) Suddenly there was a great earthquake, so that the foundations of the prison were shaken; and immediately all the doors were opened and everyone's chains were loosed.

(27) And the keeper of the prison, awaking from sleep and seeing the prison doors open, supposing the prisoners had fled, drew his sword and was about to kill himself.

(28) But Paul called with a loud voice, saying, "Do yourself no harm, for we are all here."

(29) Then he called for a light, ran in, and fell down trembling before Paul and Silas.

(30) And he brought them out and said, "Sirs, what must I do to be saved?"

(31) So they said, "Believe on the Lord Jesus Christ, and you will be saved, you and your household."

(32) Then they spoke the word of the Lord to him and to all who were in his house.

(33) And he took them the same hour of the night and washed their stripes. And immediately he and all his family were baptized.

(34) Now when he had brought them into his house, he set food before them; and he rejoiced, having believed in God with all his household.

(35) And when it was day, the magistrates sent the officers, saying, "Let those men go."

(36) So the keeper of the prison reported these words to Paul, saying, "The magistrates have sent to let you go. Now therefore depart, and go in peace."

(37) But Paul said to them, "They have beaten us openly, uncondemned Romans, and have thrown us into prison. And now do they put us out secretly? No indeed! Let them come themselves and get us out."

(38) And the officers told these words to the magistrates, and they were afraid when they heard that they were Romans.

(39) Then they came and pleaded with them and brought them out, and asked them to depart from the city.

(40) So they went out of the prison and entered the house of Lydia; and when they had seen the brethren, they encouraged them and departed.

Introduction

As a Roman colony, Philippi was a proud and patriotic promoter of the Roman way of life. Because it was situated on a large hill, it was a natural military outpost. It was the place where the famous battle between the forces of Mark Antony and Octavian, later Emperor Augustus, and those of Cassius and Brutus was fought in 42 B.C. Antony and Octavian were victorious partly because of the loyal support of the people of Philippi. For their reward, they were given Roman citizenship and later, when he was emperor, Augustus exempted them from paying taxes forever. The help they gave was not considered minimal by the emperor.

Although Philippi was not as bad as Corinth, it was still a typical center of Greco-Roman paganism. Preaching the gospel in this city presented the seasoned missionary Paul with new challenges. There were few, if any, Jews who lived permanently in Philippi. We know this because it would have taken only seven males living in the city to establish a synagogue, and none existed there. Since he began his missionary work, Paul's pattern had always been to locate the synagogue in a city and go there first to preach the gospel. A different approach had to be devised in Philippi.

Paul had evidently heard about a group of women who assembled Saturday mornings by the river (Acts 16:13). Here he met Lydia, a business woman and seller of purple dye from the city of Thyatira in Asia Minor. Purple was the color worn by the royal and the rich so she may have had a prosperous business. We do not know if Lydia was Jewish or Gentile. Luke simply says she "worshiped God" but so did Cornelius, the first Gentile convert (10:2). We know she was an honest person who listened to the words spoken by Paul, and "The Lord opened her heart" (16:14). She was baptized along with her household. This could have meant family, servants or simply friends who traveled with her. At any rate, they were destined to be the Christians who formed the nucleus for the first church established on the European continent. Lydia invited the preachers to stay at her house, and because of her insistence, they consented.

Trouble on the Horizon (Acts 16:16-18)

What started out as a successful missionary campaign suddenly turned sour. As Paul went each day for prayer, probably to the same spot where he had encountered Lydia, he was followed by a slave girl who was possessed of a "spirit of divination." Burton Coffman in his *Commentary on Acts* says, "The Greek here has 'A Python spirit,' thus identifying this unfortunate girl as one coming from the pagan temple at Delphi, where the Pythian Apollo was worshiped, the python being sacred to him, and his devotees being said to have the python spirit" (Firm Foundation Publishing House, Austin, 1976; p. 316). No indication exists that she actually possessed the power to tell the future, but the pagan people believed that the evil spirit possessing her permitted her to do so. That is the reason why she was such a valuable piece of property to her owners. However, we know that demons did have knowledge about the Son of God (Matthew 8:29; Mark 1:24; 3:11; Luke 4:41; 8:28; James 2:19). The statement of the demons in control of the slave girl prove that this was the case. They used almost the same words as the Gadarene demons did in referring to Jesus as the "Son of the Most High God" (Mark 5:7).

After enduring several days of this demonic girl following them and incessantly crying out that they were "servants of the Most High God, who proclaim to us the way of salvation," Paul became greatly annoyed. He did not want the testimony of demons any more than Jesus did. Paul turned and rebuked the demon "in the name of Jesus Christ," and immediately the evil spirit departed from her (Acts 16:17-18).

In the book of Acts, only two occasions exist when Gentiles were responsible for initiating the attacks upon the church. The first incident is the one recorded here and the second is the riot that broke out later in Ephesus, headed by the men who made and sold the statues of the patron goddess Diana. In both of these cases, the real issue was money. People who had profiteered from the superstitions and sins of other people were enraged when their income was threatened.

A Good Deed Turned Bad (Acts 16:19-24)

The slave girl's masters had no regard for her or her welfare. They were concerned about only one thing – the income they saw disappear with the departing demon. These angry men took the law into their own hands, seizing Paul and Silas and dragging them into the marketplace. This would have been the forum where the Roman courts met to decide the cases brought before them. The Greek term for "magistrate" is *strategos*, the same title worn by those justices in Rome. As a colony, Philippi would have had two of these judges.

This incident is reminiscent of the mock trials of Jesus. What were the charges brought against them? Their accusers first lied saying, "These men, being Jews, exceedingly trouble our city; and they teach customs which are not lawful for us, being Romans, to receive or observe" (vv. 20-21). Neither of these charges was true. The only people they had troubled up to this point were the shysters who had victimized the helpless demonic slave girl. The charge of troubling the city easily won these accusers the support of the judges who were responsible for the peace and stability of this colony. Paul and Silas had also broken no Roman laws in existence at that time. Although most Roman citizens were devotees of the pantheon of gods, officially Rome was a democracy that tolerated many other religions within the empire.

There was one other trick these conspirators used almost to ensure that Paul and Silas would be quickly convicted and that was prejudice. They just happened to throw in the fact that these men were Jews, and that they were Romans. This could explain why Luke and Timothy were not arrested. Luke was a Gentile, and Timothy was the son of a Gentile father and may not have looked Jewish. Anti-Semitism was a sure way to arouse the hostility of the mob toward foreigners. Jews looked different, had peculiar dietary habits, refused to worship Roman gods, and expatriate Jews were usually wealthier than their Gentile neighbors.

Paul and Silas were stripped of their garments and their dignity. The lictors, or rod-beaters, were then called in, and Paul and Silas were severely beaten publicly with many stripes before the multitude. The lictors carried bundles of rods tied together around an ax, which symbolized the right of Rome to administer corporal and capital punishment. Afterward, Paul and Silas were put in the inner prison without their wounds being nursed and had their feet fastened in stocks.

A Midnight Prayer Meeting (Acts 16:25-30)

The conduct of Paul and Silas in this whole episode is remarkable. They were accosted by an angry mob, denied due process of Roman law, punished by being beaten for crimes they did not commit, and finally imprisoned unjustly. How would most people react under such conditions? What Paul and Silas did must have had the other prisoners wondering about these men. Instead of moaning and groaning, complaining about their treatment or even protesting their innocence, they "were praying and singing hymns to God" (v. 25).

The other prisoners were not the only ones listening to this unusual church service. God was also looking and listening. We do not know what Paul and Silas were praying about. However, we do know God acted quickly to change their situation. "Suddenly there was a great earthquake, so that the foundations of the prison were shaken; and immediately all the doors were opened and everyone's chains were loosed" (v. 26). Some people deny this event was miraculous. They attribute it to mere coincidence. While Luke does not specifically say that the prayers of Paul and Silas resulted in the earthquake, we are certainly left with that conclusion.

It is important to note that "everyone's chains were loosed." As remarkable as the behavior of Paul and Silas was under such duress, the response of the other prisoners is even more astounding. We would have expected Paul and Silas not to try to escape, but why did the other prisoners not flee? Paul told the jailer that everyone was still there. Remember that they had been listening to the songs and the prayers. When the sudden unexpected and unexplained earthquake occurred at the precise time that Paul and Silas were having a prayer meeting, the other prisoners made the connection.

The sleeping jailer was awakened by the earthquake, and when he saw what had happened, he naturally assumed that all of the prisoners had escaped. He drew his sword to take his own life. Roman soldiers or jailers who allowed a prisoner to escape were not treated favorably by their government. They were given the same punishment their prisoner would have received. Among all of the men in his charge, at least one would have been guilty of a capital offense requiring execution. This jailer would rather take his own life than face the humiliation of a public execution.

The desperate jailer must have been shocked when Paul called out to him, "Do yourself no harm, for we are all here" (v. 28). The jailer called for a light and ran into the inner prison. Seeing Paul and Silas, he immediately fell before them trembling and asked, "Sirs, what must I do to be saved?" It is safe to conclude that this man was a heathen. Whatever information he had about God must have come from his brief encounter with these two missionaries. Had he also heard them singing and praying? He did not inquire about any of the other prisoners. The conduct of the two men in the face of such terrible treatment struck a chord with this hardened Roman jailer.

A Late Night Bible Study (Acts 16:31-34)

Paul's answer was in response to the jailer's fearful inquiry. "Believe on the Lord Jesus Christ, and you will be saved, you and your household" (v. 31). Often, this verse is quoted as if it stands alone, but it does not. It must be read in light of the whole context. It is not a Scripture that teaches salvation by faith only, and yet it is often used that way. If this man was a heathen, he could not believe on Jesus Christ until he first knew about Him (Romans 10:14).

This verse is also incorrectly used in other ways. Some people use it to teach household salvation. This means that if the man believed and was saved by doing so, his entire household would also be saved because of his faith. The Bible plainly teaches individual responsibility for sin, which requires each offender to believe and obey (Ezekiel 18:20-22; Romans 14:10-12). Another false concept is that his household included underage children. This is used to teach the necessity of baptism for infants and small children. There is no way we can know for certain that the jailer was married, and if married, that he had children. His household could have included, in addition to family, servants and other people living under his roof (Acts 16:33). We do know that neither this passage nor any other teaches infant baptism. Only people old enough to understand the gospel, believe it and repent of their sins are suitable candidates for baptism.

Paul and Silas told the jailer he would have to believe in Jesus Christ. They then taught him what he needed to know to produce that faith in his heart. This Bible study was open to everyone who was in the house. Although we cannot know for sure what he was taught, from the sermons and writings of Paul to Gentiles we can have some idea. It would have included some historical background, some quotations from the prophets concerning the Messiah and a summary about the life and ministry of Jesus. It would have concluded with instructions about how to be saved and an invitation to meet those requirements.

If Jesus and the gospel do not make a dramatic difference in the way we behave, then we are not truly converted. The same jailer who took the bruised and bleeding men into a dungeon without concern for their welfare now washed their stripes and took care of their injuries. A true sign of repentance is the desire on the part of the sinner to make amends for his previous wrongs. After tending to their wounds, the jailer and his family were baptized.

Another indication of the changed character of the jailer is that after his baptism he took Paul and Silas into his home and fed them. Before his conversion he did not care that they may not have eaten, and he certainly would not have invited them home for dinner. At that time they were enemies; now they were brothers in the Lord. This man may not have been taught anything about brotherly love or Christian hospitality at this point in time, but he practiced both of them.

Where before in this man's household there was no hope (Ephesians 2:11-16), it now shone brightly. Where perhaps Roman gods were once honored and worshiped, the household now believed in and worshiped God. Where once the souls of the inhabitants of this house were doomed to eternal damnation, they were now heaven-bound. We do not know the mood of the family before, but it was one of rejoicing after their conversion. Redeemed people rejoice when they understand their salvation. The jailer did not rejoice until there was repentance and baptism.

What a Difference a Night Makes (Acts 16:35-39)

After a night of calm reflection, the magistrates realized how hasty their actions were in their treatment of Paul and Silas. They were caught up in mob hysteria and condemned them without a proper trial. That alone was serious enough under Roman jurisprudence, but there were more revelations to come.

The jailer was relieved and happy as he reported to his newly found brothers that they were free to go. After all, more serious consequences could have followed, even death. He was glad they could "go in peace" (v. 36). Even he must have been shocked once more when they refused this gracious offer of freedom. How much more so when Paul informed him of something that neither he nor the magistrates knew until this moment – he and Silas were Roman citizens. Paul now claimed his right as a citizen under Roman law. He had been openly beaten and imprisoned without a trial. Now those men who had infringed upon his rights wanted him to steal silently away as if nothing had happened. Paul, however, was not willing to go quietly.

Luke records that when the magistrates received Paul's message from the officers, "they were afraid" (v. 38). They had good reason to be. Rome did not look favorably upon its citizens being mistreated. The government prided itself in being protective of its own, and it was unthinkable that the men charged with providing this protection would violate their sworn duty. These once proud, arrogant officials were suddenly humbled. When they came to the prison, the official demeanor of the seasoned jurists was gone. They were more like children caught in the act of some childish mistake, pleading with their accuser not to tell their parents. They begged Paul and Silas to leave the city, and we can be sure it was with words to the effect that they were to do so without seeking vengeance for their ill treatment. But Paul wanted them to sweat long enough to understand the seriousness of what they had done.

One of the benefits of Roman citizenship was that an uncondemned citizen could not be compelled to leave a city against his will. Paul and Silas accepted their freedom, but they did not make a hasty retreat. They went first to the house of Lydia where they had been staying. Then they met with their brethren and encouraged them. After this, they calmly moved on. They did not slink away as the magistrates had hoped but left with dignity and with their heads held high.

Lessons Learned

1. We must learn to be willing to change our missionary strategy whenever we enter new fields.
2. Lydia and her household were destined to be the first Christians on the European continent.
3. Even demons believed in the power of the Son of God and trembled.
4. When they see the hope of fortune fade, greedy men often become violent persecutors.
5. Prejudice of any kind is wrong because it labels and condemns individuals without the facts.
6. The conduct of Christians under great stress can have a powerful impact on other people.

Questions

1. How were the people of Philippi rewarded for aiding Augustus in a battle with his enemies?
2. Why was there no synagogue in Philippi, and why is this fact significant?
3. What facts do we know about Lydia?
4. Did the slave girl really possess the power to predict the future? Why or why not?

5. What is the cause for which Gentiles instigated an attack on Christians in the book of Acts?
6. What false charges were brought against Paul and Silas, and what subtle information was added to almost guarantee a conviction?
7. How were Paul and Silas treated, and why was this illegal under Roman law?
8. Why is the reaction of Paul and Silas after this ill treatment so strange? If you were where they were, what would you be praying about?
9. What was the question asked by the jailer of Paul and Silas, and how did they answer him?
10. How do we know the jailer repented?

Lesson 7

Deliverance

Week of July 18, 1999

Lesson Text

ISAIAH 37:14-20

(14) And Hezekiah received the letter from the hand of the messengers, and read it; and Hezekiah went up to the house of the LORD, and spread it before the LORD.

(15) Then Hezekiah prayed to the LORD, saying:

(16) "O LORD of hosts, God of Israel, the One who dwells between the cherubim, You are God, You alone, of all the kingdoms of the earth. You have made heaven and earth.

(17) "Incline Your ear, O LORD, and hear; open Your eyes, O LORD, and see; and hear all the words of Sennacherib, which he has sent to reproach the living God.

(18) "Truly, LORD, the kings of Assyria have laid waste all the nations and their lands,

(19) "and have cast their gods into the fire; for they were not gods, but the work of men's hands – wood and stone. Therefore they have destroyed them.

(20) "Now therefore, O LORD our God, save us from his hand, that all the kingdoms of the earth may know that You are the LORD, You alone."

ISAIAH 38:1-8

(1) In those days Hezekiah was sick and near death. And Isaiah the prophet, the son of Amoz, went to him and said to him, "Thus says the LORD: 'Set your house in order, for you shall die and not live.' "

(2) Then Hezekiah turned his face toward the wall, and prayed to the LORD,

(3) and said, "Remember now, O LORD, I pray, how I have walked before You in truth and with a loyal heart, and have done what is good in Your sight." And Hezekiah wept bitterly.

(4) And the word of the LORD came to Isaiah, saying,

(5) "Go and tell Hezekiah, 'Thus says the LORD, the God of David your father: "I have heard your prayer, I have seen your tears; surely I will add to your days fifteen years.

(6) "I will deliver you and this city from the hand of the king of Assyria, and I will defend this city.' "

(7) "And this is the sign to you from the LORD, that the LORD will do this thing which He has spoken:

(8) "Behold, I will bring the shadow on the sundial, which has gone down with the sun on the sundial of Ahaz, ten degrees backward." So the sun returned ten degrees on the dial by which it had gone down.

Introduction

Hezekiah, the son of Ahaz, was one of the good kings of Judah. He was not at all like his godless father who spread idolatry throughout the southern kingdom. Hezekiah began to reign when he was 25 years old and continued for 29 years in Jerusalem, accomplishing many good things for his people (2 Kings 18:2). He came to the throne at a very critical period in the history of Judah. The Assyrian King Tiglath-Pileser had taken Aram in 732 B.C. One of his successors, Sargon II, conquered and destroyed the northern kingdom of Israel in 722-721 B.C. and carried away most of the people who were left alive. He left only the very young, the very old and the sick and infirm in the land. Judah was already under unbearable tribute to Assyria and facing the same fate.

Hezekiah came to the throne with youthful enthusiasm and a deep commitment to God. He was at the forefront of a tremendous spiritual revival. He removed the high places where idolatrous worship was conducted and his father had offered human sacrifices. He tore down the idols of Baal, cut down the Asherah poles and destroyed the brazen serpent that Moses had erected in the wilderness to heal the people bitten by fiery serpents. It had become an idol named "Nehushtan," and they worshiped it (2 Kings 18:4). Most of the elements of idolatry that Hezekiah destroyed were instigated by his father. He remodeled the temple and restored the altar of sacrifice. A more detailed list of his reforms is recorded in 2 Chronicles 29-31.

After the death of Sargon, the political situation in the region changed. Egypt was beginning to re-emerge as a dominant influence in the area. Merodach-Baladan, the ruler of Babylon, had established himself as a force with which to be reckoned. Not only did he offer stubborn resistance to Assyria, but he also encouraged other states to become involved in overthrowing her yoke. This situation encouraged Hezekiah to rebel and refuse to pay tribute (2 Kings 18:7). He also carried on a successful campaign against the Philistines who had taken some of the cities of Judah during the reign of Ahaz. Hezekiah apparently had a broader purpose in mind and that was to cement rebellion against Assyria. This was a move that Isaiah opposed. As good as Hezekiah was, he had a problem with pride, and it got him into a lot of trouble.

Sennacherib, the new leader of Assyria, proved himself to be very powerful. He secured his position in the East with two campaigns and then moved west invading Palestine in 701 B.C. This third campaign is well documented in Assyrian annals and in the biblical record (2 Kings 18:13-37; 2 Chronicles 32:1-22; Isaiah 36-37).

After defeating a combined force of Egyptians and Ethiopians who came up to aid Ekron, Sennacherib began to besiege the fortified cities of Judah. He claims to have captured 46 cities and the villages that surrounded them (2 Kings 18:13). Among these was the exceedingly strong fortress of Lachish (v. 14). It was during the siege of Lachish that Hezekiah apparently realized that further resistance against Sennacherib was senseless, and he desired to save Jerusalem from the same fate as the other cities. He sent word to Sennacherib offering to surrender and to pay whatever tribute the Assyrian king wanted. Sennacherib demanded an enormous sum of 300 talents of silver and 30 talents of gold (2 Kings 18:14). The only way Hezekiah could meet this demand was to remove all the silver out of the temple and to strip all the gold from its doors (v. 16).

However, the Assyrian king was still not satisfied. He sent an emissary named Rabshakeh, along with two others, Taretan and Rabsaris, to Jerusalem with a sizable force to demand that Hezekiah completely surrender. He attempted to demoralize the people and perhaps incite them to rise up against Hezekiah (2 Kings 18:17-35). In his remarks he blasphemed God, and this eventually contributed to Assyria's defeat (19:4). Instead of surrendering, Hezekiah laid the matter before the Lord (19:1).

After Sennacherib had soundly defeated the forces of Egypt and Ethiopia, he sent another letter to Hezekiah demanding his complete surrender once again. The letter insisted that he could not trust God to deliver Jerusalem from his hand (2 Kings 19:8-13). Hezekiah again "spread it before the Lord" (2 Kings 19:14; Isaiah 37:23). Sennacherib brought his army down and completely surrounded Jerusalem. He bragged in his annals of having caged Hezekiah up inside the city like a bird. It was this situation that brought forth Hezekiah's prayer.

Hezekiah's Prayer for Deliverance (Isaiah 37:16-20)

Hezekiah first asked God to consider the words of Sennacherib as a witness against him. The Assyrian had arrogantly asserted that God could not deliver them from his hand (Isaiah 37:10). He also compared God to the idols of the other nations he had destroyed and urged the people of Jerusalem to consider their fate. As Hezekiah stated in his prayer, these idols were made by the hands of men and "they were not gods" (Isaiah 37:19). That is why they could be so easily destroyed with fire.

Second, Hezekiah asked God to "save us from his hand that all the kingdoms of the earth may know that You are the Lord, You alone" (Isaiah 37:20). Hezekiah appealed to God to save Jerusalem to preserve His own reputation and integrity. Sennacherib had not blasphemed Jerusalem or Hezekiah, but he had blasphemed God. He had declared that God was as impotent as the idols he had destroyed. Hezekiah wanted God to prove to Sennacherib and other nations allied with him that He alone was the all-powerful, true and living God.

God Answered Hezekiah's Prayer (Isaiah 37:21-36)

Isaiah delivered God's response to Hezekiah and told him that because he had prayed, because of the arrogance of the Assyrian king, and for his "own name's sake," He would "defend the city and save it" (Isaiah 37:21, 23-24, 35). God promised Hezekiah that the king of Assyria would never come inside the city, he would not shoot an arrow against it nor would he be allowed to besiege the city (v. 33). Instead he would have to march home to Nineveh a defeated and broken man (v. 34).

That very night, God sent an angel through the camp of Assyria and killed 185,000 men. Unable to continue his attack on Jerusalem, Sennacherib marched his remaining forces back to Nineveh with his empire now tarnished by defeat from this third-rate power. He never came into Palestine again, as far as we know, although he reigned for 20 more years. One day as he was worshiping in the temple of his god, Nisroch, he was slain by two of his sons (Isaiah 37:37-38).

Deliverance from Death (Isaiah 38:1-8)

There are some difficulties with the records of Hezekiah's reign. One of the main problems is that it is not in exact chronological order. This often leads to confusion of details. The events in this chapter actually occurred before those in the previous one (Isaiah 38:6). It is almost certain that the visit of the ambassadors from Babylon came before Sennacherib's attack, since he put down Merodach-baladan's resistance before he besieged Lachish. The illness of Hezekiah also came during the threat of Sennacherib against Jerusalem and not afterward (Isaiah 38:5, 21). Many surrounding nations had sent gifts of money to Hezekiah which greatly enlarged his royal treasury. Hezekiah was lifted up with pride, and God humbled him with an illness (v. 21) that could have taken his life. Isaiah came to him and told him, "Set your house in order, for you shall die and not live" (v. 1). The king was already on his death bed, and upon hearing this news he "turned his face toward the wall and prayed to the Lord" (v. 2). God heard his prayer, healed him with a poultice, and gave him 15 more years of life (vv. 5, 21).

As a result of his healing, the news spread far and wide about the wonder that had been done in the land. It was apparently during this time that the ambassadors came from Babylon bearing gifts from Merodach-baladan. It was during this visit that attempts were made to elicit Hezekiah's help in his planned rebellion against Assyria.

Once more Hezekiah's pride got the best of him. He was so flattered to receive such attention from a kingdom so far away that he treated these ambassadors royally and showed them all of the riches of his kingdom. "There was nothing in his house, or in all his dominion that Hezekiah did not show them" (Isaiah 39:1-2). When they left, Isaiah came to Hezekiah and asked him where they had come from, and he answered, "from a far country, from Babylon" (v. 3). He then asked, "What have they seen in your house?" The king replied that "they have seen all that is in my house; there is nothing among my treasures that I have not shown them" (v. 4). Isaiah prophesied concerning Hezekiah that because he had done this thing, that all that was in his house that he had accumulated over the years would be carried to Babylon. He also told him that his sons would be taken to Babylon and that they would become "eunuchs in the palace of the king of Babylon" (vv. 6-7).

This prophecy was fulfilled many years later when Nebuchadnezzar took the city of Jerusalem. Among those who were carried away in the first deportation were several young men of the royal seed, including Daniel, Hananiah, Mishael and Azariah, who were made eunuchs in the palace of the king of Babylon (Daniel 1:1-10).

Events During Hezekiah's Added Years of Life

During this time, his son Manasseh was born in the third year of this 15-year period. He came to the throne at the age of 12 and fell under some evil influences. His reign is counted as 55 years, although part of that time was spent in exile (2 Chronicles 33:1-2). Manasseh did not follow in the footsteps of his father but followed the practices of his grandfather, Ahaz, and was even more wicked. He rebuilt the high places Hezekiah had torn down, erected new altars to Baal and Asherah poles, and worshiped the heavenly bodies as did the nations around him. Like his grandfather, he sacrificed his sons in the fire to Molech, practiced witchcraft, and shed innocent blood in Judah (2 Kings 9:11-16). God later said on several occasions that because of the sins of Manasseh, the son of Hezekiah, that He would destroy the entire nation (2 Kings 21:1-18; 24:1-4; 2 Chronicles 33:2-10 Jeremiah 15:1-4). Because of his sins, Manasseh was taken into Assyrian captivity for 25 years. He prayed to God, and He heard his prayer and restored him to the throne in Jerusalem. For the rest of his life, Manasseh attempted to undo all of the damage he had done in the first years of his reign, but his efforts were met with little success (2 Chronicles 33:12-17).

It was also during this period that Manasseh's son Amon was born. He was 22 years old when he began to reign (2 Kings 21:19). Instead of continuing the practices of his father's later years, he reverted to the earlier sinful acts Manasseh had committed. He worshiped the idols his father had served, and he "forsook the Lord God, and did not walk in His ways" (2 Kings 21:21-22). His reign lasted only two years before he was assassinated by some of his servants who apparently intended to seize the throne. Their efforts failed, and they were put to death by the people of Judah (2 Kings 21:23-24; 2 Chronicles 33:21-24). Then Josiah his son was made king when he was only 8 years old (2 Chronicles 34:1).

Josiah came under the influence of Hilkiah, the high priest who became his tutor and advisor. At the age of 20, Josiah began one of the most far-reaching reforms that Judah had ever seen (2 Kings 22:1-23:28; 2 Chronicles 34:3-35:19, 26-27). They even reached into the territory of the former kingdom of Israel. The writer of 2 Kings says that, "There was no king like him who turned to the Lord with all of his heart, all of his soul, and with all of his might, according to all the Law of Moses; nor after him did any arise like him" (23:25). Regrettably when he was only 39, he made a foolish decision to fight against Pharaoh Necho of Egypt. Necho was on his way to Carchemish to assist Assyria in her battle with Babylon and her allies. Josiah met his army at Megiddo with a far inferior force. Necho attempted to persuade him to withdraw, but instead Josiah engaged him in battle and was killed (2 Kings 23:29-30; 2 Chronicles 35:20-25).

For the next four years, Judah was under the control of Egypt. Necho appointed Josiah's 23-year-old son, Jehoahaz, to be king but removed him after three months for pro-Babylonian leanings and took him to Egypt (2 Kings 23:31; 2 Chronicles 36:1-4). Necho then appointed another son of Josiah, 25-year-old Eliakim, to be king, and he reigned 11 years until he was carried into captivity by Nebuchadnezzar. Necho changed his name to Jehoiakim. The Chronicler wrote that, "He did evil in the sight of … God" (2 Chronicles 36:1-6).

One of the saddest things about this story is that despite Josiah's sweeping reforms they had no lasting effect upon the people. The writer of 2 Kings said, "Nevertheless the Lord did not turn from the fierceness of His great wrath, with which His anger was aroused against Judah, because of all the provocations with which Manasseh had provoked Him. And the Lord said, 'I will also remove Judah from my sight, as I have removed Israel and will cast off this city Jerusalem which I have chosen, and the house of which I said, My name shall be there" (23:26-27).

Lessons Learned

1. Hezekiah and Josiah are both examples that neither heredity nor environment can determine what we do with out lives. Both of them were good kings who had bad fathers. Certainly both of these things are factors, but in the long run it is our decisions and choices in life that decide our fate. Many people born in desperate, unbearable circumstances rise above them and make something worthwhile out of themselves. Others from similar backgrounds do not make it and often blame their heredity, environment, parents, or other people for their failures. The Bible plainly teaches that we are each responsible and accountable for our own lives (Romans 14:10-13).
2. As good as Hezekiah was, he was plagued with the problem of pride. He was prideful before, during and after his confrontation with Assyria. Yet, we see that he was a humble man, and when he saw his error, he quickly repented and asked God for forgiveness. Although we should try to live above sin, Christians are

not sinless people (1 John 1:7- 2:2). Instead of judging those who are weaker in the faith, we should give them support and try to help them grow (Matthew 7:1-5; Romans 15:1)

3. "The effective, fervent prayer of a righteous man avails much" (James 5:16b). On two occasions, we see that Hezekiah prayed fervently unto God, and his prayer was heard and answered. Prayer works because God works. He does not work in the way He did in the first century through miracles, but He does work. Providence is the method through which God works today. He is not impotent. He is active in the affairs of this world. He still answers the prayers of His children (Matthew 7:7-11; 1 John 5:14-15).

Questions

1. Why did Hezekiah destroy the brazen serpent Moses had erected in the wilderness?
2. What situations contributed to Hezekiah's decision to rebel against Assyria?
3. Why did God intervene in the war between Hezekiah and Sennacherib?
4. How was Hezekiah able to pay such an enormous tribute to the Assyrian king?
5. What accusations did Sennacherib make against God?
6. What two things did Hezekiah ask God to do in response to Sennacherib's threats?
7. In His response to Hezekiah through Isaiah, what did God say He was going to do in answer to the king's prayer?
8. How did Sennacherib die?
9. How did God defeat the Assyrian army?
10. What was the illness that Hezekiah suffered?

Lesson 8

Lament

Week of
July 25, 1999

Lesson Text

2 SAMUEL 1:17-27

(17) Then David lamented with this lamentation over Saul and over Jonathan his son,

(18) and he told them to teach the children of Judah the Song of the Bow; indeed it is written in the Book of Jasher:

(19) "The beauty of Israel is slain on your high places! How the mighty have fallen!

(20) Tell it not in Gath, Proclaim it not in the streets of Ashkelon – Lest the daughters of the Philistines rejoice, Lest the daughters of the uncircumcised triumph.

(21) "O mountains of Gilboa, Let there be no dew nor rain upon you, Nor fields of offerings. For the shield of the mighty is cast away there! The shield of Saul, not anointed with oil.

(22) From the blood of the slain, From the fat of the mighty, The bow of Jonathan did not turn back, And the sword of Saul did not return empty.

(23) "Saul and Jonathan were beloved and pleasant in their lives, And in their death they were not divided; They were swifter than eagles, They were stronger than lions.

(24) "O daughters of Israel, weep over Saul, Who clothed you in scarlet, with luxury; Who put ornaments of gold on your apparel.

(25) "How the mighty have fallen in the midst of the battle! Jonathan was slain in your high places.

(26) I am distressed for you, my brother Jonathan; You have been very pleasant to me; Your love to me was wonderful, Surpassing the love of women.

(27) "How the mighty have fallen, And the weapons of war perished!"

Introduction

A refrain that David used several times in his lamentation for Saul and Jonathan is "How the mighty have fallen" (2 Samuel 1:19, 25, 27). If it had not been for the fact that David gave another name to this song, "The Song of the Bow," this might well have been the title. We can understand why David would have had such feelings for Jonathan, but why he expressed the same sentiments for Saul is difficult to comprehend. Besides Saul's personal vendetta against David and his final rebellion against God's commands, Saul began as a good and devoted king.

Saul's Sincere Humility

Saul must also have been a remarkable physical specimen. The historian tells us that Saul was a "handsome young man. There was not a more handsome person than he among the children of Israel." He also informs us that "from his shoulders upward, he was taller than any of the people" (1 Samuel 9:2; 10:23).

However, despite Saul's physical appearance, Samuel found a sincere and humble young man when he came to anoint Saul king over Israel. When Samuel informed him that he would be God's chosen king over His people, he said, "Am I not a Benjamite, of the smallest tribes of Israel, and my family the least of all the families of the tribe of Benjamin? Why then do you speak like this to me?" (9:20-21). Despite Saul's protests, Samuel anointed him king as God had commanded him to do (v. 17; 10:1). Later when Saul had returned home, his uncle asked him what Samuel had said to him. He told him about Samuel telling him that his father's lost donkeys had been found, but because of his humble nature, he did not tell him that Samuel had anointed him king (10:14-16). When Samuel came to Mizpah and had called all of Israel together to announce to them who God has chosen to be their king, Saul was singled out, but he had hidden "among the equipment ("stuff" KJV)" (v. 22). Saul proved himself to be a valiant warrior and an effective leader of men (14:47-52).

Saul's Serious Sin

One of the saddest stories in Scripture is how Saul, this self-effacing young man, could have become the arrogant, self-destructive menace he was in his later years. Saul goes from shyness in his role as king to a pompous, bombastic braggart who believed he could disregard the will of God. It did not take long for the power of his office to go to Saul's head. Two years into his reign he was preparing his army to fight against the Philistines, who were "encamped in Michmash, to the east of Beth Aven" (1 Samuel 13:5-6). When the Israelites saw the armed might of the Philistines, some hid out in the caves, rocks, pits and fields around the area. Others fled crossing over the Jordan into Gad and Gilead. Saul went up to Gilgal to await Samuel's arrival, but even those soldiers who remained with him, about 600, were fearful (vv. 7, 15).

When Samuel did not arrive on the day he had specified, Saul took it upon himself to offer a sacrifice to God in violation of the Law (vv. 9, 13). When Samuel came and asked Saul what he had done, he excused his actions based upon the circumstances at the time (vv. 11-12). Samuel reprimanded him for his act and told him that because he had done this thing his dynasty would not continue and God would appoint another man to be king. Whether Saul fully recognized the magnitude of his sin and its consequences at that time is not known for sure. If he had, it seems unlikely he would have made the egregious error he made later.

The Amalekites had long been bitter enemies of Israel. They attacked the Israelites at Rephidim, but they were defeated by Israel's army led by Joshua (Exodus 17:8-13). At that time God swore to Moses that He would "utterly blot out the remembrance of Amalek from under heaven" (Exodus 17:14). Later Israel is reminded of this promise God had made (Deuteronomy 25:17-19). Samuel told Saul that the time had come for that pledge to be fulfilled. He told him to "go and attack Amalek, and utterly destroy all that they have and do not spare them" (1 Samuel 15:1-3).

Saul gathered an army of 210,000 men and pursued Amalek from Havilah to Shur (v. 7). He "utterly destroyed all of the people with the edge of the sword" and "everything despised and worthless" (v. 9). But he spared King Agag and the best of the sheep, lambs, oxen, cattle and anything else he considered good. When God told Samuel what Saul had done and that He was sorry He had ever made Saul king, Samuel "cried out to the Lord all night" (v. 11).

The next morning Samuel found Saul at Gilgal. The king told Samuel he had "performed the commandment of the Lord" (v. 13). Samuel then asked him, "What then is this bleating of the sheep in my ears, and lowing of the cattle which I hear?" (v. 14). Saul told him that he had spared Agag and that the people had spared the animals to offer as sacrifice to God. He said he only did it because the people made him do it (vv. 15, 20-21). It was then that Samuel told him that "to obey is better than sacrifice, and to heed than the fat of rams" (v. 22). He accused Saul of three cardinal sins – rebellion, stubbornness and rejecting the word of the Lord (v. 23). He told him that because he had rejected the word of the Lord, the Lord had rejected him from being king over Israel (v. 26). Samuel then announced the end of Saul's reign (v. 28). Afterward Samuel walked away and did not see Saul anymore until the day he died, but he did mourn for him (15:33-16:1).

When Saul and his sons died in battle, it was not a random act of war. It was the punishment of God upon him and his house for his disobedience (1 Samuel 28:19; 2 Chronicles 10:13-14). Three of his four sons, including Jonathan, were slain in battle along with many of the Israelites, and the Philistines occupied many Israelite cities for a time (1 Samuel 31:6-7). David himself had predicted Saul's demise (1 Samuel 26:10). When these things are considered, it is still hard to understand David's sorrow upon hearing the news of Saul's death.

The Death of Saul and Jonathan (1 Samuel 31:3 – 2 Samuel 1:16)

On the morning after Saul's visit to the witch of Endor (1 Samuel 28:3-25), the Philistines attacked Israel. Many Israelites died, including three of Saul's sons. Jonathan fought bravely by his father's side and may have died trying to save his life (2 Samuel 2:2-6). This was despite the fact that Saul had spoken harshly to Jonathan because of his loyalty to David and had tried to kill him (1 Samuel 14:36-45; 20:30-33). Saul was wounded in the battle, but was still alive. He tried to get his armor bearer to take his life, but he refused. Saul then took his own life by falling on his sword (31:4-5). When the Israelites realized that Saul and Jonathan were dead, they fled for their lives.

When the Philistines came to Mount Gilboa to gather the spoils of war, they saw the bodies of Saul and his three sons. They decapitated Saul and hung his body, along with those of his three sons, on the wall at Beth-Shan (31:10). They put Saul's head in the temple of Dagon and his armor in the temple of Ashtoreth (1 Chronicles 10:8-10; 1 Samuel 31:10). When the people of Jabesh-Gilead heard about this, they remembered how Saul had saved them from the Ammonites (11:1-11). At a substantial risk to their own lives, they came and took the bodies of Saul and his sons down from the wall of Beth-Shan and brought them to Jabesh. They cremated them and buried their bones under a tamarisk tree at Jabesh. Then they fasted and mourned for them seven days (31:11-13). David later praised them for their devotion to Saul.

David received word of the deaths of Saul and Jonathan from an Amalekite who had brought Saul's crown and bracelet to David (2 Samuel 1:10). He told David that he had been in the battle himself and had taken Saul's life in answer to his request (vv. 2-3, 7-10). David rent his own garments, fasted, mourned and wept for Saul and Jonathan until the evening (vv. 11-12). He then called the young Amalekite before him and asked why he had not been afraid to kill Saul (v. 14). David then had the Amalekite executed for destroying the Lord's anointed.

Another interpretation of this passage is that the Amalekite might have thought that David would be grateful for his killing Saul and returning his crown and bracelet so he lied about killing Saul. However, David saw through the lie – "your own mouth has testified against you" (v. 16) – and executed the Amalekite for lying.

David's Lament (2 Samuel 1:17-27)

A lesser man would have rejoiced that his old enemy was dead, but David was "a man after God's own heart," and he felt the loss deeply. Out of his sorrow, David composed a Lamentation or Lament (Hebrew: *qinah*) for Saul and Jonathan. He commanded that this "Song of the Bow" be taught to the people of Judah. Because Jonathan was skillful with the bow, many see this as David's way of especially honoring his beloved friend (v. 22). There are no unkind words about Saul in this song, and in fact there is nothing but praise for him. David's main thought is that God's anointed had been slain, and His glory had been diminished.

This song can be divided into five sections. First, there is the desire of David that the news of their deaths not be reported in the cities of Philistia to prevent the heathen women from rejoicing (v. 20). Second, a curse is pronounced upon Gilboa where Saul and Jonathan fell (v. 21). Third, David praised Saul and Jonathan for their remarkable abilities and virtues (vv. 22-23). Fourth, he calls upon the women of Israel to mourn for Saul because of the prosperity he had brought to them (v. 24). Fifth, the last and longest portion is devoted to Jonathan for the love that he and David shared with each other (vv. 25-27).

Part 1: David begins by saying that the "beauty of Israel is slain on your high places," referring to Mount Gilboa. He ends the first verse with the refrain "How the mighty have fallen," which is repeated three more times (vv. 19, 25, 27). Then David expresses remorse that the heathen women will have reason for rejoicing when they received the news of Saul's death (v. 20). Gath and Ashkelon were two of the principal cities of the Philistines. David had sought and found refuge in Gath when he was fleeing from Saul. The women of that day traditionally met their victorious army returning from battle bringing with them the spoils of war which were distributed among the women. It was an occasion of great celebration. We do not know whether David is merely taking poetic license or does not know that the Philistines have already broadcast this "word throughout the land" to "their idols and among the people"(1 Samuel 31:9).

Part 2: This section contains a curse placed upon Mount Gilboa because of what happened there. In poetic language, David asked that no dew or rain moisten its fields anymore so they will be barren. It is because "the shield of the mighty was cast away there" (2 Samuel 1:21). In that day, warriors had shields of metal or ones made of thick dried skins. They soaked these with oil for protection. David pictures the shield of Saul drying out in the sun where it fell. It would not be used again because Saul had fallen in battle.

Part 3: In this section, David hailed Saul and Jonathan for their exploits in battle. Saul had been a mighty warrior in many battles for Israel and for God's glory. Even in the refrain from the women of Israel that so enraged Saul, we can see how valiant a fighter he was. They chanted, "Saul has killed his thousands, and David his ten thousands" (1 Samuel 18:7). He also led his men into battle and did not send them out to do all of the fighting by themselves. In this final battle, he and Jonathan fought bravely side by side. Saul only stopped fighting when he was wounded too seriously to continue. Even if a man falters in his later years, should all of his worthy accomplishments be forgotten because of an act or acts of folly? David thought that Saul and Jonathan should be remembered for their bravery and remarkable virtues.

Part 4: This section calls upon the women of Israel to grieve over Saul. They had enjoyed status, prosperity and wealth under Saul's reign. They were able to enjoy many of the finer things of life such as gold jewelry and luxurious apparel. Although the borders of the kingdom were enlarged greatly under David and Solomon, it was Saul who had helped to make these disorganized tribes into a nation. With God on his side, he had forged out the territory that became the Kingdom of Israel. He had made the name of Israel one to be feared by the surrounding nations of Palestine. In his own way, he had spread the name of God among the heathen. All of this had given Israel a prosperity unparalleled before Saul's time.

Part 5: David reserved this final section, which is the longest part of the song, for his beloved friend Jonathan. This man's loyalty to David was unquestionable. He was loyal to David even at the expense of his relationship with his father. Jonathan had argued with Saul over why he hated David so, when he had been nothing but loyal to him. He risked his own life in defense of David. It was he who finally alerted David that it was time for him to flee the palace to preserve his life.

In this story, we have all the marks of a true friendship – trust, loyalty, sacrifice, devotion and, most of all, love. It is regrettable that some people have tried to turn this story into one of perversion because of David's statement that Jonathan's love for him "surpassed the love of women" (2 Samuel 1:26). When two men have that kind of love for each other, today's society considers it unmasculine and inappropriate. Why is that so? Our love for Christ and each other should be the kind that David and Jonathan shared.

Lessons Learned

1. David's feelings for Saul even after all he had done to him give us a glimpse into why he was called "a man after God's own heart" by the Lord Himself. David was able to forgive Saul for everything including the many attempts on his life. Forgiveness does not mean forgetting; it means that from that point on our treatment of the forgiven person will be as if they had never sinned against us. David's lament for Saul was not hypocritical. His love and respect for Saul overshadowed all of the bad memories he had of him. There is also the fact that Saul was God's anointed. David could not bring himself to lift up his hand against him, and he did not permit anyone else to do so without severe punishment.
2. Saul is a perfect example of how power, prestige, position or pre-eminence can cause people to think more highly of themselves than they ought to think. The man who hid from publicity came to seek the spotlight. In Jesus' parable about the rich fool, this successful farmer suffered from "I" disease (Luke 12:16-21). He used personal pronouns eight times in his conversation with himself. He is not alone. We need to watch out for the "Big I." Like Paul, if we must "glory" let it be "in the cross of our Lord Jesus Christ" (Galatians 6:14).
3. One of the greatest lessons we can learn from Saul's life is "obedience is better." Many people today imply that obedience is somehow inferior to grace. They suggest if we teach a person must obey God to be saved, we have somehow fallen

from grace and that grace and obedience are mutually exclusive. They are not. We do not reject God's grace when we obey; we accept it. Saul thought he could disregard certain commandments because of who he was. He thought he could substitute God's pattern of worship for another of his own choosing. He was wrong, and so are those today who advocate these same kinds of changes. Love demands obedience (John 14:15). John writes that one of the indications a person is saved is to "keep His commandments" (1 John 5:3). Do not say, "I love God," and then deny it by your disobedience. Actions speak louder than words.

Questions

1. What title might have been given to David's lament besides the one he assigned to it?
2. What are some of the indications of Saul's earlier humility?
3. What sins does Samuel charge Saul with?
4. Why could Saul not offer sacrifices to God at Gilgal?
5. How can we relate the mercy and grace of God with His order for the total destruction of the Amalekites and other heathen tribes in Canaan?
6. Why did David slay the Amalekite who brought him news of Saul's death?
7. To what was Saul's death attributed?
8. What are the five parts of David's lament?
9. Why did David curse Mount Gilboa?
10. For what things did David commend Saul?

Lesson 9

Intercessions

Week of
Aug. 1, 1999

Lesson Text

GENESIS 18:16-33

(16) Then the men rose from there and looked toward Sodom, and Abraham went with them to send them on the way.

(17) And the LORD said, "Shall I hide from Abraham what I am doing,

(18) "since Abraham shall surely become a great and mighty nation, and all the nations of the earth shall be blessed in him?

(19) "For I have known him, in order that he may command his children and his household after him, that they keep the way of the LORD, to do righteousness and justice, that the LORD may bring to Abraham what He has spoken to him."

(20) And the LORD said, "Because the outcry against Sodom and Gomorrah is great, and because their sin is very grave,

(21) "I will go down now and see whether they have done altogether according to the outcry against it that has come to Me; and if not, I will know."

(22) Then the men turned away from there and went toward Sodom, but Abraham still stood before the LORD.

(23) And Abraham came near and said, "Would You also destroy the righteous with the wicked?

(24) "Suppose there were fifty righteous within the city; would You also destroy the place and not spare it for the fifty righteous that were in it?

(25) "Far be it from You to do such a thing as this, to slay the righteous with the wicked, so that the righteous should be as the wicked; far be it from You! Shall not the Judge of all the earth do right?"

(26) So the LORD said, "If I find in Sodom fifty righteous within the city, then I will spare all the place for their sakes."

(27) Then Abraham answered and said, "Indeed now, I who am but dust and ashes have taken it upon myself to speak to the Lord:

(28) "Suppose there were five less than the fifty righteous; would You destroy all of the city for lack of five?" So He said, "If I find there forty-five, I will not destroy it."

(29) And he spoke to Him yet again and said, "Suppose there should be forty found there?" So He said, "I will not do it for the sake of forty."

(30) Then he said, "Let not the Lord be angry, and I will speak: Suppose thirty should be found there?" So He said, "I will not do it if I find thirty there."

(31) And he said, "Indeed now, I have taken it upon myself to speak to the Lord: Suppose twenty should be found there?" So He said, "I will not destroy it for the sake of twenty."

(32) Then he said, "Let not the Lord be angry, and I will speak but once more: Suppose ten should be found there?" And He said, "I will not destroy it for the sake of ten."

(33) So the LORD went His way as soon as He had finished speaking with Abraham; and Abraham returned to his place.

Introduction

Can mortals move God to change His mind? We know that God changed His mind when Moses prayed for Israel because God was ready to destroy them and raise up a new nation. God also changed His mind when Hezekiah was on his deathbed. When Isaiah told him to "set his house in order for you shall die, and not live," he turned toward the wall and prayed fervently to the Lord. God heard Hezekiah's prayer and granted him 15 more years of life (2 Kings 20:1-6).

The text for this lesson is about God changing His mind in answer to the prayer of Abraham. Some people might argue that this was not a prayer but a conversation. What is prayer but a conversation with God? This prayer took place at the time when God had told Abraham he would have the promised son within the next year (Genesis 18:10, 13-14; 21:1-3). Afterward, God told him that He was going to destroy the cities of Sodom and Gomorrah and their sister cities of the plain. Sodom was where Lot lived with his family (13:10-13). Abraham deeply loved his nephew and his family, and he was moved by what God had told him. He then began to beseech God for Sodom to spare Lot and his family from destruction.

Lot was more than just a nephew to Abraham. Lot's father, Haran, had died when he was young (11:28, 31). His grandfather, Terah, also died in the city of Haran where the family dwelt for a while (v. 32). Abraham, who had no children at that time, took Lot and raised him like a son (12:4-5; 13:8-11). Obviously, Abraham loved Lot because he had previously risked his life to rescue him and his family when they were taken captive by Chedorlaomer, the king of Elam, and his allies (14:12-16). On the occasion of our text, Abraham once again tried to save Lot's life. God heard and answered His request in sparing Lot's life but not in the way that Abraham expected.

God's Love for Abraham (Genesis 18:16-19)

After God had informed Abraham and Sarah that their promised son would be born, the two angels went outside the tent and "looked toward Sodom" (v. 16). Abraham followed to see them on their way. The text says, "The Lord said, Shall I hide from Abraham what I am doing?" This may have been a conversation God had with the two angelic beings, but it could also have been His reasoning concerning the matter. It is recorded to demonstrate the feelings He had for Abraham.

Verse 18 is a reminder to us that God had chosen Abraham to be the father of His nation Israel. God had also promised that through him all nations would be blessed. This shows the depth of love God had for this man. Abraham must have been a good man, a servant of God at the time he was chosen, but God could have selected anyone. Why did He choose him? One answer is given in the next verse. God knew not only what Abraham was but also what he would become. He knew he would lead his family to "keep the way of the Lord, to do righteousness and justice" (v. 19).

God Reveals Warnings of Sin (Genesis 18:20-21)

In God's revelation to Abraham, He began by explaining the sinful condition of Sodom and her companion cities. There were five cities in all, four of which were destroyed. God spared Zoar at Lot's request (19:18-25). Because Sodom and Gomorrah are usually mentioned together, some scholars believe they were twin cities.

God describes their sin as "exceedingly wicked" and "very grievous" (13:13;

18:20). Although they certainly were guilty of other sins, the most apparent sign of their depravity was their flagrant practice of homosexuality, a sin of which they would not repent (19:4-9; Isaiah 3:9; Jeremiah 23:14; Jude 7). So prevalent was this sin that the words "sodomize" and "sodomy" have become synonyms for male homosexual behavior. Homosexuality is, as Paul told the Roman Christians, a "sin against nature" (Romans 1:26-27) and an abominable sin in God's sight. People who practice it "will not inherit the kingdom of God" (1 Corinthians 6:9-11).

Sodom and Gomorrah are often used as examples of God's righteous judgment on sin (Isaiah 1:9; Lamentations 4:6; Zephaniah 2:9; 2 Peter 2:6-8). Jesus used Sodom as a warning to the people who would be living when Jerusalem was destroyed (Luke 17:28-32).

Abraham Intercedes for Sodom (Genesis 18:22-33)

Paul wrote that "there is one Mediator between God and men; the Man Christ Jesus" (1 Timothy 2:5). He is our only "Advocate with the Father" (1 John 2:1). This is the same as saying that He is the lawyer who pleads our case before the throne of God. No one else can do this for us. Every Christian is a saint, one sanctified or set part, for God's purposes (2 Timothy 2:21). We are also priests to offer up our spiritual sacrifices (Romans 12:1; 1 Peter 2:5). There is one Mediator, but there are many who are intercessors. Moses, Elijah, Isaiah, Jeremiah, Daniel and other prophets were called intercessors. Jesus intercedes for us (Hebrews 7:25), and so does the Holy Spirit (Romans 8:26). We can even intercede for other people (1 Timothy 2:1-2). Abraham interceded for Lot and for Sodom and Gomorrah.

The angels departed for Sodom, but God remained behind to discuss the matter more fully with Abraham. He asked God, "Would you also destroy the righteous with the wicked?" (Genesis 18:23). In this exchange, more is revealed about the character of Abraham. The fact that his blood relative was in Sodom played a part in his desire to spare those cities. Abraham had also saved the family from Chedorlaomer and his allies. He may have had friends among the inhabitants of the city, or it may have just been his love for people in general. Although we do not know for certain, it is possible that he did not know how sinful these five cities had become. He certainly would not have condoned their sinful practices.

At first Abraham asked God if there were 50 righteous people in these cities, would He spare them. He may have had in mind only Sodom where Lot lived because he used the singular "city," and in His reply, God mentions only Sodom (vv. 24, 26). The population of Sodom and Gomorrah alone has been estimated at 300,000. If all of the five cities were included, there would be a much greater number of people involved. Does it seem unreasonable that there would be 50 righteous people in a population of half a million? God said He would spare the city if there were 50 righteous people there. It appears Abraham knew there were not that many righteous people, and so he continued to reduce the number upon each successive request.

Abraham was expressing his faith in the goodness of God. He knew God was long-suffering and would not destroy the righteous with the wicked. He stated one of the essential truths of Scripture: God is not just the God of Abraham or Israel; He is "the Judge of all the earth" (v. 25). Abraham believed God was absolutely fair in all of His dealings with mankind. He was confident in the justice of God, believing that it was more just to spare these cities for a few righteous people than to punish a large number of wicked.

Abraham's conversation with God continues through verse 32. Some people have described this as bargaining, but we should not think Abraham was argumentative or disrespectful to God. Notice how he worded his request: "I who am dust and ashes have taken it upon myself to speak to the Lord" (v. 27), and "Let not my Lord be angry, and I will speak" (vv. 30, 32). Although Abraham was the "friend of God," he never let himself forget to whom he was speaking (2 Chronicles 20:7; James 2:23).

Abraham continues: "What if there were five less than 50 righteous; would You destroy all of the city for lack of five?" Once more God answers, "If I find there 45, I will not destroy it" (v. 28). Abraham then asks, "Suppose there were 40 found there," "30," "20," and finally, if "10" could be found would God spare the city? Each time God responds saying He would not destroy the city if any one of these numbers of righteous people could be found there. Why did Abraham stop at 10? What if he had said, "What if only five or four could be found there, would you spare the city?" We will never know because he never asked. He might reasonably have thought there were 10 righteous people there. This would have included Lot, his wife, their two unmarried daughters, their married daughters, their husbands and children.

If Abraham thought there were 10 righteous people there, he would have been wrong, because only four escaped the city – Lot, his wife, and their two unmarried daughters. But his wife perished when she disobeyed the angel's injunction and looked back toward the city (19:26). This could have been "an act of God," but it did not have to be. When she looked back, she would have paused long enough for the "fire and brimstone" containing high deposits of salt that was falling on the city to cover her completely (v. 24). This destruction, which certainly God brought on these four cities, could have come from volcanic activity or an earthquake that spewed forth molten lava from the depths of the earth. In any case, regardless of where it came from, it rained down from heaven, and it originated from actions God Himself took.

Although even 10 righteous people could not be found in Sodom, God spared Lot, and his daughters. He did not have to do that. He spared them because of Abraham's intercession (v. 29). It was purely an act of mercy on His part (v. 19). In the same way, God extends His mercy and grace to the sinful people of the world today (Titus 2:11-14; 3:5). It is not His will that "any should perish, but that all should come to repentance" (2 Peter 3:9). He would have "all men to be saved and come to the knowledge of the truth" (1 Timothy 2:4). We must accept His grace through faith in Christ, repenting of our sins, confessing our faith before men, and then being buried with Christ in baptism that His blood might cleanse us from our sins (Ephesians 2:8-9; John 8:24; Luke 13:3; Matthew 10:32-33; Romans 10:9-10; Acts 2:38; Galatians 3:26-27; Revelation 1:5).

Lessons Learned

1. God changes His mind in answer to His children's prayers. If He does not, then there is no reason to pray. James used Elijah as an example that God does hear and answer prayers (James 5:17-18). His main point was that Elijah was a good man but still only a man. God heard and answered his prayers, and He will also

hear and answer our prayers. The only thing that stands between us and answered prayers if we are faithful children of God is the asking. Jesus said, "Ask and you shall receive" (adapted from Matthew 7:7).

2. The homosexual lifestyle is a choice; a person is not made that way. Would God condemn something He Himself created? Homosexuality is still a sin. Many people today, especially young people, are confused about the nature of this lifestyle choice. Gay rights activists and supporters say it should be an acceptable alternative lifestyle. Homosexual marriage and allowing homosexual couples to adopt children is being encouraged. For whatever reason, a person may have a predisposition toward homosexuality, but he or she does not have to act upon that anymore than heterosexuals have to act upon their sexual desires. However, if they do act upon those desires, they will be lost. God's Word says that practicing homosexuals "shall not inherit the kingdom of heaven" (1 Corinthians 6:9). Homosexuals can change (v. 11). Christians should not hate homosexuals, but they should pray for them and try to help them change their sinful lifestyle.
3. Lot provides us with many good lessons. When he was given the choice by Abraham about where he would live, he chose the fertile plains of Sodom. He did this out of greed, and he did not consider the consequences of his actions. At first he "pitched his tent toward Sodom" (Genesis 13:12 KJV), then he moved into Sodom (19:2), and then Sodom moved into him. He was even one of the city fathers, because he was "sitting at the gate" (v. 1). Because of his choice, Lot lost everything he had – his home, belongings, two daughters and their children, and his wife. Even his two daughters who survived the destruction of Sodom were affected by that sinful environment. They got their father drunk and committed fornication with him. The two sons that were produced from that sinful union, Moab and Amon, fathered two tribes that became bitter enemies of Israel. "Be sure your sins will find you out" (Numbers 32:23).
4. Lot's wife also provides us with an important lesson. It was important enough that Jesus mentioned her in His warnings about the destruction of Jerusalem. The warning does have an application for us. The expression "she looked back" implies a lingering, longing look. She can perhaps be excused for her act because she had daughters back in Sodom, but her backward gaze and hesitation cost her her life. If people saved from sin by the blood of Jesus "look back" toward the world, like Demas, they may return to it and be lost (2 Timothy 4:10). "Remember Lot's wife" (Luke 17:32).

Questions

1. What actions prove God's love for Abraham?
2. Why did God choose Abraham?
3. What was the most obvious sin of the men of Sodom?
4. Why is homosexuality condemned?
5. What is a mediator, and who is ours?
6. Who intercedes for us?
7. How many righteous people would have saved Sodom?
8. How did Abraham approach God in his conversation and why?
9. How and why did Lot's wife perish?
10. Why did God spare Lot and his daughters?

Lesson 10

Joy

Week of Aug. 8, 1999

Lesson Text

1 SAMUEL 2:1-10

(1) And Hannah prayed and said: "My heart rejoices in the LORD; My horn is exalted in the LORD. I smile at my enemies, Because I rejoice in Your salvation.

(2) "No one is holy like the LORD, For there is none besides You, Nor is there any rock like our God.

(3) "Talk no more so very proudly; Let no arrogance come from your mouth, For the LORD is the God of knowledge; And by Him actions are weighed.

(4) "The bows of the mighty men are broken, And those who stumbled are girded with strength.

(5) Those who were full have hired themselves out for bread, And the hungry have ceased to hunger. Even the barren has borne seven, And she who has many children has become feeble.

(6) "The LORD kills and makes alive; He brings down to the grave and brings up.

(7) The LORD makes poor and makes rich; He brings low and lifts up.

(8) He raises the poor from the dust And lifts the beggar from the ash heap, To set them among princes And make them inherit the throne of glory. "For the pillars of the earth are the LORD's, And He has set the world upon them.

(9) He will guard the feet of His saints, But the wicked shall be silent in darkness. "For by strength no man shall prevail.

(10) The adversaries of the LORD shall be broken in pieces; From heaven He will thunder against them. The LORD will judge the ends of the earth. "He will give strength to His king, And exalt the horn of His anointed."

LUKE 1:46-55

(46) And Mary said: "My soul magnifies the Lord,

(47) And my spirit has rejoiced in God my Savior.

(48) For He has regarded the lowly state of His maidservant; For behold, henceforth all generations will call me blessed.

(49) For He who is mighty has done great things for me, And holy is His name.

(50) And His mercy is on those who fear Him From generation to generation.

(51) He has shown strength with His arm; He has scattered the proud in the imagination of their hearts.

(52) He has put down the mighty from their thrones, And exalted the lowly.

(53) He has filled the hungry with good things, And the rich He has sent away empty.

(54) He has helped His servant Israel, In remembrance of His mercy,

(55) As He spoke to our fathers, To Abraham and to his seed forever."

Introduction

We often speak about the great men of the Bible, but there were also many great women mentioned. Some who quickly come to mind are Rahab, Deborah and Esther.

Rahab, the former harlot of Jericho, bravely hid the Hebrew spies and helped them to escape (Joshua 2:1-21). She later married an Israelite named Salmon, King David's great-great-grandfather, and is one of the few women mentioned in the genealogy of Jesus Christ (Matthew 1:5). Rahab is also held up as a great example of faith (Hebrews 11:31; James 2:25). Deborah, who along with Barak led her nation in a great victory over the Canaanites, was a prophetess and the only female judge of Israel (Judges 4-5). Queen Esther saved her people from destruction (Esther 1-6).

The two subjects of this lesson are also devout and godly women. They were not heroines in the sense that Rahab, Deborah and Esther were; they did not risk their lives to save anyone or lead their people into battle.

Although separated by many years, they have much in common. Both women became mothers of sons, giving Israel two of its greatest men. One son was born as an answer to prayer, and the other son was born of a miracle after many prayers. Both sons were given over to be devoted to the service of God. One mother, Hannah, gave Israel one of her greatest prophets and judges. The other, Mary, the virgin from Nazareth, gave the world a Savior. We learn much about praising God from the songs of the these two godly women.

Hannah

Hannah was the wife of Elkanah, a Levite of the family of Kohath, the most honored house in that tribe (1 Chronicles 6:16-48). He lived in Ramathaim Zophim (1 Samuel 1:19), which is the same as Arimathea in the New Testament (v. 1; John 19:38). Elkanah had another wife, Peninnah, who had borne him children (1 Samuel 1:2). Hannah was barren and apparently suffered harassment from Peninnah (v. 6). There may have also been some jealousy on the part of the latter because the text says that, despite her childlessness, Elkanah would give Hannah "a double portion, for he loved Hannah," suggesting that he loved her more than Peninnah (v. 5).

Elkanah went every year to Shiloh where the tabernacle was housed to worship God (v. 3). He was most likely serving his term at the tabernacle as well. When Hannah and Peninnah were at home in Ramathaim Zophim, they were apparently separated from each other. The problems between them intensified when they went up to Shiloh, where they were forced into closer contact. The favoritism of Elkanah toward Hannah worsened the situation, leaving the latter depressed, grieving and unable to eat (vv. 7-8). How long this situation had existed we do not know, but it had apparently been a long time (v. 7). On the occasion of the text of 1 Samuel, she went to the tabernacle and "prayed to the Lord and wept in anguish" (v. 10).

Hannah's prayer was motivated by her distress about her situation. Because she is mentioned first, many scholars conclude that she was Elkanah's first wife and that if she had been able to give him an heir, he might not have married Peninnah. Hannah must have realized that she could no longer bear the strain of this yearly ritual. She poured out her heart to God so fervently that when Eli, the high priest, saw her, he thought she was drunk (vv. 12-14). He approached her and chastised her for coming up to the tabernacle drunk. She assured him that she was not drunk but was in a "sorrowful spirit" (vv. 15-16). Eli promised her God would grant her request.

Hannah's faith was strong enough that she prayed specifically. Notice that she did not just pray for a child. She asked for "a male child" (v. 11). You would think if someone wanted a child badly enough either sex would do. Her prayer was not a selfish one, because she wanted a boy so she could give Him to the service of God. We need more mothers and fathers with Hannah's attitude of service.

In her prayer, Hannah offered herself as an instrument through whom God could work. She presented herself as totally willing to be the mother of this son. The text indicated that she persisted in prayer until the child was born (vv. 19-20). When her son was born, she named him Samuel, meaning "heard by God" (v. 20). After he was weaned, she took him up to the tabernacle just as she had promised God (vv. 11, 22-24). He was under a Nazarite vow (v. 11), and he would serve at the sanctuary, not for a specified period of time as other Levites, but for all of his life. She did not just lend Samuel to God; she gave him to God forever (v. 22).

Hannah's Song of Praise (1 Samuel 2:1-10)

This song, which is itself a prayer (v. 1), came out of Hannah's joy when she finally released her son to Eli to begin his life of dedication to God. We have to be impressed that there is no indication of sadness or depression in her words. Imagine praying for a son as long as she did and then giving him up. However, she did not see this as a sacrifice; she saw it as a blessing given her by the Lord (1:27). She saw herself as merely giving back to God what He had given her in answer to her prayer (v. 28). God blessed her by allowing her to have a son who could be an instrument for fulfilling His glorious purpose for Israel and for the world. Her joyful song is a prayer of praise and thanksgiving.

In the first section of her song, Hannah rejoiced because of who God is. He was her Lord, her Master and the Ruler of her life. He will overcome her enemies, so she had no need to fear them. God had given her salvation. Her expression of joy at her salvation is similar to that of David when he confessed his sin to God (Psalm 51:12). When forgiven sinners fully realize the meaning of God's gracious gift, they will also praise God.

Hannah praised Him for His holiness. In Him there is no darkness, no infirmity or corruption. Unlike the corrupt idols worshiped by the heathen tribes around Israel, He is pure and holy. There is no other God. He is a Rock, strong and stable. He is immovable and unshakable. If we are anchored in Him, we have no need to fear the future. Jehovah is also the God of knowledge and the source of all wisdom (Psalm 94:8-12; Ecclesiastes 2:26; James 1:5). He should be judged by His actions (1 Samuel 2:3).

In the second part of her song of praise, Hannah rejoiced because of the sovereign rule of God. He humbles the mighty and exalts the lowly (Matthew 23:11-12; 1 Corinthians 1:20-29). To people who are rich and think they need nothing, He will bring to poverty (1 Samuel 2:5, 7-8; Matthew 6:19-21; 1 Timothy 6:10, 17-19; James 5:1-6; Revelation 3:17-18). For people who are hungry, He will provide what they need to sustain them (1 Samuel 2:5; Psalm 37:25; Matthew 6:25-34). As He did with Hannah, God opens the womb of the barren (1 Samuel 2:5; Genesis 21:1-2; 25:21; Luke 1:18, 24-25, 57-58). He can also make childless people who had been fruitful (1 Samuel 2:5; 15:33; Leviticus 20:20-21; Jeremiah 22:30). Hannah praised God because He is the Giver and Sustainer of life (1 Samuel 2:6; Acts 17:28). He takes life, but He also restores it. The bodies of the departed dead now asleep in the dust of the earth "will hear His voice and come forth" to be gloriously transformed (John 5:28-29; 1 Corinthians 15:50-57). He is the same God who framed the world and set the earth upon its pillars (1 Samuel 2:8; Genesis 1:1-2; Job 26:7).

In the third part of this song, Hannah rejoiced because of God's care for His saints. He guards their feet to keep them in the right way (1 Samuel 2:9). The psalmist said, "The steps of a good man are ordered by the Lord, and He delights in his way" (37:23). Jeremiah said, "O Lord, I know the way of man is not in himself; It is not in man who walks to direct his own steps" (10:23). In His prayer of example, Jesus taught us to pray that God would not allow us to be led into temptation (Matthew 6:13). The meaning of these scriptures is clear; God will do all He can to keep us on the right path, but we must choose to walk in it (Isaiah 35:8; Matthew 7:13-14).

In the final part of Hannah's song, she rejoiced because of the future plans of God for His people. Many scholars agree this is a prophetic statement. The first part deals with the judgment of the wicked (1 Samuel 2:10). This is reassurance for the righteous that the people who trouble them shall not escape justice. When that "great and terrible day" comes, they will not find any place to hide (Revelation 6:12-17; 20:11-15). The last section undoubtedly refers to Jesus sitting upon the throne of judgment for which purpose God will strengthen His hand (1 Samuel 2:10; Matthew 25:31-46; John 5:22).

Mary

When God chose the parents for His Son, He chose people He knew would raise Christ according to the Law. They were always careful to do so (Luke 2:21-22, 41-42, 51-52). Mary, His mother, was a virgin living in the city of Nazareth. She was espoused to "Joseph, who was of the house of David" (1:27). God sent an angel to her to relate the amazing news that she had been chosen to bear the Savior of the world (vv. 29-33). At first Mary was troubled at the angel's appearance; then she was stunned by his message. How could she bear a son "since she did not know a man"? (v. 34). The angel then explained: "The Holy Spirit would come upon her, and the power of the Highest would overshadow her" (v. 35). The angel then told her that her cousin Elizabeth was also expecting and was in the sixth month of her pregnancy (vv. 36-37). Mary was convinced of the angel's words and referred to herself as "the maidservant of the Lord," meaning she was ready to accept the responsibility God had placed upon her because she belonged completely to the Lord – body, soul and spirit (vv. 36, 38, 46-47).

Mary was, as the angel told her, "blessed … among women, but she was not divine (Matthew 12:47-50; John 2:2-4). The idea of the Immaculate Conception is the invention of clerics and is not taught in Scripture. Mary and Joseph had other children after Jesus was born (Matthew 13:55-56). Mary is not to be worshiped or prayed to. She was a vessel through whom God sent His Son.

Mary's Song (Luke 1:46-55)

After the angel left, Mary went up to the hill country of Judah to visit Elizabeth and share their joy. When she entered the house, and "Elizabeth heard the greeting of Mary, … the babe leaped in her womb" (v. 41). The Holy Spirit filled Elizabeth, and she began to praise God for this wonderful thing He had done (vv. 42-45). At this point, Mary began to praise God with a song that came forth from her heart out of the immense joy she felt. In this song, Mary uses many scripture quotations, mostly from the Psalms, but there is certainly a reference to the song of Hannah, especially in verses 49-53. The song is called "The Magnificat" because of the translation of verse 46 in the Latin Vulgate that reads, "*Magnificat anima mea Dominum.*" The emphasis of the song is on what God has done (vv. 49, 51-54). The song can be divided into three sections.

The first section concerns what God had done for Mary. She rejoiced first because He was her "Savior" (v. 47). Mary did not see herself as worthy of the honor that had befallen her, but she was amazed God had "regarded her lowly estate" and had blessed her in a way that she would be remembered by "all generations" (v. 48). Indeed, we honor Mary for who she was, but we do not pay homage to her. Notice that she does not praise her name, but she praises God because of the mighty deed He had done for her and because His name is holy (v. 49).

In the second part of the song, Mary rejoiced because of what God had done for all others who feared Him (v. 50). He had extended His mercy to them (Titus 3:5). Mary mentions three groups in particular whom the Lord had blessed: the helpless, the humble and the hungry (Luke 1:51-53). These people were at the mercy of the mighty and the rich (vv. 52-53). God would avenge them and scatter the proud and pull the mighty from their thrones so that He might exalt the lowly.

In the last part, Mary rejoiced because of what God had done for "His servant Israel." In His mercy, He had remembered His promise through Abraham (v. 54). Through Mary, He had fulfilled the prophecy of Isaiah and brought forth His Son, born of a virgin (Isaiah 7:14; Matthew 1:18-23). By bringing Jesus into the world, He had kept His promise to Abraham and to the other patriarchs. Paul tells us that Jesus, not Isaac or Israel, was the fulfillment of the "seed promise" (Genesis 15:1-6; 17:15-22; Galatians 3:16-18).

Lessons Learned

1. God often uses ordinary people, such as Hannah and Mary, to accomplish extraordinary events. Hannah was a woman who desperately wanted a son. She emerged from her shell of anonymity to prove herself to be a woman of deep conviction and deep faith in God. Mary, the mother of Jesus, came from a poor, humble background, but of all the women God could have chosen to bear His Son, He chose her. Neither of these women fought great battles, led God's people, or saved them from extinction, but they gave us two of the greatest leaders the world has ever produced.
2. Paul told the philosophers of Athens, "Truly, these times of ignorance, God overlooked, but now commands all men everywhere to come to repentance" (Acts 17:30). God was bringing His eternal purpose to completion, and in the process He had to work with the best people available. These were not perfect people, but they were head and shoulders above the people around them.
3. From Hannah, we learn a great deal about prayer. She prayed out of her sorrow and need. James says "you do not have because you do not ask" (4:2). God knows what we need even before we ask, but He still wants us to ask. As with Hannah, we may have to ask repeatedly; but if it is His will, He will answer with a yes. We must not grow impatient, but we must also remember that God is not on our time schedule, and we must trust Him to do what is right (2 Peter 3:8; Genesis 18:25). We also learn to ask specifically for what we desire. Hannah prayed for a son, not just a child. She also offered herself to be an instrument through whom God could fulfill this request.

Questions

1. What are the names of the three great women from the Old Testament mentioned in this lesson, and what was their claim to fame?
2. Why was Hannah so grieved?
3. What mistake did Elkanah make that may have contributed to the problem between Hannah and Peninnah?
4. What lessons can we learn from Hannah's prayer?
5. What are the main points of Hannah's prayer? Discuss each of these points.
6. What are the two divisions of the prophetic portion of Hannah's prayer?
7. How did Mary react to the angel's message? Why?
8. Is Mary to be worshiped? Why or why not?
9. What happened when Mary entered Elizabeth's house?
10. What three groups of people did Mary say the Lord had blessed?

Lesson 11

Boldness

Week of Aug. 15, 1999

Lesson Text

ACTS 4:23-31

(23) And being let go, they went to their own companions and reported all that the chief priests and elders had said to them.

(24) So when they heard that, they raised their voice to God with one accord and said: "Lord, You are God, who made heaven and earth and the sea, and all that is in them,

(25) "who by the mouth of Your servant David have said: 'Why did the nations rage, And the people plot vain things?

(26) The kings of the earth took their stand, And the rulers were gathered together Against the LORD and against His Christ.'

(27) "For truly against Your holy Servant Jesus, whom You anointed, both Herod and Pontius Pilate, with the Gentiles and the people of Israel, were gathered together

(28) "to do whatever Your hand and Your purpose determined before to be done.

(29) "Now, Lord, look on their threats, and grant to Your servants that with all boldness they may speak Your word,

(30) "by stretching out Your hand to heal, and that signs and wonders may be done through the name of Your holy Servant Jesus."

(31) And when they had prayed, the place where they were assembled together was shaken; and they were all filled with the Holy Spirit, and they spoke the word of God with boldness.

Introduction

Peter is an excellent character study. At times he was bold and daring, and at other times he was weak, impulsive, full of pride and inquisitive. Perhaps that is why we relate to him because he is so much like us. Jesus nicknamed him "the Rock" when he was as unstable as water. If not for his brother Andrew, who introduced him to Jesus, we might never have heard about Peter.

No one would have expected Peter to become a missionary and evangelist. As far as we know, he had no formal rabbinical training. That is why members of the Sanhedrin called him and John "uneducated and untrained" (Acts 4:13). He was raised in Bethsaida, which was located in despised Galilee (John 1:44). He later married and lived with his wife and mother-in-law in Capernaum (Mark 1:21, 29-31).

Peter was engaged in a fishing business in Bethsaida with his brother Andrew and the sons of Zebedee, James and John (vv. 16-20). He only left the fishing nets when Jesus called him to be a disciple (v. 17).

Peter often slipped and fell in his spiritual life. Once on the stormy Sea of Galilee, he walked on water toward Jesus, but when his faith failed he began to sink. He cried for Jesus to save him, and Jesus pulled him to safety (Matthew 14:31). It was not faith in himself that failed Peter because he knew he could not walk on water, but his faith in Christ faltered. As long as he kept his eyes on the Lord, he was all right, but the moment he looked away he began to drown.

Peter doubted Jesus again at the Passover meal when Jesus told the apostles that they would forsake Him before the night was over (Matthew 26:31-32). Peter protested loudly that "even if all are made to stumble because of You, I will never be made to stumble" (v. 33). Peter really believed this at the time. He proved it later in the garden when he drew the sword he had strapped to his side and sliced off the ear of Malchus, the servant of the high priest (John 18:10). He was ready to fight and die for Jesus, just as he said he would. However, instead of commending Peter for this act of bravery, Jesus rebuked him: "Put your sword in its place, for all who take the sword will perish by the sword" (Matthew 26:52).

This may explain why Peter stood with the enemies of the Lord in the palace of the high priest while Jesus was being tried (Mark 14:54). Had he not done so, he might not have denied Jesus, but he denied Him three times just as Jesus said he would (vv. 31, 67-71). When Jesus was crucified, Peter was hiding in the shadows with 10 of the other apostles, waiting to see what would happen (Luke 23:49).

Peter was still hiding with the other 10 apostles in the Upper Room in Jerusalem when Mary Magdalene came with the news that Jesus was resurrected. The apostles did not believe it and considered this to be "idle tales" (24:11). However, Peter did go with one of the other apostles, believed to be John, to check it out for himself (v. 12). Even when Peter saw the empty tomb, he did not believe (Mark 16:14). It took several more appearances to convince the apostles Jesus was really alive.

After spending 40 days with the apostles after His resurrection, Jesus assembled them on the Mount of Olives. There, He gave His parting words and ascended to the Father in heaven (Acts 1:4-12). The apostles waited in Jerusalem as Jesus told them to do until the Day of Pentecost, when they received the gift of the Holy Spirit that Jesus had promised them (2: 1-4). The same Peter who had denied Jesus, who had hid out for fear of his life, now preached the gospel with courage and conviction, and about 3,000 souls were baptized (vv. 14-41). From that point on, the dramatic change in Peter and the other apostles became apparent.

A Lame Man Is Healed (Acts 3:1-11)

Luke tells us that after the wonderful events of Pentecost the people were "continuing with one accord in the temple" (2:46). As chapter 3 opens, Peter and John were going to the temple at the hour of prayer, around 3 p.m. As they prepared to enter the Beautiful Gate of the temple, they encountered a lame beggar asking for alms. This gate was on the eastern side of the temple mount and separated the Court of the Gentiles from the Court of the Women. According to Jewish historian Josephus, it was very ornate, made of Corinthian brass, and was so large and heavy it took 20 men to close it (*Wars* V. V. 3. V 1. V 3). This was a favorite spot for beggars. People were far more generous when they were preparing to approach God in prayer.

This man was 40 years old (4:22) and had been lame from his mother's womb (3:2). He had been carried to this same spot every day for many years and was well known by the people who frequented the temple (v. 10). Imagine being in his situation. He could not go anywhere by himself but had to be carried by other people. He lived on the generosity of strangers, and his only goal in life was survival. He had nothing to look forward to except many more days like this one until he finally succumbed to death. Yet all of that was about to change.

When the beggar asked Peter and John for money, he could not have imagined they would give him a gift far more valuable. Peter fixed his eyes upon the man and said, "Look at us" (v. 4). The man looked up, expecting to receive money from them, but Peter said to him, "Silver and gold I do not have, but what I do have I give you: In the name of Jesus Christ of Nazareth, rise up and walk" (v. 6). Then Peter took the man by the right hand and lifted him up and immediately his feet and ankles received strength. When the man realized what had happened, he quickly stood up the rest of the way. Then he walked into the temple, leaping and praising God (vv. 7-8). The amazed crowd quickly gathered around to see this wonder (vv. 10-11). This incident provided Peter with his second opportunity to proclaim the gospel to a large gathering. He preached Jesus and Him crucified and called upon the people to repent (vv. 12-19).

A Good Deed Goes Sour (Acts 4:1-21)

The Jewish leaders soon heard the commotion and learned what had happened with the lame man being healed. They were "greatly disturbed that they taught the people and preached in Jesus' name the resurrection from the dead" (v. 2). Because it was late in the evening, they took Peter and John into custody and kept them overnight. The next morning they were brought before the Sanhedrin (vv. 5-7) who asked them by whose authority this lame man was made to walk. Being filled with the Holy Spirit, Peter said, "by the name of Jesus Christ of Nazareth, whom you crucified, whom God has raised from the dead, by Him this man stands here before you whole" (v. 10). How it must have stung when Peter said that there was no "salvation in any other, for there is no other name under heaven given among men by which we must be saved" (v. 12). These learned men did not know what to make of Peter and John when they saw the boldness with which they spoke because they knew they were "uneducated and untrained." They did, however, take note of the fact that they had been with Jesus (v. 13).

What was the Sanhedrin to do? They knew the masses of people in Jerusalem were aware of the miracle of the healing of the lame man. They wanted to punish Peter and John, but if they did the people might turn against them. After they discussed their dilemma, they decided to threaten Peter and John, commanding them not to preach in Jesus' name anymore and then let them go (v. 18). When the Sanhedrin delivered their edict, Peter boldly responded, "Whether it is right in the sight of God to listen to you more than to God, you judge. For we cannot but speak the things which we have seen and heard" (vv. 19-20). What a contrast between Peter in the palace of the high priest and Peter in the court of the high priest. When the Jews threatened them more, they believed they had no recourse but to let Peter and John go (v. 21).

Peter and John Report to the Brethren (Acts 4:23)

Although the persecution of Christians did not begin until later with Stephen being stoned to death (7:59), Peter and John had seen Jesus die. They knew the power of these Jewish rulers. We can assume that when they were taken prisoner, they expected to die. Yet any fears they may have had did not deter them from speaking the truth. It took great faith and courage for them to proclaim their faith in the resurrected Christ.

Once they were released, they could not wait to go to their companions and share the news. They reported all that had happened. They knew where to go, just as Peter did later when he was imprisoned by Herod and surely would have been put to death if God had not miraculously released him. He went to the house of Mary, the mother of John Mark and the sister of Barnabas, where his brethren were gathered and were praying for him (12:12). Prayer should be the first, not the last, thing we do.

A Prayer That Shook the House (Acts 4:24-31)

When Peter and John made their report, the people raised their voices "with one accord" (v. 24) and prayed to God. This appears to have been a purely spontaneous outpouring of gratitude. In the beginning of this prayer, they gave glory to God, first, for being the omnipotent sovereign creator God. Most all of the prayers in the Bible begin with a recognition of who God is and praising Him for that. It is common today in many circles for people to be more casual in their prayers. Although some familiarity may be appropriate, there are certain terms that should be avoided. "Hey, Dad" is entirely inappropriate for "Our Father Who is in Heaven." When we are struggling to make God more approachable, we must never bring Him down to our level.

Second, they recognized that God created the universe in the beginning and was still involved in the affairs of this world. They quoted Psalm 2:1-2 and acknowledged that it was prophetic and related it to the suffering Christians would experience in the defense of their faith (Acts 4:25-26). They accepted by faith that God was in control and not the kings and other rulers. Although these rulers aligned themselves to crucify Christ, they were only fulfilling God's purpose (vv. 27-28). Once more the foreordination or predetermination of God is mentioned (v. 28; see also 2:23).

Then they prayed for boldness to speak God's Word, even in the face of threats (4:29). They also asked God to confirm the spoken word with miracles of healing, signs and wonders. This is what Jesus had promised the apostles they would be able to do when the Holy Spirit came upon them (Mark 16:17-18). Before He ascended to Heaven, Jesus had told them to go back to Jerusalem, and they would receive the Holy Spirit and power (Acts 1:8). These two things, the Holy Spirit and power, are not synonymous (6:3-6; 8:5-8). The book of Hebrews makes it clear that the purpose of miracles was only to confirm the Word of God (2:1-4). Paul teaches the cessation of miracles when the completed or perfect revelation was given (1 Corinthians 13:8-12; Ephesians 4:11-16; James 1:25).

After they had prayed, the whole place where they assembled was shaken: "They were all filled with the Holy Spirit, and they spoke the word of God with boldness" (Acts 4:31). They had prayed for the ability to speak with boldness, and that prayer was immediately answered. This was not a renewal of the miracle on Pentecost but simply another demonstration of the power given to the apostles by the Holy Spirit. He appears to have empowered the apostles whenever there was need (Matthew 10:19-20; Acts 4:8, 31).

Lessons Learned

1. From Peter's struggles with his faith, we learn that even the best Christians can have moments of weakness. The Christian life is a journey and not a destination. When we are born into the family of God, we are but babes who can only drink milk (1 Peter 2:2). As we grow in our faith,we should be able to consume strong meat (1 Corinthians 3:1-3; Hebrews 5:12-14). We must not be discouraged when we fail. We need to do the same thing Peter did – get right back up and keep

pressing forward. Our journey is not over until we cross the finish line (2 Timothy 4:7).

2. If Peter had not "followed afar off" and "warmed himself by enemy fires," he might not have denied Jesus. The Lord said he would deny Him, but He did not say why. Fear kept him at a distance. John writes that "perfect love casts out fear" (1 John 4:18). Peter loved the Lord, but his love was just not strong enough at that time to overcome his fears. He also learned the hard way that the company we keep often determines how we act. It is easy to deny Jesus when you are among people who do not have faith in him. That is why we should choose our companions carefully (1 Corinthians 15:33).
3. The healing of the lame man provides a contrast between the miracles of the Bible and the so-called miracles of today. This man's healing was instantaneous. When Peter spoke the words and lifted him up, immediately his legs grew stronger, and he was able to walk and leap. There was no partial healing, and he did not return to his begging spot afterward. His life was changed permanently.
4. One of the greatest lessons in this study for us is the dramatic change that came over Peter and the other apostles after Pentecost. Their courage was not miraculous. They prayed and asked for boldness to proclaim God's message. They were emboldened, but it was not a miracle. God did not do it for them; instead, He gave them the help they needed to be what they wanted to be. He will do the same thing for us today (Ephesians 3:20; Philippians 4:13).

Questions

1. Why do we relate to Peter so much?
2. What lessons can we learn from Peter's short walk on the water?
3. What effect did Jesus' reprimand of Peter in the garden have upon him?
4. Why were the apostles so slow to believe?
5. What reminded the Jewish leaders that Peter and John had been with Jesus?
6. What two things did this prayer acknowledge about God?
7. What is an appropriate approach to God in prayer and what is not?
8. What was the purpose of first-century miracles?
9. How are the Holy Spirit and His power distinct?
10. Who was filled with the Holy Spirit after this prayer?

Lesson 12

Providence

Week of
Aug. 22, 1999

Lesson Text

ISAIAH 5:1-7

(1) Now let me sing to my Well-beloved A song of my Beloved regarding His vineyard: My Well-beloved has a vineyard On a very fruitful hill.

(2) He dug it up and cleared out its stones, And planted it with the choicest vine. He built a tower in its midst, And also made a winepress in it; So He expected it to bring forth good grapes, But it brought forth wild grapes.

(3) "And now, O inhabitants of Jerusalem and men of Judah, Judge, please, between Me and My vineyard.

(4) What more could have been done to My vineyard That I have not done in it? Why then, when I expected it to bring forth good grapes, Did it bring forth wild grapes?

(5) And now, please let Me tell you what I will do to My vineyard: I will take away its hedge, and it shall be burned; And break down its wall, and it shall be trampled down.

(6) I will lay it waste; It shall not be pruned or dug, But there shall come up briers and thorns. I will also command the clouds That they rain no rain on it."

(7) For the vineyard of the LORD of hosts is the house of Israel, And the men of Judah are His pleasant plant. He looked for justice, but behold, oppression; For righteousness, but behold, a cry for help.

Introduction

Isaiah was one of the foremost prophets, but there were other prophets before him. Jude, our Lord's brother, refers to "Enoch, the seventh from Adam" as a prophet (v. 14). The three leading patriarchs, Abraham, Isaac and Jacob are all given this title (Genesis 20:7; Psalm 105:6-15). Moses, his brother Aaron, and his sister Miriam are all called prophets (Exodus 7:1; 15:20; Numbers 12:6; Deuteronomy 18:15-22; Acts 3:22-23). With the exception of Moses, most of these would fall into the category of oral prophets.

The so-called "Golden Age of Prophecy" began with Samuel about 1,000 B.C.. He was a different breed of prophet. He was a priest, a ruler or judge of sorts, and a prophet. Samuel was an oral prophet and a writing prophet. He is credited with writing the first 24 chapters of 1 Samuel, with the rest attributed to Nathan and Gad. Samuel is considered to be the person who started the schools for prophets. There appear to have been five of these schools located at Ramah, Gibeah, Bethel, Jericho and Gilgal (1 Samuel 10:5; 19:18-24; 2 Kings 2:3, 15; 4:38-41). Many of the later great prophets, such as Elijah and Elisha, are thought to have been graduates of one of these schools. These men made predictions about the future, but they were primarily preachers delivering God's message to their people.

Isaiah, the writer of the text for this study, was at the beginning of a new golden age of prophecy. His name means "God, or Jehovah, is salvation." He was the first in a long line of writing prophets. He was the son of Amoz (Isaiah 1:1). Isaiah was a man of cultivation, culture and refinement. He is believed to have been of the aristocratic class. He was at home in the highest circles of government and had easy access to the king of Judah. Isaiah moved with grace and understanding among the wealthiest and the poorest people of the land. He is believed to have been raised in the city of Jerusalem and to have spent his entire career preaching there.

Isaiah grew up in a time of unparalleled affluence and prosperity. However, he lived to see the nation's wealth plundered and its affluence used as a means of decimation and degeneration. He received his prophetic call in the year that King Uzziah died, ca. 715 B.C. (6:1). Isaiah was without a doubt the greatest of the writing prophets, both in the content and comprehensiveness of his messages and His ability to communicate. He is called "The Messianic Prophet" because of the numerous passages concerning the Christ contained his writings. He sets forth the doctrine of Christ in such detail that insights are found here that cannot be found in any other Old Testament book. He is quoted more often in the New Testament than any other writing prophet. There are many lessons within this book that are relevant to our day. Our text provides us with one of those lessons.

Isaiah's Prophecy of the Vineyard

In the Old and New Testaments God's people are often spoken of as the Lord's vineyard (Psalm 80:15; Isaiah 27:2-6; Jeremiah 12:10; Matthew 20:1-16; 21:33-41; Mark 12:1-11; Luke 20:9-18; John 15:1-8). In Psalm 80:8-9, Israel is referred to as the vine that the Lord brought forth out of Egypt. In our text, the Lord has planted this vine in a fertile place and has protected it. Despite all He has done to make it a beautiful and productive vineyard, His efforts fail, and it produces only wild grapes that are not fit to consume. Some of the rotten fruits are stated in the verses following our text: greed, disregard for God's Word and His work, deliberate defiance of God, hypocrisy, pride and misdirected power (vv. 8-23).

This song is believed to have been constructed in connection with the yearly festivals, and Isaiah incorporated it within his prophecy to depict the relationship between God and His people.The prophet mentions "a fruitful hill," Jerusalem, and Judah, which are all references to the Southern Kingdom. However, some scholars see a reference to all of Israel as the vineyard and Judah as the choice vine. Some writers suggest that he used it initially at one of the feasts to illustrate how the people had failed to measure up to God's purpose. Because of the circumstances it describes, it perhaps was composed between 741 and 726 B.C., either in the latter days of Jotham's reign or in the early period of Ahaz's reign.

Judah boasted about its special favor with God because Israel had already been carried away into captivity by Assyria, and they had been spared. They pointed to their prosperity under Uzziah and Jotham as evidence of divine favor. Isaiah's song declares that the only divine favor or grace was in the planting of the vineyard.

The song has been variously divided. One popular division involving the entire chapter is: 1. The Song, vv. 1-7; 2. The Harvest, vv. 8-23; and 3. The Terrifying Judgment, vv. 24-30. Another division that concerns only our text is: 1. Great Investment, vv. 1-2; 2. Disappointing results, vv. 3-4; 3. Tragic Ruin, vv. 5-7. Most scholars appear to agree on this basic interpretation. The theme that runs through the song itself is the providence of God. There is a timely message in it for the world today.

God's Preparation of His Vineyard (Isaiah 5:1)

Isaiah says this song is dedicated to his "well-beloved," the people of Judah and Jerusalem. He had grown up among them. He had spent his career ministering to them. His love was deep and profound. Because of his love for them, the message he had to deliver was bitter and not pleasant to taste (6:8-13).

The "Beloved" is God, the Husbandman over His vineyard. He had brought them up out of Egypt and had planted them in the land of Canaan as He had promised to Abraham, Isaac and Jacob. The "fruitful hill" is undoubtedly a reference to the hill of Zion upon which Jerusalem is said to be situated. It was the highest and most prominent of the seven hills upon which the whole of Jerusalem sits. It is located on the most southwestern part of the city. The name "Mount Zion" eventually came to be identified with the entire city of Jerusalem. Later, Old and New Testament poets, prophets and writers used the term to refer to a type of sacred capitol. It has been used to describe the Holy Place (Psalm 87:2), God's chosen people (Psalm 51:18; 87:5), the church (Hebrews 12:22), and heaven (Revelation 14:1).

God Protection of His Vineyard (Isaiah 5:20)

Look at all of the precautions God had taken to ensure a productive vineyard. He chose the most fertile plot of land He could find. He laboriously dug up all the stones and cleared them from the land. Anyone who has ever been in the vicinity of Jerusalem knows what a task that would be. The ground all around that area is literally covered with rocks. That is why they are the weapon of choice for the Palestinians who are trying to gain their independence from Israeli rule.

God also planted in the vineyard the choicest of plants, *sorek*, a variety of vine with the greatest potential for producing the finest of grapes. This choice vine is assumed to be Judah. Once He had planted the vineyard, God built a rock wall and a hedge around it to keep out intruders. He erected a tower in the midst of it so that a watchman could see all around the area and spot potential dangers before they got close enough to damage the vines or harm the fruit. He also made a winepress in it hewn out of solid rock in which to store his wine, an indication of the great harvest of luscious grapes He expected.

How disappointed God was when the time finally came for the harvest, and the vineyard produced only wild fruit. It is hard to conceive of even wild grapes being bitter and sour to the taste. For this reason scholars have suggested a reference to a weed called labruscas, or wild vine. These vines grew in abundance in Judea and produced a poisonous berry that resembled grapes (Deuteronomy 32:32-33; 2 Kings 4:39-41). Most people seem to agree that although the variety cannot be known for certain, a wild, obnoxious plant is in mind rather than a wild, uncultivated grape vine.

God's Produce from His Vineyard (Isaiah 5:3-4)

God had given such careful attention to His vineyard that it should have produced the choicest of grapes. He then calls upon the inhabitants of Jerusalem and Judah to judge what might have gone wrong. What measures might He have taken that He did not? The form of the question suggests the answer – nothing. There was nothing He could have done to make a difference in the outcome. The fault did not lie with the Husbandman but it lay with the vineyard itself and the plants.

This part of the song is similar to Jesus' parable about the tares (Matthew 13:24-30). Although it referred to a different people, time and place, the outcome is the same. In this case, the farmer planted good seed in good ground. There was no reason to expect anything other than a bountiful and beautiful harvest. However, while the man slept, his enemy sowed tares, a noxious weed, in with the good wheat seeds. When the wheat began to raise its head, the presence of the tares was apparent. The servants were astonished and could not understand this result because they were absolutely certain that they had sowed only good seeds in the field. The owner assured them that they had done nothing wrong but that an enemy was responsible. When asked if they should gather out the tares and destroy them, he expressed concern that they would also pull up the good plants with them. So he said, "Let them both grow together until the harvest, and at the time of the harvest I will say to the reapers, 'First gather together the tares and bind them in bundles to burn them, but gather the wheat into my barn'" (v. 30).

God's Pronouncement Against His Vineyard (Isaiah 5:5-6)

What do you do with an unproductive grapevine? God said He would take away the hedge He had grown around the vineyard and burn it with fire. The wall He had built He would break down. Although it is not believed that the vineyard was Jerusalem itself, there is certainly an allusion to the destruction that would come upon the city when the Babylonians captured it. When God removed His hedge of protection from it, they overran the city. They tore down the walls and then burned the city with fire. Imagine the Babylonian soldiers trampling down the city as they marched through, desecrating every inch of it.

The judgment against Israel is explained in more detail in the last part of this chapter in a series of "woes" (vv. 8-30). These woes were pronounced against five groups: 1. the powerful monopolizing landowners whose houses would be destroyed and left desolate (v. 8); 2. the intemperate and frivolous citizens who would either lose their lives or be carried into captivity (vv. 11-13); 3. people who labored at iniquity and made evil their work and did not believe God's prophets when they pronounced their doom (vv. 18-19); 4. people who blurred the distinction between good and evil in word and in action; they presumed to know it all and rejected the word of the wise prophets (v. 20); and 5. people who indulged in alcoholic drink and rejected the claims of people who came to them with righteous causes; they would be consumed as dry grass by a raging fire and their roots would rot and decay (vv. 22-24). This judgment would come in the form of powerful nations who would come upon them (vv. 26-30).

God's Punishment of His Vineyard (Isaiah 5:7)

What a sad state of affairs this was. Israel had been carefully selected and every caution had been taken to ensure a good result of justice and righteousness (v. 7). Instead, it produced a dismal crop of injustice and oppression. The righteous and oppressed wept and cried out for God to avenge the wrongs done to them (v. 7). The righteous and Holy God could not turn a deaf ear to their cries, but justice had to prevail to spare them and to preserve His name.

Jesus answered the question of what to do with an unproductive vine in His parable about the vine (John 15:1-8). In this parable He said He was the Vine, and Christians are the branches (v. 5). As long as we remain connected to Him we will be productive, and God will be glorified (vv. 5, 7-8). If we are unproductive branches, we will be cut down and cast into the fire. This is unquestionably a reference to the final judgment (Matthew 25:31-46; Revelation 20:10-15; 21:8).

Lessons Learned

1. Considering the current state of affairs in our nation, there is a grave warning here for us. This nation had been blessed by God as no nation before it. It was founded by God-fearing men and women who honored His Word. It had within its borders some of the most fertile and productive land in the world. It could conceivably produce enough food to feed the entire world if it ever became necessary. Despite God's blessings upon them, they squandered their inheritance and turned their backs on their heritage. Unless we turn back to God in humble repentance, we will meet the fate of other nations who have forgotten God.
2. The parable about the vine teaches us about the need to be productive branches. What is the fruit of a grapevine? It is grapes. What is the fruit of a Christian? Is it not other Christians? Should we not be reproducing after our own kind? Can God be pleased with the fact that evangelism is almost non-existent in our communities? When we spent more time teaching and converting people to Christ than we did arguing among ourselves, the Lord's vineyard, His church grew. We must once again take the Great Commission seriously and stop allowing it to be the Great Omission.
3. The wicked shall not escape the vengeance of God. Often it seems that the wicked are getting away with something. They seem to prosper while the righteous suffer. We sometimes envy them, but we should not. You would not want to trade places with them on the Day of Judgment.

Questions

1. Who was the first prophet mentioned in Scripture?
2. What was the principle job of a prophet?
3. Who started the school of the prophets?
4. What does Isaiah's name mean?
5. What is the Lord's vineyard today?
6. Who was the "well Beloved," and who was the "beloved" Husbandman?
7. What precautions did God take to ensure a good harvest?
8. Who was the enemy in the parable about the tares?
9. What was Judah's punishment for being unproductive?
10. What fate awaits the unproductive on the Day of Judgment?

Lesson 13

Ongoing

Week of
Aug. 29, 1999

Lesson Text

LUKE 18:1-8

(1) Then He spoke a parable to them, that men always ought to pray and not lose heart,

(2) saying: "There was in a certain city a judge who did not fear God nor regard man.

(3) "Now there was a widow in that city; and she came to him, saying, 'Get justice for me from my adversary.'

(4) "And he would not for a while; but afterward he said within himself, 'Though I do not fear God nor regard man,

(5) 'yet because this widow troubles me I will avenge her, lest by her continual coming she weary me.' "

(6) Then the Lord said, "Hear what the unjust judge said.

(7) "And shall God not avenge His own elect who cry out day and night to Him, though He bears long with them?

(8) "I tell you that He will avenge them speedily. Nevertheless, when the Son of Man comes, will He really find faith on the earth?"

ACTS 6:1-4

(1) Now in those days, when the number of the disciples was multiplying, there arose a complaint against the Hebrews by the Hellenists, because their widows were neglected in the daily distribution.

(2) Then the twelve summoned the multitude of the disciples and said, "It is not desirable that we should leave the word of God and serve tables.

(3) "Therefore, brethren, seek out from among you seven men of good reputation, full of the Holy Spirit and wisdom, whom we may appoint over this business;

(4) "but we will give ourselves continually to prayer and to the ministry of the word."

ROMANS 12:12

(12) Rejoicing in hope, patient in tribulation, continuing steadfastly in prayer.

1 THESSALONIANS 5:17

(17) Pray without ceasing.

Introduction

If the Bible teaches us anything about prayer, it teaches that our God is a prayer-hearing and prayer-answering God. Yet there is no area of revelation about which there is more skepticism. So often Christians pray, believing the entire time that it will not do any good. Such prayers are wasted breath and energy. James says, "But let him ask in faith with no doubting, for he who doubts is like a wave of the sea driven and tossed by the wind. For let not that man suppose that he will receive anything from the Lord; he is a double-minded man, unstable in all his ways" (1:6-8). Later in his book, James says that the "effective, fervent prayer of a righteous man avails much" (5:16). Then he uses Elijah as an example to illustrate his point. Elijah prayed that it would not rain on the earth, and it did not rain for three and one-half years. After his confrontation with, and defeat of, the prophets of Baal on Mount Carmel, he prayed again, and it began to rain torrentially (vv. 17-18). The whole point of his illustration is that Elijah was only a human being, and God heard and answered his prayer. If He would hear and answer Elijah's prayer, He will hear and answer our prayers too. If we do not believe in the power of prayer, then let us stop praying.

Charles Hodge, in his book *Prayer: The Voice of Faith,* writes, "I do not believe in prayer ... I believe in God; therefore, I pray" (Resource Publications, 1996; p. 11). He also says, "Prayer is power because God is God. Prayer works because God works! Prayer moves the hands that move the world" (p. 18). Prayer is powerful because God is powerful. Yet so many of our prayers are powerless. This causes us to wonder if prayer really does do any good. The problem is not with prayer; it is with our understanding of it or use of it and our belief concerning it. When we change these things, prayer will change things for us.

In Prayer Persistence Pays (Luke 18:1-8)

This parable teaches the same lesson that Jesus taught earlier when His disciples asked Him, "Lord, teach us to pray"(11:1). After giving them His example prayer, He told the parable about the friend at midnight to illustrate that God will answer our prayer, but we must be persistent (vv. 5-8). A man had company late one night and did not have enough food, so he went to borrow some from his neighbor who was already in the bed. The neighbor, disturbed from his rest, said in essence, "Go away! I'm in bed. My family is in bed. The doors are locked, and I will not get up and give you any bread." However, because the man continued to knock and to ask, his neighbor got up and gave him what he wanted. Jesus made the point that in our prayers to God we must continue to "ask, and it shall be given you; seek, and you will find; knock, and it will be opened" (v. 9). God knows what we need before we ask, but He still wants us to ask. Sometimes He wants us to ask and ask again.

In the companion parable in Luke 18, Jesus told the parable about the persistent widow. In this story, a widow seeks justice for some injustice done to her. The judge to whom she appealed does not "fear God nor regard man" (v. 2). At first he would not give her the justice she sought; but later, because she "troubled him by her continual coming," he gave in to her demands. This parable is used to illustrate that God hears the cries of His children who are oppressed and who seek justice, and when it is time, He will avenge the wrongs done to His elect. Jesus said, "He will avenge them speedily" (v. 8). There is a disturbing question at the end of this verse that almost seems out of context: "Nevertheless, when the Son of Man comes, will he find faith on the earth?" The thought of Jesus returning in the clouds of heaven and not finding faithful people left on Earth is frightening. However, the context of the statement is in connection with people believing in prayer and continuing to pray.

Church Leaders Need to Pray Continually (Acts 6:1-4)

When a church begins to grow, the devil steps in and tries to to stop it. That is exactly what happened in Jerusalem. On the Day of Pentecost, about 3,000 souls were added to the church (2:41). God continued to add "to the church daily those who were being saved" (v. 47). By the time of Peter's temple sermon, there were 5,000 men who had become Christians (4:4). After Ananias and Sapphira were disciplined by God and put to death for their intended deception, "Believers were increasingly added to the Lord, multitudes of both men and women" (5:14). But along with this growth, there came growing pains.

In Acts 4, there is the beginning of persecution of Christians. In chapter 5, there is the need for discipline. Then, in chapter 6, there is murmuring and complaining. Only dead churches have no problems. One of the great disgraces in the church today is the fights and fusses that end in congregational division. If we have the spirit of Christ in us, there is no problem that will arise in the church that cannot be resolved by God's people in God's way.

Our text here in Acts 6 teaches how the church should handle any problem. We do not know if the complaint about the Grecian Jewish Christians was real or imagined. They were the ones who saw discrimination in the way the daily provisions were being handled, and the Palestinian Christians were most likely the ones in charge of this distribution. Even if the problem was not real, their concerns were and had to be addressed promptly. The first thing we must not do is ignore a problem, thinking that it will go away or try to sweep it under the rug and forget about it. This is the way churches split. When people see a problem in their church and approach the elders about it, and if nothing is done, the pressure builds until it finally erupts in an explosion of departing members. Problems must be met head on, and they must be resolved in a scriptural way with agreement from all sides to accept the decision. That is what happened here, and as a result the Jerusalem church did not split but continued to grow (vv. 5-7).

When the problem was presented to the apostles, they were still serving as the leaders of the church. We do not read about elders in the Jerusalem church until Acts 11:30. At this time, the apostles were acting in the role elders would later fulfill (Ephesians 4:11). The apostles devised a plan to correct the problem; they called "the multitude of the disciples together" to explain their position and to enlist their cooperation in resolving the conflict (Acts 6:2).

The first thing they did was make it clear that they could not leave the important work in which they were engaged to "serve tables" (v. 3). It is not that serving tables was demeaning to them or that it was not a good and necessary work, but they had been appointed by Christ to be His personal ambassadors to the world (1:6-8). As important as resolving this problem was, the apostles could not neglect their primary function as preachers. It is easy, for preachers especially, to get sidetracked. There are many urgent matters demanding their time and attention, but a preacher's primary function is to preach. In order to preach they must devote adequate time to study. Preachers, elders and congregations need to understand this. A lot of people do not understand it. They think that the church exists to serve them. They think it is a social service agency, a benevolent institution, or a dispenser of recreation, but that is not the reason for the church's existence. We may use the means mentioned to fulfill the churches' missions, but they are not the mission (Luke 19:10). It is God's savings institution. It is the only one He has ordained to make known His "manifold wisdom" to the world (Ephesians 3:10). Let us never be guilty of neglecting important needs, but let us take care of the most important need first.

The apostles were engaged in two important ministries: "prayer" and the "ministry of the word" (Acts 6:4). These men prayed continually. How often do our elders pray for the sheep under their care? How often do we pray for our congregation, for our elders, deacons, preachers and members? Do we pray for the success of our work? For peace and harmony to rule? Do we pray for the lost of our community and our world? If we had more praying, we would have less complaining.

When the church selected the six men, all of whom it seems lived outside of Palestine, to serve tables, the apostles prayed and laid their hands on them to impart spiritual gifts to them. They asked God's blessings upon these men. No work can succeed without God. We should never begin any program or make any plans or decisions without first asking God for help and guidance and to bless what we are about to do. Perhaps the reason many of our plans and programs do not succeed is because we do not ask for His help, and we try to do it on our own. When we do this, we are doomed to failure.

All Christians Need to Pray and Never Stop (Romans 12:12; 1 Thessalonians 5:17)

Paul makes these two statements to show the need for Christians to pray always. First, Paul writes to the Roman Christians, encouraging them to be "continuing steadfastly in prayer" (12:12). The word used here for "steadfastly continuing" in the Greek is a form of the word *proskatereo*. It refers to being strong towards something, to be steadfast and unwavering. It also means "devoted," and this text is translated "be devoted to prayer" in another translation (NASB). A person who has the strength to continue living the Christian life will be a person who prays continually.

When Paul wrote to the congregation at Thessalonica, he encouraged them to "pray without ceasing" (1 Thessalonians 5:17). The meaning is obviously not that we must always be praying, but it is that we must be constantly in an attitude and disposition of prayer. We must leave the line open and the receiver off the hook. The Greek word used here implies "constantly recurring," and not "continually occurring." One preacher said he began his prayer in the morning and closed it at night. If we do that, we can add something at any time in the day. We do not need to always fall down on our face or our knees to pray. At any time in our day, whether walking, riding, sitting, standing or kneeling, we can talk to our heavenly Father with the full assurance that He hears and will answer our prayers.

This brings up the question of how God answers prayer. God always answers the prayers of his faithful children (1 John 5:14-15). We often equate answered prayer only with a "Yes." "No" is also an answer. In the garden Jesus prayed three times, "O My Father, if it is possible, let this cup pass from me; nevertheless, not as I will, but as You will" (Matthew 26:39, 42, 44). God did not take the cup of death away, but He did answer His Son's prayer. Paul prayed three times for his thorn in the flesh to be taken away, but God did not take it away. Instead He gave him something better: the strength to bear it (2 Corinthians 12:9). God may answer with a "Yes," or He may say "No," or he may say "wait awhile," but He will answer in His time and in His way.

Lessons Learned

1. Faithless prayers are like trying to start a car without an engine. You can have the key, but when you turn it nothing will happen. When we pray, we must believe or else it is hypocrisy. Real faith is not just believing God can, but it is also believing that He will. Even the faith of a tiny mustard seed can move mountains (Matthew 17:20). There are not many mountains being moved today. In fact, we are struggling under the ant hills that threaten to engulf us. Our greatest sin in praying is failing to pray.
2. The parable about the friend at midnight and the persistent widow teach us to keep asking, seeking and knocking. God rewards persistence. This is seen in the story about Hannah, the mother of Samuel, who prayed for a son (1 Samuel 1:12). How long she prayed, we do not know, but the language suggests that she asked continually. Finally, God gave her what she asked for (v. 20).
3. Whenever a church begins to grow, Satan will step in and stop it if he can. A dead or dying church is not a threat to him but a thriving, growing one is. He will use discouragement, and often it will come from the most unexpected sources. When problems arise in a church, they must be met head on and resolved as quickly as possible. We must not let such matters interfere with the greatest work in the world, the Lord's work.
4. The mission of the church is described in the words of Jesus when He was describing His mission. He said "the Son of Man has come to seek and to save that which was lost" (Luke 19:10). We can use many different tools to accomplish this objective, but we must never lose sight of the goal. The church exists to preach the gospel and save lost souls. We must not allow ourselves to get sidetracked or derailed in fulfilling this objective.

Questions

1. What point is James making using Elijah as an illustration?
2. What was the reason for Jesus telling the parable about the persistent widow?
3. What was the problem in the Jerusalem church in Acts 6?
4. How was the problem in Acts 6 resolved?
5. When are elders first mentioned in Acts?
6. In what two ministries were the apostles engaged?
7. What is the meaning of *proskatereo*?
8. What did Paul mean by saying "pray without ceasing?"
9. How does God answer the prayers of his children?
10. What did Jesus mean by saying that if we had the faith of a "grain mustard seed" we could "move mountains?"